SEA
G. BATUR
Kintamani
DANAU BATUR
DANAU BRATAN
GUNUNG AGUNG
G. BATUKAU
BUKIT SERAJA
P. Batukau
P. Besaki
P. Kehen
Tirta Empul
Gunung Kawi
BANGLI
Payangan
Sangeh
Blakiuh
Pedjeng
Ubud
Pliatan
Bedulu
Mas
Sidan
GIANJAR
Lebi
Selat
Udjon
Bug Bug
Kusambe
Blayu
Mengwi
Kediri
Kapal
Sibang
Lukluk
Batubulan
Kesiman
Sanur
Kedaton
N. SERANGAN
Benua
OCEAN

Baris Gedé—ceremonial war dance

Portrait of Ayu Ktut

The beach in Sanur

Island of BALI

MIGUEL COVARRUBIAS

with an album of photographs by
Rose Covarrubias

PERIPLUS EDITIONS
Singapore • Hong Kong • Indonesia

Published by Periplus Editions (HK) Ltd with editorial offices at
61 Tai Seng Avenue #02-12, Singapore 534167

This edition published by arrangement with Alfred A. Knopf, Inc.

ISBN 978-0-7946-0562-9

Distributed by:

Indonesia
PT Java Books Indonesia
Kawasan Industri Pulogadung
Jl. Rawa Gelam IV No. 9; Jakarta 13930, Indonesia
Tel: (62) 21 4682-1088; Fax: (62) 21 461-0206
cs@javabooks.co.id

Asia Pacific
Berkeley Books Pte. Ltd.
61 Tai Seng Avenue, #02-12
Singapore 534167
Tel: (65) 6280-1330; Fax: (65) 6280-6290
inquiries@periplus.com.sg
www.periplus.com

North America, Latin America & Europe
Tuttle Publishing
364 Innovation Drive
North Clarendon, VT 05759-9436 U.S.A.
Tel: 1 (802) 773-8930; Fax: 1 (802) 773-6993
info@tuttlepublishing.com
www.tuttlepublishing.com

Printed in Singapore

08 09 10 5 4 3 2 1

Acknowledgment

A BOOK ABOUT THE LIFE AND traditions of the far-away island of Bali naturally involves in its preparation the cooperation of many companions on the island as well as scholars, translators, artists, and the makers of other books. I am grateful to all of them—too many to mention here. I am particularly indebted to Walter Spies and my many Balinese friends, especially my host, Gusti Alit Oka, and his family; to Edith J. R. Isaacs, who so patiently and sympathetically criticized and edited the manuscript; to Maimai Sze for invaluable assistance in the final preparation of the book; and to the Guggenheim Award which enabled me to make a second trip to Bali to complete and check my material. Rose Covarrubias' cooperation speaks for itself in the photographs which are so essential a part of the book.

Contents

Illustrations

The colored illustrations were reproduced through the courtesy of The Condé Nast Publications, Inc.

Foreword

IS IT POSSIBLE FOR A BOOK TO become so legendary that it defines the place it is written about? I remember as a student going to an exhibition of new Balinese art in Sydney, and seeing a shrine in the corner of the gallery—a niche illuminated by a single light source—and on that shrine was an original edition of Miguel Covarrubias' *Island of Bali*. Despite it being "popular" literature, I had already found the book invaluable in my studies, but this elevation added a new dimension to my understanding of the legend of Bali. If there is one book that made Bali's reputation as the fabulous island of dreams, as the paradise of nature and culture, then it is this book.

Miguel Covarrubias (1904-1957) is one of Mexico's cultural heroes. Although he left his native country for the United States as a young man and subsequently traveled widely in Europe and Asia, he and Rose (Rosa) Covarrubias (1895-1970) made important contributions to the development of modern Mexican national culture. In any exhibitions of modern Mexican art, Miguel Covarrubias has a place along with his friend Diego Rivera. Covarrubias made his name as a caricaturist, working in popular magazines such as *Vanity Fair*, where he was commercially successful. But as the illustrations to his books show, he had the hand and eye of a gifted artist, and by 1940 he was being exhibited along with Mexico's other great artists in the Museum of Modern Art in New York. Covarrubias wrote on the US and Mexico and made a significant contribution to Mexican archeology, but it is *Island of Bali* that is his most famous work. Both Miguel and Rose added a significant cosmopolitan dimension to the identity of Mexico, as among their long list of friends and acquaintances were George Gershwin, André Gide and Frido Kahlo. At the same time, the Covarrubiases contributed to an international culture in which Bali had a special place.

During the late 1920s, Bali was beginning to acquire a reputation as an exotic center amongst the glittering elite of New York. Miguel and Rose Covarrubias, looking for new experiences outside the US and Europe, embarked on a journey by steamship to Asia in 1930.

Although highlights of their trip included Shanghai, it was Bali that really captivated them, and induced them to stay for nine months. The arrival in Bali was not that promising: the northern port of Buleleng, everybody's first glimpse of Bali in those days, was a mixture of urban colonial influences and ethnic groups from all over Asia and beyond. Its rusty tin roofs and small shops gave it an uninspiring provincial air. The real shock of Bali came in the drive south, with the broad vistas of rice fields, the pockets of rainforest that still had wild boar and even tigers, and the picturesque villages that were compact islands of thatch in the middle of verdant green. Miguel and Rose were lucky to have an introduction to the European artist Walter Spies, who took them all over the island, showing them exorcistic trance dances where spirits entered the bodies of little girls accompanied by the mass chanting of half-naked men, strange temples which were populated by monkeys, and temple ceremonies where masked dancers enacted the history of Bali's kingdoms.

Most of Bali was only colonized at the beginning of the twentieth century. Bali in the 1930s was not necessarily the ideal place that many imagined it to be. The island had been reduced to a subsistence level of economy after the Great Depression smashed the prices of commodities on which the island's colonial rulers, the Dutch, depended. Miguel and Rose arrived on the island just as the Depression was hitting home. The privation that Balinese experienced was deep, many were impoverished and had to sell heirlooms to survive. In such a situation, foreigners with independent incomes could live like kings, and frequently did. The same poverty that afflicted many Balinese proved to be attractive, in that it meant that Balinese maintained many of their religious practices and aspects of pre-colonial lifestyles. However much they might have aspired to modern life, economic circumstances denied it. But the foreigners who came to the island were also fleeing aspects of the modern world, and were entranced by the strong sense of tradition on the island.

When, with funding from the Guggenheim Foundation, Miguel and Rose returned to Bali in 1933 for another year's stay, Bali's tourist industry was just beginning to take off, although it was not until the late 1930s, after the 1937 publication of *Island of Bali,* that tourist numbers reached the thousands.

The Covarrubiases' experiences of Bali obviously benefited from the fact that Westerners on the island at the time took status from the colonial system, and from much higher incomes than the Balinese. But in Miguel's case, as a Mexican in Bali, local people perceived him to be much closer to themselves, and the fact that he dressed as they did, ate as they did, and went enthusiastically to all their ceremonies and temples meant he was received as almost Balinese. Before he arrived on the island, he started learning the Malay language that is the predecessor of modern Indonesia, but soon found that he had to learn Balinese to really communicate, a task that he took to with great skill. He was taken into the confidence of cultural experts, told traditional stories and taken to places in ways that exceeded even the usual high standards of Balinese hospitality.

Even in the late 1970s, during one of the periods when I was living in Bali, there were people who remembered Covarrubias. Pak Kompiang, my host in Denpasar and one of those great raconteurs for whom oral history must have been invented, saw my copy of the book and said "Ah, Miguel Covarrubias, yes, I helped him find magical drawings. I went up to Klungkung and found these magical incantations for him." Since I was going to live in Klungkung, a place of magic, Pak Kompiang gave me a protective formula from his research in the 1930s to help me with my fieldwork. I never doubted Pak Kompiang's story, but thought that the Covarrubias notes must have been thrown away. It was not until the publication of Adriana Williams' and Yu-Chee Chong's carefully researched *Covarrubias in Bali* that pages from Covarrubias' notebooks, with magical drawings (*rerajahan*) and mystical incantations, came into public view. The notebooks tell us a lot about how *Island of Bali* was written, about the author's fascination with details of Balinese culture that were craftily distilled into one or two pages of his book, and about how he cultivated relations with Balinese in order to search out information from all over the island.

While perhaps he might not have given enough credit to his Balinese research assistants—and to Rose's role in the research—it is not so much the raw material as Covarrubias' deft rendering of it into lively prose and telling anecdotes that makes *Island of Bali* so great. The scholarship that went into the book is formidable, from Dutch translations of medieval poems, to studies in German and French of Asian dance and religion, to one of Bali's first works of modern literature, I Wayan Gobiah's *Nemoe Karma*. This thorough research into primary and secondary literature was matched by a tireless approach to fieldwork. The couple made a home in the walled compound of I Gusti Alit Oka in Belaluan, a relative of my friend Pak Kompiang, in the center of the South Bali capital of Denpasar. Since Gusti Oka was an aristocrat of some status, he gave them entrée into many different aspects of Balinese high culture that they might otherwise have been denied. Life with Gusti Oka's extended family opened up insights into Balinese daily life, but to get the full range of experiences Miguel and Rose traveled all over the island, risking the mosquitoes and even crocodiles to camp out in tents with Spies and other companions. Through Miguel's accounts, and Rose's accompanying photographs, we can trace their movements backwards and forwards from the North Bali port of Buleleng to the coast at Sanur, then to the central village of Ubud and to the eastern village of Iseh up in the mountains of Karangasem in search of even more unusual temples or ceremonies. The cars they used were rare vehicles at the time, owned by the few European residents and members of Balinese royal families. But in their journeys they also used traditional boats, and trekked through forests to find remote ancient temples.

While some of the book was written in the thrall of the charismatic but yet-to-be-famous painter Walter Spies—and Covarrubias may have had advice from their friend on Bali, the leading anthropologist Jane Belo—he set his own stamp on the book and worked closely with the leading Balinese musicians and artists of the day—people such as the composer Agung Mandera (who had participated in the Paris Colonial Exposition of 1931) and the painters Agung Sobrat and Ida Bagus Made Togog. Miguel's host on Bali, Gusti Oka played an important role in introducing him to the cultural life of the island. Belaluan, where he lived, was then the center of the best orchestra in Bali. This gamelan played for the guests of the new Bali Hotel, and was the first to be recorded by Westerners fascinated by Bali's unique music. Through the Belaluan orchestra the Covarrubiases met some of Bali's best dancers, including the little girls who danced the fabulous Legong, among them Ni Pollok, who later married a much older Belgian artist before becoming a leading contributor to the post-War rebirth of tourism in Bali in her role as an entrepreneur.

This book is an encyclopedia of Bali. In a manner that no twenty-first century author would dare to use, Covarrubias ranges in his descriptions from outlines of myths, to ethnographic descriptions of rituals, to lucid discussions of food, clothing and hair-dos, to intimate details of how Balinese have sex (and how did he know?). This book withstood the critical scrutiny of leading contemporary anthropologists such as Ruth Benedict, just as today it is still on the reading lists of university courses on Bali.

Island of Bali's great strengths are also its weaknesses. This book defines the myth of Bali the paradise, by carefully bringing together all the elements of previous Western writings praising Bali, and then slyly adding an idealization of a perfect Bali, removed from the influences of modern Western life, that were beginning to capture the interest of Balinese. Yet this is an ambiguous idealization, one that seeks to give power and recognition to Balinese while criticizing Dutch colonialism. The last criticism was a commonplace of Western writers, who seemed less averse to imperialism than to putting down the Dutch. Covarrubias took on the anti-Dutch sentiment of Anglo-Saxon writers, but recognized the critical role played by some Dutch civil servants in trying to deal with the massive social upheavals Bali experienced in the 1930s.

Just as he adopted the ethnographic details of earlier accounts of the island, Covarrubias picked up on, and strengthened, many of the clichés about Bali—"everybody in Bali seems to be an artist"; "the Balinese have little need of cash to procure the daily necessities of life"; "no other race gives the impression of living in such close touch with nature". Nevertheless, Covarrubias continually refers to aspects of modern life on Bali, of education. Western clothing covering the women's bare breasts, a sex industry involving young men, and changes in property rights. This ambiguity is part of the power of the book; *Island of Bali* is at once a nostalgic document describing a pre-colonial world, and a portrait of great cultural and social change. It remains relevant to us for both reasons. While the book may be of great use to a tourist industry that recalls the island before the landscapes were overbuilt and the rivers polluted, it also demonstrates how Balinese have coped with the rest of the world, and so provides some important clues about the capacity of Balinese to adapt.

Adrian Vickers
Professor of Southeast Asian Studies
University of Sydney

Introduction

TODAY ALMOST EVERYBODY has heard of Bali. To some it means a smart place to go, one of the many ports in a round-the-world cruise; to others it brings mental images of brown girls with beautiful breasts, palm trees, rolling waves, and all the romantic notions that go to make a South Sea Island paradise. In general the popular knowledge of Bali ends there. But only six years ago, when I sailed with Rose for the remote island, no one seemed even to have heard of the place; we had to point it out on the map, a tiny dot in the swarm of islands east of Java. We had seen a splendid album of Bali photographs (*Bali*, by Gregor Krause), and gradually we had developed an irresistible desire to see the island, until one spring day of 1930 we found ourselves, rather unexpectedly, on board the *Cingalese Prince*, a freighter bound for the Dutch East Indies. In New York we were told that Malay was the language of the islands and that we must learn it to be understood there. So on the six weeks' voyage through the Panama Canal, across the Pacific Ocean, and down the China Sea, we took daily lessons in elementary Malay from a sailor on board, a young Javanese who joined the ship to see the world, but who was disappointed because, he said, all he had seen was the sea around him, for when the boat docked he seldom had a chance to go ashore. When we reached Java we found we should have been helpless without the little Malay we had learned on board ship.

We had our first unforgettable glimpse of Bali at dawn when the little K.P.M. steamer approached Buleleng—a high dark peak reflected on a sea as smooth as polished steel, with the summit of the cone hidden in dark, metallic clouds. As we were rowed ashore, Buleleng came out of the mist: the eternal tin roofs and dilapidated Chinese houses, the concrete steamship office, and the scraggy coolies of every small port of the Indies. Landing on the primitive wooden pier, we received the inevitable welcome of Patimah, a gay and dignified middle-aged Balinese "princess" from whom one rents a car to go to the south of the island. Patimah is a famous woman: tales go about that she was saved by the Dutch from being burned alive at the cremation of her husband, the king of Bali. The truth is that she was visiting in Buleleng at the time the Raja[1] of Klungkung was killed with his whole court when he opposed the Dutch army. Patimah escaped death by submitting quietly and remaining in Buleleng. There she married a henpecked Muslim, changed her religion and became the prosperous owner of a silver and brocade shop and of a fleet of fine motor-cars for hire. The traveler succumbs easily to her charm, her lively sense of humor, and her hospitality when she serves coffee on her veranda, and he seldom fails to buy a hammered silver bowl or a brocade scarf. But some Babbitt has taught unsuspecting Patimah that a typical American greeting is: "Shake the bottle!" followed by a significant gesture of the hand. This is the only English she knows.

After the coffee interlude the traveler is hurried into his car, and while his baggage is being tied on, he is told that he is going to Denpasar, the capital of the South, "center of Balinese culture," where are the only large, comfortable hotels. The car darts through narrow streets lined with dingy little shops of cheap crockery and cotton goods run by emaciated Chinese in under-shirts or by Arabs with forbidding black beards. Javanese in black velvet skull-caps mingle with Dutch officials in pith helmets and high starched collars, but the beautiful Balinese of steamship pamphlets are not to be seen anywhere. The people on the streets are ugly and unkempt, and instead of the much publicized beauties, there are only uninteresting women in not very clean blouses. The car drives through Singaraja, the capital, with its neat Dutch bungalows, its gasoline stations, and the house of the Resident, with its imposing driveway flanked by two monstrous cement snakes. Leaving the town, the car passes miserable villages and occasional gingerbread temples with tin roofs; it climbs the mountain side, the villages become more and more scarce, it grows colder and colder, and soon the tourist is shivering in a cloud of fog. He begins to suspect that he has been deceived. A few wild-looking people wrapped in blankets appear on the road riding on small ponies, and soon a double row of wooden shacks with more tin roofs announces Kintamani, the village on the rim of the crater of the Batur, where a beautiful view of the volcanoes has been promised. Ten chances to one it will be foggy and the tourist will see nothing, so he goes into the elaborate resthouse of the K.P.M. to have a drink and warm up.

[1] So spelled here to differentiate it from "Rajah," an Indian ruler.

Soon he is on the road again; the car winds and turns sharp curves down the mountain, the fog vanishes, and the air becomes warmer and clearer. Tropical vegetation reappears, and riding among tall palms and enormous banana trees, he enters Bangli, which is at last like the Bali of the photographs. With lessened suspicions, he rides through many beautiful villages and fantastic terraced rice fields covered with every shade of tender green. At a sharp curve a large tire sign indicates arrival at his destination—Denpasar. His car drives noisily up to the Bali Hotel, pride of the K.P.M., and he is shown to a clean and sanitary room wth a hospital bed through the middle of which, lengthwise, stretches a hard, round bolster, the so-called "Dutch wife." On the veranda of the hotel at tea time there are always pretty Balinese girls who sell curios, plainly junk, but they are not to blame. They have discovered that the tourists generally prefer hideous statuettes made by beginners or the gaudy weavings dyed with anilines to the fine old pieces of wood-carving or to the sumptuous ancient textiles that now rarely find their way into the curio market.

Denpasar is a glorified Buleleng. In the great "alun-alun," the playground of Denpasar, stolid Hollanders play tennis and drink beer near young Balinese playing soccer in striped sweat-shirts, shorts, and spiked shoes. All around the square are the homes of the leading white residents, neat and bourgeois, small bungalows with enormous pink embroidered lampshades on every porch and well-kept front gardens of imported roses. The business street leading to the market consists, as in Buleleng, of the same squalid shops, provision stores, gasoline pumps, a small Chinese hotel, and curio stalls with mass-production "Balinese art," all kept by the same Chinese compradors, the same bearded Bombay merchants with eagle-like beaks, dressed like burlesque comedians in incongruous tall fezzes, embroidered slippers, pink sarongs, and European vests worn over shirts with tails out, bargaining excitedly with husky bare-breasted Balinese women.

After the first bewildering days, when we had recovered from the shock of such distressing impressions as these, we began to "discover" the real Bali. Only a block away from the square, on the dirt-paved lanes adjacent to the main avenues, where the peace is not broken by mad automobiles running over pigs and chickens, we found the typical mud walls of the compounds, the thatched gates protected by mysterious signs—a dead chicken nailed flat on a wall, or a little white flag inscribed with cabalistic symbols. These were the proper setting for the lithe brown-skinned women returning from market with baskets of fruit on their heads and for the men in loincloths sitting in groups around the baskets in which they kept their favorite fighting cocks. Energetic women thresh rice or bathe quite unconcerned in the ditch by the roadside, and serious naked children play in the middle of the street with a cricket they have just captured. From behind the walls come occasional tinkling sounds of practicing on a *gamelan*.

As we became more and more familiar with our new life, and our ears grew accustomed to Malay, we made friends among the Balinese. We were already weary of the stolid prudishness of Dutch hotel life, and since we could not afford the high rates much longer, we looked for another place to live. Houses for rent that were not in the Arab, Chinese, or European quarter were non-existent in those days, but somehow we became attached to the household of our first Balinese friend—Gusti Alit Oka, an intelligent and dapper young man, prince by birth, carpenter by profession, and musician by choice. He agreed to rent us one of the pavilions of his house and undertook to improve our Malay. Our household consisted of the young prince's wife and child, two widowed aunts, and an old servant, a retainer of his father, the great warrior who was killed with his brother the Raja of Badung in their last desperate stand against the invading Dutch army twenty-nine years ago, when our host was a baby. Like a true Balinese prince, Gusti had his "man," an amiable but exceedingly ugly retainer, by name Katel, who followed his master admiringly wherever he went. We settled in Gusti's house, bought a few chairs and tables, had beds made, and hired a few nonchalant servants: a *jongos* who insisted his name was "Dog," a cook, and a chauffeur. We bought a decrepit Chevrolet and gave ourselves up to the full enjoyment of the island, going from feast to feast, dances, and cremations.

It was my good fortune to have made friends in those days with Walter Spies, Bali's most famous resident. The son of a German diplomat in Moscow at the outbreak of the World War, Spies was already well known in Europe as a painter in 1923, when I had admired and cut out reproductions of his paintings of Russia from the *Kunstblatt*, never thinking he was to become one of my closest friends. As fine a musician as he is a painter, Spies studied the music of the Tatars while interned in the Urals during the war years. After the war he ran away from disorganized Europe to the East until he reached Java, where he was called by the Sultan of Yogyakarta to organize and lead a Western orchestra. He lived for years in the Sultan's court learning their music. Then one day he went to Bali on a visit and has remained there ever since, and may, perhaps, for the rest of his life. In his charming devil-may-care way, Spies is familiar with every phase of Balinese life and has been the constant source of disinterested information to every archeologist, anthropologist, musician, or artist who has come to Bali. His assistance is given generously and without expecting even the reward of credit. Much of his enthusiasm and energy has gone to help the work of others, but he has achievements of his own: he was the first to appreciate and record Balinese music, he has collected every pattern of Balinese art, has contributed to Dutch scientific journals, has created the Bali Museum, of which he is the curator, and has now built a splendid aquarium. An authentic friend of the Balinese and loved by them, I feel he has contributed more to the prestige of the white man than the colonial despots who fail to impress the discriminating Balinese by the policy used to bluff natives into submission.

The months went by as we roamed all over the island with Spies, watching strange ceremonies, enjoying their music, listening to fantastic tales, camping in the wilds of West Bali or on the coral reefs of Sanur. Walter loves to collect velvety dragonflies, strange spiders and sea slugs, not in a naturalist's box, but in minutely accurate drawings. For days at a time he would sit in his tent drawing them, because once dead, their beautiful colors disappeared. He was temperamental when he went into seclusion to paint, he would work incessantly for months on one of his rare canvases, great pictures that made the Balinese exclaim: "Beh!" with their mouths wide open in astonishment, and that were snatched by prosperous art-loving travelers who were lucky enough to find Spies with a finished painting. There were never two paintings in his house at once. He paints dream-like landscapes in which every branch and every leaf is carefully painted, done with the love of a Persian miniaturist, a Cranach, a Breughel or a *Douanier* Rousseau.

When I could speak fair Malay, I discovered it was not enough. Malay was the trade language between Balinese and foreigners, spoken mainly by the new generations of the towns, so I started to learn a little Balinese to be able to understand the most interesting people of the island—the older men and women—but just then we had to leave our new home to return to America. On the way back we stopped in Paris, where the Colonial Exposition was going on. There we found friends from Bali—the Cokordes of Ubud, feudal lords of Spies's village, the leaders of the troupe of dancers and musicians that were the sensation of the exposition. With them I continued to study the difficult Balinese language, because I had then and there made up my mind to return to Bali as soon as possible. I had some random notes, and Rose had taken hundreds of photographs. Someone in Paris suggested publishing an album of the pictures, with text from the notes, which I later decided were disconnected and quite unsatisfactory. We had grown so homesick for Bali that the only thing left to do was to return, so in the summer of 1933, partly assisted by a generous scholarship from the Guggenheim Foundation and partly with our savings, we sailed back to Bali.

At first we were disappointed; the tourist rush was in full swing and we began to hear that missionaries, unknown in Bali up to the time we left, were making converts, and everybody talked of trouble on their account. In Denpasar a great many women had taken to wearing clumsy blouses, the young were developing contempt for Balinese ways, and the people complained of poverty, another novelty in Bali. Dutch gold currency had gone up, and even there, where trade is unimportant, prices had crashed to bottom levels. Only twenty-five cents could be obtained for one of the great sheafs of rice that before brought ten times as much; a cow could be bought for five guilders, and a pig for one. The Balinese were unable to obtain cash to pay back taxes, and their lands were being sold at auction. Newly acquired luxuries—imported articles—took their precious cash, and at first the situation seemed desperate. We feared we had made a mistake in returning, and to escape the tourist-ridden, commercial Denpasar, we went to live with our friend Spies in his beautiful house in Campuhan, in the mountains near Ubud. We remained there for a few months among new Balinese friends, guided by the experience of Spies, working and collecting the material for this book.

But we missed our old friends and the activity of our former village home. We were convinced that it was in the district of Badung, around Denpasar, despite the superficial changes, that the most sumptuous feasts were held and dances and plays were most frequent. I had now a teacher and translator who gave me daily lessons and helped with manuscripts. With Spies and the teacher, we moved the entire household back to Belaluan, to our old house, the home of Gusti Oka, who had in the meantime married a new wife, a beautiful young princess. Our dear friend Siloh Biang, Gusti's first wife, had fought with Sagung, her rival, and had run away to her mother, but our return brought Siloh Biang back. She preferred to remain with us in our part of the house rather than with Gusti and his new wife, and we often had to act as mediators in their family quarrels. At times this created difficult diplomatic situations. Some of our old friends had died, others had married or moved away, and the little dancers who only left our front porch to go to bed at night had grown into serious young women of thirteen or fourteen years of age. We became again members of the quarter of the village, the *banjar* of Belaluan, home of one of the finest orchestras on the island, the *gong belaluan,* of which Gusti was a member. We had open door to the frequent local festivals, and within our compound we had opportunity to observe the daily life of the Balinese and to collect first-hand information for this book. The details given here, however, cannot be taken as applying to the entire island; each community has its own code, and what is law in one place is often ignored in the next. No two festivals are carried out in exactly the same manner and there are no two temples exactly alike. The general principles are the same everywhere, but the details vary from place to place and from caste to caste, and the traditions of the ancient mountain villages are different from those of the districts under the influence of the former rulers; to note them all would require an entire book for each custom or ceremony.

Not having made a systematic study of anthropology or of Oriental religions, the objective of this book is limited to the attempt to present a bird's-eye view of Balinese life and culture, both of which are inextricably bound to their deep-rooted beliefs and to their logical and harmonious living. The Balinese still retain their traditions and hold to their own manner of life, but they are only too willing to adopt every new idea, good or bad, brought into their island by merchants, tourists, unsuitable education, and missionaries. The only aim of this book, therefore, is to collect in one volume all that could be obtained from personal experience by an unscientific artist, of a living culture that is doomed to disappear under the merciless onslaught of modern commercialism and standardization.

PART I

NOTE ON PRONUNCIATION

THE BALINESE LANGUAGE is a difficult one to pronounce properly; it abounds in subtle sounds—two sorts of *d's, t's, a's, e's,* etc. At present there is an officially recognized system, taught in Balinese schools, for the spelling of Balinese words in Latin characters. However, for English-speaking readers this system would be confusing and a few of these rules of spelling have been modified here for the sake of convenience.

In general all consonants are pronounced as in English. The former Dutch *dj* which sounds like *j* in "jam" is now spelled as *j* in modern Indonesia, and the Dutch *tj* with a sound of *ch* as in "church" is now spelled as *c*. The Dutch *j* has been changed to *y* as in *wayang, nj* is changed to *ny—i.e., njepí: nyepí*—pronounced as in "canyon." The *ng* sound typical of Malay languages should be pronounced as one sound, as in "ringing"—*peng'iwa* and not *pen'giwa*.

All vowels are pronounced as in Spanish or Italian: *a* as in "artistic," *i* as in "miss," *o* as in "photo"; *e,* however, is short and hardly pronounced unless accented, *é, è,* when it is as in "egg" or "eight." The most important modification of the Dutch spelling is that *oe* has been changed to *u,* pronounced as in "bull" or like the *oo* in "fool." This is to be remembered especially in connection with geographical names as they appear in old Dutch maps; for example, Kloengkoeng, Oeboed, are now spelled Klungkung, Ubud.

Always in a word ending in *a,* this letter has a sound rather like the last *a* in "America," or as in "odd." Other phonetic signs have been omitted.

CHAPTER ONE

The Island

THE MALAY ARCHIPELAGO lies directly on the volcanic belt of the world. Like the backbone of some restless, formidable antediluvian monster, more than three hundred volcanoes rise from the sea in a great chain of islands—perhaps all that remains of a continent broken up in prehistoric cataclysms—forming a continuous land bridge that links Asia with Australia. Because of its peculiar and fantastic nature, its complex variety of peoples, and its fabulous richness, the archipelago is one of the most fascinating regions of the earth. It includes famous islands like Java, Borneo, Sumatra, New Guinea, the Philippines, and the hysterical island-volcano of Krakatau. Such freaks of nature as the giant "dragon" lizards of Komodo, the colored lakes of Flores, the orangutans, the rafflesia (a flower over three feet in diameter), and the birds of paradise, are to be found nowhere else. The population of the islands ranges from such forms of primitive humanity as the Negritos, the Papuans, the Kubus, who seem only a few steps away in the evolutionary scale from the orangutan, to the supercivilized Hindu-Javanese, who over six hundred years ago built monuments like Borobudur and Prambanan, jewels of Eastern art.

Through the centuries, civilization upon civilization from all directions has settled on the islands over the ancient megalithic cultures of the aborigines, until each island has developed an individual character, with a colorful culture, according to whether Chinese, Hindu, Malay, Polynesian, Muslim, or European influence has prevailed. Despite the mental isolation these differences have created, even the natives believe that the islands once formed a unified land. Raffles, in his *History of Java,* mentions a Javanese legend that says "the continent was split into nine parts, but when three thousand rainy seasons will have elapsed, the Eastern Islands shall again be reunited and the power of the white man shall end."

One of the smallest, but perhaps the most extraordinary, of the islands, is the recently famous Bali—a cluster of high volcanoes, their craters studded with serene lakes set in dark forests filled with screaming monkeys. The long green slopes of the volcanoes, deeply furrowed by ravines washed out by rushing rivers full of rapids and waterfalls, drop steadily to the sea without forming lowlands. Just eight degrees south of the Equator, Bali has over two thousand square miles of extravagantly fertile lands, most of which are beautifully cultivated. Only a narrow strait, hardly two miles across, separates Bali from Java; here again the idea that the two islands were once joined and then separated is sustained by the legend of the great Javanese king who was obliged to banish his good-for-nothing son to Bali, then united to Java by a very narrow isthmus. The king accompanied his son to the narrowest point of the tongue of land; when the young prince had disappeared from sight, to further emphasize the separation, he drew a line with his finger across the sands. The waters met and Bali became an island.

The dangers lurking in the waters around the island suggest a possible reason why Bali remained obscure and unconquered until 1908. Besides the strong tidal currents and the great depths of the straits, the coasts are little indented and are constantly exposed to the full force of the monsoons; where they are not bordered by dangerous coral banks, they rise from the sea in steep cliffs. Anchorage is thus out of the question except far out to sea, and the Dutch have had to build an artificial port in Benoa to afford a berth for small vessels.

One of the volcanoes, the Gunung Batur (5,633 feet), is still active. In the center of the old crater an enormous amphitheater ten miles across by a mile in depth rises like a dark blister, the smoking cone of a more recent crater (see map), its sides covered with the black lava spilled out into the great bowl of the older crater in the latest eruption. It is said that this lava has not yet cooled deep down, and when the rain water seeps through the cracks it turns into clouds of steam. Half-circling the new crater is the peaceful, misty Lake Batur, its shores dotted with the ancient villages of the oldest present inhabitants of the island. In former times the prosperous village of Batur rose at the foot of the volcano, but today only the villages across the crater remain, those on the safe side of the lake. One day the Batur began to growl and in 1917 it burst into a violent eruption accompanied by earthquakes. The whole of the island was affected, and 65,000 homes, 2,500 temples and 1,372 lives were lost. The lava engulfed the village of Batur, but stopped at the very gate of the temple. The villagers took the miracle as a good omen and continued to live there. In August 1926, however, a new eruption buried the sacred temple under the molten lava, this time with the loss of one life, an old woman who died of fright. The people of Batur, unable to break the spell that links their destinies to the mountain, rebuilt their village high up on the rim of the outer crater, renamed it Kububatur, and will probably remain there until again driven away by the anger of the volcano.

According to legend, Bali was originally a flat, barren island. When Java fell to the Muslims, the disgusted Hindu gods decided to move to Bali, but it became necessary for them to build dwelling-places high enough for their exalted rank. So they created the mountains, one for each of the cardinal points. The highest, Gunung Agung, was erected at the east, the place of honor; the Batur at the north; the Batukau at the west; and since there had to be one for the south, the raised tableland (the Bukit) of Bukit Pecatu became the seat of the patron of the south.[1] The Batur is venerated in its neighborhood, and the Batukau

[1] In other versions, the mountains from East Java were moved to Bali. In the *Catur Yoga* it is recorded that the Gunung Agung went to the center, the Batur to the north, Mount Recani (the peak of Lombok) to the east, the Bukit to the south, and Batukau to the west.

is holy to the villages on its slopes, but it is the Gunung Agung, Bali's highest mountain (10,560 feet) that is most sacred to the whole of the island. Half-way up the mountain is the mother temple for all Bali, the great Besakih with its impressive stone gate and its hundreds of towers thatched with sugar-palm fiber. The Gunung Agung is regarded as the Navel (*puséh*) of the World. It is to the Balinese what Kailasa and Meru are to the Hindus of India. As Mahameru it is the Cosmic Mountain, the Father of All Humanity.

To the Balinese, Bali is the entire world. Knowledge of the other nations of which they are conscious—China, Java, and Europe—does not influence their belief in the least. They are simply other worlds that have no relation to their own conception of the earth. There is an old manuscript which gives a description of the structure of the world. Although not very highly regarded by scholars, it gives us the popular Balinese conception of the cosmos, especially as it justifies their faith that Bali is the world. The following are excerpts from a free translation:

"At the bottom of everything there is magnetic iron, but in the beginning there was nothing, all was emptiness; there was only space. Before there were the heavens, there was no earth, and when there was no earth, there was no sky. . . . Through meditation, the world serpent Antaboga created the turtle Bedawang, on whom lie coiled two snakes as the foundation of the World. On the world turtle rests a lid, the Black Stone. There is no sun, there is no moon, there is no night in the cave below (the underside of the stone); this is the underworld, whose gods are the male Batara Kala and the female Setesuyara. There lives also the great serpent Basuki. . .

"Kala created the light and Mother Earth, over which extends a layer of water. Over this again are consecutive domes or skies, high and low; one of mud (which dried to become the earth and the mountains); then the "empty" middle sky (the atmosphere), where Iswara dwells; above this is the floating sky, the clouds, where Semara sits, the god of love. Beyond that follows the "dark" (blue) sky with the sun and the moon, the home of Surya; this is why they are above the clouds. Next is the Perfumed Sky, beautiful and full of rare flowers, where live the bird Cak, whose face is like a human face, the serpent Taksaka, who has legs and wings, and the *awan* snakes, the falling stars. Still higher in the sky *gringsing wayang*, the "flaming heaven of the ancestors." And over all the skies live the great gods

THE BALINESE COSMOS
The World Turtle, Bedawang, and the Supreme Being, Tintiya
by Ida Bagus Togog, of Batuan

who keep watch over the heavenly nymphs."[2] Thus we have it that the island rests on the turtle, which floats on the ocean.

As the last Asiatic outpost to the east, Bali is interesting to the naturalist as an illustration of the theory of evolution. In 1869 Alfred Russel Wallace discovered that the fauna and flora typical of Asia end in Bali, while the earlier, more primitive biological forms found in Australia begin to appear in the neighboring island of Lombok, just east of Bali. Here the last tigers, cows (*banteng*), monkeys, woodpeckers, pythons, etc., of Asia are not to be found farther east, and the cockatoos, parrots, and giant lizards predominate. Bali has the luxuriant vegetation of tropical Asia, while Lombok is arid and thorny, like Australia. Wallace drew a line across the narrow straits between Bali and Lombok, the deepest waters in the archipelago, to divide Asia from Oceania.[3] Today, however, scientists are more inclined to regard the islands as a transitional region.

As in all countries near the Equator, Bali has an eternal summer with even, warm weather, high humidity, and a regular variation of winds, but the unbearable heat of lands similarly situated is greatly relieved by sea breezes that blow constantly over the descending slopes of the four volcanoes that form the island. The seasons are not distinguished as hot and cold, but as wet and dry. It is pleasantly cool and dry during our summer months, when the south-easterly winds blow, but in November the northwest monsoon ushers in six months of a rainy season so violent that it makes everything rot away, growing green whiskers of mold on shoes that are not shined every day. Then the atmosphere becomes hot and sticky and the torrential rains that lash the island cause landslides that often carry enormous trees into the deep ravines cut into the soft volcanic ash by the rivers, themselves red with earth washed from the mountain. Brooks and rivers swell into huge torrents (*banjir*) that rise unexpectedly with a deafening roar, in front of one's eyes, carrying away earth, plants, and occasional drowned pigs, destroying bridges and irriga-

[2] This is from the *Catur Yoga*, a popular manuscript which I translated for the sake of practice on the language. It consists of ideas on cosmogony, mythology, legends of the creation of man, etc., ending in a confused set of rules for cremation and Balinese genealogies. The second half of the manuscript is extremely obscure, full of errors, and appears incomplete, perhaps owing to careless copying of an older palm-leaf book.

[3] Wallace divides the archipelago into Indo-Malayan (west of Bali) and Austro-Malayan (east of Lombok), until Sumbawa, where he draws another line to divide the Malayan from the Polynesian islands.

tion works. It is not unusual for a careless bather to be surprised by a sudden *banjir* and to be carried away in the muddy stream.

It is only natural that in a land of steep mountains, with such abundant rains, crossed in all directions by streams and great rivers, on a soil impregnated with volcanic ash, the earth should attain great richness and fertility. The burning tropical sun shining on the saturated earth produces a steaming, electric, hothouse atmosphere that gives birth to the dripping jungles that cover the slopes of the volcanoes with prehistoric tree-ferns, pandanus, and palms, strangled in a mesh of creepers of all sorts, their trunks smothered with orchids and alive with leeches, fantastic butterflies, birds, and screeching wild monkeys. This exuberance extends to the cultivated parts of the island, where the rice fields that cover this over-populated land produce every year, and without great effort, two crops of the finest rice in the Indies.

Despite the enormous population, the lack of running water has kept the western part of the island uninhabited and wild. The few remaining tigers, and the deer, wild hog, crocodiles, great lizards, jungle cocks, etc., are the sole dwellers in this arid hilly country covered with a dusty, low brush. Curiously enough, the Balinese regard this deserted land *(Pulaki)* as their place of origin. They explain in an old legend that a great city, which still exists, once flourished there, but has been made invisible to human eyes by Wahu Rahu, the greatest Brahmana from Java, who was forced to flee from the capital, Gelgel, to save his beautiful daughter from the king (by caste his inferior) and who found refuge in *Pulaki* by making the city invisible to the wicked king and his followers.

Another arid region in contrast with the extravagant fertility of the island is the peninsula of limestone called *Bukit* by the Balinese which rises to a height of 700 feet above the sea. This curious tableland, which shows every indication of having once been at the bottom of the ocean, is joined to the mainland by a low, narrow isthmus, but its sides rise almost vertically from the sea, and on the extremity of a long narrow rock, with a straight drop of 250 feet, is the fantastically situated temple of Uluwatu, one of the holiest in Bali. This projecting rock is believed to be the ship, turned to stone, of Dewi Danu, the goddess of waters.

The mountains with their lakes and rivers are the home of the gods and the sources of the land's fertility, and they stand for everything that is holy and healthy. To the Balinese everything that is high is good and powerful, so it is natural that the sea, lower than the lowest point of land, with the sharks and barracuda that infest the waters, and the deadly sea-snakes and poisonous fish that live among the treacherous coral reefs, should be considered as *tenget*, magically dangerous, the home of the evil spirits. Few Balinese know how to swim and they rarely venture into the sea except to bathe near the shallow beaches, and then they go only a few feet from the shore. There are small settlements of fishermen who brave the malarial coasts of Kuta, Sanur, Benoa, and Ketewel, but in general fishing is done on a small scale, either with casting-nets, or in beautiful prows shaped like fantastic "elephant-fish" *(gajah-mina)* with elegant stylized trunks, and eyes to see at night. With their triangular sails apex downward, they go far out to sea at sunset to procure the giant sea-turtles required at the frequent banquets of this feast-loving people. Most Balinese seldom eat fish and remain essentially a rice-eating race. Their repugnance for the sea may be due to the same religious fear of the supernatural that prevents them from climbing to the summit of the great mountains. The Balinese feel that the heights are for the gods, the middle world for humans, and the depths and low points for the spirits of the underworld. They dread the unholy loneliness of the beaches haunted by demons and they believe that the coastline is under the influence of Jero Gedé Mecaling, the Fanged Giant, who lives on the barren island of Nusa Penida. They are one of the rare island peoples in the world who turn their eyes not outward to the waters, but upward to the mountain tops.

CHAPTER TWO

The People

LIKE A CONTINUAL UNDERSEA BALLET, the pulse of life in Bali moves with a measured rhythm reminiscent of the sway of marine plants and the flowing motion of octopus and jellyfish under the sweep of a submarine current. There is a similar correlation of the elegant and decorative people with the clear-cut, extravagant vegetation; of their simple and sensitive temperament with the fertile land.

No other race gives the impression of living in such close touch with nature, creates such a complete feeling of harmony between the people and the surroundings. The slender Balinese bodies are as much a part of the landscape as the palms and the breadfruit trees, and their smooth skins have the same tone as the earth and as the brown rivers where they bathe; a general color scheme of greens, grays, and ochres, relieved here and there by bright-colored sashes and tropical flowers. The Balinese belong in their environment in the same way that a humming-bird or an orchid belongs in a Central American jungle, or a steel-worker belongs in the grime of Pittsburgh. It was depressing to watch our Balinese friends transplanted to the Paris Fair. They were cold and miserable there in the middle of the summer, shivering in heavy overcoats or wrapped in blankets like red Indians, but they were transformed into normal, beautiful Balinese as soon as they returned from their unhappy experience.

Today the beauty of the Balinese has been exploited to exhaustion in travelogues and by tourist agencies, but as far back as 1619 records mention that Balinese women were in great demand in the slave markets of Bourbon (Reunion), where "they brought as much as 150 florins." The traffic in Balinese slaves continued until 1830, and today there is a colony of Balinese in Jakarta, the descendants of former slaves. Their reputation for beauty is well justified: the majority of the population are handsome, with splendid physique and with a dignified elegance of bearing, in both men and women of all ages. From childhood the women walk for miles carrying heavy loads on their heads; this gives them a great coordination of movement, a poised walk and bodily fitness. Old women retain their strength and do not become bent hags. We were astonished at times to discover that the slender, straight silhouette we had admired from a distance belonged to an old lady with gray hair, walking with ease under forty or fifty pounds of fruit or pottery. Unless physically disabled, elderly people never admit that they are too old or too weak for activity; to "give up" would be dangerous to physical and spiritual health and would render a person vulnerable to attacks of a supernatural character.

Ordinarily free of excessive clothing, the Balinese have small but well-developed bodies, with a peculiar anatomical structure of simple, solid masses reminiscent of Egyptian and Mycenaean sculptures: wide shoulders tapering down in unbroken lines to flexible waists and narrow hips; strong backs, small heads, and firm full breasts. Their slender arms and long legs end in delicate hands and feet, kept skillful and alive by functional use and dance training. Their faces have well-balanced features, expressive eyes, small noses, and full mouths, and their hair is thick and glossy. Because they are tanned by the sun, their golden-brown skin appears generally darker than it really is, and when seen at a distance, people bathing are considerably whiter around their middles, where the skin is usually covered by clothes, giving the impression that they wear light-colored pants. Watching a crowd of semi-nude Balinese of all ages, one cannot help wondering what the comparison would be should men and women of our cities suddenly appear in the streets nude above the waist.

Their character is easy, courteous, and gentle, but they can be intense and can show strong temper if aroused. They are gay and witty; there is nothing that a Balinese loves more than a good joke, especially if it is off-color, and even children make ribald puns that are applauded by grown-ups. It is perhaps in their mad sense of humor, the spirit of Rabelaisian fun with which they handle even such forbidding subjects as religion and death, that lies the key to their character. The adjective "childish" or "childlike," so often misapplied to primitive peoples, does not suit the Balinese, because even the children show a sophistication often lacking in more civilized grown-ups. They are resourceful and intelligent, with acute senses and quick minds. Once, when I mentioned the goodness of a very short friend, the immediate reply was: "How could he be otherwise, he is so small!" One day Spies's monkey got loose and ran all over the house upsetting and breaking things. All the Balinese boys chased the monkey, but it let them come to within a few feet of it and then leaped out of reach onto the roof or a tree. The only one who did not join in the chase was Rapung, our teacher of Balinese, because he was a newcomer to the household and the monkey snarled and sprung at him every time Rapung passed near where it was tied: they hated each other. When it became plain that the monkey could not be captured so easily, one of the boys had the bright idea of having everybody pretend to attack Rapung, imitating the monkey, making faces, and squealing at him. Soon the monkey forgot that he himself was persecuted and joined in the attack, but when he was most aggressive someone grabbed him.

The pride of the Balinese has not permitted the development of one of the great professions of the East: there are no beggars in Bali. But this unique distinction is now threatened by tourists who lure boys and girls with dimes to take their pictures, and lately, in places frequented by tourists, people are beginning to ask for money as a return for a service. Ordinarily even a child would be scolded and shamed by anyone who heard him ask something from a stranger. A gift must be reciprocated and we were often embarrassed by the return presents of our poor neighbors. We gave Ktut Adi, a little dancer of eight, a scarf of no great value; one day soon after she came to us with a basket of rice, some eggs, and a live chicken, carried by her mother because the load was too great for her. Children of the neighborhood that Rose had treated for infected wounds always came back with presents of fruit, cakes, or rice which they handed casually to our house-boy, never mentioning them to us, as if they wanted to avoid making a demonstration of their generosity. Even children have a strong sense of pride.

The aristocracy is despotic and arrogant, but the ordinary people, although used to acknowledging the superiority of their masters, are simple and natural in an unservile and unsubmissive way. By the threat of passive disobedience and boycott they kept the princes from overstepping their bounds. Europeans complain that the Balinese make bad servants; they are too free, too frank, and do not respond to the insolent manner that the white man has adopted as "the only way to deal with natives."

Their moral code consists in maintaining their traditional behavior, observing their duties towards their fellow villagers and paying due respect to the local feudal princes. Among themselves they are kind and just, avoiding unnecessary quarrels and solving their disputes by the simplest and most direct methods.

The villages are organized into compact boards or councils, independent of other villages. Every married man—that is, every grown man—is a member of the council and is morally and physically obliged to co-operate for the welfare of the community. A man is assisted by his neighbors in every task he cannot perform alone; they help him willingly and as a matter of duty, not expecting any reward other than the knowledge that, were they in his case, he would help in the same manner. In this way paid labor and the relation of boss to coolie are reduced to a minimum in Bali. Since the world of a Balinese is his community, he is anxious to prove his worth, for his own welfare is in direct relation to his social behavior and his communal standing. Moral sanctions are regarded as stronger than physical punishment, and no one will risk the dreaded punishment of exile from the village, when a man is publicly declared "dead" to his community. Once "thrown away," he cannot be admitted into another of the co-operative villages, so no misfortune could be greater to the Balinese than public disgrace. This makes of every village a closely unified organism in which the communal policy is harmony and co-operation—a system that works to everybody's advantage.

By their ingenuity and constant activity they have raised their main occupation, the cultivation of rice, to levels unsurpassed by other rice-growing nations. Being essentially agriculturists, they are not interested in navigation and trade; living the easy life of the tropics, they are satisfied and well fed. The majority work the land for themselves, so they have not yet become wage earners and have enough freedom and leisure left to dedicate to spiritual relaxation. They are extraordinarily fond of music, poetry, and dancing, which have produced a remarkable theater. Their culture, unlike that of their cultural ancestors, the Javanese, is not yet in frank decline. Even the common people are better agriculturists, better craftsmen and artists than the average Javanese. The Balinese are by no means a primitive people.

Moreover, unlike the natives of the South Seas and similar races under white domination, the Balinese are not a dying people; far from that, in the last ten years a constant increase in the birth-rate has been recorded. The 1930 census gave the population of Bali as 1,148,000 people, or about 500 to the square mile, an enormous figure when compared with the 41 per square mile of the United States. This includes the foreign population: 7,935 Chinese, 1,544 Arabs and other Muslims, and 411 Europeans, of which only a small percentage are of pure European stock, the rest being Eurasians and certain Balinese, Javanese, Chinese, and Japanese who are given equal standing with Europeans by a decree making them "Staatsblad Europeanen."

For those interested in knowing something of the racial origins of the Balinese, it may be added that they are by no means a pure race, but a complicated mixture of the native aborigines, with superimposed layers of higher cultures of various types.[1] The Balinese are descendants of a pure "Indonesian" race mixed with the Hindus of Central and East Java, who were themselves Indonesians of Hindu culture, with Indian and Chinese blood. To these mixtures are further added traces of the Polynesian and Melanesian, the result being a picturesque variety of types among the Balinese: from the noble Hindu and Northern Chinese, to the Malay-Javanese, Polynesian, and even Papuan. While some have sleek hair, high nose bridges, and cream-yellow skins, some are dark and curly-haired like South Sea Island-

[1] The ancient inhabitants of the Malay Archipelago were "Indonesians," also called Malayo-Polynesians, Austronesians, Malaysians, and so forth. Of these, pure branches are to be found today in the Dayak of Borneo, the Batak of Sumatra, the Toraja of Sulawesi, and the Igorot the Philippines. They are called by anthropologists "Proto-Malaysians" to differentiate them from the "Deutero-Malaysians," those with Hindu, Chinese, and Arabic mixtures.

The original Indonesians perhaps came to the islands long before our era, probably from Southern China about 2000 B.C. (Heine-Geldern), found extremely primitive aborigines of the Vedoic or Negrito type already there, perhaps the most undeveloped form of humanity. The Indonesians spread their culture over the islands and introduced the cultivation of rice, outrigger canoes, domestic animals—pigs, dogs, chickens, and water-buffaloes—ironwork, mats, pottery, megalithic monuments, and probably the making of tapa cloth. They were often head-hunters and cannibals, and Dr. D. J. H. Nyessen suggests that they may have been the ancestors of the Polynesians.

The islands were at the crossroads of the ancient sea-routes, favored by winds and currents, so the natives mixed freely with the peoples of neighboring regions: India, China, Arabia, and the Melanesian and Polynesian islands. The Hindus established great colonies that became powerful empires, like Majapahit in Java and Srivijaya in Sumatra, and they exerted a marked influence upon the Indonesians, but they did not come in great numbers and were eventually absorbed. The same happened to the Chinese, who had come to Java since the beginning of our era, and it is possible that part of the army of Kublai Khan became incorporated into the native population around 1292, when Chinese influence predominated over the Hindu. I have been told by Chinese scholars that at one time they considered Bali as their colony.

ers. Some have large almond eyes, often with the "Mongoloid" fold, convex noses, and fine mouths; others have the concave, flat, broad noses, the squinty eyes, bulging foreheads, and prognathic jaws of the more primitive Indonesians. Thus the Balinese of today are the same people as the Hindu-Javanese of pre-Muslim Java, in the sense that they both underwent the same racial and cultural influences.

THE ANCIENT SURVIVAL: THE BALI AGA

At one time the island was populated by pure Indonesians, an ancient people who filed and blackened their teeth. They lived in small communities, family clans ruled by a council of Elders who acted as the priests of their religion. Their cult centered in the worship of the powerful spirits of nature, and especially those of their ancestors, with whom they continued to live, a great family of both the dead and the living. Occasionally, by means of mediums and sacrifices, they brought their ancestral spirits down to this earth to protect them. They buried their dead or simply abandoned them in the jungle to be carried away by the spirits, and it is possible that they even ate parts of the bodies in order to absorb the magic power inherent in their ancient headmen.

The pure descendants of these people, calling themselves Bali Aga or Bali Mula, the "original" Balinese, still live, isolated and independent, in the mountains where they found refuge from imperialistic strangers. Hidden in the hills of East Bali, near Karangasem, lies the village of Tenganan, where the most conservative of the Bali Aga preserve the old traditions with the greatest zeal. Tenganan is a rabidly isolated community, socially and economically separate from the rest of Bali, almost a republic in itself. It is shut off from the world by a solid wall that surrounds the entire village, which is meant to keep outsiders away, and is broken only by four gates, each facing one of the cardinal points. Of these gates, three open to the gardens and plantations of the village, but the main gate is so narrow that a stout person has difficulty in squeezing through. Such is the obsession for isolation in Tenganan that there is an official specially appointed to sweep the village after the visits of strangers, to obliterate their footprints.

We became acquainted with I-Tanggú, a youngish man with fingernails four inches long, who was the *perbekel* of Tenganan, the representative of his village with the Dutch Government. We were surprised to find him quite sociable. Once we played host to him in Denpasar and from then on we were often invited to visit Tenganan. Unlike the rest of the villages in Bali, there is hardly any vegetation around the Tenganan houses, which are all exactly alike and are arranged in rows on each side of stone-paved avenues. In the central place is the council house where the Elders meet, a long shed about ten feet wide by some seventy feet long, strongly built and apparently very old. Farther along are other buildings for public use, the purpose of some kept a secret. The most curious are the unique mill for grinding *kemiri* nuts to obtain oil, and the wooden Ferris-wheel, usually dismantled, in which the women revolve for hours in a strange rite. The dwelling of I-Tanggú is just like all the others: a small gate reached by a flight of steps leads into a court in which are the sleeping-quarters, the kitchen, and a long house for relatives and for storage. There is also a small empty shrine where the spirits may rest when they visit their descendants.

The people of Tenganan are tall, slender, and aristocratic in a rather ghostly, decadent way, with light skins and refined manners. The majority of the men still wear their hair long. They are proud and look down even on the Hindu-Balinese nobility, who respect them and leave them alone. They live in a strange communistic or, rather, patriarchal-communalistic system in which individual ownership of property is not recognized and in which even the plans and measurements of the houses are set and alike for everybody. The village of Tenganan owns communally enormous tracts of fertile and well-cultivated lands that fill every need of the village and make it one of the richest in the island. I-Tanggú told me this legend of how the land came to belong to the village:

"Hundreds of years ago, long before the Hindu-Javanese settled in Bali, the powerful king Bedaulú lost his favorite horse. Brokenhearted, the king sent the men of whole villages in all directions with orders to find the stray horse. The Tenganans went eastward[2] until,

[2] The people of Tenganan claim to have come originally from the district of Bedulu, named after King Bedaulú, near the once holy city of Pejeng. The Bratan people, a branch of the same family, are supposed to have gone northward in search of the horse. But having failed, they did not dare to return and still live near Singaraja in Desa Bratan, where they constitute a special caste of silver-workers, and where Patimah has her silver shops. The Tenganans still recognize their alliance with the people from Bedulu and make special visits to them at the feasts of the temple of Samantiga. The people of Bedulu also go to Tenganan on special occasions to make offerings.

after days of travel, they found the corpse of the horse. The king asked them to name their reward, but their spokesman said they wanted only the land where the horse was found; that is, the area covered by the smell of the carcass. Although the horse had been dead for many days under the tropical sun, Bedaulú considered this a modest request and sent an official with a delicate sense of smell to measure off the land, starting from the place where the horse lay. Accompanied by the chief of Tenganan, he walked for days, but no matter how far the two went, the smell seemed to follow them. Finally the official was exhausted and could go no farther; he said he considered the land already covered enough, and the Tenganans were satisfied. When the official left, the chief pulled from under his clothes a large piece of the rotten flesh of the horse."

I-Tanggú told me the story as we went up to the top of a hill to look at one of the remains of the famous horse; the penis, "which had turned to stone." On the summit, under a large tree, was the relic, a long river stone shaped like a phallus by the action of water. Passing people had left offerings on top of it. I-Tanggú also said that the people of Tenganan are not permitted to work their vast lands with their own hands, but hire other Balinese to do the agricultural work for them. The aristocratic communists of Tenganan go to the plantation only to make *tuak*, beer from sugar palms.

On the way down the hill, I was allowed a glimpse of the sacred temple of Tenganan, of which we had heard mysterious reports. It was a small enclosure under a great banyan tree surrounded by a low wall of uncut stones roughly piled up. Inside were a few mounds of the same stones, reminiscent of altars, and in one of them there was a larger stone with what appeared to be a natural cavity. I could not go into the enclosure because no outsider is ever permitted to enter it. I-Tanggú could not divulge the purpose of such a primitive "temple" and could not even name the deities worshipped there, but he added mysteriously that there were three of them! It seems extraordinary that this pile of stones is the only sacred, "essential" place of worship for the Tenganans, who are expert carvers and fine artists.[3]

Just outside the village I had seen a regular Balinese-style temple

[3] This extraordinary village must not, however, be taken as a typical Bali Aga community. Tenganan was deliberately cut off from the natural development of the rest of Bali and remains today a unique, rabidly conservative, and strictly tribal community that seems to take pride in doing things "differently," even from the rest of

with fine roofs and elaborate carvings, but this, I-Tanggú said with contempt, did not mean much to them and was more for the use of their Balinese guests and coolies, perhaps as a concession to the official cult of the island, so that they would not be considered as savages, people without a "proper" temple.

The clubs of virgins (*seka daha*) and of adolescent boys (*seka truna*), who are still untouched by the magical impurity supposed to come from sexual intercourse, are an interesting feature of Bali Aga villages not to be found among the Hindu-Balinese. In Tenganan a ceremonial meeting is held for them once a year. The virgins wear golden crowns covered with quivering flowers of beaten gold, and are dressed from the armpits to the ground in bright silk scarfs which they hold between jeweled fingers, often tipped with four-inch artificial fingernails made of solid gold. They appear dancing the *rejang*, arranged in line from the smallest baby, a year old, perhaps, to the grown girls who on past occasions have failed to obtain a husband. They dance accompanied by the *gamelan selunding*, an ancient, rarely heard orchestra that has great iron sound-plates, struck energetically by the old men of the village with oversize wooden hammers. This dance could not be more archaic and simple: standing in a double line, they fling the scarfs slowly away, first to one side, then to the other, half turning the body each time. In the long intervals between movements they stand motionless with downcast eyes until a change of position is announced by the orchestra. This is the whole dance; a slow-motion version of the stilted feminine dances of Java, giving one an unearthly feeling of suspended movement, and bearing no

the Bali Agas. Institutions that are the very essence of Balinese culture, such as the shadow-plays (*wayang kulit*), are unknown, while others are even forbidden. Many rites and festivals peculiar to Tenganan do not exist elsewhere.

Dr. E. V. Korn has made an exhaustive study of the Tenganan people (*De doorpsrepubliek Tnganan Pagringsingan*), but their religious concepts remain obscure, perhaps even to the Tenganans themselves. Like the other Balinese they worship the Gunung Agung and rule their life by the eternal principle of orientation—high and low, right and left. They venerate shapeless stones (*batú menurun*), considered to be the fragments of the famous horse of Oucé Seraya, stones that are the symbols of "origin" of totemic groups that are sharply divided into "right" and "left." The people of Tenganan were influenced by distorted ideas from an early version of pre-Majapahit Hinduism and have a vague notion of the Hindu Trinity, headed, however, by Indra, generally a minor deity, who is to the Tenganans the same as Siwa-Iswara, the supreme god, "Lord of the Center," with the *kubu* (home) of "Sanghyang" (Brahma) at the right and that of "Ijeng" (Wisnu) at the left. One of their lonely temples, or, rather, tabooed enclosures, is supposedly the reflection on this earth of the heavenly lake of Indra.

relation to the exuberant vitality of the Balinese dances we were accustomed to see.

Soon boys in their best clothes and wearing krisses begin to appear and form a group at the other end of the dancing-space, watching the girls. When enough boys have gathered, the music stops and the audience, mostly women, shows a lively interest. The music begins again, playing the theme for the *abuang*, a dance in which the boys express their preferences. One by one the girls step to the front to show themselves in a short posed dance with their eyes on the ground and their arms tensely out-stretched. Each of the marriageable girls has her chance, but the boys are shy and at first nobody takes up the challenge.

The *abuang*

It is only after the girls have danced a second or third round that one of the boys overcomes his shyness, walks up to his favorite girl when her turn comes again, and takes his place in a stately dance. If she is pleased, she will continue to dance with him until the bar of music is over, but if she dislikes the boy, she leaves the floor and goes back into line while the crowd laughs at the rejected suitor.

Marriage restrictions are peculiar in Tenganan; their isolationist law allows no one to marry outside the village, and even there only within certain rules as to family and caste. There was, for instance, the daughter of the priest who was already past marriageable age, but who could not find a husband since there were no unmarried men of her class. This continual inbreeding perhaps accounts for the decadent and aristocratic type of the people. A Tenganan who marries outside the village or breaks one of their taboos is thrown out of the village; such exiles have formed a small village of their own just outside the main gate, but they are never again admitted into the mother community.

The Balinese have often accused the Tenganans of cannibalism, which is of course indignantly denied and about which the Tenganans are extremely sensitive. But people from Karangasem and even renegade Tenganans tell naïve stories like this:

In olden days there were celebrations in which aged men were sacrificed and eaten, and once there were none left in Tenganan. For a long time the council had planned to rebuild the *balé agung*, the assembly hall, already in ruins. The wood for the pillars had been cut by the old men years before and was dry and well seasoned. But when the work was started and the time came to put up the pillars, the workers could not proceed, because nobody knew which was the bottom and which the top of the logs. In all Bali it is forbidden in a construction to stand a log "upside down"—that is, in the opposite direction from which it grew. Work on the *balé agung* was interrupted and there was worry and confusion, until a young man announced that, if they swore to stop eating their old men, he would find a way to locate the right end of the logs. After long deliberations the council agreed and presently the young man produced his own grandfather, whom he had kept hidden for years in a rice granary. The old man measured each log, tied a rope in the exact center, and had it lifted up; the end closer to the roots was heavier and the log tilted in that direction, so the council could proceed with their work, and old men could continue to live.

I have been told by Balinese that in Tenganan today a corpse is washed with water that is allowed to drip into a sheaf of unhusked rice placed under the body. The rice is then dried in the sun, threshed, and cooked. After the burial a human figure is made of the cooked rice which is served to the dead man's descendants, who proceed to eat it, each asking for some part—the head, an arm, and so forth—a funeral dinner that may well signify the ritual eating of the corpse to absorb its magical powers. This, of course, is pure hearsay which I could not verify through my Tenganan friends.

The Balinese also believe that human beings were sacrificed in Tenganan to make dyes for their famous ceremonial scarfs, the *kamben gringsing,*[4] a cloth that, because it is supposed to be dyed with human blood, has the power to insulate the wearer against evil vibrations and is prescribed at all important Balinese rituals. These scarfs, in which the warp is left uncut, are much in demand by the Balinese. The *kamben gringsing* is a loosely woven, narrow scarf of thick cotton with intricate designs in rich tones of rust-red, beige, and black against a yellowish background. The process of dyeing and weaving

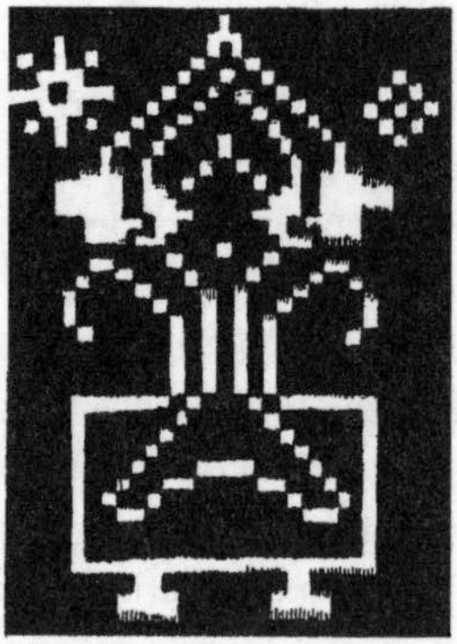

Human motifs woven on the *kamben gringsing*

is unbelievably long and complicated, and over five years are required from the time the cotton is prepared to the finished scarf, according to Korn. The threads are left in each of the dyes for months, macerated in kemiri oil for months to fix each color, and then dried in the sun for months after each stage. The design is obtained by the double "*ikat*" process (*ikat,* "to tie"): that is, the threads of both the warp and weft are patterned previous to the weaving. To do this warp and weft are stretched on frames, and groups of threads are tightly bound with fibers at certain points before they are dipped into the dye, so that the tied part remains uncolored to produce the design. This is repeated with each color, the part already dyed also protected by the fiber bind-

[4] *Kamben* means simply "cloth," "article of dress"; *gringsing* means "flaming," "mottles" like an orchid. Single *ikat,* where only the warp is "ikated," is common throughout Indonesia, and some are famous, like the large shawls from Sumba, Sumbawa, Roti, and Flores, which are highly prized; but a "double *ikat*" is extremely rare; besides those from Tenganan, others known are from Gujerat in India and simple shawls made in Zurich, Switzerland (according to Ikle).

ing. When the threads are finally colored and ready to be woven, the design of the weft is fitted exactly into the one on the warp, and a mistake spoils the work of years. Taking into consideration the laboriousness of the dyeing, the painstaking, difficult weaving, and the mystery that surrounds the secret process, it is easy to understand why the popular mind has endowed the *kamben gringsing* with such extraordinary powers. In Tenganan the scarfs are an essential part of ceremonial dress, and I-Tanggú told me that if he sold his he would lose his place in the village council. Only the finest scarfs are worn in Tenganan; imperfect ones or those in which the dyes fail to produce the required tones are sold to outsiders.

In North Bali, on the slopes of the Batur, above Tejakula, is the Bali Aga village of Sembiran, where even the daily language is different from that of the rest of Bali. There, as in Tenganan, the "temple" is a group of rough stone altars surrounded by a neglected fence. It is hidden in the jungle near the edge of a deep ravine, a dangerous haunted place, where not even the people of Sembiran would venture alone. In Sembiran the dead are not buried; after washing the corpse, it is wrapped in new cloth, carried to the edge of the ravine, and deposited on a bamboo platform with offerings, consecrated water, and the belongings of the deceased. There it is left for three days; if, after that, it has not disappeared, this means that the spirits did not care to take it, so it is thrown unceremoniously into the ravine to be eaten by wild beasts.

There are many other mountain villages that have resisted the influence of Hinduism. Although not as extraordinary as Tenganan and Sembiran, they are equally conservative Bali Aga, like Trunyan on the shores of Lake Batur, where the largest statue in Bali is kept, that of Ratú Gedé Pancering Jagat, powerful patron guardian of the village. There is Taro, the home of Kbó Iwá, a fearful giant of pre-Hindu days who was so great that there was never enough food to feed him and he went about eating people. To provide him with a place to sleep, the villagers of Taro built the longest council house in Bali. He is supposed to have carved all the ancient monuments and sculptured caves with his own fingernails. In the highlands between the Batur and the Bratan, the Gunung Agung and the Batukau, there are many Bali Aga villages, and in some, like Selulung, Batukaang, and Catur, there are remains of ancient and primitive monuments; stone statues and small pyramids, some of which are purely Indonesian in character, while others show early Hindu, perhaps Buddhist influence. In the Bali Aga villages there is much that remains of the ancient race who once inhabited all of Bali, but who were to become the fascinating Balinese of today.

NOTES ON THE HISTORY OF BALI

It seems difficult to reconcile the soft-mannered, peace-loving Balinese we know with the intrigue and violence of their turbulent past. For a thousand years the history of the island is a series of wars and heroic episodes that reached a dramatic climax only thirty years ago when the Balinese made a desperate but futile last stand against a modern army.

Bali was under the rule of Javanese kings from the earliest days of Hindu Java, but we first hear of Balinese dynasties in the tenth century of our era. In 991 A.D. a child was born of a Balinese king and a Javanese princess. He was named Erlangga and was sent to Java to marry a princess and to become a local chief in the kingdom of his father-in-law. Dharmawangsa, the ruler, was murdered suddenly and Erlangga took charge, saving the kingdom from total collapse and bringing it into even greater glory. Erlangga ruled during thirty difficult years, creating a strong bond between Java and his native Bali, which was then governed by Erlangga's brother in his name. Then, as befits a model hero of Hindu ideas, Erlangga suddenly renounced the kingdom he had made great and died a hermit under the guidance of his religious teacher, Mpú Bharada. Erlangga's kingdom was nearly destroyed by a plague supposedly brought by the dreadful witch Rangda, queen of evil spirits, who was, according to historians, Erlangga's own mother. Out of the mythical struggle between the magic of the witch and that of the great king, arose the legend *Calon Arang* (see Chapter 10) that made Erlangga the most famous figure of Balinese mythical history.

In later years Bali became independent of Java, but was again subjugated in 1284 by the army of Kertanagara, the king of Singasari (of the Tumapel dynasty). Singasari was destroyed eight years later by the new dynasty of Majapahit, and Bali again became free, only to be reconquered in 1343 by General Gajah Mada for King Rajasanagara, under whom the entire Archipelago became a vassal of Majapahit. During the next hundred years the power of the empire was undermined by civil wars and revolts in the colonies, and soon the great empire went into decline. The Balinese revolted against Majapahit time and again, but the uprisings were put down in memorable battles, after which military figures like Arya Damar and Gajah Mada became rulers of Bali and to them the present Balinese aristocracy traces its origin. Gajah Mada was sent to Bali to subjugate the king of the Balinese Pejeng dynasty, Dalem Bedaulú, who was supposed to have had the head of a pig. He was the owner of the famous horse of Tenganan. Bedaulú was a semi-demoniac character of supernatural origin who refused to recognize Majapahit supremacy. (See page 31.) He was defeated by Gajah Mada, and Bali once more came under Javanese rule.

The expeditions of Gajah Mada were the last military displays of the empire. In the meantime Muslim missionaries were becoming influential in Java and were converting princes who proclaimed themselves sultans of their districts, repudiating their allegiance to Majapahit. Soon peaceful propaganda turned into armed force; Muslim fanatics made war on Majapahit, which finally collapsed after it was weakened by internal trouble. Stutterheim is of the opinion that the empire's destruction came gradually somewhere about the year 1520. However, in the more picturesque but less reliable historic records (*babad*)[5] it is stated that Majapahit fell in 1478 under the reign of Brawijaya V (Krtabhumi, according to Stutterheim). Brawijaya was told by his chief priest that after forty days the title of Raja of Majapahit would cease to exist. The king had such implicit faith in the prediction that at the expiration of that time he had himself burned alive. His son, unable to withstand the Muslim invasion and not daring to disobey the sentence of the priest, escaped to his last remaining colony; followed by his court, his priests, and his artists, he crossed over into Bali, settling on the south coast of Gelgel, at the foot of the Gunung Agung. There he proclaimed himself the king of Bali, the Dewa Agung, the hereditary title of the Rajas of Klungkung. The Dewa Agung divided the island into principalities which he gave to his relatives and generals to govern. By degrees these local chiefs grew independent of the Dewa Agung and became the Rajas of the smaller kingdoms into which Bali was later divided.[6]

[5] Raffles: *The History of Java.*

[6] Badung, Gianyar, Tabanan, Mengwi, Bangli, Klungkung, Karangasem, Buleleng, and Jembrana.

It was of extreme significance for the cultural development of Bali that in the exodus of the rulers, the priests, and the intellectuals of what was the most civilized race of the Eastern islands, the cream of Javanese culture was transplanted as a unit into Bali. There the art, the religion and philosophy of the Hindu-Javanese were preserved and have flourished practically undisturbed until today. When the fury of intolerant Islamism drove the intellectuals of Java into Bali, they brought with them their classics and continued to cultivate their poetry and art, so that when Sir Stamford Raffles wanted to write the history of Java, he had to turn to Bali for what remains of the once great literature of Java.

THE DUTCH

The Balinese princes prospered and soon started out for new colonies, extending their influence to the East and conquering the neighboring islands of Lombok and Sumbawa. In 1510 the Portuguese adventurer Alphonso de Albuquerque discovered Sumatra and made voyages to the "Spice Islands" to procure valuable cargoes of pepper, cloves, and nutmeg, all the while fighting pirates, hostile Malays, and Javanese. In 1597 a fleet of Dutch ships, headed by a former employee of the Portuguese, Cornelius Houtman, discovered Bali. He and his men fell in love with the island and made excellent friends with the king, a good-natured fat man who had two hundred wives, rode in a chariot drawn by two white buffaloes which he drove himself, and owned fifty dwarfs whose bodies had been distorted into resemblance of kris handles. After a long sojourn in the island, some of the Dutch returned to Holland to report the discovery of the new "paradise;" others refused to leave Bali. The news created such a sensation in Holland that in 1601 the trader Heemskerk was sent to Bali with presents of all sorts for the king, who in turn presented him with a beautiful Balinese lady.

The relations between the Indies and Europe later were darkened by the appearance of the Dutch East India Company, an organization of merchants and traders whose goal was the unlimited exploitation of the islands. They promoted wars, seized lands, established monopolies of opium (if a native was caught selling opium he was put to death), and collected revenues from the natives that were even greater than those exacted by the local princes. The traders used every possible means to gain the favor of the Rajas in order to control Bali, bringing gifts to them of Persian horses, gilt chairs, red cloth, wines, brass candelabra, and so forth. Not meeting with much success, they resorted to political intrigue, selling arms to the enemies of the Balinese while offering assistance against those they had armed, in exchange for concessions.

Meantime the Balinese had completed the conquest of Lombok (1740). There the Dutch tried to influence the Balinese governors to become independent of Bali and join the "Honorable East India Company." After two centuries of ruthless operation the company, already bankrupt and decayed, attracted such unfavorable criticism that the Dutch Government was forced to assume control, and in 1798 the Dutch East India Company went into inglorious collapse.

In the following years trouble started for the Balinese; the sultan of Surakarta, in Java, ceded to the Dutch "rights" he did not have over Bali, but they took no steps to claim them. The Balinese princes recognized Dutch supremacy, but retained their local autonomy. In 1846 the question of the ancient right of the Balinese to confiscate the cargo of wrecked ships brought the first Dutch military expedition against North Bali, which, after a series of battles, ended in Dutch control over the northern states of Buleleng and Jembrana in 1882. The Balinese princes were made to sign a treaty in which piracy, slavery, and the exercise of shore rights were forbidden and in which they promised not to permit the establishment of any other European power in Bali.

In 1885 there was a rebellion of Sasaks, the vassals of the Balinese in Lombok, while in Bali internal wars broke out among the various Rajas. Sasaks were brought to Bali and forced to fight. During these wars the united states of Badung and Klungkung annexed Mengwi and they all turned against the troublesome Raja of Gianyar. The Sasak chiefs complained to the Dutch, asking to be freed from the tyranny of the Balinese princes. The Dutch were becoming alarmed at the friendly advances of the Balinese towards the English, and officials were sent to negotiate a peace. They were unsuccessful and even apologies demanded for insults to the envoys were refused.

THE LOMBOK WAR

In 1894 the Dutch landed an elaborate military expedition in Lombok and sent an ultimatum to the Lombok Raja, who was under the influence of Gusti Gedé Jilantik, Raja of Karangasem, a friend of the Dutch. The terms of the ultimatum were accepted and the Raja agreed to pay a "war indemnity" of one million guilders. Conferences were held between the Balinese and the Sasaks, and everybody seemed satisfied. The army remained in the capital for a few weeks giving military demonstrations while waiting for the payment of the indemnity. Soon there were rumors of dissension between the old Raja and the princes, and the Balinese began to appear less friendly; the camps were no longer visited by the princes, and one day the women did not even come to market. This was the signal for the Dutch to prepare for the defense.

That night they were attacked by fierce rifle-fire through holes made in the thick walls of the palaces and houses around the Dutch encampments. Orchestras played continuously and all night the great alarm-drums were beaten. The Dutch returned the fire as well as they could in the darkness, trying to demolish the stone walls of the palace, but without much success. Captain W. Cool, an eyewitness, relates: "The noise was deafening and bullets were falling fast around us. . . . Added to all this was the ear-splitting sound of the tomtoms and the war cries of the Balinese as an accompaniment to the hammering and boring of the walls." Every bivouac was besieged by an invisible foe. On the dawn of the third day the army retreated towards the sea, leaving nearly one hundred dead and three hundred wounded. Among the dead was General Van Ham, second in command. A regiment was taken prisoner and was marched along the lines of Balinese soldiers; Captain Cool tells us that "they were all armed, yet they maintained a respectful attitude. Not an offensive word was said or a threatening hand raised." The starving prisoners were fed with white rice and drinks of orange and coconut water. The wounded were provided with fresh bandages. After a sojourn in the palace they were released with a letter from the Crown Prince stating that he was releasing the prisoners as a gesture of friendship and as proof that he wished to end hostilities. But the letter was ignored by the commander-in-chief, and at the seashore the decimated army erected new fortifications protected by the warships at anchor.

When the news of the defeat reached Java and Holland, the press flared up with indignation against "the sinister treachery" of the Balinese. Immediately large reinforcements of men and heavy artillery were sent from Java. New fortifications were built and the Sasaks were forced to fight against the Balinese. The offensive was started against the capital, the army advancing cautiously, bombarding the villages along the way, and burning them to the ground after the Sasaks had looted them. Mataram and Cakranegara, the two residences of the princes, were shelled and the Dutch succeeded in blowing up their arsenals and rice stores. The city of Mataram was captured first. Men and women, caught unawares, stabbed themselves rather than fall into the hands of the soldiers. Once occupied, Mataram was ordered razed to the ground. Every wall was laid low and all the trees chopped down. The work of destruction took over a month. Next came the attack on Cakranegara, the last important city of the Balinese in Lombok. They defended it tenaciously, but could not long resist the effects of artillery, and every palace and house that showed resistance was soon in flames. The Crown Prince, Anak Agung Ktut, the greatest enemy of the Dutch, was killed. The city was taken, the old Raja captured and exiled to Jakarta, where he soon died of a broken heart. Thus ended Balinese rule in Lombok. The new conquest cost the Dutch 214 dead and 476 wounded, besides 246 who died of sickness and fatigue.

CONQUEST OF SOUTH BALI

In Bali, things continued in a state of turmoil. The allied states of Badung, Klungkung, and Bangli united to make war on Gianyar. In 1900 the powerful prince of Ubud, Cokorde Gedé, influenced the Dewa Manggis, Raja of Gianyar, to ask for help from the Dutch Government. An army was sent immediately to protect Gianyar, which was automatically annexed by the Dutch. In May of 1904 the small Chinese steamer *Sri Koemala,* coming from Borneo, was wrecked and looted in Sanur, on the south coast of Bali. The owners held the Dutch Government responsible and demanded three thousand silver dollars' damages and the punishment of those culpable. Official embassies were sent to obtain the amount from the Raja of Badung, Anak Agung Madé, who refused. The dickering went on for two years, but finally the Dutch, angered because the prince could not be made to pay, ordered the closing of Badung to all exports and imports and asked the co-operation of the bordering states. All of the independent princes refused to close their frontiers. That was the beginning of the struggle for supremacy between the Dutch and the Balinese

Rajas. The people themselves were, for the most part, indifferent. To them the victory of one side or the other meant chiefly a change of masters, somebody else to whom to pay taxes.

In the fall of 1906 the Raja definitely refused to meet the demands and on the 15th of September a large military expedition landed in Sanur, only three miles from Denpasar, the capital of Badung. Here the people remained indifferent to the presence of the soldiers, because, being under the influence of the peace-loving Brahmanas, they were unconcerned with the troubles of the Raja. But at dawn of the following day an army of Balinese with golden spears, coming from Denpasar, made a surprise attack. The fighting went on all day; a few Dutch soldiers were wounded, but hundreds of Balinese were killed in the unequal fight, and by evening the Balinese were forced to retreat. The Dutch remained in Sanur for a few days, occasionally giving concerts for the Balinese, ironically playing the *Sourire d'amour* on their brass band. When the advance on Denpasar was started, the army was opposed all the way, but when they came to the palace of Kesiman, just outside the town, they found it deserted. There the acting ruler had been killed by a priest in an argument over whether they should oppose the Dutch. It is curious that inside the palace they found two bronze cannon that had belonged to Napoleon, bearing the date 1813 and the Napoleonic "N," together with a number of muskets from 1620.

Early on the morning of September 20 the navy bombarded Denpasar, shells falling on the palace and the houses of other princes, setting them on fire. This caused the civilian population to flee, leaving the Raja with only about two thousand men. Soon after the bombardment the army was reported near Denpasar; the Raja expected that the attack would be directed against the main entrance of the palace on the south side, as their military law would require, but unexpectedly the army turned and made for the north. Inside, the household had been worked up to a state of frenzy, almost a trance; everything of value was destroyed and the palace was set on fire. The king, seeing his cause lost, told his followers that to defend the palace was hopeless, but anyone who wished could follow him into a *puputan,* a "fight to the end." The only honorable thing left for him was to die a dignified death, rather than be exiled like the Raja of Lombok, to die away from Bali, and without the proper rituals of cremation. In a moment the Raja, his Pungawas, his generals, and all his relatives, men and women, were ready, dressed in their best and wearing their finest gold krisses. The women were even more enthusiastic than the men; they were dressed in men's clothes, short white loincloths caught between the legs, covered with jewelry, and with their hair loose. They carried krisses and spears broken in half to be used more effectively at close range. At nine in the morning the fantastic procession left the palace, with the Raja at the head, carried on the shoulders of one of his men, protected by his gold umbrellas of state, staring intently at the road in front of him, and clutching in his right hand his kris of gold and diamonds. He was followed by silent men and entranced women, and even boys joined the procession, armed with spears and krisses. They marched on through what is today the main avenue of Denpasar towards Kesiman, and when they turned the corner, the Dutch regiment was only three hundred yards away. The commander, astonished at the sight of the strange procession, gave orders to halt; Balinese interpreters from Buleleng spoke to the Raja and his followers, begging them anxiously to stop, but they only walked faster. They came within one hundred feet, then seventy feet, then made a mad rush at the soldiers, waving their krisses and spears. The soldiers fired the first volley and a few fell, the Raja among them. Frenzied men and women continued to attack, and the soldiers, to avoid being killed, were obliged to fire continually. Someone went among the fallen people with a kris killing the wounded. He was shot down, but immediately another man took his place; he was shot, but an old woman took the kris and continued the bloody task. The wives of the Raja stabbed themselves over his body, which lay buried under the corpses of the princes and princesses who had dragged themselves over to die upon the body of their king. When the horrified soldiers stopped firing, the women threw handfuls of gold coins, yelling that it was payment for killing them; and if the liberating bullet did not come soon enough, the maddened women stabbed themselves. When they had nearly all been killed, a new group approached, led by the Raja's brother, a twelve-year-old boy who could hardly carry his spear. The interpreters again tried to stop them, but were ignored, and they were all shot down.

The way to the burning palace was now free, except for the hundreds of corpses that covered the road. Everywhere lay broken spears and krisses with gold handles studded with enormous diamonds and rubies in pools of blood. On the side of the Dutch there was only one man killed, a sergeant stabbed by a woman.

In the afternoon of the same day the army attacked the palace of the neighboring Raja of Pemecutan, but the Balinese met them with artillery-fire that caused some losses among the Dutch. Near the palace another *puputan* took place: the insane old Raja, dressed in yellow silks and carried in a gold sedan chair, followed by his wives and Pungawas, went out to meet the army after setting the palace on fire. Soon all were killed. When the palace was taken, the last obstacle to the conquest of Badung, the tired soldiers returned to Denpasar, but their victory tasted of a terrible moral defeat.

The people returned to their houses. All night long, hurried wholesale cremations were held while the Dutch buried their dead. The next morning a young Pungawa came to see the commander. He said he had been away the day before and had missed being killed with the rest, so he asked to be shot by the soldiers. When he was refused, he drew his kris and stabbed himself before he could be prevented. The Balinese then gave up their arms.

A few days later Gusti Ngurah Agung, the Raja of Tabanan, came with his son to speak to the Resident. He had changed his gold umbrella for a green one in sign of submission. He wanted to surrender on condition that he be allowed to retain his title and have the same rights as the Raja of Gianyar and Karangasem; Resident Liefrink replied coldly that he must be deported from Bali until an answer to his request came from the Government. He would be held in the palace for the night and on the next day would embark for Lombok. Next morning both the Raja and his son were found dead; the son was poisoned, supposedly by an overdose of opium, and the old Raja had cut his throat with a blunt *sirih* knife. Thus the state of Tabanan fell to the Dutch.

Two years later the Dewa Agung of Klungkung remained the only independent Raja, but he was "insolent," and the stories of Lombok, Denpasar, and Pemecutan were repeated; an armed force was sent to punish him and another great *puputan* took place in the main avenue of Klungkung; the highest Raja in Bali was killed, with his whole family.

Two of the women who survived the Denpasar *puputan*, sisters of the Raja, were aunts of Gusti Oka, the young prince in whose house we lived. They are now white-haired old ladies, but they remember every detail of the struggle and one showed me two bullet wounds in her side. Gusti was only two years old at the time and he was rushed to another village with his little cousin, the present Regent of Badung, but Gusti's father was killed and his house destroyed. Another relative of the Raja who survived the massacre told us she fainted when she was cut in the face by the spear of a falling man. All she remembers was "the cool hissing of the bullets" in her ears; she added: "like music."[7]

The army remained in Bali until 1914, when it was considered that Balinese resistance was sufficiently controlled, and the army was replaced by a police force. The Dutch then reorganized the Government of the island along the lines it had under the Rajas; those who had been favorable to the Dutch, their allies in Gianyar and Karangasem, were allowed to retain their autocratic rights over the people of their districts and were given certain supremacy over other ruling princes, mostly the descendants of the former Rajas. They were made puppet regents, responsible to the Government for the behavior of their subjects and for the payment of taxes, which they collect through relatives whom they appoint as chiefs, *pungawa*, of the districts under their control. Each regent is, however, supervised by a Dutch Controller, who is supposed to act as his "elder brother" and whose orders are called recommendations.

NOTE ON MAYA DANAWA

Jane Belo in "A Study of Customs Pertaining to Twins in Bali" (see Bibliography) quotes the legend of Maya Danawa and the origin of Delam Bedaulú from the Balinese manuscript *Usana Bali*:

"It was long ago, in the time when the great mountain, the Gunung Agung, had just been made. A fierce and terrible Detya, Maya Danawa, was in power over the land. He was jealous of the gods and did not allow the people to give them offerings. The gods banded together to fight the demon and a war ensued in which many people were killed.

"Finally Batara Indra was able to overpower Maya Danawa, but in killing him his plan was to make him alive again, dividing him into a male and female part, to become the first Raja of Bali. The spirit of the demon was placed in a coconut flower, and on the slopes of the Gunung Agung the

[7] The official details, dates, and so forth of the conquest of Denpasar come from the account of a witness, Dr. H. M. Van Weede: *Indische Reisherinneringen* (Haarlem, 1908).

gods came and blessed it, and out of the coconut flower they made to come two children, a boy and a girl, who were called Mesula-Mesuli."

The boy and girl twins married and had children, also twins, who continued to rule in Pejeng. These twins also married and had more twins, until a seventh generation of twin Mesula-Mesuli. The last male of these twins rejected his black and ugly sister in marriage for a girl dancer, thus breaking the line of royal twins. The last twin born was endowed with great magic powers; he could allow a retainer to cut his head off and replace it without harm to himself. But one day the head fell into a river and was lost, carried away in the rushing stream of a sudden *banjir*. The retainer in desperation cut off the head of a pig and placed it on the shoulders of the king, who from then on had to live on a high tower and forbade his subjects to look up at him. He was seen, however, by a small child who passed unnoticed and who spread the news of the pig-headed king, who became then known as Bedaulú, He-Who-Changed-Heads.

In the manuscript *Catur Yoga* we came across additional details of the great war between the gods and Maya Danawa:

> ". . . The gods were defeated by Maya Danawa and driven back to where a spring of poisoned water had been created by the demon. The thirsty gods drank and died, all except Indra, who struck the ground and produced a spring of the elixir of immortality, *amreta*, with which he was able to revive the gods." The local of this spring is supposed to be the holy spring of Tirta Empul near Tampaksiring. The gods attacked again, Maya Danawa was wounded, and his blood flowed into the great river Petanu that runs near Blahbatu. Today the waters from this river may not be used to irrigate rice fields because it is believed that rice watered by it will, when cut, exude blood.

CHAPTER THREE

The Community

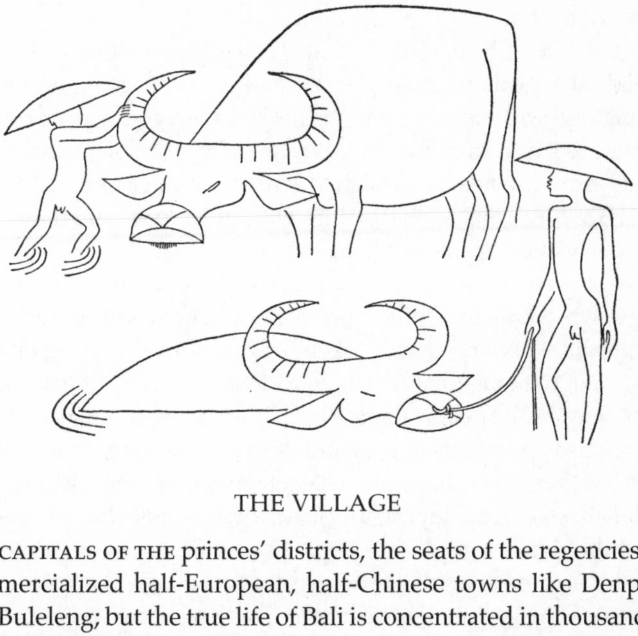

THE VILLAGE

THE CAPITALS OF THE princes' districts, the seats of the regencies, are commercialized half-European, half-Chinese towns like Denpasar and Buleleng; but the true life of Bali is concentrated in thousands of villages and hamlets. With their thatched roofs they lie buried under awnings of tropical vegetation, the groves and gardens that provide for the needs of the villagers. Out of the chartreuse sea of rice fields they surge like dark green islands of tall palms, breadfruit, mango, papaya, and banana trees.

Underneath the cool darkness, pierced only by the shafts of sunlight that sift through the mesh of leaves, are the houses hidden from view by interminable mud walls that are broken at regular intervals by long narrow gates. All the gates are alike: two mud pillars supporting a small roof of thick thatch, giving access to each household by a raised doorstep of rough stones. In front of every gate is a stone bridge, or, simpler still, a section of coconut tree trunk to ford the deep irrigation ditch that runs invariably along both sides of the road.

A simple village consists of family compounds, each completely surrounded by walls, lined on each side of a wide well-built avenue that runs in the direction of the cardinal points; from the mountain to the sea, the Balinese equivalent to our "north" and "south." The villages grew as they spread in these directions, and the Dutch had only to pave the main streets and extend them through the rice fields to obtain the five-hundred-mile net of automobile roads that covers this small island.

The Balinese, being still essentially pedestrians, took good care to shade the roads with large trees, and every morning and every evening one sees the people in the streets, men going to work nonchalantly beating rhythms on their agricultural implements, or returning from the fields overloaded with sheaves of rice heavy with grain. Poised women come and go with great loads or shiny black clay pots on their heads. If it happens to be market day in the village, at dawn the roads are crowded with husky people from the near-by villages who come to sell their produce—piles of coconuts, bananas, or vegetables, pottery, mats, baskets, and so forth—carrying on their heads even the table that serves as a stand. If there is a feast in the village temple, the people parade in yellow, green, and magenta silks with fantastic pyramids of fruit and flowers, offerings to the gods, in a pageant that would have made Diaghilev turn green with envy.

Naked children play at the gates by the bell-shaped baskets where the fighting cocks are kept. Each morning the baskets are lined out on the street so that the roosters may enjoy the spectacle of people passing by. Small boys wearing only oversize sun-hats drive the enormous water buffaloes, which in Bali appear in two colors, a dark muddy gray, and a pale, almost transparent pink, an albino variety. A water buffalo will not hesitate to attack a tiger; their ponderous calm and their gigantic horns are awe inspiring to Europeans, who have been told that their odor infuriates the buffaloes. They have often charged white people for no apparent reason, although the smallest Balinese boy can manhandle the great beasts. They love to lie in the water and be scrubbed by their little guardians, who climb all over them and hang from their horns when they take them for their evening bath. The buffalo tolerates the children perhaps as a rhinoceros tolerates the birds that eat the ticks on its back.

The Balinese raise a fine breed of cattle, a beautiful variety of cow, with delicate legs and a long neck, that resembles overgrown deer more than ordinary cows. Ducks are driven in flocks to the rice fields, where they feed on all sorts of small water animals. Their guardian is a boy or an old man who leads them with a little banner of white cloth on the end of a bamboo pole topped by a bunch of white feathers. This he plants on the ground and he can then go away for the rest of the day, sure that his ducks will not wander away. At sundown the trained ducks gather around the flag waiting to be taken home. When the duck-guardian arrives, the flock is all together, and at a signal from the flag, they march home, straight as penguins and in perfect military formation.

All Balinese domestic animals are rather extraordinary; chickens are killed constantly by rushing automobiles, but their owners make no provision to keep them from the road except the low bamboo fence that bars the house gate, and that is intended, perhaps, more for the pigs, which in Bali belong to a monstrous variety that surely exists nowhere else. The Balinese pig, an untamed descendant of the wild hog, has an absurd sagging back and a fat stomach that drags on the ground like a heavy bag suspended loosely from its bony hips and shoulders.

The roads are particularly infested with miserable dogs, the scavengers of the island. Most dogs are attached to the house they protect and keep clean of garbage, but they reproduce unchecked and there are thousands of homeless living skeletons, covered with ulcers and mange, that bark and wail all night in great choruses. The Balinese

are not disturbed by them and sleep peacefully through the hideous noise. The curs are supposed to frighten away witches and evil spirits, but I could never discover how our neighbors knew when it was an ordinary mortal and not a devil that the dogs barked at; they always awoke when a stranger came into the house at night. Such dogs were undoubtedly provided by the gods to keep Bali from perfection.

The Balinese make a clear differentiation between the dwelling-grounds and the "unlived" parts of the village, those for public use such as the temples, assembly halls, market, cemeteries, public baths. The village is a unified organism in which every individual is a corpuscle and every institution an organ. The heart of the village is the central square, invariably located in the "center" of the village, the intersection of the two main avenues: the big road that runs from the Balinese "North-South" and a street that cuts it at right angles from "East-West." Consequently the crossroads are the center of a Rose of the Winds formed by the entire village; the cardinal directions mean a great deal to the Balinese and the crossroads are a magic spot of great importance.

All around and in the square are the important public places of the village; the town temple (*pura desa*) (A), with its hall of assembly (*balé agung*), the palace of the local feudal prince (B), the market (C), the large shed for cockfights (*wantilan*) (D), and the tall and often elaborate tower where hang the alarm tomtoms (*kulkul*) (E) to call to meetings, announce events, or warn of dangers. Also important to the village life is the ever present *waringin* (F), a giant banyan, the sacred tree of the Hindus, planted in the square. Under its shadow take place the shows and dances given in connection with the frequent festivals; market is also held there in villages that do not have a special market enclosure. In ancient villages the *waringin* grows to a giant size, shading the entire square and dripping aerial roots that, unless clipped before they reached the ground, would grow into trunks that unchecked might swallow up a village. A beautiful village *waringin* is an enormous rounded dome of shiny leaves supported by a mossy, gnarled single trunk hung with a curtain of tentacles that are cut evenly at the height of a man; but in the *waringins* that have grown freely outside the village, the tree spreads in every direction in fantastic shapes. The aerial filaments dig into the earth and grow into whitish trunks and branches emerging at illogical angles and filled with parasite fems, a dreamlike forest that is in reality a single tree.

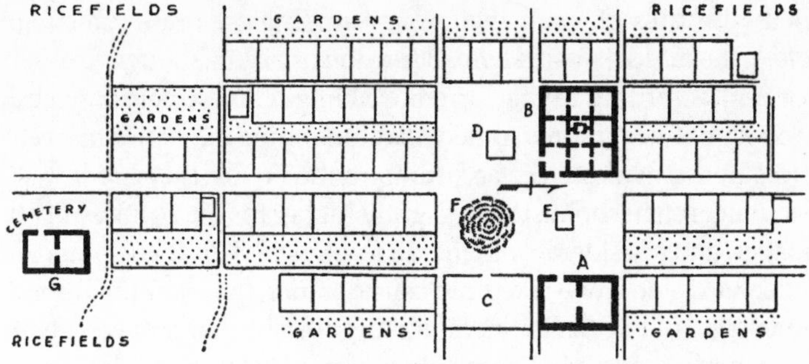

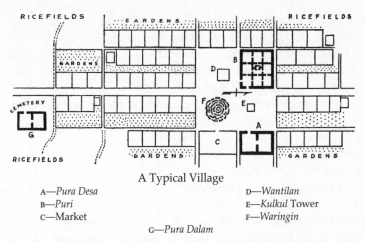

A Typical Village

A—*Pura Desa*
B—*Puri*
C—Market
D—*Wantilan*
E—*Kulkul* Tower
F—*Waringin*
G—*Pura Dalam*

Somewhere in the outskirts of the village are the public baths and the cemetery, a neglected field overgrown with weeds and decaying bamboo altars, with its temple of the Dead (G) and its mournful *kepuh* tree, a sad and eerie place. The bathing-place is generally a cool spot shaded by clusters of bamboo in the river that runs near the village, where all day long men and women bathe in the brown water in separate modest groups. Some villages have special bathing-places with fancy water-spouts and low walls of carved stone, with separate compartments for men and women. Tejakula in North Bali is famous for its horse bath, a special compartment that is larger and even more elaborate than the baths for the people.

THE MARKET

Important towns have great utilitarian markets of cement and galvanized tin where shrewd Arabs and Chinese keep regular shops of cloth and imported knick-knacks, but the average *desa* holds market under the shadow of the *waringin* or under square shades of straw mats like umbrellas. A few people sell there every day; the "big" market takes place every third day of the religious calendar. There are "market associations" organized in groups of three *desas* that work together, holding market in rotation every day in each of the three villages. The women are the financiers that control the market; one seldom sees men in it, except in certain trades or to help carry such a load as a fat pig. Even the money-changers are women, who sit behind little tables filled with rolls of small change, *kepeng*, Chinese brass coins with a hole in the middle, worth a small fraction of a cent (about five to seven to a cent according to the current exchange). These coins are strung into rolls of two hundred, called *satak* (one string of twenty-five cents). Prices in the market vary according to the buyer; they are lowest to the villager in his home town, slightly higher for the Balinese of other villages, and considerably higher to foreigners. This is customary and understandable if one takes into consideration the communal spirit of the village and of the Balinese. It is significant that an average meal in the market costs a Balinese only twenty-five *kepeng* or about two or three American cents. The Balinese do not count in the present Dutch monetary system of guilders and cents; among themselves they use only the smallest unit, the *kepeng*, and the largest, the *ringgit*, big silver coins (worth two and a half guilders) that are normally divided into 1,200 *kepeng*. The Balinese cannot visualize a foreigner using *kepengs* and when I bought peanuts or a banana at a food-stand and they did not have Dutch pennies for change, the women vendors were amused to see me pocket a heavy string of *kepengs*. Accustomed to dealing in hundreds and thousands, they have acquired a surprising knowledge of mathematics, and the women can add, subtract, multiply, or divide with the speed of an adding machine. To test this ability we used to ask the women of our household for multiplications of numbers of several ciphers; with mysterious operations of a few *kepengs* spread on their laps, they always found a quick and accurate result.

The market reaches its height about noon, when it is hard to walk through the crowd of semi-nude women. At that time the animation is very great and the market resounds with the excited bargaining, the constant coming and going of people, and the squealing of the pigs that are mercilessly stuffed into baskets or carried in the arms of the women like babies. The thousand smells of coconut oil, flowers, spices, and dried fish combine to make the pungent smell so characteristic of Balinese markets. The soft browns and yellows of the women's skirts and the bright-colored sashes they wear, the graceful movements and unconscious beauty of their poses, make of the market a show as interesting to watch as their luxurious and spectacular feasts. The excitement subsides gradually in the late afternoon, when the women return home loaded with the merchandise they have bought or with the empty baskets balanced on one corner, in the most absurd defiance of the laws of gravity, by the heavy strings of *kepengs* that record the day's sales. Most markets have a little shrine for the goddess of fertility and of gardens, Dewi Melanting, also the deity of the market, to whom the vendors make small offerings for good luck.

THE SOCIAL ORDER

It was surprising to discover the extent to which the question of rank obsesses so simple and democratic a people as the Balinese. In our house every time Gusti came near, everyone scrambled down the veranda steps to place themselves at a level lower than his. Once in Ubud we received a visit from two little girls, high-caste dancers of ten. They were to spend the night in the house, but they would not sleep unchaperoned and a servant was appointed to watch over them; when they heard he was to sleep in the attic, twenty feet up, they snatched their pillows and ran upstairs, not to be defiled a second longer by an inferior located above them. They perferred to sleep on a hard bench rather than in the bed made for them, while the poor servant had to sleep on the floor. Once we visited a high priest, who invited us to remain for lunch; when the food came he apologized for having to ask us to sit down, because, he said, "the gods would not like it" if he, a Brahmana, placed himself at a level lower than ours. We observed similar situations over and over again among people of all classes.

Five centuries of feudal domination by an aristocracy have made the Balinese so conscious of caste, the determination of a man's place in society by his birth, that the whole of their social life and etiquette is molded by this institution. A member of the aristocracy is constantly on the look-out so that his inferiors may keep to their appointed level and address him in the language of respect. Princes still demand the adulation and kowtowing of their former vassals, although now their power has ended and their prestige is greatly diminished. Caste rules today are largely restricted to the observance of established formulas of etiquette even among the princes, who were always fairly liberal. Caste relations are relaxed and simple compared with the absurd intolerance of India. But the common people take for granted the divine superiority of the aristocracy and are so thoroughly accustomed to arrogance that they submit to the demands of caste etiquette as a matter of duty.

By far the most strict of social taboos is that on intermarriage. A man may marry any woman he wishes as long as she is of equal or lower caste, but under no circumstances may a low-caste man marry a woman of a higher class. For such a man even to have relations with a woman of the royal or priestly castes was a crime punished in olden times by the death of both; the woman perhaps stabbed by a member of her disgraced family, the man thrown into the sea in a weighted sack, the most degrading of deaths. Today punishment is simply exile of the guilty couple to the wilds of Jembrana or the little penal island of Nusa Penida. But like everything else in Bali, special concessions can be made if the difference of castes is not very great and the man is influential; in some cases the affair has been settled by fines, annulment of the marriage, or a special edict raising the man's caste.

ETIQUETTE

Despite strict caste regulations, the code of etiquette is simple and reasonable; a general air of frankness and friendliness prevails in daily intercourse, and it is only in the presence of an arrogant prince that the common man has to humiliate himself; even more polite treatment is given to a high priest. From the beginning a stranger is struck by the extreme politeness and gentle manners, even in the lower classes. The strongest criticism that can be made of a person is that he has no manners. Such a freak should be avoided.

One is greeted on the road with the words: "*Lungga kija,* Where to?" and a visitor is welcomed with: "*Wau rauh,* Just arrived." These are formulas not to be taken in their literal sense. A visitor takes leave by asking to be excused: "*Tiang pamit,*" the answer to which is simply "Yes," "*Ingé*" There are no other words for greeting or for goodbye. It is not polite to answer a question with monosyllables, and one should not point with the index finger. It is better to use the words for the cardinal points to indicate direction, but if one must point, it should be done with the thumb, holding the rest of the hand closed.

The Balinese are constantly paying visits to one another, but no one would dream of making a formal visit without bringing along a gift of some sort: fruit, rice, eggs, or chickens, given casually and received without a word of thanks. It is taken for granted that the present is appreciated by the acceptance of it, but if one wants to be over-polite, one says: "*Tiang nunás,* I want it" or "I like it" (*idéh* in the common language). An object is handed with the right hand while touching the elbow with the left, and it is received with the same gesture.

The gift problem became acute for us as we entered into a competition with our friends and neighbors for more and more valuable presents. Someone would arrive with a basket of eggs or rice; we repaid the visit taking a cheap headcloth. On the next visit they came with piles of fruit and even live chickens, so we had to rush to the market to buy a batik shirt or a bottle of Javanese perfume. We generally ended by exchanging brocades, krisses, and so forth for pieces of silk, flashlights, and fountain pens. The Balinese are very much concerned with the price paid for an object, and they always insisted on knowing what we paid for a present, until we realized that it was a great mistake to remove the price tags. When we bought new glasses or new plates, Dog, our house-boy, washed them carefully around the label so as not to rub off the price.

It is necessary to be properly dressed to pay or to receive a visit. The breasts of men and women should be covered by a special breast-cloth, a *saput* for men and a *selendang* for women. People in the house always dashed for their breast-cloth, usually an ordinary foreign towel, when a special guest arrived. Immediately the visitor was provided with green coconuts to quench his thirst, with cigarettes and betelnut. Up-to-date Balinese like to offer soda-pop, coffee and Chinese pastries. The chewing of betelnut is the first gesture of hospitality and the main social pastime of the entire archipelago. To chew betel, a piece of the green nut of the betel palm is dabbed with a little lime, wrapped in pepper leaves, *sirih,* and the whole chewed together with a large wad of shredded tobacco that is held under a monstrously protruding lower lip. The combination of betel, *sirih,* and lime produces an abundant flow of saliva, red as blood, and the betel addict spits constantly, leaving crimson splotches wherever he goes. After certain guests departed our house-boy always had to wash the veranda steps because they looked as if a murder had been committed on them. Today betel-chewing is not favored by the younger generation, not only because it looks so disagreeable, but because it spoils the teeth. The older the person, the fonder he is of betel, and the ingredients are always kept on hand in boxes with little compartments or in special satchels of woven pandanus. Old men without teeth have a special bamboo tube with an iron rod to mash the various ingredients together. The *sirih,* betel, and lime are presented to guests in little ready-made packages often beautifully decorated with streamers of delicately cut-out palm-leaf. They are called *canang* or *baséh,* a gift.

A host must act as servant to his guests, himself attending to their comfort and not partaking of the refreshments. Meals are also served by the host, even if he has servants and assistants, and he can eat only after the guests have finished. If the visitors come from another village, they are expected to stay for the night and even for days at a time. The place of honor in the house is then assigned to them. After a reasonable period of time the visit is repaid and the presents reciprocated.

Very strict are the rules between men and women. On public occasions men and women keep to themselves in separate groups, and people from Gianyar are shocked to see the sexes mingle in Badung while watching a show. In the same manner the people of Badung are disgusted because in Tabanan men and women bathe near together. It is rude to look into a public bath and even worse to enter it unless to bathe. Then the other bathers become figuratively invisible. Great courtesy is shown even among people who are intimate and it is extremely unusual for a man to "get fresh" with a girl in public; should it happen, the man would be severely punished. Thus a woman can confidently remain in her house while her male relatives are away at work, and a girl can go anywhere without fear of being approached by a stranger. Girls of high caste usually go chaperoned. Lovers are particularly careful not to show their emotions in public.

To neglect releasing a loud belch after a meal would be taken by the host as a sign that the food was not satisfactory. In general the Balinese are very frank in actions that would be out of the question among us, such as clearing the throat, spitting, and so forth. These are perfectly normal actions no one needs to conceal.

But the key to Balinese etiquette among the castes consists in the language spoken and in keeping at the proper level. Under no circumstance should a common man stand higher than an aristocrat. If a lowly person has to pass a nobleman who is sitting, he stoops in front of him until he is reasonably far away, and to address his superior he must squat or sit on the ground clasping his hands together in front of his chest or over his left shoulder. To retire, after begging leave, he walks backwards, stooping and holding his hands clasped.

LANGUAGE

When two strange Balinese meet, as for instance on the road, they call each other as *jeró*, a safe, polite way of addressing someone whose title is unknown. Since there are no outward signs of caste, the appropriate titles cannot be used and all the words for "you" (*caí, nyaí, naní*) are extremely familiar and derogatory. Strangers talk in the middle language, a compromise between the daily speech and the polite tongue. Should, however, one be of low caste and the other a nobleman, it would be wrong for them to continue talking in this manner, and one of the two, probably the high-caste man, will ask the other: "*Antuh linggé*? Where is your place (caste)?" which is answered by the other man's stating his caste. Then the usual system is adopted; the low man speaks the high tongue and the aristocrat answers in the common language.

When I started to study Balinese I found it disturbing to hear the people around the house talking in the daily language and then suddenly shifting to high to address Gusti, our landlord-prince, who answered them in the common language. The high and low tongues are not two dialects or even variations of the same languages, but two distinct, unrelated languages with separate roots, different words, and extremely dissimilar character. It was always incongruous to hear an educated nobleman talking the harsh, guttural low tongue, while an ordinary peasant had to address him in the refined high Balinese.

The low language is the everyday tongue spoken by equals at home, at work, and at the market. It is undoubtedly the native language of the island and belongs to the Malayo-Polynesian dialects, the aboriginal languages of the archipelago. The high language is similar to Javanese and is of Sanskrit-Javanese origin. It is flowery, and rich in shades of meaning; I have been told that to speak it well, one should know about ten different words to express the same idea. Few Balinese can speak the high language well, and the ordinary peasant generally ignores it, except perhaps for standard expression to address a superior. The peasant learned to listen only when he became a vassal of the Hindu-Javanese feudal lords, who had to learn the language of the island, but they demanded to be addressed in their own, high tongue by the unworthy natives. The natural politeness of the Balinese perhaps gave birth to the middle language, used when in doubt of a man's caste.

It is an important rule that one may not use high terms when speaking about oneself; it would be poor taste to call one's head by the elegant term *prabú*, instead of the common word *sirah*, or to refer to one's feet as *tiokor* instead of *batis*. It would be a dreadful insult to speak of someone's head as *tandas,* meaning the head of animals.

The type of language used in conversation is prescribed by one of the strict rules of caste etiquette, and the use of the wrong form is a serious offence. A prince has to be addressed as "highness" (*Ratú* or *Agung*), but he and the people of his caste talk to everybody in the low language, except perhaps to their parents, elder brothers, and members of the priestly caste, the Brahmanas. Polite people (not all high-born people are considered polite) are supposed to address old people in the high language.

There is still a fourth language, the Kawi, used on ritual occasions, in poetry and classic literature. It is archaic Javanese, in which nine out of ten words are Sanskrit; but the knowledge of Kawi rests almost entirely with the priests and scholarly Balinese.

The language problem of Bali has been further complicated by the addition of Malay, now officially the language of the Dutch East Indies. It is taught in the schools and is spreading rapidly among the Balinese youth because it is considerably simpler than the difficult Balinese and is free of the caste regulations. Thus a modern Balinese scholar would require five languages for social and cultural intercourse: the high, middle, and low Balinese, plus Kawi and Malay. Such a linguist is not rare today in Bali.

THE CASTES

The Hindu caste system as it is found today in Bali was not firmly implanted until after the conquest by the famous Gajah Mada. Then Hindu-Javanese rule was definitely established and the island was divided into vassal territories paying tribute to the local princes that were given control. The natives lived under a class system of their own long before that time, however. They had their ranks, with a sort of aristocracy that combined government and priesthood.

Hindu-Javanese penetration did not reach many of the remote mountain communities, which remained outside the feudal territories. There, even today, live the conservative old-fashioned Balinese, entrenched against the landlords, regarding them as intruders. In these villages the Hindu castes are not recognized and the descendants of the primitive aristocracy proudly retain their titles and their authority. At the top of the long list of native ranks are the *pasek* and the *bandesa,* the heads of the two central institutions of the old-style community: the temple of "origin," and the assembly hall, ritually belonging to the "right" and "left." I was told that a girl of these castes who marries a man of the Hindu aristocracy is publicly renounced by her family and spiritually "thrown out" of the village. Also held in respect are the blacksmiths, a caste in themselves, *pandé,* the ancient firepriests who made the magic krisses, symbol of the family's virility. Even Brahmanas, highest among all classes, must use the high language when addressing a *pandé* who has his tools in his hands.

In the tributary districts the natives coordinated their castes with those of the new nobility, in a great scale of ranks that have now become so muddled through intermarriage that they appear confused even to the Balinese themselves. The original castes still remain as subdivisions of the fourth and lowest of the Hindu castes, the Sudras, who constitute about ninety-three per cent of the population of Bali.

The Hindu-Balinese nobility is divided into the three well-known groups: the priests, Brahmanas (Brahmins of India); the ruling royalty, Satrias (Ksatriyas); and the military class, Wesias (Vesiya). They are supposed to originate directly from the gods. According to the legends, the Brahmanas sprang out of the mouth of Brahma, the Satria from his arms, and the Wesia from his feet. Perhaps the reason why the common people look upon their nobility with such respect is that they have still an unshaken belief in their divine origin. The true Balinese religion consists mainly in the worship of the family ancestors, with the patriarch-founder of the village as the communal god. Thus it was easy for the conquerors to establish their own dead kings as ancestral gods, since they, too, descended from canonized kings and holy men who were in turn descendants of the highest divinities. This fitted perfectly with the Balinese idea of rank and with their cult of ancestors. In many legends the great kings and religious teachers of the past were considered as reincarnations of gods, so I was never surprised when a priest or a prince assured me in all seriousness that his family descended from Indra or Wisnu, or some such divine character.

Such is the caste complex of some Balinese that I often found silly boys from Denpasar posing as members of the higher castes when they visited a strange town where they were not known. Some common people say that once they were of a higher caste and that their present state is due to faults committed by their ancestors. Good behavior on this earth brings a raising of caste in the next incarnation, and bad behavior the opposite; consequently social position in the world of men is the result of behavior in former lives. Many Wesias claim that their families were Satrias lowered in rank while they were ordinary humans; such was the case of the ancestor of the royal families of Badung and Tabanan, the legendary Arya Damar, who was lowered to a Wesia. On the other hand, the Balinese insist that the Raja of Karangasem was a Wesia who had himself elevated to the Satria caste after the fall of the Klungkung dynasty.

The "highest of the high," the Brahmanas, claim descent from the great priest Wau Raúh, who wandered all over Bali in legendary times creating children with women of all classes, even the servant women of his wives. These children, the future priests, were the heads of the various Brahmana families, some of which are higher than others, according to their purity of blood on account of the origin of their various mothers. The Brahmanas are further divided into two sects: the Siwa and Bodda, the descendants of the two famous brothers, the religious teachers Mpú Kuturan and Mpú Bharada, who created the laws for the Balinese. A distinction is made between initiated Brahmanas, the priests, and the uninitiated.

It is generally recognized that the Brahmanas are higher than the Satrias, but a great undercurrent of disagreement and animosity has always existed between them on this account. The Satrias resented having to pay homage to the Brahmanas, and the legends and historical records are full of instances of the feud created by their struggle for caste supremacy. Kings were deposed by adventurers supported by Brahmanas; high priests cursed rulers and drove them to commit suicide, and often they had to flee and hide to protect their daughters from arrogant princes who wished to take them as wives, thus affronting their superior caste pride. Once in a *jauk* performance I saw a typical story enacted: The Raja of Bali, the Dewa Agung of Klungkung, wanted to prove that Brahmanas were fakers when they claimed supernatural powers. He placed a duck in a well and sent for the highest priest in the country so that he could prove his magic power by guessing what was in the well. The priest said that it was a great serpent, a *naga*. The king laughed in his face and uncovered the well; a huge *naga*, fire streaming from its nostrils, shot out and coiled around the king's body and would have crushed him to death if the priest had not killed the *naga* with a miraculous arrow. From then on, the princes did not dare to question the supremacy of the

Brahmanas. This legend is still commemorated at the cremation of Satrias, when the Brahmanic priest shoots arrows at the *naga banda*, the serpent that conveys the soul to heaven. (See page 351.)

But the dispute still goes unsettled, with the priest's sphere of influence restricted now to purely religious duties. Brahmanas are devoid of administrative powers, but serve as judges in the courts; they could not be sentenced to death and did not pay taxes to the princes, but instead had to pray for the well-being of the land. Their own regulations forbid them from attending cockfights or making money in commerce. They are exalted and aloof, but ordinary people secretly laugh at them; there is a popular story, *Pan Bunkling*, in which the hero is constantly poking fun at Brahmanas and their philosophy. The Brahmanas can be identified by the titles of Ida Bagus for men and Ida Ayú for women, both meaning "Eminent and Beautiful."

Satrias are supposed to be the descendants of the former rulers, and many claim to be of the family of Sri Krisna Kapakisan, the great overlord that ruled Bali at the time of Gajah Mada. He was supposedly born of a heavenly nymph and a stone Brahmana (Korn). The Satria caste is divided into two main groups; the Satria Dalem, the descendants of the ruling princes, and the lesser Satria Jawa, those of the prime ministers' families. Today Satria blood is very mixed, owing to intermarriage with the lower castes, some of which are considered even lower than the higher Wesias. The Satrias are called by the titles of Ratú, Anak Agung, Cokorde, and so forth. Among the lesser groups are the Predewa and the Pangakan (who bear the titles of Prebagus and Presanghyang).

The members of the third caste, the Wesias, are better known in Bali by their title of Gusti, also subdivided into many groups. The highest, the Pregusti, are the descendants of Arya Damar, the predecessor of Gajah Mada. The lower Wesias are the descendants of the lesser Javanese princes and Pungawas. The Gustis are the majority of the Balinese nobility and are often politically influential.

Certain professions are unclean, and if practiced within the village pollute the *desa*, such as the indigo-dyers, pottery-, palm sugar-, and *arak*-makers. Although Korn claims there are no real outcastes in Bali, I was told by everybody that indigo-dyers belong to a special caste, the *pamesan*, who are forbidden by traditional law to use wood or cotton in their cremation bier, which should be open, without a roof, and devoid of ornaments. They said that the *pamesan* are often rich and careful to conceal their origin. When it is mentioned that someone is a *pamesan*, it is done in a pitying whisper. There was a scandal in Denpasar about someone who had maliciously accused another of being a *pamesan*. This may perhaps point to a trace of the idea of the outcaste.

The aristocracy divides the population of Bali into "insiders" (*dalem*), which are themselves, those who live within the palace; and the "outsiders" (*jaba*), the common people. From the point of view of the great majority of the Balinese, this is a fallacy, since it is the nobility who are the real outsiders. The feudalism of the Hindu aristocracy was curiously only superimposed on the Balinese patriarchal communism, and centuries of feudal rule have failed to do away with the closed independence of the village communities. Thus the nobility is left devoid of voice where it concerns the inner affairs of the community, despite the Pungawas and Perbekels they appoint to keep an eye on the villagers.

THE ORGANIZATION OF THE VILLAGE

One moonlight night the "tock tock" of a *kulkul* attracted us towards the temple of the wind-swept, ancient town of Kintamani, on the rim of the foggy crater of the Batur. On the road we joined an old man carrying a torch who informed us they were calling the village members to the monthly meeting in the *balé agung*, the "great house," the council hall of the community. It was a long shed with a raised platform running along its entire length and with a thick thatch of sugar-palm fiber, faintly lit by a primitive oil lamp. There sat the village Elders, cross-legged, in two rows facing each other, talking quietly, each in his allotted place and carefully avoiding the empty seats of those who had not yet arrived. Slowly the platform filled up. When everybody was present, the old headman of the council called the roll while two assistants went around with flashlights to see that everybody was properly dressed: wearing the ceremonial breast-cloth, and a kris.

Thus the Elders of the old villages like Kintamani meet at each full moon to partake of a ceremonial banquet in the company of their gods. The assistants distributed the food from a large basket, placing a heap of parched rice with a ring of beans around it in front of each man, served by a specified ritual number of handfuls. After the distribution of food was over, the oldest member sat at the extreme end of the *balé agung* in an attitude of prayer and recited a rousing speech to invite the ancestral spirits, the *pitara,* to join in the banquet. With a clear voice he called: "*Kakí! Kakí*! Grandfather! Grandfather!" followed by the formula of invitation. Then he took his seat again at the head of the council, by the side of the little raised wooden throne dedicated to the village forefathers. Then everybody relaxed, breaking the tense silence; they discussed village affairs, the improvements of the temple, the coming feast, and gossiped for a while before wrapping the remaining rice in banana leaves to take home.

The ceremony was a clear example of the religious significance of the social organization of the village; the close relationship between the cult of the ancestors and the administration of the community. A Balinese village is a self-contained, independent community, a little republic ruled by a council of representative villagers (*krama desa*), in which everyone has equal rights and obligations. The independent village is called a *desa,* a term we shall employ to designate the legal, "complete" village that has the three reglementary temples: (1) the civil temple (*pura desa*), where the main celebrations are held and where the *balé agung* is located; (2) the temple of "origin" (*pura puséh,* the "navel"), the ancient shrine of the earlier days of the community, dedicated to the symbolical patriarch-founder of the village; and (3) the temple of the dead (*pura dalem*), out in the cemetery.

Such a village is economically and politically independent of all others, except for a curious relation of blood. It often happens that various neighboring villages are united by a strong bond into an association of related villages which worship a common original ancestor and with a common temple of "origin," located in the oldest village of the group, which they recognize as a "head" or "mother" village. From this it is supposed that the other villages sprung, and when they grew became independent. Such village associations cooperate with one another by sending offerings and representatives to the temple feasts of the other *desas*.

Just as the temple of origin is the shrine of the Great Ancestor, so the *balé agung* is the home of the spirits when they visit their descendants, the symbolical throne of their authority. Like everything in Bali, the *balé agung* is divided into "right" and "left," with the chiefs and council members classified in the same manner. They sit on the long shed either at the right or at the left, on a spot set by their rank. New members act as attendants without a seat, but at the meetings squat on the ground outside the shed, until a seat at the end of the club-house is left to them by the death of a member. They advance progressively with age, the entire line moving up each time there is a vacant seat, until they reach the higher places towards the head of the *balé agung*. The headmen keep a record of each member's position in the building, in which the names of the members are written on the palm-leaf.

Every normal married man who owns a house or a plot of land in the village territory is compelled to join the village association, and his refusal would be punished by the denial of every assistance, confiscation of his property, and possibly even exile from the village. Theoretically all the land in Bali belongs ultimately to the gods, who lease it to the Balinese to work it and live from it; consequently landownership in an absolute sense cannot exist in the Balinese mind. Thus the *desa* authority, as representative of these gods, controls the land of the village, the homes, private and communally cultivated rice fields, grazing-lands, and the grounds left wild (*pecatu*) that provide bamboo, rotan, pandanus, wood, and so forth. From the lands adjoining the *desa* a worthy member may obtain an agricultural plot or the ground for his home. If someone has to move to another village and is justified in leaving, he asks to be released from the association and has the right to take with him the value of his share of the village property, but his land and his house return to the *desa*. His property is confiscated without compensation, Korn says, if he leaves the society without explanation.

The headmen of the association, the *kliang desa*, rules the village in the name of the council. He is usually elected by common approval, but his office may be hereditary if the son of a popular chief is believed to possess his father's virtues. Should he be found to be undesirable, he is politely asked to resign and a new *kliang* is elected. A good village chief is a popular and influential man although he may be poor and simple. Once elected and after the choice has been sanctioned by the gods, he cannot decline to hold office, except under severe penalty. Even then his services are not rewarded, and the advantages he enjoys by his position are insignificant; he receives a slightly larger share of land, perhaps a double share of the food distributed from offerings, and he is free of certain duties. He does not receive any salary despite the burden of his obligations and responsibilities; he has to administer the society, preside over the meetings, manage and organize all of the *desa* festivals. He shares the executive duties of the *desa* with the *penyarikan*, a lesser official (who is not, however, under his authority), a scribe and a number of messengers, none of whom are rewarded.

Under the rule of the princes the system was greatly undermined, especially where the villages grew too large to be effectively managed by such a simple patriarchal organization. In the conquered territories the lands were gradually taken away from the *desa* and its authority was weakened until the function of the *desa* is now reduced to the upkeep of the village institutions, the celebration of village festivals, and religious ceremonies. The *desa* remains, however, the bulwark of the *adat* law, the net of traditional regulations owned by each village, in which all possible cases are carefully worked out in the most remarkable simple logic.

THE BANJAR

As the *desa* government lost control over the social and economic organization and as the village grew, simultaneously with the power of the local prince, it became divided into smaller communities within the *desa*, quarters or wards, the *banjars*: co-operative societies of people bound to assist each other in marriages, home festivals, and especially during the expensive cremations. The various *banjars* of a village take part in the *desa* activities, assisting in the repair and improvement of the temples and contributing to the village festivals. The *banjars* have recaptured a great deal of the administrative power that the *desa* lost to the princes, although they are subject to the present-day Government (that of the Dutch through the princes), but they remain socially independent within their territory, with their boundaries generally established by the main road on one side, the lesser streets on another, and the rivers and ravines on the outskirts of the village. They have often rice fields worked communally to provide for their banquets and to enlarge their income, which is mainly derived from fines and entrance fees, kept in a communal bank that lends money to needy members. Everyone enjoys absolute equality and all are compelled to help one another with labor and materials, often assisting a member to build his house, to prepare his son's wedding, or to cremate a relative.

Membership is compulsory; after marriage a man receives a summons to join the *banjar*. He is given ample time, but if after the third summons he has not joined, it is considered that he deliberately refuses to comply and he is declared morally "dead," is denied even the right to be buried in the cemetery, and is boycotted from all communal activity.

Like the *desa*, the *banjar* is ruled by a *kliang banjar*, elected by the members, with the choice approved by the gods through consultations with mediums. The *kliang* of the *banjar* is not remunerated for his difficult work, except for the honor attached to his position and certain insignificant concessions like extra rice at banquets, a small percentage of the fines collected, and presents from members who receive special services, like part of the reward offered for lost cattle, for surveys, for assistance in marriages, and so forth. He cannot decline to serve and can be deposed if found unsatisfactory.

The *banjar* has considerable property: It owns its meeting halls, the *balé banjar*, a club-house without special religious significance, with its drum-tower to call to meetings. The *balé banjar* is provided with a kitchen and with all sorts of cooking implements: pots and pans, chopping-blocks, knives, etc., which are lent to members who require them. The *banjars* also own the village orchestras and the dancing-properties—costumes, masks, and head-dresses—which are stored in a *gedong*, a brick building where they are safe from theft or fire.

The men spend most of their spare time in the *balé banjar*, gossiping, trying out their fighting cocks, watching a rehearsal of a play or of the orchestra, or just sitting. If the *banjar* is prosperous, it takes great pride in giving elaborate banquets with music and entertainment. These may happen at the great national festivals, at the anniversary of their little *banjar* temple, or at the inauguration of a new roof, a new orchestra or dancing-group. But also the private festivals of the members become *banjar* affairs, and *banjars* like Belaluan, where we lived, celebrated feasts with staggering frequency. Only the men may prepare banquet food, and often we were awakened in the middle of the night by the *kulkuls* calling them to kill the turtles and the pigs for a feast. Banquet food takes long to prepare and the animals have to be slaughtered in the middle of the night to ensure the freshness of the meat and of the sauces in the difficult climate of Bali. After two in the morning before a feast everybody was busy; the men chopping meat, cooking, scraping coconuts, building sheds and altars; the women carrying water, making offerings, cutting out ornaments of palm-leaf or wrapping individual packages of *sirih* and betel for the guests.

By noon the banquet took place, the men sitting in the *balé banjar* in two long rows facing each other with their individual mountains of rice, pig, and turtle meats served in large squares of banana leaf, drinking *tuak* and making loud jokes. When the meal was over, *kendis* of water were passed so that the guests could wash their hands and mouths. The rest of the day and most of the night was spent watching cockfights, plays, and dances.

Most important of *banjar* property is a little communal temple (*pamaksan*). If the *banjar* grows beyond the function of village quarters, or "ward," its *pamaksan* temple may become a temple of "origin"; then they will build their formal village temple (*pura desa*), their temple of the dead, out in the cemetery, and, having the three reglementary temples (*kahyangan tiga*) that every complete community needs, they will ask for independence from the village and will become a full-fledged free *desa*.

In the old mountain villages the *desa* system has remained untouched by the influence of the princes. Before the advent of the Dutch, they controlled their states through district landlords, the Pungawas, usually members of the prince's family, who appointed lesser tax-collectors, the Perbekel, one in every village. A Perbekel ruled only with the interest of his master in mind, often disregarding the local *adat*, with the result that he was regarded as an intruder and remained a complete outsider in the affairs of the village. Thus the system was saved because these agents had to be content with collection of taxes and the enforcement of princely orders. But the Balinese could always find regulations to curtail the power of the princes, and if their demands interfered too much with traditional institutions, the people simply boycotted them and refused to obey.

Following the conquest of Bali, the Dutch found the *desas* divided into many small spheres of influence: the princes, the *desa* chiefs, *banjar* heads, and so forth. In the hasty reorganization of the political system they centralized the Government for control of the complex conglomerate of *desas*, logically enough, following the system of the princes, creating Government districts headed by Dutch officials assisted by the former landlords. They preserved the prince (Regent), the Pungawa, and the Perbekel to see that the taxes were paid. Finding the *desa-banjar* relationship incompatible with Western management, they redivided the villages, often in an arbitrary way, and renamed the towns and *banjars*, ignoring their traditional connections. The *desa* became simply any "big" village, and the *banjar* was simply "hamlet" or "quarter of the village." What was close by was joined together, and what was separated by distance was cut off, forming the so-called Government *desas* and Government *banjars*. There are cases of *banjars* merged into one, and small *desas* degraded into *banjars* or joined with other small *desas* to make a large *desa* worthy of the name, despite the fact that it might have more than one *balé agung*. These new villages exist in official documents, but not in the Balinese mind, forcing the people to make a strong distinction between the "Adat Desa" and the "Gouvermen' Desa."

LAW AND JUSTICE

A "bad man" does not have a chance in the strict communal Balinese system. Everyone is so dependent on the co-operation and goodwill of others that he whose conduct is not good, or who in some way fails to be in harmony with his community, becomes a boycotted undesirable.

In Bali moral sanctions carry greater weight than physical punishment; light faults bring automatic fines, the confiscation of property, or temporary suspension from the society; but the punishment for major offences ranges from the dreaded boycott from all *desa* activities to permanent exile, total banishment from the village. Since the death penalty has been abolished by the Dutch, the fearful formula of declaring a man "dead" is now the capital punishment. A man expelled from his village cannot be admitted into another community, so he becomes a total outcaste—a punishment greater than physical death to the Balinese mind. It often happens that a man who has been publicly shamed kills himself.

In the *adat* law of every village the line of conduct for every act of the villagers is carefully set down. In a general way, the most serious crimes are those that seriously impair the well-being of the community and most especially acts that would weaken the village magic, such as temple vandalism, theft from the gods, arson, running amuck, and murder, some of which may be punished by the killing of the offender on the spot. Everybody has to report, armed, immediately upon the signal of alarm (the fast continuous beating of the large *kulkul*), to be ready to extinguish a fire or to stop a man that has gone temporarily insane and has run wild. In Denpasar one afternoon the alarm call was sounded. It was the siesta hour, but instantly everybody was up and out; they grabbed sticks, spears, agricultural implements, or whatever was at hand and rushed out, some on bicycles, towards the sound of the *kulkul*. Everybody in the *banjar* turned out and on the road we even met the old judge, our neighbor, who could hardly walk, but who tagged along brandishing a great sword. It turned out to be simply a fire that was quickly extinguished with everybody's aid. When the excitement was over, we returned home with the crowd, listening to their reminiscences of recent cases of alarm and of men who ran amuck and were killed on the spot. Desecration or theft of temple property, if at night, can also be punished with immediate death. One night in a village near Kesiman two men were caught in the act of robbing the temple. The alarm was sounded and the villagers killed the two men as they put up a fight. They showed us the weapons that were taken from the thieves.

Other serious offences are the consistent failure to perform village duties, disobedience to officials, refusal to pay fines, repeated absence from meetings, theft of village property, especially of legal village documents, adultery, incest, bestiality, rape of an immature girl, witchery, the cutting of certain trees, theft of irrigation water, or damage to another's property, like allowing cattle to trample a planted field. Crimes against the prince, or even against Brahmanas, are severely punished, but they do not affect the spiritual cleanliness of the village—one more instance of the position of the aristocracy as outsiders. An old man told us that in former times a prince might kill or mutilate a man for offences against caste, as, for instance, for a common man to have had relations with a noble girl. A man who stole from the prince might have had his hands cut off.

Once we had the opportunity to observe the old-fashioned manner in which an ordinary thief is punished: Passing through Silekarang, we met a strange procession led by an old man who carried two sheaves of rice on a pole. There were flowers and leaves decorating the sheaves, and he wore red hibiscus on his gray hair. His wrinkled brown body was smeared with broad streaks and crosses of white paint all over his face, chest, and back. He was followed by a mock retinue of some fifty men carrying green boughs, yelling and beating little bamboo *kulkuls*. They informed us that the old man had stolen the rice and that the shameful parade was his punishment. Should he have refused to comply, he would have been thrown out of the village. We asked the men if a jail term, as would be the punishment in Denpasar, would not be more severe or more effective than a single afternoon of public disgrace, but they were all emphatic that it was just the reverse; a thief, they said, treated in this manner will never steal again, while locking him up in the Government jail would not help anybody; they would give him free food, he would not be shamed, and besides the company would make him worse.

As the parade resumed the march with the resigned old man at the head, a compassionate passer-by handed him a little package of betel and *sirih* to chew on the way. Later I was told in Ubud of a similar case where the thief was paraded all over the town with the pair of old shoes he had stolen, hung around his neck. It was significant that during our entire stay in Bali, with the house always open and filled with Balinese visitors, we never lost anything.

THE COURTS

The Balinese like to settle their differences peacefully, and if possible to come to an agreement among themselves. Otherwise they apply to the village chiefs, the *kliang* or the *penyarikan* of the *desa* or *banjar* to act as mediators for a friendly settlement. Disputes concerning rice fields or irrigation water are settled by the council of a special agricultural society, the *subak*. Should it become necessary to adopt a strong decision, the village council votes for a verdict.

In any case the village heads leave no stone unturned for a quick settlement of the affair to prevent its becoming involved in a legal court procedure, which is always distasteful to them, and it is only as a last resort, when all other resources have failed and passions are very much aroused, that the Balinese will appeal to the official high tribunal, the *kerta*.

The repugnance of the people against having to appeal to the *kerta* is only part of the Balinese policy of keeping the princes from interfering too much in their affairs. The *kertas* are the courts of the princes and they are generally composed of three Brahmanic priests who act as judges. They are assisted by a number of *kancas*, "lawyers," and a scribe.

Trials take place in a special shed, built over a high stone or brick platform. The Kerta Gosa, the court house of Klungkung, one of the inevitable sights of Bali, is already famous because of the lurid paintings that cover the entire ceiling, depicting the punishments that await a law-breaker in hell. The court house is beautifully decorated; two stone serpents flank the stairs that lead to the platform where the judges sit on great gilt chairs.

A trial must be conducted with the greatest dignity and restraint. There are rules for the language employed, the behavior of the participants, and the payment of trial expenses. It is interesting that court procedure resembles that of cockfights in its rules and terminology. On the appointed day the plaintiff and the defendant must appear properly dressed, with their witnesses, and their cases and declarations carefully written down. An absentee or one whose case is badly stated loses his suit. The *kancas* read the statements of each party and then those of the witnesses in their successive order. No one is allowed to speak unless he is addressed. Talking excessively or too loud, quarrelling, or pointing at the judges is punished by a fine. When the case has been thoroughly stated, the witnesses have testified and the evidence has been produced, the judges study the statements and go into deliberation among themselves until they reach a decision.

Besides the witnesses and the material evidence, special attention is paid to the physical reaction of the participants during the trial, such as nervousness, change of color in the face, or hard breathing. Dr. Korn writes that in former times there was a curious official, the *batú tumpeng*, also to be found at cockfights, whose participation in the procedure was to sit silently, watching and listening, so that he could form an unprejudiced opinion. After the judges reached a decision they submitted their verdict to the *batú tumpeng* and if he did not agree, they had to confer anew. As an absolute neutral, he informed the contestants of the decision.

The most important evidence is the swearing of the oath of truth that either one of the two parties (it is never foreseen which) will be required to take. After the verdict is announced, the judges will specify the type of oath and who shall take it. Then the date is set by the religious calendar. There are "little" and "big" oaths, all terrifying in their content, but with varying effects; some will affect only the person of the perjurer with minor misfortunes, but in the "big" oath all of his descendants, even unto the third generation, will be cursed by dreadful calamities.

Although the curse may be averted by obtaining an expensive neutralizing formula from a dishonest high priest, taking an oath is an extremely serious and dangerous performance that must be accompanied by elaborate ritual. The man about to swear appears in the temple with all his relatives, even small children, with his head bare and wearing white clothes, symbol of cleanliness. He sits cross-legged among the offerings, holy water, and incense, facing the *penyarikan,* who begins to read the text of the oath in a loud, relentless voice, enumerating the calamities that will curse him and his family, who appear anxious and worried. Then the *penyarikan* tears the palm-leaf in which the text of the oath is written and puts the ribbons of it into a jug of holy water. The man drinks the water and makes a reverence with a flower while he is sprinkled with the remaining water, after which the pot is dashed to the ground and broken. He and his descendants have good reason to be frightened at the swearing of the oath; Krause gives us the following version of it:

". . . Perjurers and their accomplices shall be confounded by every evil and be struck by lightning. When they go into the forest they shall become entangled in the creepers, losing their way, running here and there without finding the right road. Tigers shall attack them. They shall dash against the rocks, their skulls split open, and their brains spill out. On the crossroad they shall be crushed by falling trees. In the fields they shall be struck by lightning from a clear sky, be bitten by poisonous serpents, and torn to bits by the horns of buffaloes. They shall fall into deep rivers where pointed stones will cut their chests open, their bones will be dislocated, and the blood flow from their veins. Their corpses shall sink to the bottom of the waters. When they are at sea they shall be attacked by crocodiles. The Sumdang-Aal and the Peh fish shall bite them and the poisonous sea-serpent Lempe strike them, and sea-monsters swallow them. In their houses they shall be the prey of all sorts of sickness and they shall die unnatural deaths. No one shall help them, and during their sleep they shall die while dreaming, they shall die standing up, they shall die while eating or drinking. Neither they, nor their children, their grandchildren, nor their great-grandchildren, shall again be men on this earth. They shall reincarnate as maggots, clams, worms, and serpents. Such is the curse upon perjury as is ordained by Ari Candana and Angasti, and the Eminent Gods of the East, North, South, West, and Center. . . . They, their children, grandchildren, and great-grandchildren shall know no further happiness from now on."

CHAPTER FOUR

Rice, Work, & Wealth

ACCORDING TO LEGEND, the Balinese originally had only the juice of sugar-cane as food. Out of pity for the human race, the male god of fertility and water, Wisnu, Plutonic Lord of the Underworld, came to earth in disguise to provide them with better food. He raped an unwilling Mother Earth to fertilize her and give birth to rice, and she became known as Sanghyang Ibu Pretiwi, the Smitten Grandmother. Then Wisnu made war on Indra, Lord of the Heavens, to induce him to teach men how to grow rice. Thus, as the principal source of life and wealth and as a gift from the gods, rice was born from the cosmic union of the divine male and female creative forces represented in earth and water.

Besides white rice (*bras*), there are red (*gaga*) and black (*injin*) varieties. These the Balinese conveniently coordinated with their symbolic notion of the relation between color and direction by the explanation that the seeds were provided by Sanghyang Kesuhum Kidul (Brahma), the patron of the South, who sent four doves with seeds of the four cardinal colors: white, red, yellow, and black. Since there was no yellow rice, the seed of that color became turmeric (*kunyit*), an important condiment.

Poor people, or those living in districts where water is not abundant, live on corn and sweet potatoes, foods considered inferior to rice, and taken to be transformed male and female attendants of Dewi Sri, wife of Wisnu, goddess of agriculture, fertility, and success. To the Balinese Dewi Sri represents all that is good and beautiful and she is their most popular deity. She has been placed, perhaps with the advent of Hinduism, above Dewi Melanting, the native goddess of seed and plants, who, as daughter of Dewi Sri, remains the goddess of gardens and markets. Dewi Melanting spends half the year above the earth and the other half below; or, as Dr. Goris puts it, "she has first to undergo death under the black earth before she can come to new life."

Since man lives off rice and his body and soul are built from it, rice itself is treated with reverence and respect and the whole rice culture has developed into an elaborate cult. There are endless magic-ritual acts to make the rice grow big and strong, or so that water shall not be lacking, or to prevent the pollution of the land and the loss of seed by theft, birds, and mice. From planting-time until harvest the growth of rice is watched with as much anxiety as the life of a child. The Balinese are famed as the most efficient rice-growers in the archipelago. They raise two crops of fine rice a year with such success that they have more than sufficient for the needs of the population, often having enough left over to sell or give away. Even agricultural experts admit that modern methods could not improve the already excellent results, due perhaps to the intense striving of the Balinese for improvement, their communal, co-operative agricultural societies, and their Burbank-like system of seed selection.

The most striking element of the Balinese landscape is the ever present rice field, the *sawah,* a patch of land filled with water held by dikes cut out of the red earth. Every available piece of ground to which it is humanly possible to bring water, even to mountain heights, is made use of. The receding man-made terraces, like flights of gigantic stairs, cover the hills and spread over the slopes and plains. When they are first filled with still water they are like mosaics of mirrors that reflect the clouds. Later they are sprinkled with the dainty blades of the newly planted rice in an all-over pattern of chartreuse on a ground of brown ooze. This thickens eventually into a tender yellow-green carpet which turns to a rich gold ochre as the grain ripens, finally leaving only dry, cracked mud after the harvest. The landscape is continually changing, and as the crop begins or ends, a familiar surrounding is so transformed as to become almost unrecognizable.

THE SUBAK

The rugged, mountainous nature of the island, closely furrowed by deep ravines, makes irrigation extremely difficult. Water is led from the mountains to the various levels of cultivated land by an elaborate system of canals, dams, bamboo pipes, and even long tunnels cut through solid rock, to the dikes that permit the *sawah* to be flooded or drained at will. Solid matter is filtered off and pools are made for sand deposits to prevent the clogging of the rice fields.

It is obvious that small landowners could not carry out, alone, the tremendous task of attending to the work of irrigation. It became necessary for them to organize into *subaks*, agricultural co-operative societies, "water boards" that control the equitable distribution of water to their members, all those who take water from a common source. The objectives of the *subak* are to give the small agriculturist the assurance that he will not lack water, to police the dams effectively so that strangers will not divert the water supply, to settle disputes, and to attend to the communal rice festivals. In the village the society assumes full social, technical, and administrative authority in all matters concerning irrigation and agriculture.

Like the village and ward associations, the *subak* is presided over by elected headmen, the *kliang* and *penyarikan subak*, with their assistants (*pangliman*). The *subak* leaders open and preside over the meetings, see that the decisions and rules are carried out, impose fines and penalties, and act as treasurers of the organization. They keep written records of the names of the members and of all transactions and proceedings. The offices of the *subak* leaders are unrewarded, except, as in the case of other societies, for certain privileges such as extra shares of water and a small percentage of the fines collected. Every man who owns rice fields is compelled to join the *subak* and to carry out orders. Members may be allowed to buy off their services, but they must be present when important repairs are made, even though they may pay others to do their share of the work.

Once a month, or oftener if necessary, a general meeting is held in the little temple of the *subak*, a small shrine dedicated to the agricultural deities, built out in the middle of the rice fields. Attendance is compulsory and an absentee who is not properly justified is fined. When the members have gathered, the headman reads the roll, communicates the improvements and repairs to be carried out, reports on the relations of the society with higher officials[1] and with other *subaks*, and accounts for money received in fines and fees as well as what has been spent in materials, offerings, and so forth. Important decisions are reached by majority vote. When all business is settled, the headman adjourns the meeting and an informal social gathering follows in

[1] The various *subaks* of a district are under the control of an official, the *sedahan*, a sort of minister of agriculture, now under a Government salary.

which tobacco, *sirih*, and refreshments are served by appointed attendants. If the *subak* is a prosperous one, there may even be a banquet.

Like other Balinese associations, the spirit of the *subak* is essentially communal; all members abide by the same rules, each one being allotted work in relation to the amount of water he receives. Certain stipulations are made to prevent individuals from holding more land than would be convenient to the community. A man who has more land than he can work is compelled to share the produce with people appointed to help him.

RICE CULTURE

Before any work is done in the rice fields, an expedition composed of the *kliang*, a priest (*pemangku*), and four or five *subak* members goes to the holy sources of water such as Lake Batur, or Besakih in the Gunung Agung. They take offerings with them to gain the goodwill of the deities of the lake or of the sacred spring. Some water is brought back in a bamboo container (*sujang*) wrapped in a new cloth and hung with strings of *kepeng*, topped by a bunch of beautiful mottled red and green *andong* leaves for decoration.

At the return of the expedition the *sujang* is deposited on an altar in the temple of the *subak*. It is believed that the deities of the holy

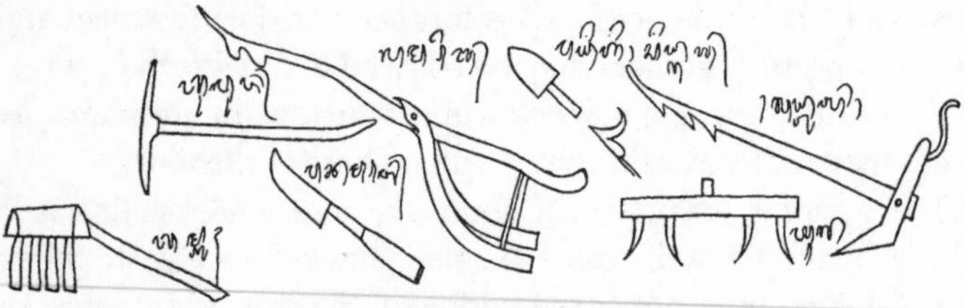

Agricultural implements

water are embodied in the container, and a feast (*mapag*) is given in honor of the divine guests. To entertain them so that they will not leave, the *subak* members perform dances and burn incense in braziers. The fields are sprinkled with holy water and the rest is poured into the common canal of the *subak* so that all the fields may benefit by it. The feast over, the necessary repairs are made, with more offerings so that the water will flow through the proper channels. Then the water is let in to flood the dry soil, and all *subak* members meet again to take a vow not to steal from one another. The land is cleansed with a great offering to the evil spirits and cockfights are staged to satisfy their thirst for blood.

When planting-time arrives, the land is plowed over and over again, and harrowed to incorporate with the soil the weeds and rice straw that serve as fertilizer. In some places the land is effectively plowed, in a spirit of festivity and sport, in great bull races (*megrumbungan*) held before a new crop is planted. The expense involved in entertaining the many guests with a banquet has made the bull races rare nowadays, but they are still to be seen in North Bali, where there are many rich peasants. Besides the amusement derived from the race, the chance for gambling, and the utilitarian plowing of the field, the feast is considered a good investment, because the gods, pleased by the gay and colorful spectacle, are expected to repay the donor with a plentiful harvest.

The race is held in a flooded rice field between rival teams of specially trained bulls. The oxen are crowned with ornaments of tooled gilt leather, and silk banners decorate their yokes. Enormous wooden bells, often three feet across, are attached to their necks. Bets are placed as the contending teams are lined up with their drivers standing on the rakes to which the bulls are hitched. At a signal from the referee, they are off with a speed one does not usually associate with plowing oxen. The yelling drivers, on the rakes that glide along the mud, whip and entice the bulls to run across the field, always with an elegant gait. Their heads are raised high, forced up by the great thumping bells, giving them an added elegance. However fast they may run, the referee gives his decision not to the fastest, but to the team with the most stately bearing.

It is typical of the Balinese to place style before mere physical speed.

When the field is prepared, the mother-seed, which has been picked from the largest and most beautiful ears, is soaked for two days and two nights, then spread on a mat and sprinkled with water until the germ breaks through. A nursery plot is prepared in a corner of the field to receive the young sprouts, which must be planted on a propitious day set by the religious calendar. They remain in the nursery for about two months; then when they have developed enough, they are pulled out, washed, pruned, tied in bunches, and exposed to the air for one night. By this time the *sawahs* are clean and ready to receive the young plants; offerings (*sujuk*) to Dewi Sri are made again and the owner of the *sawah*, with his own hands, plants the first nine sprouts in a small group at the uppermost corner of the plot. He begins with a single central one; then one to the right; one towards himself (in the direction of the sea behind him); then to the left; towards the mountain in front; and finally to the four intermediate points, in the following order:

9	5	6
4	1	2
8	3	7

This is to represent the Nawa Sangga, the magic Rose of the Winds, the Balinese cardinal directions (*pengider-ideran*):

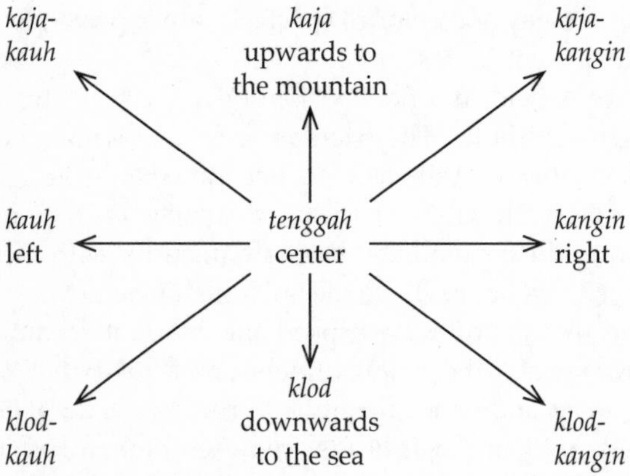

A more detailed explanation of this important ritual principle by which the Balinese rule their actions will be given later, but for the sake of convenience let it be understood that the points correspond, in principle, to our North, South, East, West, and Center, remembering that the point called *kaja*, which we shall call "North," is invariably towards the Gunung Agung or the local great mountain, and the *klod*, "South," is always towards the sea.

After the nine cardinal points have been established, the rest of the seedlings are planted all over the field, the plants stuck into the mud in rows at intervals of one hand-span. Often the owner of the field gives a party at this time to bring himself luck. Soon the rice becomes green and new shoots appear, but then the rice requires the utmost care; it must be properly weeded and should have plenty of water. Offerings (*sayut sarwa genep*) are made to protect the tender plants from caterpillars, and again, after forty-two days, more offerings (*dedinan*) are made to celebrate its feast day. In about three months the grain makes its appearance; then the rice is said to be pregnant, and just as women with child long for sour foods, the offerings made then include sour fruits, as well as eggs and flowers. A stylized figure of a woman (*cili*), made of palm-leaf, provided for this occasion with male sex organs, is presented with the following speech repeated three times: "Pst, pst, look at the woman with testicles (*Psu, psu, jero, m'baleh loh mabutoh*)." Somehow this is supposed to help with the pregnancy of the rice. The three-month feast day is celebrated with another feast called *mebijukung*. By this time the grain has spread all over the field, and the water is drained off so that the rice may ripen quickly.

The menace of birds and mice then makes its appearance. To scare the birds away, the whole *sawah* is covered by an intricate network of strings hung with palm-leaves and all sorts of dangling objects (cloth barred), set in motion by a single rope operated by a boy who watches the field constantly from a high platform built for the purpose. Life-size scarecrows are erected, but soon the birds become familiar with them and will not be frightened away. Then watchmen circulate among the fields beating bamboo drums and cracking loud bamboo slapsticks. Should the *sawah* become infested with mice, a campaign is conducted against them; large numbers are caught and killed, but a pair is set aside and later released to atone for the killings. Then a ceremonial cremation in miniature disposes of the dead ones. Should it happen that rice is stolen, the *sawah*-owner takes food to the rice field and leaves it there, saying: "Whoever stole my rice, let him return and be content with this food. I ask that my rice may multiply so that I shall get mine back."

When the grain is ripe, the *subak* members prepare for the *ng'usaba nini*, the great harvest festival. Cockfights are held again in the rice temple and the following day is declared *nyepi* for rice fields: a day of absolute stillness, requiring the suspension of all activity, when no one may enter a field under penalty of a fine. Two days before cutting the rice, small offerings are made to the irrigation inlet, and boughs of the *dapdap* tree, decorated with little faces of palm-leaf, are stuck at the four corners of the field to keep evil influences away. The next step is the making of the Rice Mother (*nini pantun*), two sheaves of rice, one male, the other female, the Rice Husband and

Wife.[2] The two sheaves are fastened together and tied to a branch, which is stuck in the ground near the main irrigation inlet. Then the cutting of the rice may proceed.

In Bali only men plant and attend to the rice, but women and even children help with the harvest. Everybody wears coats and great sun-hats of bamboo for protection against the burning rays of the sun. The line of reapers moves like a living row of enormous mushrooms, cutting the rice with small iron blades set in wooden frames, just large enough to be hidden in the palm of the hand. The stalks are cut one by one and tied later into huge bunches. When all the rice is cut, the Rice Mothers of the various *sawah*-owners are dressed in a skirt of new white cloth held at the middle of the sheaf by a rope of white yarn, a small apron (*lamak*), and a silk scarf. The head-dress is represented by the ends of the stalks, ornamented with flowers and cut-out palm-leaf in the form of a fan, often with a human face added, drawn on a heart-shaped piece of palm.

We witnessed a harvest festival in Ubud: the dressed Rice Mothers were ceremoniously assembled in the little rice temple out in the fields, decorated for the occasion with pennants (*penyor*)—tall bamboo poles hung with lacy ornaments of palm leaf—and with beautiful *lamaks*, strips many feet long, made of the young yellow leaves of the coconut or sugar palm pinned together with bits of bamboo, covered with delicate patterns representing moons, stylized girls, trees, and so forth, cut out of the mature leaves of palm, dark green lace against a background of lemon yellow.

The crowd started for the village in a long procession with music. The women carried the offerings and the Rice Mothers on their heads. The men wore hats freshly woven of coconut leaf, bristling with flowers and ferns. The parade stopped at the village temple, where the decorated sheaves were blessed by the temple guardian. This cere-

[2] The male is larger and consists of 108 stalks, while the female has only 54 stalks. The people of Badung agree that the sheaves are male and female, but in Ubud, Gianyar, they claim it is only female. They also make two sheaves, one larger than the other, but they are confused when pressed to explain the reason for the two sheaves. They call the *nini pantun* also by the names of *dewa padi* or *dewi istri*, "rice deity" or "divine wife." *Nini pantun* means simply "rice mother." Perhaps the association of feminine names and ideas has obscured the bisexual significance of the two sheaves. Van Eck says that the Rice Husband and Wife are ceremoniously wedded in the granary: "Increase ye and multiply without ceasing." I was told in Gianyar that the rice stalks used to make the mother should be stolen from various rice fields, but in Badung they appeared shocked at this idea.

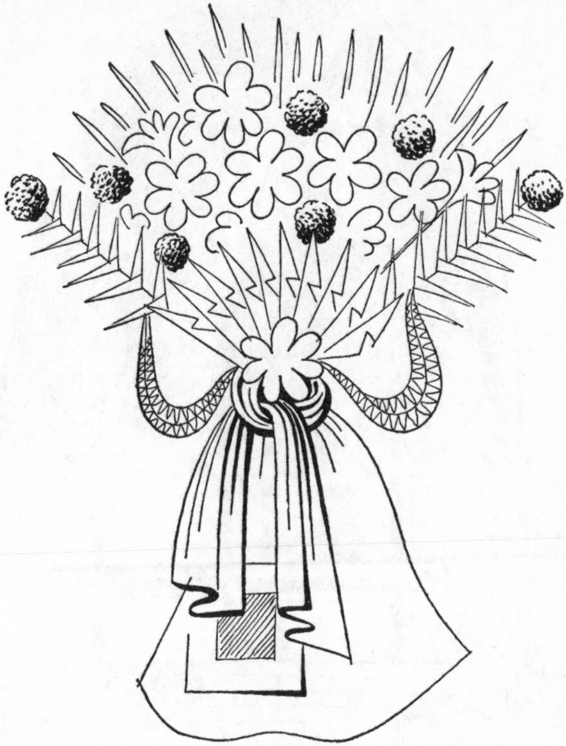

Rice Mother

mony was called *mendak nini*, "to bring back the Mother." Each family took its Rice Mother to its own granary, which was also decorated with *penyors* and *lamaks* to receive it. The Rice Mothers were deposited on cushions on special wooden thrones inside the granaries, and I was told that they would remain there until eaten by rats. Not even famine could justify eating the rice of the *nini*; whoever ate the Rice Mother would be considered as low as a dog. After the ceremony the cut rice was brought home to be stored in the granary until needed.

The rice granaries (called according to size and shape *lumbung, glebeg, jinan, klumpu,* and *klimking* in the order of their importance) are a good indication of the economic status of a family. They are tall buildings with steep, high roofs of thatch resembling the Melanesian yam houses in shape. A granary is supported by four wooden pillars with wide circular capitals to prevent rats from climbing up. Custom demands respectful handling of rice. It must be

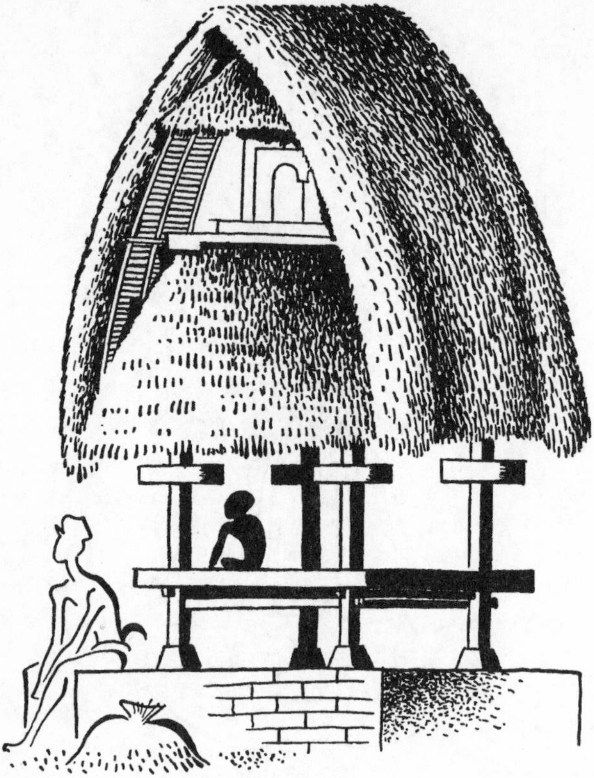

A granary (*lumbung*)

fetched in silence and only in the daytime. A person who climbs into a granary should be in a normal state of physical and spiritual health and may not chew betelnut.

DISTRIBUTION OF LABOR

In Bali one may see a woman laying bricks or breaking stones to pave a road, or find men in the market in Denpasar sitting at their sewing-machines making blouses for women, but it would be unthinkable for a woman to paint a picture or to climb a coconut tree; a man would be disgraced if seen performing work that is the perquisite of women.

The labor allotted to each sex is sharply defined; all heavy work requiring manly attributes—agriculture, building in wood or thatch, the care of cattle—as well as most of the trades and crafts, such as carpentry, wood- and stone-carving, painting, writing, playing musical instruments, is the work of men. Women own, raise, and sell chickens and pigs, but only men care for cows, buffaloes, and ducks. Since men dislike working for wages, the women of the lower classes are obliged to engage as coolies transporting building-materials, carrying coconuts to sell to the Chinese for making copra, delivering charcoal, or obtaining broken coral from the beach to make lime. Although only men build Balinese houses, women are the house-painters and work as masons in constructions of Western style.

Domestic duties such as fetching water for the kitchen, threshing rice, making flour, weaving, and making domestic offerings are performed by women, but men take an equal interest in the care of children and are proud to carry their sons everywhere. While the daily food is cooked by women, only men may prepare the pork and turtle dishes for banquets, and rice may be cooked by both. When at harvest-time both sexes help cut the rice and carry it home, every woman holds one of the heavy sheaves on her head, and the men carry two, one on each end of a pole swung across the shoulders. It is a rule that a woman carries only on her head and a man on on his shoulders, except for offerings and holy objects, which must be carried on the head.

Children assist their parents in the daily work, the boys taking care of the ducks and cows and weeding the rice fields; or, if their father is a craftsman, they become his apprentices. Little girls help their mothers to carry loads, to cook, to weave, or sell in the market. The activity of the women seems to increase with age; by far the most active person in our household was Gusti's aunt, a proud old woman over sixty. Women of the common class carry even greater loads than the young, but she, being a *Pregusti,* could not carry loads. Her hands, however, were never still and she was reputed the best maker of offerings in the *banjar*. Endowed with a knowledge acquired only by age, elderly women are essential to the religious festivals and many act as priestesses.

Although old men are mainly concerned with sitting in the *balé banjar* discussíng literature, chewing *sirih,* and drinking *tuak,* they also have duties to perform: they are the leading members of the village association, the priests, witch-doctors, story-tellers, and of course the teachers of writing, poetry, and the arts. Old men are often duck-shepherds, guiding the flocks of ducks to the fields and back.

At one time the dramatic arts were restricted to the men, although older women danced in religious ceremonies. But today girls have successfully invaded the theatrical field. In general the condition of Balinese women is better than in other Eastern countries. A woman has definite rights; the income she derives from the sale of her pigs, her weaving, or the garden produce she sells in the market is her own, and she may dispose of her belongings without the knowledge of her husband. Most women are not only economically independent, but contribute to the expenses of the household. A woman's debts are her own and her husband is not liable for them. The women keep the finances of the family and control the markets.

THE ECONOMIC ORDER

With agriculture as the main occupation of the people and the basis of wealth, the question of the ownership of land is of great importance. Bali presents the amazing spectacle of a land where the deep-rooted agrarian communalism of the people has continued to exist side by side with the feudalism of the noble landlords. We have seen that the true Balinese village is an independent economic and social unit, ruled by a council of villagers with voting power, equal rights for all, and ownership of land restricted by village regulations. The lands are communally cultivated to maintain the village festivals, and even the ground on which the houses stand is village property that can be reclaimed if the tenant abuses his privileges. Since the land and its products belong to the ancestral gods, the idea of absolute property is not firmly rooted among the Balinese. In our household nobody objected when neighbors came and cut flowers and banana leaves without permission.

Alongside the Balinese commune is the contrasting influence of medieval princes who have tried, without success, to abolish the village organization and the religion that motivated it, to replace it by feudal rule with an official cult under their control. Passive disobedience at first, and Dutch supremacy later, left the princes in the position of impoverished nominal aristocrats, who, despite the fact that they represent the Government, are excluded from the administrative management of the villages. Through their co-operative societies, the *banjars* and *subaks*, the Balinese have recaptured some of their village autonomy. However, the communal system has suffered considerably in the feudal territories where the princes have held sway; the communal lands sometimes became part of the estate of the local prince, who gave grants of lands to his vassals in exchange for servitude, and gradually ownership of the land in these districts became more and more individualistic, developing a class of organized small landowners. Village ground cannot legally be disposed of, but *sawahs* have been pawned when there was great need of ready cash. Land has never become a commodity, however, and today the agriculturist is protected to a certain extent by the law forbidding the sale of agricultural lands to foreigners, perhaps one of the wisest laws passed by the Dutch Government.

Economic inequality is not as striking in Bali as elsewhere. Until recently almost everybody wore the same type of clothes, all went barefoot and lived in thatched houses. At first sight they all seemed happy and prosperous. The majority of the population has a roof, enough to eat, and some big silver dollars buried under the earthen floor of the sleeping-quarters. Yet there are some who are extremely poor while others are considered rich. There are people without lands or a house of their own, living a parasitic life of slavery, a remnant of feudalism, attached to the household of a master and eating whatever is given them. A rich family is one who has *sawahs*, a house with a gate of carved stone, a large rice granary, an ornate family temple, and a well-built pavilion for guests. They may have some fine cloths put away and heirlooms in the form of gold jewelry, a kris with a gold sheath and handle set with precious stones and a number of silver or gold vessels, all of which can be pawned in one of the Government pawnshops in case of need.

In general the Balinese have little need of cash to procure the daily necessities of life. Normally the cost of living is extremely low and food and the requirements for shelter are produced by the Balinese themselves. A meal in a public eating-place may cost as much as twenty cents, but, having rice, the cash expense for food for an entire family in the home amounts only to a few pennies, perhaps only enough to buy salt and spices. Fruit and vegetables are grown in the gardens adjoining the house; pigs, chickens, and ducks are raised at home to be killed on special occasions or for offerings which the people themselves eat after the gods have consumed the essence. Fuel consists of the fallen dry leaves and stems of the coconut trees.

The housing-problem is simple. Entire families live together in ancestral compounds, and a modest house can be built almost overnight out of bamboo and thatch at a very low cost. People without means or without a house simply go to live with a relative, "sharing a kitchen" in exchange for small services and assistance in the general housework, or procure land from the village and gradually build their own household. The daily clothing consists of a *kamben*, a piece of cotton worn like a skirt, and a headcloth, with an added shirt or blouse in the more "modern" districts. A complete ordinary outfit of clothes costs about two guilders ($1.36 at the time of writing): one guilder for the skirt, fifty cents for the headpiece and fifty cents more for the shirt. Amusements are free and transportation is mainly by foot, leaving medicines and luxuries to be bought for cash.

It was always a mystery to us how the Balinese made the money they seemed to spend so lavishly in extravagant festivals and in beautiful clothes. They never appeared to work regularly for wages, and outside of the market, in which alone business was transacted, they never seemed interested in commerce. The men were always busy in the rice fields, but rice cannot be considered an important source of cash income. The Balinese grow rice for personal consumption and for offerings, selling only what is left over from the second planting, which they regard as unfit for offerings to the gods.

Their main source of income is in the sale of cattle and pigs, and of coconuts for making copra; a second source is from coffee, rice, and tobacco which they sell for export to Chinese middlemen. The trades and crafts are incidental sources of income and in the markets one may see people selling pottery, mats, baskets, and so forth, together with the vendors of vegetables, dried fish, spices, and flowers. Some craftsmen, such as the gold and silver-workers, the blacksmiths, carpenters, weavers of palm, and pottery-makers, have regular incomes, but they remain independent artisans. The Balinese men work for wages only spasmodically and as an adventure. In the larger towns they engage as chauffeurs, clerks, and servants—positions which are regarded as superior. With the affluence of tourists, some now derive an income from the sale of sculptures, paintings, silverwork, weavings, and so forth.

Ruled by the principle of live and let live, landowners allow others without land to share their crop in exchange for help. There are, however, organizations of laborers (*seka mejukut*) who work the earth for a communal wage. They are paid by time recorded by water-clocks (*ganji*) similar to those used in cockfights: a half coconut-shell with a small hole in the bottom, placed in a basin of water, the time it takes to sink being the measure. The fees are arranged by the head of the group.

At the present time, however, the economic balance has, temporarily at least, ceased to exist. With taxes and imported commodities on the increase, and the price of Balinese products for export at rock-bottom levels, the whole population has come to find itself in need of cash, not in *kepengs* (Chinese cash valued at a fraction of a cent with which they buy the daily necessities), but in Dutch guilders worth from five hundred to seven hundred *kepeng* according to the exchange. There is no demand for their insignificant products, and the deflated Dutch currency has become harder than ever to obtain.

The Balinese are more and more eager for the "advantages of civilization" in the form of inferior foreign cloth, bicycles, flashlights, aniline dyes, and motor-cars, and if their miserable earnings are not taken away by the Arab merchants it is only because they are already due for back taxes. Besides a tax on each household, there is a *sawah* tax (*pajeg*) and a tax (*upeti*) on dry grounds bearing coconut and coffee trees. The most hated of taxes is that paid every time a Balinese kills a pig, no matter how small, for which he needs a certificate. This has led to clandestine slaughter and with it the reduction of the pig supply, and the reward promised to denouncers has introduced the element of discord into otherwise unified communities. Dr. Korn, the authority on Balinese sociology, says that the population would prefer an export tax on cattle to the troublesome slaughter tax.

With the relentless drain of the island's wealth, poverty, too, is on the increase and the Balinese are threatened with the loss of their lands through failure to pay taxes. They have been forced to sell whatever they possessed of value—antiques, fine brocades, jewelry, and even the bits of gold that decorate their krisses—to tourists and gold-hoarders, while theft and prostitution are on the increase. It is to be feared that if present conditions continue, the simple and well-organized life of the Balinese will be seriously disrupted and their institutions will collapse as a result of the unavoidable social unrest.

CHAPTER FIVE

Everyday Life in Bali

THE HOUSE

AS AN ORGANIC UNIT, the structure, significance, and function of the home is dictated by the same fundamental principles of belief that rule the village: blood-relation through the worship of the ancestors; rank, indicated by higher and lower levels; and orientation by the cardinal directions, the mountain and the sea, right and left. The Balinese say that a house, like a human being, has a head—the family shrine; arms—the sleeping-quarters and the social parlor; a navel—the courtyard; sexual organs—the gate; legs and feet—the kitchen and the granary; and anus—the pit in the backyard where the refuse is disposed of.

Magic rules control not only the structure but also the building and occupation of the house; only on an auspicious day specified in the religious calendar can they begin to build or occupy a house. On our arrival we were able to secure a new pavilion in the household of Gusti only because the date for occupation set by the priest was still three months off. We were strangers immune from the laws of magic harmony that affect only the Balinese and we could live in the house until the propitious day when the priest would come to perform the *melaspasin*, the ceremony of inauguration, saying his prayers over each part of the house, burying little offerings at strategic points to protect the inmates from evil influences.

A Balinese home (*kuren*) consists of a family or a number of related families living within one enclosure, praying at a common family temple, with one gate and one kitchen. The square plot of land (*pekarangan*) in which the various units of the house stand is entirely surrounded by a wall of whitewashed mud, protected from rain erosion by a crude roofing of thatch. The Balinese feel uneasy when they sleep without a wall, as, for instance, the servants must in the unwalled Western-style houses. The gate of a well-to-do family can be an imposing affair of brick and carved stone, but more often it consists of two simple pillars of mud supporting a thick roof of thatch. In front of the gate on either side are two small shrines (*apit lawang*) for offerings, of brick and stone, or merely two little niches excavated in the mud of the gate, while the simplest are made of split bamboo. Directly behind the doorway is a small wall (*aling aling*) that screens off the interior and stops evil spirits. In China I had seen similar screens erected for the same purpose and once I asked a Balinese friend how the *aling aling* kept the devils from entering; he replied, with tongue in his cheek, that, unlike humans, they turned corners with difficulty.

The pavilions of the house are distributed around a well-kept yard of hardened earth free of vegetation except for some flowers and a decorative frangipani or hibiscus tree. But the land between the houses and the wall is planted with coconut trees, breadfruit, bananas, papayas, and so forth, with a corner reserved as a pigsty. This is the garden, the orchard, and the corral of the house and is often so exuberant that the old platitude that in the tropics one has only to reach up to pluck food from the trees almost comes true in Bali.

Curiously, bamboo is not grown within the house. If it sprouts by itself it is allowed to remain, but its growth is discouraged by indirect means. Such is the magic of bamboo that only old people may tackle the dangerous job of planting it or digging it out, and the first lump of earth dug must be thrown as far away as possible. It is said that if this earth touches someone, he will surely die, and it is only on certain days that work concerning bamboo may be safely undertaken. Yet life in Bali would have developed along different lines had bamboo not existed on the island. Out of bamboo they make the great majority of their artifacts; houses, beds, bridges, water-pipes, musical instruments, altars, and so forth. It is woven into light movable screens for walls, sun-hats, and baskets of every conceivable purpose. The young shoots are excellent to eat, while other parts are used as medicine. I was told that the tiny hairs in the wrapping of the new leaves are a slow and undetectable poison like ground glass and tiger's whiskers. Bamboo combines the strength of steel with qualities of the lightest wood. It grows rapidly and without care to enormous size.

Social and economic differences affect but little the basic structure of the home. The house of a poor family is called *pekarangan*, that of a

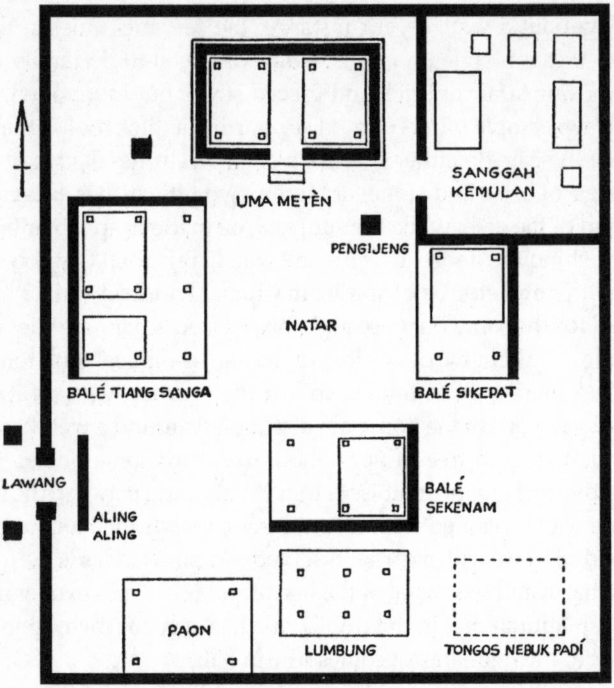

A typical *pekarangan*—plan of Gedog's house

nobleman is a *jeró*, and a Brahmana's is a *griya*, but these differences are mostly in the name, the quality of the materials employed, the workmanship, and of course in the larger and richer family temple. The fundamental plan is based on the same rules for everyone. Only the great palace (*puri*) of the local ruling prince is infinitely more elaborate, with a lily pond, compartments for the Raja's brothers and his countless wives, a great temple divided into three courts, and even special sections for the preservation of the corpses and for the seclusion of "impure" palace women during the time of menstruation.

The household of Gedog, our next-door neighbor in Belaluan, was typical; the place of honor, the higher "north-east" corner of the house towards the mountain,[1] was occupied by the *sanggah kemulan*, the

[1] Endless ill luck would follow whoever ignored the laws of rank and built a dwelling at a level higher than a temple. The Balinese have resented the building of a Government rest-house on a hill above the holy temple of Tirta Empul in Tampaksiring, and our servant Pugog insisted he could not bring his wife to Campuan because the temple across the ravine was at a lower level than the house, and intercourse with a woman there could only result in a catastrophe.

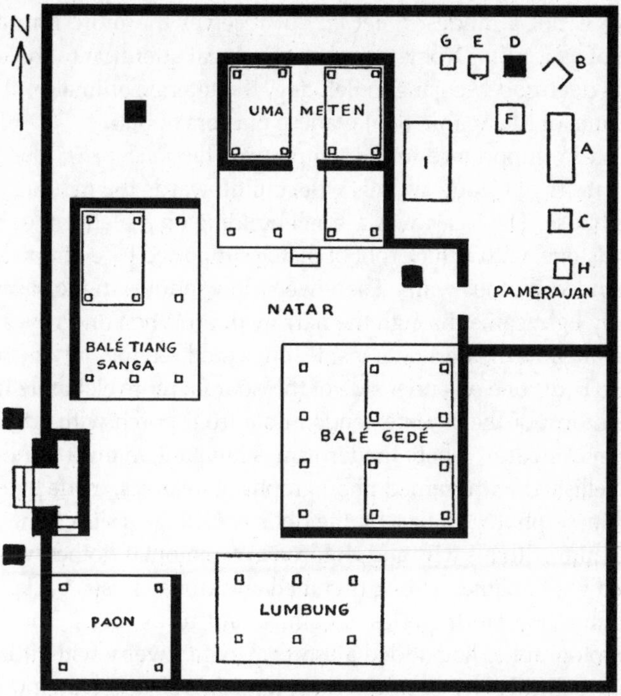

Plan of a *jeró*, the house of a man of means

A—*Kemulan*
B—*Padmasana*
C—*Menjangan Seluang*
D—*Gedong* for Gunung Agung
E—*Sarén*
F—*Tajok*
G—*Taksú*
H—*Ngrurah*
I—*Balé Piasan*

family temple where Gedog worshipped his ancestors. The *sanggah* was an elemental version of the formal village temple: a walled space containing a number of little empty god-houses and a shed for offerings. The main shrine, dedicated to the ancestral souls, was a little house on stilts divided into three compartments, each with a small door. There were other small shrines for the two great mountains—the Gunung Agung and Batur—and for the *taksú* and *ngrurah,* the "interpreter" and "secretary" of the deities. In Gedog's house the altars were of bamboo with thatch roofs, but in the home of Gusti's uncle, the noble judge who lived across the road, the family shrine was as elaborate as the village temple, with a moat, carved stone gates, brick altars, and expensive roofs of sugar palm fiber. Such a temple is not a modest *sanggah,* but receives the more impressive name of *pamerajan*. Noble people pay special attention to the shrine for the deer-god Menjangan Seluang, the totemic animal of the descendants of Majapahit, the Javanese masters of Bali.

Next in importance to the temple was the *uma metén,* the sleeping-quarters of Gedog and his wife, built towards the mountain side of the house. The *metén* was a small building on a platform of bricks or sandstone, with a thick roof of thatch supported by eight posts and surrounded by four walls. There were no windows in the *metén* and the only light came through the narrow door. When one's eyes grew accustomed to the darkness inside, one could see the only furniture, the two beds, one on either side of the door. In more elaborate homes the platform of the *metén* extends into a front porch with additional beds. In Denpasar, where modernism is rampant, many a front porch is embellished with framed photographs of relatives, made by the local Chinese photographer. By the door of Gedog's *metén* hung a picture of him with his wife and children in ceremonial clothes, violently colored with anilines, sitting dignified and stiff against a background of stormy clouds, draperies, columns, and balustrades. The generous photographer had added all sorts of extra jewelry with little dabs of gold paint. I have seen the most amazing objects hanging in the porches of Balinese homes: dried lobsters, painted plates representing the snow-covered Alps, Chinese paintings on glass, old electric bulbs filled with water, aquatic plants growing out of them, postal cards of New York skyscrapers, and so forth; objects prized as exotic, rare things, as we prize their discarded textiles and moth-eaten carvings. In one house we found a picture of Queen Wilhelmina; we asked who she was and the quick reply came: "Oh! *itu gouvermen*—That is the Government." The *metén* is the sanctuary of the home; here heirlooms are kept and the family's capital is often buried in the earth floor under the bed. Normally the heads of the family sleep in the *metén*, but being the only building in which privacy can be secured, they relinquish it to newly-weds or to unmarried girls who need protection. They shut themselves into it at night, but otherwise the entire life of the household is spent outdoors on the porch or in the surrounding open pavilions, each provided with beds for other members of the family.

The other three sides of Gedog's courtyard were occupied by three open pavilions; on the left was the *balé tiang sanga,* the social parlor and guest house, and two smaller pavilions were on the right (*balé sikepat*) and back (*balé sekenam*) where other relatives slept with the children and where the women placed their looms to work. In the lowest part of the land, towards the sea, were the kitchen (*paon*) and the granary (*lumbung*). Rice was threshed in a cleared space (*tongos nebuk padi*) behind the granary. As in every household, there were two small shrines (*tugú*), one west of the *metén*, the other in the middle of the courtyard, the *pengijeng* perhaps dedicated to the spirit of the land, "His Excellency the Owner of the Ground" (*Ratú Medrwé Karang*).

Such is the general pattern of the home of a family of the average class that has rice fields and is economically comfortable. The better homes often have more elaborate pavilions, one of which may become a *loji* (a Dutch word) by enclosing half of the pavilion with four walls, leaving the other half as an open veranda. This will provide a second sleeping-quarter for a married son. In the houses of the well-to-do the social hall is often a great square pavilion (*balé gedé*) with an extraordinarily thick thatch roof supported by twelve beautifully carved posts. A well-built *balé*, the archtype of Balinese construction, is a masterpiece of simplicity, ingenuity, and good taste. It consists of a platform of mud, brick, or stone reached by three or four steps and covered by a cool roof of thick thatch. The roof is supported by more or less elaborate wooden posts (*tiang*), the number of which determines their name and function. Thus a *balé* is called *sike pat, sekenam, tiang sanga,* or *balé gedé,* according to whether there are four, six, nine, or twelve posts. Definite rules dictate the dimensions and designs of these posts, 23 lengths of the index finger (*tujoh*), or about seven feet, being the standard height of a house post. It has already been mentioned that the house must stand "upright"; that is, the bottom of the posts should be the end nearest to where the roots were in the tree. The roof is built of *lalang* grass sown on the long ribs of coconut leaves, placed close together like shingles and lashed to the bamboo skeleton of the roof with indestructible cords of sugar-palm fiber, with an extra thickness of grass added to the four corners. Then the roof is combed with a special rake and the lower edge is neatly evened with a sharp knife. Such a roof, often a foot and a half in thickness, will last through fifty tropical rainy seasons. The beams that support the roof are ingeniously fitted together without nails, and are held in place with pegs made of heart of coconut wood. Generally one or two sides of the *balé* are protected by a low wall and between the house posts are built-in beds or platforms of wood with

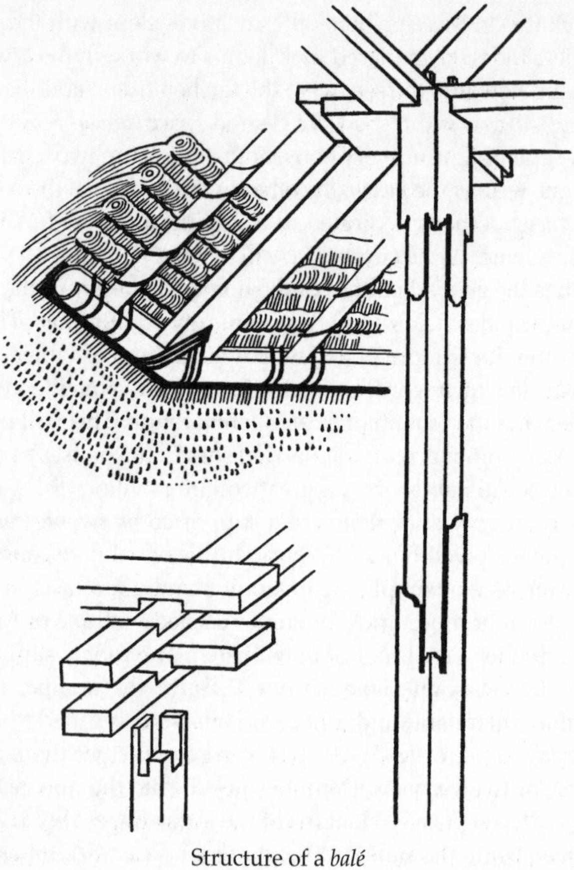

Structure of a *balé*

springs of bamboo, also called *balés*, where distinguished guests sit cross-legged to eat, or where, with a mattress added and screened by a curtain, they are put up for the night.

In Belaluan everybody was up even before the first rays of the sun outlined the jagged tops of the coconut palms, awakened by the raucous crowings of the fighting cocks. In the indigo semi-darkness of the dawn the women were busily sweeping the yard and bringing water from the village spring. The first thought of the men was for their pets; to line up the bell-shaped cages of the fighting cocks out on the road by the gate so that the roosters might "amuse themselves watching people go by." The cages of the cooing doves were strung up on high poles for them to enjoy the morning air and the sunshine, and the flocks of pigeons, trained to fly in circles over the house, were released for their morning exercise. As protection from birds of prey, they had small brass bells around their necks that produced various humming sounds as they flew round and round until they tired, when they came down to be fed.

After a refreshing bath the men started for the fields without breakfast, taking along a snack—rice boiled inside of little diamond-shaped containers of palm-leaf called *ketipat*. More substantial food was taken to them later if they had to remain in the fields all day, but they returned at noon for lunch if there was not much work or if the *sawahs* were near. Meanwhile the women fetched sheaves of unhusked rice from the granary, spread them on the ground to dry in the sun, filled the *gebah*—the large water basin in the kitchen—and started the fire for the day's cooking. A kitchen is a simple roof of coarse thatch supported by four posts, with a bamboo platform at one end—the kitchen table—and a primitive mud stove at the other. Often a crude figure is modeled out of the same clay of which the hearth is made to preside over the kitchen. It is called *brahma*, not the supreme lord of the Hindus, but simply meaning "fire," an animistic fire god.

The food that Balinese gourmets eat at festivals is as elaborate as any in the world and will be described later in detail, but the daily meal is extremely simple. A mound of boiled cold rice with salt and chili pepper was sufficient, our house-boy Dog claimed, to keep body and soul together for a Balinese like himself. The daily diet of Gusti and his noble family was the same cold white rice (*nasi*, a synonym for food in general), helped, however, by a side dish of vegetables chopped together with a dozen or so of spices, aromatics, grated coconut and the hottest chili pepper in the world.

Gusti's wives did the cooking; Siloh Biang prepared the rice while Sagung scraped coconut in a *kikian*, a board bristling with little iron points, chopped the ingredients for the sauce, or fried them in coconut oil in an iron pan (*pengorengan*). Some eat their daily rice simply boiled in a clay pot, but in our household they preferred it steamed; they washed the grain repeatedly until the waters lost their milky color and came out transparent, boiled it for a while, and when it was half done put it into a funnel-shaped basket (*kukusan*) covered with a heavy clay lid (*kekeb*) and steamed the whole over a special pot (*dangdang*) of boiling water. From time to time some of the boiling water was poured over the rice with a ladle of coconut shell to prevent it from drying up and sticking together. The result was a deliciously dry, separate rice that served as a medium for the peppery sauces. The food was prepared with cleanliness, everything carefully washed first, and the food covered until eaten with squares of banana leaf.

As soon as the rice was done, they prepared a tray of offerings

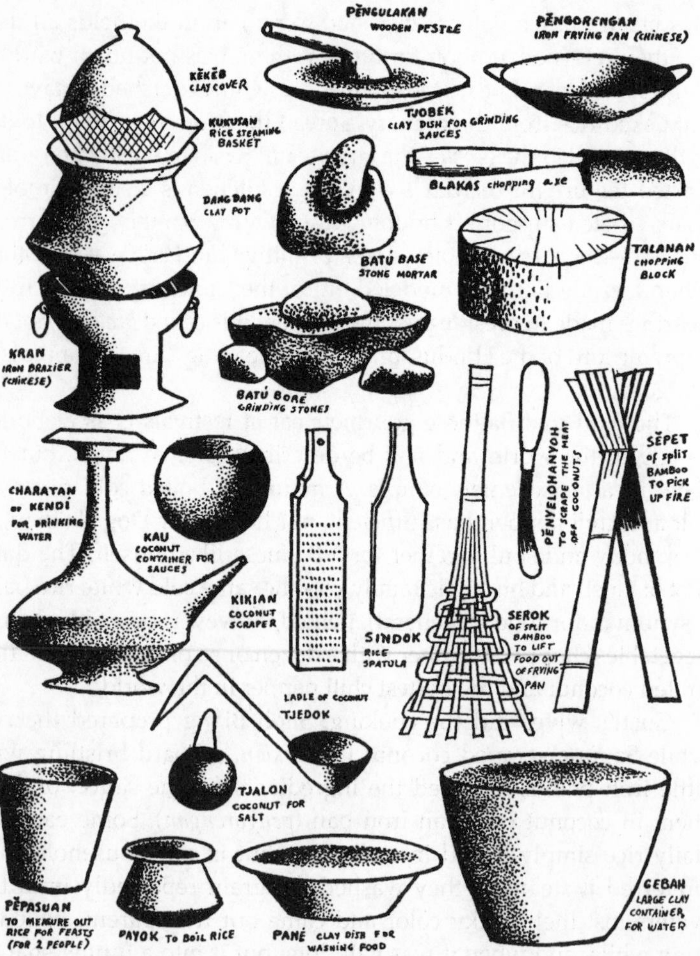

Kitchen Utensils

(*ngejot*) for the spirits that haunt the house: little squares of banana leaf, each with a few grains of rice, a flower, salt, and a dash of chili pepper. No one could eat before the little portions were distributed in front of each of the house units: at the entrance of the family shrine, in front of the sleeping-quarters, in front of the little altar in the middle of the court, at the well if there is one, and finally at the gate. The woman who distributed the offerings was followed by the eternally hungry dogs, who unceremoniously ate the grains of rice as soon as the offering was placed on the ground. Nobody cared, however, since they were intended for evil spirits, which might, perhaps, be embodied in the dogs.

There were no set meal hours and they ate whenever they felt hungry. A little before noon the men returned from work after taking a bath in the spring or in a river and sat casually somewhere near the kitchen, often turning their backs silently on each other because a person who is eating should not be spoken to. Each was given his portion of rice with its complementary sauce in a square of banana

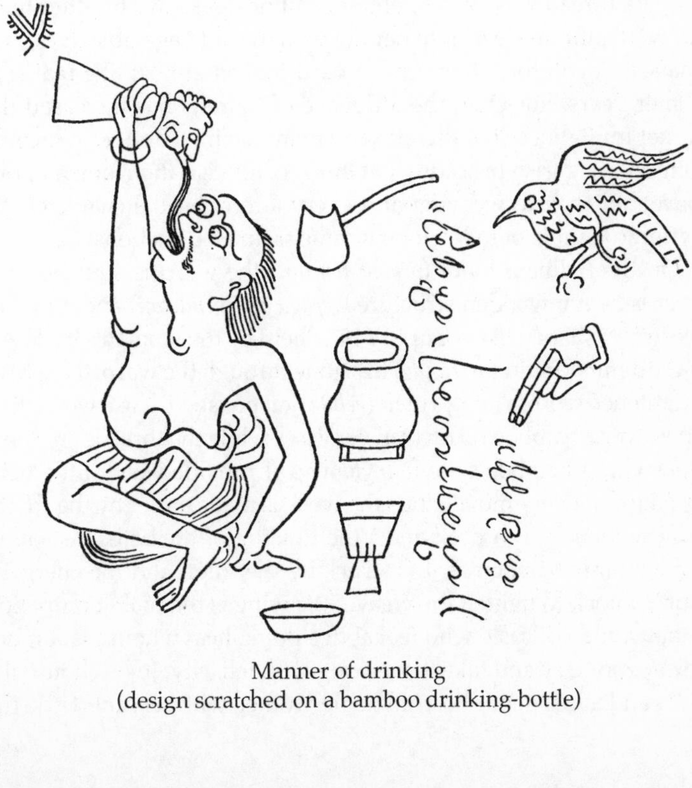

Manner of drinking
(design scratched on a bamboo drinking-bottle)

leaf which he held in the hollow of the left hand while the right acted as spoon and fork. The use of dishes and cutlery is to the Balinese an unclean and repulsive foreign habit. Balinese who use plates invariably place a square of banana leaf over them. When finished, the leaf dishes were simply thrown to the pigs; no dishes were left to wash. A *kendih* of water was passed around after the meal, each drinking in turn and at a distance from it, letting a continuous jet of water fall into the open mouth, the lips never touching the spout. (When we tried to drink like the Balinese we succeeded only in choking or drenching ourselves.) The mouth and fingers were rinsed, and after emitting a loud belch of satisfaction the men took a nap or went to the *balé banjar* to chat before resuming work. Generally the women ate after the men were finished, then fed the pigs, and spent the rest of the afternoon weaving, threshing rice, or simply delousing each other, a great social pastime.

For a while it seemed as if the art of hand weaving would be wrecked by the ever increasing importation of foreign cloth. Chinese silk thread was hard to obtain, aniline dyes gave brighter hues and were infinitely easier to handle than the old vegetable dyes, and Japanese rayon for a few cents a yard looked almost like real silk. In later years, however, the affluence of tourists has increased the market for Balinese handicrafts and many women derive an income from selling garish brocades. On our second visit the women of our household took to weaving and every afternoon the characteristic rhythmic sounds of many looms came from all directions.

On the Balinese loom (*prabot tennun*) the warp is stretched between a heavy wooden structure (*cecaga and pendalan*) and a sort of yoke (*épor*) shaped like a Cupid's bow held by the woman's back. After the bamboo spindle (*tunda*) has gone through the warp, the weave is tightened with a long ruler (*belida*) of polished hard wood that slides over a bamboo drum (*pengrorogan*), while the threads are separated with a bamboo tube (*bungbunggan*) provided with little bells that jingle at every move. Thus the work is made easier by the rhythmical sequence of three sounds: the tinkling of the bells, the sound of the hollow bamboo as it is struck by the ruler, and the energetic double knock to tighten the weave. Weaving is the main occupation of the women of caste who feel above doing heavy house labor, but they are not lazy and take to weaving with tenacity. In our house the wives and aunts of our host, all noble-women with servants to do the

Loom (*Prabot Tennun*)

A—*Pendalan*	G—*Belida*
B—*Cecaga*	H—*Srat*
C—*Pengrorogan*	I—*Sumpil*
D—*Selaran*	J—*Apit*
E—*Bungbunggan*	K—*Èpor*
F—*Yerinring*	L—*Tunda*

housework, remained all day glued to their looms and often continued working into the night by the faint light of a petrol lamp.

Towards evening the ground of the house shook, resounding with deep, rhythmic thumping—the women threshing the rice for the next day's meal. Two women pounded the rice in wood mortars with long, heavy pestles, each dropping her pestle alternately in unfailing, perfectly timed intervals, catching it on the rebound with the other hand. Then the rice was separated from the husk by swishing it around in flat bamboo trays, the centrifugal force throwing the chaff towards the outside.

Everybody bathed again when the work for the day was done; by then the sun had begun to set and the atmosphere had cooled, so it was time to put on clean clothes, *cempaka* blossoms in the women's hair, great hibiscus behind the ears of the men, and to go visiting or take a stroll and be admired. Back from work, the men sat in groups at the gates or in the middle of the road talking and fondling their fighting cocks until the sun dropped behind the curtain of coconut palms. Sunset[2] comes suddenly in the tropics and in a few seconds it was night, when the lamps were lit and it was time to eat dinner, the cold food left from lunch. There were many ways of spending an evening; elderly men fond of *tuak*, palm beer, belonged to "*tuak* associations" and met at the *balé banjar*, summoned by a special tomtom. Or if there was a rehearsal of the village orchestra or a meeting at the *balé banjar*, the men sat talking things over until they were tired, going to bed about nine or ten. But if there was a feast in the neighborhood, or one of the frequent theatrical performances, the whole family went to watch the show, remaining until it was over, long after midnight.

BALINESE COOKING

Although the daily meal was frugal, the Balinese seemed exceptionally well fed, and people were always nibbling at something. They were continually eating at odd hours, buying strange-looking foods at public eating-booths, in the market, at the crossroads, and particularly at festivals when the food-vendors did a rushing business in chopped mixtures, peanuts, and bright pink drinks. Every day a young vendor came into the compound and invariably found many customers. For five cents she served a large piece of delicious roast chicken with a strong sauce, accompanied by a package of rice that sold for an extra penny. Even small children, accustomed to look out for themselves, bought their snacks from the street vendors, waiting silently for their

[2] The Balinese divide the day into eight periods (*dauh*) established by the position of the sun in the sky:

"One o'clock" (*dauh pisan*)	about 6 a.m., when the sun appears behind the trees.
"Two o'clock" (*dauh roh*)	about 8 a.m.
"Three o'clock" (*dauh telú*)	10 a.m.
"Four o'clock" (*dauh tepat*)	at noon.
"Five o'clock" (*dauh lima*)	about 2 p.m.
"Six o'clock" (*dauh nam*)	at 4 p.m.
"Seven o'clock" (*dauh pitú*)	at 6 p.m., when the sun goes down.
"Eight o'clock" (*dauh kutus*)	when it grows dark and the lamps are lit.

Generally the Balinese simply point to the place of the sun in the sky to indicate an hour. The night is divided thus: from sunset (*penalekan*), then midnight (*tenggah lemang*), to *galang tanah*, before dawn, when the earth becomes visible. Friederich mentions that in Badung there was a special *kulkul* in a clock-tower in which the hours were struck.

orders to be mashed and wrapped in neat little packages of banana leaf, paying for them with the *kepengs* they kept tied in their sashes.

Balinese food is difficult for the palate of a Westerner. Besides being served cold always, food is considered uneatable unless it is violently flavored with a crushed variety of pungent spices, aromatic roots and leaves, nuts, onions, garlic, fermented fish paste, lemon juice, grated coconut, and burning red peppers. It was so hot that it made even me, a Mexican raised on chili peppers, cry and break out in beads of perspiration. But after the first shocks, and when we became accustomed to Balinese flavors, we developed into Balinese gourmets and soon started trying out strange new combinations. Siloh Biang understood our appreciation of their delicacies and often brought Rose new dishes to taste. Babies are fed the peppery food as soon as they are weaned and will not touch food without spices and peppers. Most Europeans, used to beef and boiled potatoes, simply cannot eat Balinese food, but on the other hand no Balinese of the average class can be induced even to touch European food, which is *nyam-nyam* to them—that is, "flat and tasteless."

A Brahmanic priest we occasionally visited told us that under no circumstances may Balinese eat the following: "human flesh, tigers, monkeys, dogs, crocodiles, mice, snakes, frogs, certain poisonous fish, leeches, stinging insects, crows, eagles, owls, and in general all birds with moustaches"! We assured him nobody ate such things, but he remarked that it was well to keep it in mind anyway. Being of the highest caste and a priest besides, he could not touch the flesh of cows, bulls, and pork, eat in the streets or in the market, drink alcohol, or even taste the food from offerings from which the essence had been consumed by the gods. Members of the high nobility—Brahmanas and Satrias—are forbidden to eat beef, but many of the lesser Gustis do not mind eating it.

Outside of these prohibitions the common people eat everything that walks, swims, flies, or crawls. Chicken, duck, pork, and more rarely beef and buffalo are the meats most commonly eaten, but the people are also fond of stranger foods such as dragonflies, crickets, flying ants, and the larvae of bees. Dragonflies were caught in a most amusing manner; boys and girls wandered among the rice fields waving long poles, the ends of which were smeared with a sticky sap. The supposedly "rank-conscious" dragonflies must always stand in the highest branches and all the boy had to do was to hold the stick above the place where a fly stood; it flew onto the sticky end of the pole and was caught in the trap. Great numbers were obtained in this curious manner, their wings taken off, and the bodies fried crisp in coconut oil with spices and vegetables. Great delicacies are also the scaled ant-eater (*klesih*), the flying fox (a great fruit bat), porcupines (*landak*), large lizards (*alú*), wild boar, squids, rice birds, from the *glatek* to the minute *petingan*, which was eaten bones and all, and all sorts of cray-fish. In every food-stand we saw small fried eels from the rice fields, looking suspiciously like shrivelled baby snakes. Although dogs are included in the list of what not to eat, they are eaten in some of the remote villages in Klungkung and Gianyar, but the rest of the Balinese will have nothing to do with people of such disgusting habits.

With meat eaten only occasionally, the diet of the Balinese consists, besides rice, corn, and sweet potato, of vegetables and fruits, of which they have a great variety. Besides eggplant, papaya, coconut, bananas, pineapples, mangoes, oranges, melons, peanuts, and so forth, there are others unknown among us, such as the delicious breadfruit (*timbul*), jackfruit (*nangka*), acacia leaves (*twi*), greens (*kangkung*), edible ferns (*pakú*), and extraordinary fruits such as *salak*, a pear-shaped fruit that grows on a palm, tastes like pineapple, and is covered by the most perfect imitation snakeskin; the delicate *jambú*, fragrant *waní*, the *rambutan* (a large sort of grape inside of a hairy transparent pink skin), the famous mangosteen (*manggis*) (for which a prize was offered by Queen Victoria to anyone who found the way to bring the fruit in good condition to England), and the stinking durian (*duren* in Bali). A good deal has been written both in favor of and against this spiky sort of custard apple, whose putrid smell has been compared with every decaying or evil-smelling thing from goats to rancid butter. The meat of the durian is a creamy custard, the undefinable flavor and texture of which develops into a passion among those used to eating it. Most Europeans, however, object to its offensive smell to such a degree that they forbid their servants to bring durian within a distance of their house. The fruits are eaten raw and the vegetables are boiled or fried after being washed carefully in a special bowl. The Balinese peel vegetables away and not towards themselves, as is done in the West. Although the Balinese are not fond of sweets, they make a delicious dessert of coconut cream with cinnamon, bananas, or breadfruit steamed in packages of banana leaf.

We have seen that the women are reduced to the routine of cooking the everyday meal, but when it comes to preparing banquet food, it is the men, as is universally the case, who are the great chefs and who alone can prepare the festival dishes of roast suckling pig (*bé guling*) and sea-turtle (*penyú*), the cooking of which requires the art of famous specialists. Few *banjars* enjoyed as great a reputation for fine cooking as Belaluan; there the great banquet dishes were prepared most often because the *banjar* was prosperous, and there lived famous cooks who were always in great demand to officiate at feasts. People spoke with anticipation when Pan Regog or Madé directed the preparation of epicurean dishes such as "turtle in four ways" or the delicious *saté lembat*.

On the road coming from the seaport of Benoa we often met men from Belaluan staggering under the weight of a giant turtle flapping its paddles helplessly in space, and then we knew they were preparing for a feast. For days before the banquet of the *banjar* four or five stupefied turtles crawled under the platforms of the *balé banjar* awaiting the fateful moment when, in the middle of the night, the *kulkul* would sound to call the men to the gruesome task of sacrificing them. A sea-turtle possesses a strange reluctance to die and for many hours after the shell is removed and the flaps and head are severed from the body, the viscera continue to pulsate hysterically, the bloody members twitch weirdly on the ground, and the head snaps furiously. The blood of the turtle is carefully collected and thinned with lime juice to prevent coagulation. By dawn the many cooks and assistants are chopping the skin and meat with heavy chopping axes (*blakas*) on sections of tree-trunks (*talanan*), are grating coconuts, fanning fires, boiling or steaming great quantities of rice, or mashing spices in clay dishes (*cobek*) with wooden pestles (*pengulakan*).

The indicated manners of preparing the turtle are the afore-mentioned four styles:

lawar: skin and flesh chopped fine and mixed with spices and raw blood;
gecok: chopped meat with grated coconut and spices;
urab gadang: same as above, but cooked in tamarind leaves (*asam*);
kiman: chopped meat and grated coconut cooked in coconut-cream.

Coconut (*nyuh*) is an essential element for fine Balinese cooking. Grated coconut meat is mixed with everything, frying is done exclusively in coconut oil, coconut water is the standard drink to refresh one's guests, and a good deal of the food is cooked in rich coconut cream, *santén*, made by squeezing the grated coconut over and over into a little water until a heavy milk is obtained. Food containing coconut does not keep and must be eaten the same day.

Santén enters also into the composition of the other delicacy essential to banquets, the *saté lembat or leklat*. This is a delicious paste of turtle meat and spices, kneaded in coconut cream, with which the end of a thick bamboo stick is covered and which is then roasted over charcoals. The *saté* lembat is presented with an equal number of ordinary *saté*, little pieces of meat the size of dice strung on bamboo sticks "*en brochette*" and roasted over the coals, eaten dry or with a sauce. Rose was always poking around where cooking was going on, and to her I owe the following recipe for preparing the *saté lembat* given to her by the Belaluan cooks, who warned her, however, that it was a most difficult dish to prepare:

Take a piece of ripe coconut with the hard brown skin between the shell and the meat and roast it over the coals. The toasted skin is then peeled off and ground in a mortar. Next prepare the sauce: red pepper, garlic, and red onions browned in a frying-pan and then mixed with black pepper, ginger, turmeric, nutmeg, cloves, *srá* (pungent fermented fish paste), *isén* and *cekóh* (aromatic roots resembling ginger), *ketumbah, ginten,* and so forth, adding a little salt, all mashed together with the toasted coconut skin, and fry the mixture until half done. Take red turtle meat without fat, chop very fine, and add to the sauce in a bowl, two and a half times as much meat as sauce. Add one whole grated coconut and mix well with enough *santén* to obtain a consistency that will adhere to the sticks, not too dry or too wet. Knead for an hour and a half as if making bread. Meantime sticks of bamboo of about ten inches long by a half-inch thick should be made ready and rounded at one end. Take a ball of the paste in the fingers and cover the end of the stick with it, beginning at the top and working down gradually, turning it all the time to give it the proper shape, then roast over the coals until done.

The *saté* can be made of pork or chicken, but turtle remains the favorite of the Balinese of Denpasar. Turtles are expensive (about twenty dollars for a good-sized one), and ordinarily pork, chicken, or duck is the dish served at more modest feasts. They may be prepared in the form described above, in *satés, lawar, gecok,* or simply split and roasted with a peppery sauce. Duck is stuffed and steamed (*bebek betutu*). Although the expression: "He has to eat banana leaves" is used to give emphasis to someone's extreme poverty, a delicious dish and a great delicacy is the *kekalan,* made of tender shoots of banana leaves cooked in turtle blood and lime juice. Balinese cooking attains its apotheosis in the preparation of the famous *bé guling,* stuffed suckling pig roasted on a spit, the recipe for which was also given to Rose by the Belaluan cooks:

After the pig has been killed, pour boiling water over it and scrape the skin thoroughly with a sharp piece of coconut shell. Open the mouth and scrape the tongue also. Cut a four-inch incision to insert the hand and remove the viscera. Wash the inside of the pig carefully with cold water. Run a pointed stick through the mouth and tail and stuff the pig with a mixture of:

red chili pepper (*lombok*)	*bogaron, tinké* (nuts resembling ginger)
garlic	*cekoh* (an aromatic root of the ginger family)
red onions	black pepper (*merica*)
turmeric (*kunyit*)	*srá* (concentrated fish paste)
ginger (*jahé*)	aromatic leaves (*saladam* or *ulam*)
salt	and *ketumbah,* a variety of peppercorn.

Chop all these ingredients fine, mixing them with coconut oil. Stuff the pig with the mixture, placing inside a piece of coconut bark, and then sew up the cut. To give the skin the proper rich brown color, bathe the pig, before roasting, in turmeric crushed in water, and rinse off the excess root. Make a big wood fire and place the pig not directly over it, but towards one side. Forked branches should support the end of the stick that serves as a spit, one end of which is crooked to be used as a crank by a man who turns the pig constantly (*guling* means to turn), while another man fans the fire to direct the flame and smoke away from the pig. The heat should be concentrated on the head and tail and not in the middle so as not to crack the skin of the stomach.

After a few hours of slow roasting the juiciest and most tender pork is obtained, flavored by the fragrant spices, inside of a deliciously brittle skin covered with a golden-brown glaze. Few dishes in the world can be compared with a well-made *bé guling*.

When the food is ready and the guests are assembled, sitting in long rows, they are served by the leading members of the *banjar* and their assistants, who circulate among them carrying trays with pyramids of rice and little square dishes of palm-leaf pinned together with bits of bamboo, containing chopped mixtures, *satés*, and little side dishes of fried beans (*botor*), bean sprouts with crushed peanuts, parched grated coconuts dyed yellow with *kunyit*, and preserved salted eggs. Others pour drinks; *tuak* (palm beer), *brom*, a sweet sherry made from fermented black rice, or more rarely *arak*, distilled rice brandy. More frequently water alone is served; it is only old men who are fond of alcoholic drinks, drinking, however, with moderation and never becoming drunk. During our entire stay in Bali we never saw a man really drunk, perhaps because the Balinese dread the sensation of dizziness and confusion, of losing control over themselves.

COSTUME AND ADORNMENT

At home and at work the Balinese like to be free of excessive clothing; ordinarily the dress of both men and women consists simply of a skirt called *kamben* (the women wear an underskirt—*tapih*) of Javanese batik or domestic hand-woven material, and a headcloth. The women wear this skirt wrapped tight around the hips, reaching down to the feet and held at the waist by a bright-colored sash (*bulang*). A long scarf (*kamben cerik*) in pale pink, yellow, or white cotton completes the costume. Young girls love gay batiks from Pekalongan, full of birds and flowers in red and blue on a white ground, or hand-woven skirts of yellow and green for feasts, but older women prefer conservative brown and indigo or black silk enlivened by a green, yellow, or peach sash. The scarf is generally thrown over one shoulder or wound around the head to keep the hair in place, but it also serves as a cushion for a heavy basket carried on the head, or to wrap over the breasts when appearing in front of a superior or entering the temple, because, although the Balinese are accustomed to go nude above the waist, it is a rule of etiquette, for both men and women, that the breast must be covered for formal dress. This is purely a formula and does not imply that it is wrong to go with uncovered breasts; often the cloth is worn loosely around the waist, leaving the torso free; but even modernized Balinese, who generally wear a shirt or blouse, wrap the breast-cloth across their chest or around their middles when they wish to appear properly dressed.

For daily wear the men also wear a *kamben*, a single piece of batik reaching from the waist to a little below the knees, tied in the front and leaving a trailing end that falls into pleats. The *kamben* can be pulled up and tied into an abbreviated loincloth when the men work in the rice fields. An indispensable part of the men's dress is the headcloth (*udeng*), a square piece of batik worn as a turban and tied in an amazing variety of styles. Each man ties his *udeng* in a manner individual to himself, taking good care that the folds form a certain pattern and that the end sticks out just right. Conservative Balinese wear the *udeng* with a corner high like a crest, but the young generation prefers small tight turbans with the four points neatly arranged in different directions. Children generally wear only a lock of hair on their foreheads, but little girls learn feminine propriety by wearing a skirt many years before the boys. Priests dress all in white and one can recognize a high priest (*pedanda*, "staff-bearer") because he goes bareheaded and carries a staff (*danda*) topped by a crystal ball (*suryakanta*, "the glitter of the sun"), symbol of his authority.

It is unfortunate that new fashions in dress are introducing a new sort of class-consciousness. Young elegants feel superior and "emancipated" from the old-style peasant class when they wear a Malay *sarong*, a tube of cloth worn snug at the back, folded in front in two overlapping pleats and held at the waist by a leather belt. With the *sarong* go a pair of leather sandals, a common shirt, too often with the tails outside, and a European-style coat. This is the costume of school-teachers, clerks, chauffeurs, and those in frequent contact with Europeans, who will, in the long run, set the fashion for the rest of the population.

All women in North Bali have worn the Malay blouse (*baju*) for over half a century, since they were ordered to wear blouses by official decree "to protect the morals of the Dutch soldiers." Women of the Southern nobility started to wear *bajus*, and the fashion is rapidly spreading all over Bali. The Balinese form of *baju* is clumsy and ill-fitting and does not suit the huskier Balinese women as it does the slim Javanese. Many women cannot afford more than one *baju* and often let it go without washing. A girl who looks elegant and noble in the simple and healthy dress of the country, appears vulgar when "dressed up" in a tight *baju* of cheap cotton, not always clean, usually worn pinned up at the breast with a rusty safety-pin.

Those accustomed to associate nudity with savagery often refer to the Balinese as "charming primitive people unconcerned with clothes," but however scant and simple their daily costume may be, they love dressing up, and for feasts they will wear as elaborate a dress as they can afford, or borrow one rather than appear poorly clothed to parade at the feast. At temple feasts, weddings, and cremations one still sees middle-aged men in the elaborate ceremonial dress of former times: the white *kamben* with a trailing end, a rich piece of brocade (*saput*) tied over the breast with a silk scarf (*umpal*) in which is stuck the ancestral *kris*, weapon and ornament,

Ceremonial costumes of woman and man

the sheath of precious wood and ivory, the hilt of chiseled gold glittering with rubies and diamonds, crimson hibiscus over their ears. Few costumes in the world have the dignified elegance of the ceremonial costume of a noblewoman: the underskirt dragging on the ground in a train of silk and gold; the torso bound from the hips to the armpits; first is a strong *bulang*, a strip of cloth fifteen feet long, covered by a *sabuk*, another strip of silk overlaid with gold leaf; with

Gelung agung

gold plugs through her ears, her hair dressed in a great crown of real and gold flowers, with the forehead reshaped with paint and decorated with rows of flower petals, two small disks of gold pasted to the temples; walking with poise in a procession with other girls dressed like herself, in a display of style, beauty, and dignity. The costumes for dramatic performances are as spectacular as any in our ballets; diadems of fresh flowers and helmets of gold set with col-

Pusung gonjer

ored stones, the body wrapped from head to foot in bright-colored silks to which bold designs in glittering gold leaf are applied by a special process in truly theatrical style.

A Balinese woman is seldom without flowers in her hair, and during festivals one sees a bewildering variety of head-dresses. They are then well aware of their beauty and take special pains with the arrangement of the hair, fixed ingeniously without pins and without the help of a mirror. The hair is combed back with a fan-shaped comb, the end rolled into a bundle (*pusung*) that protrudes to the left and is held in place tucked under strands of the woman's own hair. Unmarried girls leave a loose lock (*gonjer*) that hangs down the back or over one shoulder. Ordinarily the flowers are simply caught between the hairs, sometimes suspended in the *gonjer* or over the forehead, dangling from a single invisible hair.

Each type of head-dress receives a special name, from the simple flower arrangement worn at lesser feasts to the *gelung agung*, the diadem worn by noble brides. The *gelung agung* is an enormous crown of fresh flowers; sprays of jasmine, *sandat*, and *bunga gadung*, mixed with flowers of beaten gold mounted on springs that quiver at the slightest motion of the head. A beautiful forehead that describes a high arch coming down at the temples is obtained by painting it with a mixture of soot and oil. Little acacia blossoms or yellow flower petals are carefully pasted in a row in the blackened area to emphasize the outline of the brow. They are called *trangana*, meaning a "constellation." Girls who have reached puberty cut two locks of hair, brought from the middle of the head, over the ears in two curls (*semí*), stiffened with wax to keep them in place.

Men do not wear any ornaments except flowers and perhaps a bracelet of *akar bahar*, a black sort of coral supposed to prevent rheumatism, but women love jewelry and it is extraordinary that outside of dancers or children the Balinese are one of the rare people in the world that do not wear necklaces. In ancient times men and women wore ear-rings, and ancient statues show that, like the Dayaks of Borneo, they distended their ear-lobes until they hung below the shoulders, weighted down by heavy gold ornaments. Today some men have pierced ears because when children they wore leaf-shaped ear-ornaments (*rumbing*) of gold set with precious stones.

Little girls distend the holes of their ear-lobes with rolls of dry leaf or with a nutmeg seed until the hole is large enough to receive the large rolls of lontar leaf for everyday or their replicas of gold (*subang*) for feasts. The *subangs* are hollow conical cylinders of beaten gold three inches long by one in diameter, closed at one end, imitating in shape the palm-leaf *subang*. Only girls wear them and after marriage they consider the wearing of *subangs* a coquetry that is out of place, although married women of high caste may wear them at feasts. Rings of gold set with rubies are popular, but the most fashionable today are those set with an English gold guinea. Bracelets are in good taste only if made of gold and tortoise-shell set with rubies, star sapphires, or little diamonds.

The Balinese are as fastidious in the care of their bodies as they are about dress, and people of all classes, conditions permitting, make almost a cult of cleanliness. They bathe frequently during the day, whenever they feel hot or after strenuous work, but two baths a day are the rule, in the morning and evening, before each meal.

Many villages have formal baths with separate compartments for men and women, divided by carved stone walls and provided with water-spouts in the shape of fantastic animals, or simple natural pools or streams fitted with bamboo pipes and low walls. Often the favorite bathing-place is a shallow spot in the river where men on one side, women on the other, squat on the water, remaining for a long time in animated conversation, scrubbing themselves with pumice stone that removes superfluous hair and invigorates the skin, or rubbing their backs with a rough stick or against a large stone placed there for the purpose. In a river near Gianyar we often saw a group of women sitting in the water in a circle, their feet radiating from the center, gossiping until after dark.

There are strict rules of etiquette for bathing-places; for example, sexual parts should be concealed even among persons of the same sex. A man simply covers himself with one hand not to offend his fellow bathers. It would be unthinkable for a man to look deliber-

ately at a nude woman although she may be bathing within sight of everybody in the irrigation ditch along the road. It is customary to give some indication of one's presence on approaching a public bath. Women wade into the water raising their skirts to a respectable level, a little above the knee, and after considering the possibilities of the place sit suddenly in the water, quickly taking off the skirt. The process is reversed in getting out of the water: the skirt which has been lying on a stone or held in one hand, is gathered up in front of the bather and dropped like a curtain as she stands up. She wraps it around her hips and walks off without bothering to dry herself.

Besides the ordinary village bathing-places there are sacred pools and bath-houses, some of which have magic or curative qualities. There it is customary to leave a small offering for the spirit of the spring before bathing. The most famous of these is the sacred pool of Tirta Empul in Tampaksiring, one of the holiest temples of Bali, where a special compartment has been devised for menstruating women.

The Balinese admire a smooth, clear skin the color of gold, and pretty girls have a mortal dread of being sunburned, so they do not like to go unnecessarily into the sun. The skin is kept in condition by rubbing and massaging while bathing, afterwards anointing the body with coconut oil and *boreh,* a yellow paste that refreshes the skin when hot or gives it warmth after exposure to the rain. *Boreh* is made of mashed leaves, flowers, aromatic roots, cloves, nutmeg, and turmeric (*kunyit*) for coloring.

In olden times men wore the hair long, but nowadays the younger generation cuts it short like Europeans. The women's hair should be long, thick, and glossy, heavily anointed with perfumed coconut oil in which flowers are macerated. The hair is kept in condition by washing it in concoctions of herbs.

When a Balinese has nothing to do he squats on the ground and pulls hairs from his face with two coins or with special tweezers, and women remove the hair under the armpits with porous volcanic stones. Some men wear moustaches, which are considered elegant, but only priests wear beards. It is a sign of distinction to wear the fingernails long, often four inches or more, showing that the wearer does not have to do manual work. Priests may wear the nails of both hands long, but the average well-to-do Balinese lets them grow only on the left hand. In Tenganan I have seen young girls wearing nail-protectors five inches long made of solid gold.

The teeth are ceremoniously filed at puberty to shorten them and make them even. Old-fashioned Balinese blacken them with a sort of lacquer that supposedly protects the teeth from the devastating effects of betelnut. However, since betel-chewing is losing favor, young people keep their teeth white by polishing them with ashes, although in many cases the molars are blackened, and the front teeth left white. The custom of filing and blackening the teeth, which is widespread throughout Malaysia, has its roots in animistic ritual, to avoid having the long, white teeth of dogs. In Bali today the teeth are filed mainly for aesthetic reasons, since long teeth are ugly.

It is plain that the refined and sensitive Balinese make the most of their daily routine, leading a harmonious and exciting, although simple existence, making an art of the elemental necessities of daily life—dress, food, and shelter.

CHAPTER SIX

The Family

The wedding of Rama and Sita (*from a Balinese painting*)

"AFTER THE WORLD, the mountains, and the cardinal directions were created, and there were trees, fruits, and flowers, the gods made four human beings out of red earth, whom they provided with utensils to work with and houses to live in. Batara Siwa, the Supreme Lord, next made four mature girls for wives of the four men. The god of love, Batara Semara, made mating a pleasure so that the women would be fertilized, and eventually the four couples had many children: 117 boys and 118 girls, who grew, became adolescent, married, and had children. But there remained a girl without a husband. Broken-hearted, she went into the forest and there found the stump of a jackfruit tree (*nangka*) which Siwa had carved, to amuse himself, into the likeness of a human being. The girl made love to the wooden figure and became pregnant. Out of pity for her, Semara gave life to the figure so that she also could have a husband, and the couple became the ancestors of the *ngatewél* clan," whose totem is the *nangka* tree.[1]

Another legend tells us that "the gods concentrated to make human beings and produced two couples; one yellow in color: Ketok Pita and Jenar; another red: Abang and Barak. From the yellow couple was born a boy, Nyoh Gading, `Yellow Coconut,' and a girl named Kuning. The second couple had also two children, a boy named Tanah Barak, `Red Earth,' and a girl Lewék. Yellow Coconut married Lewék; Red Earth married Kuning; and their descendants did the same until the population of Bali was created."[2]

There are endless tales like these relating the origin of the Balinese to magic or ordinary unions of the eternal male and female principles, elements of great importance in the religion around which their life revolves. Their supreme deity is *Siwa*, the esoteric combination of all the gods and all the forces of nature, he who is the hermaphrodite (*wandú*) in the sense that within him are the male and female creative forces, the complete, perfect unity. Men and women must imitate their gods to attain some of that divine "completeness" by uniting to form families that worship common ancestors in the family shrine of each Balinese household. The various families that compose a village all worship in turn a common ancestor, the village god represented by the "Navel," the *puséh*, the temple of common origin. Family ties are consequently the most important factor in Balinese life; a continuous sequence that relates the individual to his family, to his community, and to the total of the Balinese people in a relationship that represents race and nationality to them. A woman who marries a Chinese, a Muslim, or a European automatically ceases to be a Balinese.

A Balinese feels that his most important duty is to marry as soon as he comes of age and to raise a family to perpetuate his line. A bachelor is in Bali an abnormal, incomplete being devoid of all social significance since only settled married men can become members of the vil-

[1] The author's free translation from the *Catur Yoga*.

[2] Korn: *Het Adatrecht van Bali*.

lage association. Even *pedandas*, the high priests, do not conform to the ascetic abstention favored by orthodox Hindus and invariably marry.

Thus every Balinese centers all his hopes in having children, preferably male children, who will look after him in his old age, and, most important of all, sons who will take the proper care of his remains after he is dead, performing the necessary rites to liberate his soul for reincarnation, so it will not become an aimless wandering ghost. From paintings and temple reliefs, they are familiar with the fate that awaits the childless in Hades, the *swarga*, where a woman who dies without children is condemned to carry a gigantic worm suckling at her useless breasts. A man who does not obtain children from his wife has the right to divorce her and get back the money he paid for her; or if she dies or runs away, he remarries as soon as possible. Often the sterile wife will herself suggest and even provide for a second wife for her husband. There are, however, many childless couples that because of personal attachment or for economic reasons remain monogamous and are content to borrow or rather be given a child by a neighbor or a relative to bring up as their own.

CHILDBIRTH

To follow the development of their sexual life we shall begin the cycle of birth, childhood, adolescence, marriage, and birth again, with the event of pregnancy, a great blessing to every Balinese household.

Most people we talked to had a quite correct idea of the physiology of procreation; they said that the man's seminal fluid (*semara*, named after the god of love), coming in contact with the "female semen," turns into blood in the womb, forming a ball which, fed by the woman's own blood, eventually takes human form and develops into a child. Along with this almost scientific notion goes the belief that a child is the reincarnation of an ancestor whose life-giving spirit comes down to earth in the form of dew, which is inadvertently eaten by the parents, the process of gestation taking place after intercourse.[3]

[3] Jane Belo ("The Balinese Temper") reports that a woman is popularly supposed to have within her a *manik*, a "gem," which grows into a child after it is "hit" during sexual intercourse, and that after the birth of the child she gets a new *manik*. The people of Badung with whom I discussed the subject never mentioned the *manik*, which they perhaps translated for my benefit as the "female semen." The *manik* idea is quite in the manner of thought of the Balinese and could symbolize the ovum.

With children generally welcome, birth control is rarely practiced, although it is not unknown to unmarried girls who do not want to become pregnant. Apparently the only method of prevention they know is for the woman to stand up after intercourse and free herself of the seminal fluid. There are medicines to cause abortion and to make a woman sterile, but both ideas are criminal and fall within the category of black magic.

In Bali a woman with child is free of rigid taboos, and her life is carried on as usual. Omens are taken carefully into consideration, and special attention is paid to exorcizing obnoxious spirits, the *butas*, that persecute her at this critical time, but her real enemies are then the *leyaks*, the witches that infest Bali, whose main diet consists of the blood of pregnant women and the entrails of unborn children. However, for a small sum her husband can procure amulets from the local priest or witch-doctor; magic words and symbols drawn on a piece of paper or cloth, hung at the house gate or carried on her belt to keep the *leyaks* away. Ordinarily a pregnant woman may do as she pleases, and in Badung she may even enter the temple. In later months, for obvious reasons, she may be more secluded and has to observe certain prohibitions, the natural ones of diet and hygiene; bathe oftener and avoid certain foods, such as too much pepper, octopus, eggplant, and a kind of mango. But, as in Malaya and other parts of Indonesia, her husband may not cut his hair until after the child is born.

When the time approaches for childbirth (*medal, lekad*; i.e., "to come out") certain magic (*penyesáh*) is practiced so that the child will be born easily. Particularly effective is a shoot of coconut palm naturally ingrown into a loop. This is soaked in water and held over the woman's head so that the water will drip into her mouth. It is recommended also to pass or stand under the cage of a dove that has a natural bald spot over the heart.

Sexual questions are simple and natural matters to the Balinese, and our friends discussed them freely when, in the evenings, they gathered on our front porch to talk. Once when the conversation was led onto the subject of childbirth the women described their own experiences eagerly while the men added details the women had overlooked. The most convincing authority was Rapag, a boy of fourteen who had witnessed the birth of his four sisters. They said that most women have their children easily, and as an example they told of a woman who lived next door who had had her child unexpectedly while she was alone in the groves. She carried the baby home and they claimed that two days later she was already selling in the market.

Frequently even the assistance of a midwife is dispensed with and only expert women relatives aid the woman. As a rule the husband should be present. There is no special place where the child should be born. When the time comes, the woman is placed half-seated on a new mat, supported from the back by a woman, while another helps her, through massage, to deliver the child. The umbilical cord (*udal, unsang*) is tied and cut with a sharp knife made of bamboo (iron may not be used). Then the child is washed, and there is a curious ruling that demands that the woman drink—or just taste—three times out of the water. The placenta, together with the umbilical cord, some blood (*gateh*), and afterbirth water (*yieh nyom*)[4] are placed in a "yellow coconut" (*nyoh gading*), which is wrapped in sugar-palm fiber and buried in front of the sleeping-quarters (*metén*), that of a boy at the right, that of a girl at the left of the entrance. A fire is built over the place where the coconut is buried and a bamboo altar with offerings is erected over the spot.

At first the child is fed with a porridge of boiled rice flour (*bubur*) or a little palm-sugar and meat from a young coconut. In easy cases the woman recovers on the same day and is able to walk and give the breast to the child. They believe that the first milk is "hard" and indigestible, and before feeding the baby, the mother milks her breast, making the first milk fall on the house wall. The only explanation for this strange idea is the eternal answer that it is custom. Ordinarily, they say, a woman will have "pains in her insides" for about three days, after which time she can perform her usual work. It is not considered that the mother's milk is sufficient for the nourishment of the child; she gives the baby the breast every time he cries, but he is also fed with *bubur*, and even with a banana previously chewed by the mother.

The child is weaned after three birthdays (*otonan*), two and a half of our years, when the mother puts a mixture of lime and palm-sugar to her nipples; but it is not unusual to see children of four being suckled still.

Special songs are used to amuse or put the child to sleep, Balinese nursery rhymes (*cecangkrima*) sung to a slow beautiful tune. Here is an example: —

[4] There are special ritual names for the umbilical cord (*sulabir*); the placenta (*jalaer* or *banaspati*); the blood (*barak*); and the water (*mokaer*).

> "Tadpoles, fishes, and beetles from Bedulu, where are you going southwards? To where the boats land. What will you sell there? My insides that have fallen out. How far did they fall? As high as a thousand pigs. What doctor gave you medicine? The one with the beard and the topknot. Where does he live? In front of the little *warú* tree where the *kulkul* hangs. With what do they beat the *kulkul*? With sticks of heart of sandalwood and *tengulun*. Who beats it? The big ironsmith who is there crouched asleep."[5]

After the birth of the child, he and his parents become impure (*sebel*), the man for three days, during which it would be dangerous for him even to climb a tree, the woman and the child for forty-two days. Offerings are made during this time: when the navel of the child has healed; when he is twelve days old; and at the expiration of the forty-two-day period, when the husband, the mother, and the child are restored to normalcy by the priest, who blesses them in an elaborate ceremony of purification.

The birth of a freak, whether from a woman or from an animal, is an evil omen for the community, the presage of an approaching disaster that can only be averted by elaborate purification ceremonies. But should an unfortunate woman give birth to a boy and girl twins (*kembar buncing*), the entire village falls under the curse of the "child blunder," *manak salah*, as the dreadful calamity is called. The "incestuous union" of the brother and sister in the mother's womb is a wrong that can only be wiped out by the most complete and troublesome of exorcisms.

As soon as the happening is discovered, the alarm-drum is sounded to declare the village polluted (*sebel*); the temple doors are closed and hung with forbidding pandanus leaves, a sign of taboo (*sawén*), so that no one will enter. No celebrations of any sort can be held and the entire social life of the village is paralyzed until the long crisis that ensues is over and the village is again made normal.

The guilty parents and the baby twins are rushed to some unholy

[5] "Cingcing koka beduda di Bedaulú, nyaí kija menglodan? Tiang kadap ka prau. Nyen nyaí ngadap? Iseng basang suba laboh. Lamon apa labohé Mengceléng ají siú. Balian apa kenubadin? Balian jengot maka kuncung. Apa mediwangé Warú cenek mengantung kulkul. Apa penepakné Les cendana, les tengulun. Nyén kenepak? I pandé gedé melingkúh."

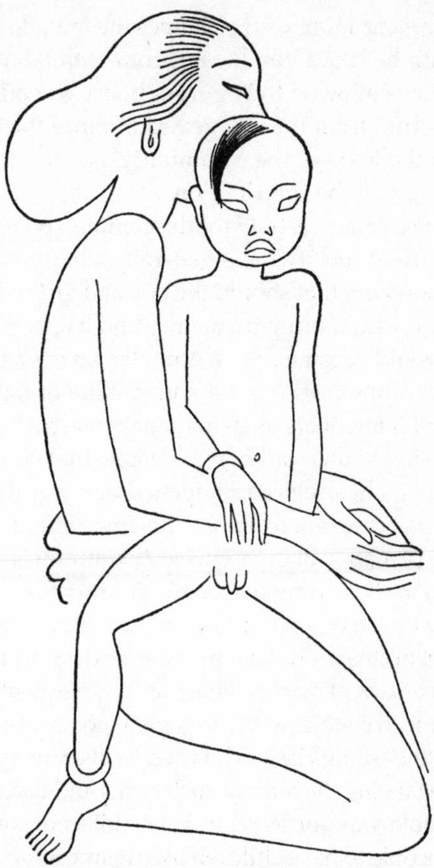

spot, generally the cemetery or more rarely the crossroads, together with the house in which the twins were born, which is dismantled and hastily rebuilt there. The couple and the twins are condemned to live in exile for forty-two days, guarded by a number of watchmen, who remain with them until the period of banishment is over, when the house is ceremonially burned to the ground before they all return to the village to perform the *mecaru*, the great ceremony of purification. (See "Nyepí," page 252).

It is at this point that serious trouble starts for the unfortunate father of the twins; he must pay all expenses for the costly purification offerings and ceremonies by selling his property if he has no ready cash. If the amount obtained is not enough, the townspeople have to raise the rest, but should the man be totally destitute, the village advances the money. In old times the man became a slave of the village until he could buy his freedom with labor, but today in many places he is allowed to beg from house to house, authorized by a special permit from the village heads. Since the purpose of his begging is for the good of the community, no one may refuse him, no matter how small the contribution.

This strange calamity is only for the common people. Among the nobility the birth of such twins is generally a happy omen and people of high caste claim that should the boy and girl twins marry each other, the union would bring prosperity and happiness to the country and they would become rulers. A nobleman explained to me that when a couple of his class has led a model life of faithfulness unto death, they will reincarnate as twins "again married in the mother's womb," returning to their old home. Despite this idea, however, the marriage of twins has seldom happened and my Balinese friends knew of only one case where a noble boy married his twin sister.

A logical explanation of these curiously contradictory customs has been given by Jane Belo in her thorough "Study of Customs Pertaining to Twins in Bali" (see Bibliography); on the native side, as originated by the dread of brother and sister incest so widespread among primitive peoples, a breach of marital taboos and consequently a crime. The native idea came in conflict with the general policy of establishing the superiority of the ruling class, who tried to liberate themselves from the curse by legalizing the birth of such twins and declaring that such was the desirable way for Rajas to have children; consequently for the common people to have children like them was an affront to their superiority. Jane Belo points also to an endless variety of concepts relating to twins in Bali, differing from district to district and even from one village to the next—a typical attitude in regard to everything in Bali, with the general trend as described above. However, the birth of twins of the same sex (*kembar*) does not bring pollution to the village and passes as an ordinary happening, although again, as in everything else, there are exceptions to the rule.

THE LIFE OF CHILDREN

Forty-two days after birth, when the child is blessed by the priest, he is given anklets and bracelets of brass and silver in place of the black strings that he wore tied around his wrists since he was seven days old. His ears are pierced, and a thread is passed through each hole so that three months later he can wear little flower-shaped ear-rings of gold. Around his neck is tied a necklace composed of various amulets that will protect him and influence his growth: a silver tube containing a dried piece of the child's own umbilical cord, some colored glass beads, a piece of black coral (*akar bahar*), an ancient coin, and a tiger's tooth or a piece of tiger bone. This is all the child wears until he is about seven years old, but little girls are given a skirt and a sash three or four years before. The repugnance of the Balinese for actions characteristic of animals causes them not to permit children to crawl on all fours, and before the child is three months old he may not even touch the earth and is carried everywhere.

Offerings are made when the child is three months old (*nelubulanin*) and again at his first anniversary (*otonan*) when the child is 210 days old, one Balinese year. Then he is dressed in rich brocades and is given gold bracelets, anklets, a necklace set with rubies and sapphires, and a gold disk with a ruby in it, which is pasted on the child's forehead. His hair is then cut (*ngutangin bok*), and his head is shaved clean except for a lock of hair on the forehead that is never cut; otherwise he would become ill. On this date the priest blesses the child again, while offerings are made to the family shrine, to the sun, and to the evil spirits.

The well-to-do make a big occasion of the first birthday and give a banquet with theatrical performances, but it is a rule for all to give a shadow-play as a part of the ceremonies. After the first anniversary less attention is paid to birthdays; the third year has a special significance and perhaps the mother will make some offerings in subsequent years, but grown people forget about them and soon lose track of their ages.

On his first birthday the child receives his magic name from the priest, who writes various propitious names, obtained through a divination, on pieces of palm-leaf which he burns. The name given to the child is that which can be made out most clearly from the charred remains, or the one that takes the longest time to burn. This is a secret name that no one ever hears and soon even the father forgets it. A baby is simply called "the child of so-and-so," but eventually he is given a personal name by his parents. Even this name has an influence over his life and should he become sick often, the name is to blame and a more appropriate one is chosen by the priest or the

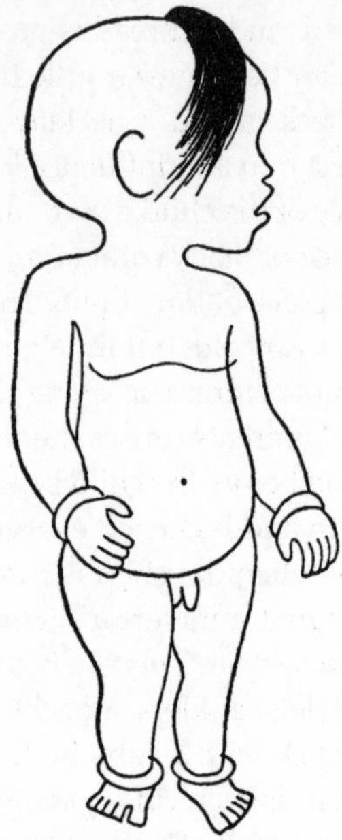

witch-doctor. Boys and girls are called by their names, but it would be poor manners to do so after the child has grown up. A personal name is private property and it is always patronizing to call a person by his name. High-caste people keep their names secret and go through life called only by their caste titles.

Most commonly used are the words that refer to the order of a person's birth: the first child of Sudras is called *Wayang*; *Putú* or *Gedé* for high castes; the second child is *Madé* or *Nengah*; the third is *Nyoman*; and the fourth is *Ktut*. The order is repeated for subsequent children. Satrias add the word *Ngurah* to their other titles to indicate the purity of their descent (for example, Anak Agung Ngurah Gedé). The words for father (*bapa*) and mother (*memé*) have a very elastic application; every uncle and aunt is called *bapa* and *memé*, and every cousin is a brother or sister, but a well-bred young man calls his father *gurú* ("teacher"). Elderly people are called grandfather (*pekak*) or grandmother (*dadong*) as a sign of respect in the same way that a young man calls his older friends "elder brother" (*blí*), while a girl is called "sister" (*embok*). After a Sudra couple have children their name changes to "Father or Mother of so-and-so." Our servant Dog, the father of little Muluk, was called Panmuluk and his wife was known as Menmuluk. Gusti's wife, a woman of high caste, was called Gusti Rake, but after she became the mother of Gusti Gede she became known as Gusti Biang Rake, *biang* being a polite term for "mother."

From the time the child can walk, he is left to himself and falls in the care of other children. Small girls know how to take care of babies with the same proficiency as their mothers and it is common to see babies carried on the hips of girls only slightly older. The child learns early to be self-sufficient and is free to wander all over the village and to do as he pleases. A child is often called *idewa*, "a god"; he is not considered responsible for his actions, because, as they say, "his mind is still undeveloped" and it is the god within him that acts through his body. At home there is no regular discipline and no pampering; the parents do not intimidate their child, but rather coax him into obedience as an equal. And he is never beaten; if a mother loses patience and strikes her child, he would, in all probability, strike back and she would be mortified and would grieve over her rash impulse. The sensible Balinese say that if a child is beaten his tender soul will be seriously damaged.

Frequently the father is inclined to be more demonstrative than the mother, and it is common to see a man with his child in his arms, taking him everywhere and talking to him as if he were a grown-up. It is extremely rare to hear a child cry. Thus the child grows among other children as a member of a children's republic, with an independent life of its own. Often groups of children go out on expeditions, remaining away from home all day. When they get hungry they can buy food from a public stand with the pennies that are given to them every day. Only by the independence and lack of pampering can one explain the well-mannered seriousness and the self-sufficiency of Balinese children. With no special behavior set for children apart from that of grown-ups, the mentality of a Balinese child develops quickly. Nothing is hidden from him; he listens to all conversations of grown people and observes the acts of animals, so his sexual education begins as soon as he is able to talk. A child in Bali knows facts about which an adolescent in the West is totally ignorant, and we knew children under five who could make erotic jokes. Their sense of responsibility became patent to me when I became the guest of a small boy in whose house I had spent the night. The next morning he took me for a walk to see his village, showed me the temples, and introduced me to the local prince; then we went to the market to see the good-looking girls of the village and he told me the story of the love affairs of each, while he bought fried peanuts from his favorite vendor to treat me. He even offered me some of his own cigarettes; it is normal for little boys and girls to smoke and they show preference for a certain brand of tobacco perfumed with cinnamon and cloves in little cigarettes wrapped in corn husk that sell six for a penny.

A boy assists his father in the work at home and in the fields, and cares for the cattle, driving the cows and buffaloes and bathing them at sunset. He learns his father's trade, and by the time he is about eight or ten he has a good knowledge of practical matters. Besides the hybrid education that the Balinese now receive in the Dutch schools, a boy learns to read and write in Balinese characters from his father or his *gurú*; mythology, ethics, and history he learns from watching plays and puppet shows, where he can pick up literary terms and become a scholar. Little girls learn from their mothers to cook, weave, thresh rice, and make offerings. Although the higher education is rather the attribute of men, women are not barred from acquiring knowledge, and even peasant women show high spirits and a keen mentality.

ADOLESCENCE

A boy comes of age gradually and unconsciously, but the first menstruation of a girl (*nyacal*) is an important event and when this condition arrives to the daughter of a prince, the village *kulkul* is beaten to announce that the little princess is now a woman of marriageable age. As soon as the fact is discovered, the girl is secluded in the sleeping-quarters, and the veranda is enclosed with screens of woven palm-leaf, leaving a small entrance. Men are strictly forbidden to go into the place. The girl becomes automatically *sebel*, unclean, and remains in seclusion until the menstrual period is over and until the auspicious day when she will be purified by the priest. Then a great feast is given by her family to celebrate her reappearance into the world as a mature woman.

We assisted at the purification feast of Madé Rai, one of the *legong* dancers of Belaluan, who had just come of age. When we arrived at her house, Madé Rai was being dressed inside the house, surrounded by busy women who came and went with clothes, jewels, and flowers. The platform of honor of the *balé gedé*, the reception hall, was filled with great offerings of palm leaf, fruit, and flowers, and the high priest, the *pedanda,* waited to perform the purification, sitting cross-legged on the high *balé* with an air of aloof importance, his intriguing paraphernalia ready in front of him. Madé Rai made her triumphal appearance among exploding firecrackers, carried on the shoulders of Regog, the strong man of the *banjar,* and dressed in the ceremonial costume of her class: a skirt of *prada,* silk with applications of gold leaf, a scarf of brocade around her budding breasts, *subangs* of gold in her ears, and a crown of gold flowers. She was deposited on a mat before the priest, who proceeded with his *maweda,* magic prayers recited with an accompaniment of mystic gestures with the hands. The priest sprinkled her with holy water and occasionally flung flowers towards the girl. Certain offerings, "moons" of palm-leaf and long brooms, sexual symbols, were held in front of her while she fanned their essence towards herself with graceful gestures of her dance-trained hands. The holy water that the priest had consecrated was poured on her hands through a rice-steaming basket (*kukusan*); she drank the water with reverence, wiping her wet palms on her forehead. This ended the ceremony and Madé Rai could then go to pray at the temple of origin of her family (*pura dadia*). She was taken in procession, carried on a palanquin preceded by flags and spears. On arriving at the temple she knelt on a cushion in front of the principal shrine and she prayed with the other members of her family, while the old men sang *kekawin* poems that described the beauty of the *dedari,* the nymphs of heaven. The procession returned home and the guests were entertained with plays and dances to celebrate the fact that Madé Rai, the little girl that a few days before roamed unconcerned all over the *banjar,* had become a beautiful woman of fourteen.

The custom of filing the teeth has a deep significance among primitive peoples, usually as a form of initiation ceremonies at puberty. Others tattoo or scar their bodies, and even Westerners, who are horrified at the absurd customs of savages, practice initiation tortures in the form of saber duels, beatings, featherings, or simply breaking their noses at college football games.

The Balinese file their teeth when a boy or a girl comes of age; not in sharp points like some Africans, or down to the gums like the Sumatrans and other Indonesians; but they simply file off a small portion of the upper incisors and upper canines to produce an even line of short teeth, also wearing them down to smooth their outer surface. Undoubtedly the custom of filing the teeth (*mesangí, mepandés*) had its origin in initiation rites. As we have seen, the teeth are not only filed to make them beautiful, but also blackened, and it is possible that, like the custom of cutting the rice stalks at harvesting-time with a small blade carefully hidden in the palm of the hand, the filing and blackening of the teeth may in some way be connected with the fear of offending, or hurting, the rice soul. Today, as I have said, young people are giving up chewing betelnut, and the custom of blackening the teeth is disappearing. It is mostly elderly people who display black caverns for mouths, oozing with blood-red betel juice.

The filing should be performed preferably at puberty, but the ceremony is expensive because of fees, guests, banquet, offerings and so forth, and usually only the well-to-do can afford it then. Although it is no longer regarded as essential, many people have their teeth filed later in life if they were not filed during youth. It is believed that a person may be denied entrance into the spirit world if his teeth are not filed, and often the teeth of a corpse are filed before cremation so that he will not look like a demon, a *raksasa*, the long canines of whom stick out through the cheeks like a wild boar's.

The filing takes place on an auspicious day after the person is blessed by a *pedanda*. The boy or girl may not go out of the house the day before and Van Eck tells of a Brahmanic rule that demands that the person remain in the dark for three days. The operation is performed by a specialist, generally a Brahmana, who knows formulas by which his tools—files and whetstones—are blessed "to take the poison out of them," to make the operation painless. The patient is laid on a *balé* among offerings, the head resting on a pillow which is covered with a protective scarf, *gringsing wayang wangsul*, one of the magic cloths woven in Tenganan, the warp of which is left uncut. The body is wrapped in new white cloth and assistants hold down the victim by the hands and feet. The tooth-filer stands at the head of the *balé* and inscribes magic syllables (*aksara*) on the teeth about to be filed with a ruby set in a gold ring. The filing then proceeds, taking from fifteen minutes to a half-hour, endured stoically with clenched hands and goose-flesh, but without even a noise from the patient, who is given a rest from time to time, so that with the help of a mirror he can see the results. Often he makes suggestions and even complains when the teeth are not yet short enough.

During these pauses the patient spits the filings into a small "yellow" coconut adorned with a palm-leaf fan and flowers. When the filing is over, the boy or girl, paler than usual, but apparently not suffering pain, takes the coconut with the filings over to the family temple, where it is buried just behind the ancestral shrine. We questioned a girl who had just come out of the trying experience about her sensations and she assured us that she felt "shivers," but no pain; she seemed happier and smiled more freely than before.

Among the puritanical Bali Agas of the mountains, adolescent boys (*truna*) and girls (*daha*) are considered pure people not yet contaminated by sexual intercourse. In those ancient villages the inhabitants are divided into four separate clubs: of men, of women, and of "virgin" boys (*seka truna*) and girls (*seka daha*), whose purity is jealously preserved, since they have special rites to perform in the systematic village magic: the care of divine heirlooms too dangerous for less pure people to handle. Consequently, in the strict communities of the Bali Aga, sexual license on the part of a boy or girl is a crime against the village magic and is proportionately punished.

This is not the case, however, among the ordinary Balinese villages, where boys and girls lead a freer sexual life. There matters of sex are not solemn, mysterious prohibitions, and it is natural that in coming of age they should continue to have sexual relations that started in the character of play, incompletely of course, during childhood.

The average Balinese does not attach great importance to virginity and it is not difficult for a divorcee, a widow, or even a woman who has committed adultery to marry again. Low-caste girls have many occasions to meet boys and often carry on affairs, kept secret because of natural shyness. The Balinese are extremely discreet in their intimate relations; lovers are never seen together in public, and it would be unpardonable manners for a man to make insinuations to a girl in public. It is not unusual for girls to take the lead and "make eyes" (*saling sulang*) at boys, or give encouragement to a shy suitor with some sort of small present.

Girls of high caste are usually chaperoned and their chances of meeting boys are considerably fewer. For the princes, whose mentality is more "Oriental" than that of the less prejudiced average Balinese, a virgin (*gentan,* in the absolute sense of the word) is highly desirable. Where feudalism still holds sway, a prince may order a subject of his to reserve his pretty daughter for him when she comes of age, and there are cases of Satrias and Brahmanas who kidnapped a girl of their own caste immediately after the first menstruation. Such cases are shocking to most Balinese, however, and there are rules and penalties against premature marriages. In general, the average marriageable age is eighteen for boys and sixteen for girls. A noble Balinese friend once told me that he could tell a virgin at first sight from the texture of her skin, the shape of her breasts, the muscles under her arms, and even the shape of the mouth; but he added sadly that now that so many girls wear blouses it has become more difficult to tell!

Young people meet at the market, at harvesting-time, when everybody helps to cut the rice, at the river, and so forth, but especially

Dagang

at the frequent village celebrations and nocturnal theatrical performances, when the boys meet their friends and make new conquests. An attraction at all festivals is the pretty *dagangs*, girls who run small stands of food, drinks, cigarettes, and *sirih*. They sit behind little tables illuminated by petrol lamps, scraping coconuts, grinding sauces, and serving drinks, surrounded by a circle of admirers who squat on the ground, joking with them on the pretext of buying a pennyworth of peanuts or a package of cigarettes. Some girls know that it is best to remain cold and indifferent, attending to their business, while others are gay and friendly and can answer cleverly to the boys' wisecracks.

To the Balinese, the average features of Nordics are not to be admired; sharp noses, prominent chins, white skin, blue eyes, blond

hair, and so forth are distasteful to them. They compare blond hair to that of albinos', but red hair is still worse, since only witches and some devils have red hair. Only dogs, monkeys, and evil characters have long, prominent teeth and hair over their bodies. For the Balinese taste, the skin should be smooth, clear, and devoid of superfluous hair, which they call *bulú*, "feathers," to differentiate it from the "proper" hair of the head, which is called *rambut*. The hair of women should be thick, black, and glossy; goddesses are represented with hair down to their knees. The complexion should not be too dark and a girl with a golden skin is considered beautiful even if other requirements are missing. The face should be round, the eyes bright and almond shaped, but not too large, while the mouth must not be too small, with full arched lips and short even teeth. The already mentioned outline of the forehead is important. It must be high and narrow, in a deep arch coming down to the temples. Moles and beauty spots are admired, and it is believed that a woman who possesses a small mole in the area of the lips is destined to marry a Raja who will have to remain faithful to her. Perfume, either in the form of aromatic oil or as fresh flowers, is necessary to enhance one's attractiveness, and whenever there is a crowd the pungent smell of *cempaka* and *sandat* blossoms, mixed with that of coconut oil, fills the air.

The body should be small but well proportioned, the hips and waist narrow, and the breasts round and full; a woman should never be too fat nor too thin. Women are less particular about their men and the rules are not so well defined; vitality, strength, a well-proportioned body, and a smooth skin devoid of hair are the physical requirements of a man in a woman's eyes.

THE LOVE LIFE OF THE BALINESE

Romanticism only flourishes where traditional barriers for the free and natural relations between men and women are strongest. Consequently the practical and unrestrained Balinese in love does not idolize the woman he desires, but goes directly to the point. If he feels strongly attracted by a girl, he does not pretend a platonic interest and must culminate his desire by sleeping with her. A direct solicitation constitutes his declaration of love: "Do you want? (*Kayun? Nyak?*)." The only words in Balinese for "love," *kayun, suka, deman, nyak,* all mean "desire," "to like," and "to want," while stronger terms like *lulut* and *tresna* have a certain illegal connotation, as in adultery (*mamitra*). Without a word in their vocabulary for the abstract idea of romantic love, the Balinese does not develop a morbid unhappiness when failing in love. A man who is refused by a girl may be unhappy for a while even as among us, but soon he will forget her and fall in love with a less recalcitrant girl.

Should the man be accepted, the affair may be developed into attachment that will in most cases lead to marriage. It is not infrequent that the couple may live together—*gendak*—before marriage, although not exactly in sin, since *gendak* is permitted as a sort of a trial marriage, not yet made legal in public and before the gods. Often in a prearranged marriage the couple is allowed *gendak,* and there are regulations that protect the woman against desertion and that make children born in the *gendak* period legal. Even among the more puritanical Bali Agas *gendak* appears in the traditional village law, as in the following excerpt from the law of the village of Lumbuan in the Bangli mountains:

> ". . . the *desa* orders a man accused of intimacy with a woman to take her as wife, making the offerings and ceremonies mentioned above. Should the man refuse to marry her, he has to pay the *penyeheb* (a roast pig) and *tumbakan* (a cow), while the woman will pay only the *tumbakan* to clear her impurity and the pollution of the village (*sebel*). Should there result a child, it belongs to the woman. If it is not known who the man was, the woman is responsible and must provide the *penyeheb* and *tumbakan* within an allotted time."
>
> (*Bawanagara*, T. 11, No. 8/9, 1933.)

This attitude must not be interpreted as one of promiscuity; the Balinese like to marry young, and a man after love has usually marriage in view. However, a girl is not too easily persuaded and puts off her suitors, often too long, and the boy is either bored and leaves her or is obliged to use stronger methods.

Shy people who are after success in love may employ the services of professional matchmakers (*cetí*) or those of a magician to make a reluctant girl yield. To appear beautiful in the eyes of a desired person certain amulets are employed, most often ancient Javanese bronze disks with a hole in the center like Chinese coins, which are carried on the belt. Those used by men (*pipis arjuna*) have an image in low relief of their semi-divine, romantic hero Arjuna, while those used by women are the so-called "moon-coins" (*pipis bulan*). The moon-coins I had occasion to observe seemed to me simple old *kepengs* in

Amulet of love magic (*Arjuna* coin)

which the border was not properly centered, producing an accidental design like a new moon. These coins, in reality ancient amulets, are believed to have been made by the gods and not by humans; I was told that they are found lying around the temple at night if it is the wish of the gods to present one with a magic coin. The lucky owners often lend them or rent them to prospective lovers for rather high prices. They are kept wrapped in a little rag, covered with ointments and flower petals so that they will not "die" and become useless.

In more difficult cases an infatuated person has recourse to powerful love magic (*guna pengasih*); incantations that resemble other sorts of secret magic and that consist of a charm (*serana*) and a spoken formula (*mantra*). Typical charms are twin coconuts or twin bananas, and even more effective are the saliva of a snake, the tears of a child, the oil from a coconut that has been dragged around by a child, or that from a coconut tree under which a pregnant woman has sat. "The silken net" (*i jaring sutra*), "the crawling serpent" (*i naga bilad*), and the "constant weeping" (*i tuntung tanggis*) are among the names of formulas used to obtain a difficult girl. The desired person must be anointed inadvertently with the above-mentioned charms after the corresponding magic formula has been recited over them.

There are other ways to get a girl, such as the *pengacap*, "stealing her thoughts through concentrated mental effort" (*kenáh*); thinking of the beloved at all times: when eating, putting food aside for her, and on going to sleep calling her mentally until she is made so unhappy and uncomfortable that she cannot work, eat, or sleep until she is with the man who operates the magic.

I was told of a special magic way to obtain a girl for "only one night," which is to remain throughout the night looking intensely at the flame of a lamp made out of a new coconut, freshly made oil, and a new wick, remembering the girl's face. On the following day she will not be able to refuse the man. A girl will also fall in love with a man who succeeds in feeding her a *sirih* leaf (to chew with betelnut) on which has been inscribed an image of a *cintia*, "the Unthinkable God," with enormously exaggerated sexual organs.

Besides these innocent and harmless procedures, there is a black and evil sort of magic (*pengiwa*) when a man or a woman wants to take revenge on a lover; to tie a hair of the victim to a bird which is afterwards released will make the person lose his mind. Another way to make a lover go insane is to make an image of the person using something that belonged to him: a piece of his underclothes, hair, nail-clippings, or earth from his foot-print, but with the head either at the place of the sex or at the feet; the whole then inscribed with magic syllables and a formula said over the image.

Menstrual blood anointed on the head of a man infallibly destines him to be henpecked.

The love technique of the Balinese is natural and simple; kissing, as we understand it, as a self-sufficient act, is unknown and the caress that substitutes for our mode of kissing consists in bringing the faces close enough to catch each other's perfume and feel the warmth of the skin, with slight movements of the head (*ngaras, diman*) in the manner which has been wrongly called by Europeans "rubbing noses." In general, the love practices of Westerners seem to the Balinese impractical and clumsy, especially in relation to intercourse, for which the general adopted form is the man kneeling, the woman reclining, a posture such as Malinowsky describes of the Trobriand Islanders in his *Sexual Life of Savages*. The Balinese believe that too hasty intercourse can only result in a deformed child. I have insisted that the Balinese are frank in sexual matters, although the terminology for the sexual act is governed by definite rules: there are extremely refined terms like the classic *akrida*; usual ones, *metemú*, "to meet;" and unmentionably coarse ones (*mekatuk*). There are, besides, terms used for animals, such as *metungan* and *mesakí*.

The taboo against incest (*salah timpal*) extends to certain spiritual relations; it is incest to sleep with the daughter of one's teacher, who is considered as his pupil's spiritual father. A real child cannot marry an adopted brother or sister, and among the Bali Agas cousins are equally forbidden to marry, although the rest of the population does not always agree, especially the nobility, among whom such marriage is often considered desirable. Tabooed for sexual relations are albinos, idiots, lepers, and in general the sick and deformed. Making love to a woman of a higher caste is a dreadful breach of caste rules and a dangerous one if discovered—I have mentioned that in old times the couple was killed—although it is not unthinkable that a Sudra boy may have a secret love affair with a noble girl.

It is my impression that sexual abnormality is not prevalent among the Balinese and if it exists at all among the common people is due purely to mercenary reasons. The people are naturally languid and affectionate; it is usual for people of the same sex to embrace each other, to hold hands, to huddle together for a nap at public places; and even old men are often seen walking down the road hand in hand. This has given outsiders the impression that Balinese boys are effeminate, although, on the other hand, I have been asked by a naïve Balinese why it is that white men so often prefer boys to girls. I could only deny his strange idea, but later I found the explanation when I observed the alarming number of mercenary homosexuals around the hotels at night. In general the idea of homosexuality is inconsequential to the Balinese, and a boy known as a professional homosexual eventually falls in love with a girl, marries her, and becomes normal. There are in Bali curious individuals called *bencí*, interpreted by the Balinese as "hermaphrodites"—a condition which is characteristic of gods, but bad and ridiculous among humans. The *bencí* are men who are abnormally asexual from birth (impotent, according to the Balinese), who act and dress like women and perform the work of women. In Denpasar there was one of these pitiable creatures, a man who dressed like a girl and talked in falsetto, selling food at a public stand in the main street. It was a great joke of the village boys to sit by the *bencí* and make him offers of marriage. He answered coyly and even seemed to enjoy the puns.

Prostitution had not, until recent years, flourished in Bali, but there are in the Balinese language terms that differentiate between a woman who prostitutes herself for pleasure (*demangan, jalir*) and a mercenary prostitute (*nyudal, nayang*), a type that is rapidly increasing in the centers where there are foreigners.

Bestiality (*salah karma*) is a dreadful crime against the spiritual health of the community and is supposed to make the country "sick" (*panas*) with epidemics, loss of crops, and so forth. In former times both animal and offender were thrown into the ocean; today the animal is generally drowned and the man exiled or put in jail. In any case a great ceremony of purification with animal sacrifices (*mecaru*) is necessary to cleanse the land. Bestiality is so horrifying to the Balinese that they can only explain it as bewitchment on the part of the man, to whom the animal appears as a beautiful woman.

MARRIAGE

As with everything in Bali, marriage customs differ from district to district and from caste to caste; from marriages by free choice, and others prearranged by the parents, to kidnapping with violence. Often what is commonplace in one village is unknown in another, and no general rule can be established that applies to the entire island. I shall attempt, therefore, to give only a general outline of marriage practices and to note what we had opportunity to observe in the districts in which we lived: Badung and Gianyar. It is in detail, however, that the ceremonies vary; the fundamental principles for the different sorts of marriage remain the same everywhere.

Ngrorod. In Bali the honeymoon usually precedes the wedding; the average boy in love with a girl makes his marriage arrangements directly with her, and outside of his father, perhaps, and a few friends from whom he needs help, he keeps his intentions secret until the day, previously agreed upon between the boy and girl, when he will steal her. Shy couples simply run away together to the house of a friend, as a rule in another village, where they spend their honeymoon in hiding. But the Balinese love spectacular kidnappings. The girl arranges for her clothes to be taken secretly to their future hide-out, and on the appointed day she is captured somewhere on the road, in the fields, or in the river by the kidnapping party, led by her suitor. She is expected to kick and bite her abductors in sham self-defense, and although there may be witnesses, no one would dream of interfering, unless they are relatives of the girl, in which case they are supposed to put up a great fight. In Denpasar it is stylish to rush the girl away by hired motor-car.

At her home, as soon as her disappearance is discovered, her enraged father is supposed to run up the alarm-drum-tower and beat the *kulkul*, asking who took his daughter; but of course no one knows. Even a searching party may be organized simply for the fun of it; after a while they return breathless but empty-handed. Should it be known, however, that the girl has been abducted against her will (*melagandang*), the pursuit is real and the kidnapper may be badly beaten and even killed if caught by the girl's relatives. In Badung even forceful kidnapping is legal if the girl is taken in daytime and not from her house; then, as often happens, if the girl chooses to remain with her forced husband, the marriage is legalized by the proper offerings and ceremonies and by the payment of a stipulated amount to her family; otherwise the marriage is annulled and the boy fined or jailed.

Special offerings (*sesayut tabúh ráh* and *makala-kalaán*) have been

Kidnapping (*from a Balinese painting*)

taken beforehand to the hide-out, and once safely there, it is law that the couple must consummate the wedding before the offerings have wilted. This is extremely important as these offerings alone make the marriage binding. They constitute what is called "the small legalization" (*masakapan alit*), and without them the union would be considered an ordinary, illegal affair. Thus the couple is made husband and wife before the gods, and it appears as if the elaborate ceremonies (*makasapan, nganten*) that follow every wedding are rather the official, public confirmation of it. They consist in the eternal purification by a priest's prayers and holy water, plus additional magic acts to ensure the couple a lucky and fruitful marriage. The great marriage ceremony is supposed to take place within the customary forty-two days after the kidnapping, but in some cases it has been performed considerably later if there is not enough money immediately available for the expensive festivities.

The couple remains in hiding, going out as little as possible, until the ransom money has been paid to the girl's father, all arrangements are concluded, and a lucky day established for the return of the couple. Representatives of the boy—his father or his friends—go, if possible on the day the girl is taken, to inform her parents and to try to placate them, since tradition demands of them to appear outraged although they may approve of the boy. The girl's relatives do not participate in the marriage ceremonies, and it is significant that after marriage the girl takes leave of her ancestral gods and adopts her husband's. The emissaries go to the girl's house wearing krisses and in refined language they point to the virtues of the boy, to his good intentions, and to the advantages of the union. Reluctantly the girl's father gives in, but not until the amount of the "bride-purchase" money (*patumbas wadon*) has been settled. I was told in Denpasar that the sum may vary from ten thousand to forty thousand *kepeng*, eight to thirty-two *ringgit* (silver dollars)[6] or even to as much as a hundred *ringgit*, which in normal times would be equivalent to 125,000 *kepeng*, quite a fortune for people that buy with *kepeng* the daily necessities of life.[7]

[6] Normally a *ringgit* is worth one gold dollar: two and a half guilders. There were 500 *kepeng* in one guilder in 1930, although in 1933 the Dutch guilder had gone up to 700 *kepeng*.

[7] In Buleléng brides are more expensive than in South Bali; Liefrink stated the price there as from 400 to 600 *ringgit*, and Van Eck put it between 100 guilders to 600 (or from 40 to 240 *ringgit*), but Dr. Korn, the latest authority, mentions in his *Adatrecht* that in Balinese law documents the sum is seldom above 20,000 *kepeng* (16 *ringgit*), and consequently the price would be lower for a girl of low caste. The price is further depreciated for widows, the divorced, and so forth, while the rate goes up to foreigners, for palace women, or in case of forceful kidnapping. Perhaps the rate is exaggerated and it is possible that brides are getting cheaper with the gradual impoverishment of Bali. It is not without reason that Korn believes that the ransom money cannot be taken literally as a price for the girl, since the trousseau she takes along is often more valuable than the money paid for her. The ransom for a widow is not paid to her parents but to her parents-in-law. In prearranged marriages (*mapadik*) there is no ransom money, since many presents and personal services are made by the bridegroom to the girl's father. There is no money paid if the bride's father has no male descendants and he wishes to adopt his son-in-law as a *sentana*, a legitimate son for the purpose of inheritance. Korn suggests that the money is paid rather as ransom to the house gods and not to the parents.

Mapadik. It may happen that the head of a prominent family of caste requests the daughter of a friend or relative as wife for his son to bring two great families closer together by a bond of blood. Such prearranged marriages are decided upon at times when the boy and the girl are still children, and the marriage is performed as soon as possible after the girl comes of age and before they fall in love with someone else. This must not be misconstrued as a form of the much publicized child-marriage of India; such marriages are rare, they do not take place until the girl is a woman, there is no law that enforces them, and there is always divorce to undo an undesirable union. Besides, if a girl suspects she is to be married against her will, she can arrange secretly to be kidnapped by a boy she likes. The *mapadik* marriage, or marriage by request, takes place more often with willing grown boys and girls of the nobility, to whom it is always desirable to marry within their caste, being of course more dignified than the customary *ngorod,* marriage by elopement. The father of Gusti's second wife, a noble chief (*pungawa*), once lamented that all his three daughters had been stolen in *ngorod* and that his hopes that Sagung might have been asked for were frustrated when Gusti took her. *Mapadik* marriage is in general the old-fashioned, respectable way for the feudal aristocracy to marry and perhaps originated with them, although, curiously enough, it is still prevalent among the Bali Agas of the mountains.

Arrangements for the *mapadik* are started by the boy's father, taking a ceremonial present of clothes, a ring, food, and *sirih* to the girl's relatives, who accept by chewing the *sirih* and giving in return a present in the girl's name. These acts establish the marriage contract, although it can be dissolved by infidelity on the part of either of those concerned. The boy continues to visit at the house of his future bride, bringing presents regularly and performing small services for his prospective father-in-law.

It is not uncommon that a betrothed couple may be permitted prenuptial intercourse (*gendak*) until the time comes for the official legalization, the great marriage festival. Among the aristocracy, to whom the girl's virginity is of importance, the defloration of the bride acquires a certain ritualistic, barbaric aspect. In Ubud, where old-style customs are still maintained, I was told of the procedure by which a *mapadik* marriage is consummated, a description which agrees with that given by De Kat Angelino in his *Huwelijksrecht*:[8]

[8] Quoted by Korn in *Het Adatrecht van Bali.*

. . . The girl is dressed and then wrapped in yards of cloth like a mummy, until she is unable to move. She is locked in the *metén* from the inside with a number of female attendants. The groom arrives in gala dress and wearing his kris, followed by his retinue, and when he comes to the locked door, he sings in *kidung*, answered in song by one of the old women inside.

"I, So-and-so, son of So-and-so, request to be allowed to enter this house. Whoever is inside please open the door."

"He who wants to enter must be an important person who can pay me ten *ringgit*; then I shall open."

"If you unlock the door, one hundred gold pieces is not too much; much less the ten *ringgit* you request."

The servant opens the door and receives the money from the bridegroom, who enters with his friends. They pick up the helpless bride, lay her on the *balé*, cut the wrappings, and leave the couple alone. After a period of time the groom steps out and announces the marriage consummated; female attendants examine the girl to verify her defloration, and the couple is bathed—the man in the river—and dressed again. They stand in front of the offering called *sesayut tabúh ráh*, "to end virginity," and are blessed by the priest. Ten days later they dedicate the offering *tetebasan* and prepare for the great legalization ceremony, which takes place in five days.

Masakapan. It is essential that the great wedding festival take place on a propitious day set by the high priest, the *pedanda*. *Mapadik* marriages are calculated to take place on the fourth or the tenth month, but for *ngorod* the date is set on a good day of the week called *ingkel wong*, one out of every six weeks, in which affairs concerning human beings are propitious (there are, besides, weeks set aside for domestic animals, for birds, trees, fish, and bamboo). After their honeymoon a runaway couple returns to the home of the boy's father for the legalization ceremony, brought in grand procession, carried on palanquins to the accompaniment of cymbals and gongs, *kulkul* beats, and fire-crackers.

In Pemecutan we assisted at the belated marriage feast (*masa-kapan*) of a Gusti people. Among the higher castes, who like to appear rich and extravagant, there is considerably greater ceremony than at the weddings of the common people. Often formal invitations written on palm-leaves are sent to near relatives, in which is stated the nature of the wedding present that they should bring along—the one I saw asked for four ducks—thus keeping the present tactfully within the means of the donor and avoiding repetitions. In this manner the relatives co-operate in meeting the expenses, for among such families there are always innumerable guests of rank to be lavishly entertained with banquet food and theatricals. Early in the morning the house of our aristocratic friend in Pemecutan began to fill with impressive noblemen dressed in their best and wearing jeweled krisses, who arrived with retinues of women and attendants bearing presents. The teeth of the bride and groom had not yet been filed and the greater part of the morning was spent in the hair-raising task, while the *wayang* music played in a corner of the crowded courtyard, mingling with the crashing of the cymbals and gongs of the orchestra that played out on the street. The male guests sat in the places of honor drinking coffee, eating pastry, and chewing betelnut, listening casually to two professional story-tellers that sat in the middle of the court reciting the erotic passages of the great literary classic, the *Arjuna Wiwaha,* also a rule at weddings, one man chanting verses in musical Kawi language, while the other translated with rich and expressive tones into guttural everyday Balinese. The women wandered about among offerings and presents, in and out of the *metén* where the bride was being dressed, while the boy's father played host, seeing that everybody was taken care of, and directing the assistants who distributed trays of food and poured drinks.

After the teeth-filing was over, the bride and groom simulated domestic activities: she washed a handful of rice and cooked it in a clay pot over a small fire; the groom cut a branch of *twí,* the sort of acacia leaves used as a vegetable, which they cooked together in another pot. Next they were led to a platform erected in the courtyard, a bed with mattress and pillows in which was placed the offering *tetagpulú,* two truncated cones wrapped, one in black, the other in red thread, each topped by a fan of palm-leaf. They sat on the bed, the boy cross-legged, the girl kneeling, and made reverences (*sembah*), bringing their joined hands three times to their foreheads, each time holding between their middle fingers little *sampian,* fans of palm decorated with flowers. Next the food they had cooked together was brought to them on silver platters, and, with their necks joined by a Tenganan scarf with the warp left uncut, they had to feed each other some rice and *twí.* Their movements were hampered by the scarf and they were shy and clumsy. The guests thought this extremely funny and laughed heartily, making the couple turn red with embarrassment. They gave each other water to drink from a *kendih,* but the crucial test was the mutual chewing of *sirih,* betelnut, to which they were not accustomed. The boy chewed the *sirih* reluctantly, making wry faces, handing some already chewed to his bride. This concluded the first half of the ceremony, until the afternoon, when the priest would come to perform their ritual purification.

I was told that among the common people the girl walks three times around the offerings (*pangulapan*) holding the *tetagpulú* in her arms, while two of the boy's relatives hold a string across her path. She walks on until the string breaks (*benang tebusan*). Later the couple walks again three times around a small *dadap* tree specially planted for the occasion, the girl with a platter of rice on her head, the boy carrying on his shoulder a pole loaded with good stuff such as coconuts, a chicken, and a duck. Then they sit side by side behind the priest or witch-doctor (*balian*) and pray while he dedicates the offerings. They also take a meal in public—an act which appears to have a special significance, since only a married couple would ever be seen together eating in public.

The blessing by the priest to purify the couple that we witnessed, at the wedding of a prominent prince of Gianyar, was exceptionally elaborate. Three great sheds had been specially built: one for the ceremony, another for the banquet, and a third for the entertainment. The principal shed was surrounded by offerings brought by the prince's vassals, and there were tables and chairs for the guests of honor, Balinese noblemen and Dutch high officials, while the populace crowded on the outside. Facing towards the right of the mountains, *kangin,* was a high platform filled with all sorts of great marriage offerings, and in the middle of the platform sat the venerable high priest of the prince's family among his ritual accessories. To the left of the shed was an altar for the sun, fifteen feet high, and at the right a story-teller gave a performance of *wayang lemah,* a shadow-play without a screen.

A murmur of admiration arose from the crowd as the bride and groom came out of the house, resplendent in gold and jewelry. They stood first at the right of the priest, who faced away from them. Old women attendants burned coconut husks and sticks of incense, then touched their hands and feet with an egg and with some of the offerings. Then they moved to the other side, at the left, and knelt on the ground making reverences, the *sembah,* with fans of palm-leaf adorned with flowers of different colors. There were two chairs ready behind the priest, and the couple sat on them, the groom at the right, while the attendants waved symbols of purity—a live white chicken and a white duck—in front of them. They were given various sorts of holy water to drink and various foods to eat—eggs, rice, and *satés*. The priest turned towards them, shook a long grass broom at the couple, and gave them salt to taste. Next he sprinkled them with holy water and later drenched them with ladles of it, poured through a rice-steaming basket, held by the women over their heads, just as in the coming-of-age ceremony of Madé Rai. A sort of shield of palm-leaf was waved at them and each took a blade out of it and placed it folded in the head-dress. More prayers were said by the priest in the direction of the couple, and on finishing he gave each a flower which was also placed in the head-dress.

Next came curious actions with two ropes made of red, black, yellow, and white string, weighted at the ends with *kepengs*. These were passed under the arms and across the backs of the bride and groom, the four ends held by the priest while he recited a prayer. Then the ends of the ropes were crossed over their chests and thrown back. The priest gave the couple a ladle of holy water to drink, and continued praying while the couple fanned towards themselves the essence of the prayer, doing the same again when the priest held in front of them a bundle made of the colored ropes, which in the meantime had been removed by the attendants. The ceremony concluded with a long prayer (*maweda*) performed by the priest towards *kangin;* a combination of Sanskrit formulas recited silently, accompanied by swift and intricate gestures of the hands, alternated with ringing a bell and flinging away various sorts of flowers. After the purification the banquet was served and the guests spent the rest of the night watching plays and dances.

The woman "follows" the man and lives in his home. Either the eldest or the youngest son inherits the paternal home, but other sons usually build a house of their own on an empty lot given by the village to a newly-wed couple. The first duty of the man is then to build a temporary *sanggah kemulan,* his family shrine, made of bamboo and thatch, which is replaced later on by a more solid structure of brick and wood, when the old one has fallen into decay. It may happen, however, that a man commits *nyebuhin*, going to live in the house of the girl with whom he is infatuated. A man who runs after a girl in this manner is disgraced; he loses all rights to the paternal home and lives as a servant of the girl's family. The opposite may also happen and a *ngungahin* marriage takes place, when a girl, supposedly bewitched, forces herself upon a man.

Ordinarily there is at home a strong feeling of equality, of politeness, and friendly frankness in the relationship between husband and wife, and the woman is by no means the proverbial slave of Oriental countries. She is well aware of her rights, she manages the house and the finances of the family, and at times she even keeps her husband. We have seen that the majority of the women of average class work and have their own incomes. They own their clothes, their jewelry, and the household utensils, as well as the pigs and chickens of the house. The man, of course, owns the house itself, the rice fields, the cattle, and his implements, and inheritance is invariably along the male line. The woman has absolute rights over her income and owns her share of the money earned by their combined efforts, although the husband is the administrator of this money. In general the man is the acknowledged master of the household and represents the family before the law and before the gods, who are his own ancestors.

But once a month, during menstrual time, a wife's life is not a happy one; to her physical handicap is added the powerful taboo of pollution (*sebel*) which then falls upon her: she is forbidden to go into the temple, into the kitchen or the granary, or to the well. She may not prepare food nor, of course, make offerings or participate at feasts, and the wife of a high priest may not even speak to her exalted husband. No man would dream of sleeping in the same room with a woman in this condition; the average man moves into the house of a friend, but the wife of a nobleman has to look for a place to sleep, far from her husband. In the palace of a prince there is often a secluded compartment where his wives retire while menstruating. When the period is over, a woman has to be purified again with sprinkling of holy water before she can resume normal life. Perhaps because the Balinese believe that a man can be bewitched, losing all his will to the woman who can anoint his head with menstrual blood, they have such mortal horror of being near a woman during the time of menstruation.

The Balinese are reputedly polygamous, but the great majority—about ninety-five per cent—have only one wife. It was generally believed that there are considerably more women than men in Bali, but the last census (1930) gives the figures as 561,874 males as against 576, 543 females, or 49.35 per cent men and 50.65 per cent women, a percentage of women that is even below normal. Men of the nobility often have two, three, four, and even more wives, and old records mention Rajas with as many as two hundred. This is a thing of the past, however, and there are few people today who can afford more than one wife. But the Balinese are naturally polygamous and it is common for men to have lovers and for women to take the extramarital relations of their husbands as natural.

If a man brings home a second wife, the first is not expected to show jealousy, but unpleasant situations develop if the man takes a new wife without the knowledge of his first wife. Such was the case in our household and we often had to mediate between the two wives of our host in violent squabbles that exploded for the most trivial causes. I remain under the impression, however, that it was often wounded pride rather than sentimental jealousy that brought about the tense situations, and with other families of polygamous Balinese we knew this was so. The younger wife of a friend took care of the elder wife's child, and when they visited us together one would have taken them for sisters, such was the affection they showed for each other. Often another woman with whom to share the house means company and help to the first, and thus she is welcomed, especially if the new wife was chosen, as often happens, by the first wife.

Two wives in one home have separate houses to sleep in and often they do not even live together. Many Balinese live with the first wife in the ancestral home and keep their subsequent wives in other houses and even in different villages, visiting them once in a while and only bringing them together at festivals where they all must pray together. They agree that this is the most convenient arrangement, and our harassed host confided to me that in future lives he would be wiser and would marry only once.

The free and easy status of women of the average class is not enjoyed by women of the aristocracy; their husbands are absolute masters and they live restricted and secluded in the palace, the *puri*, usually going out only in groups to festivals. The first wife of the same caste as the husband (*padmí*) enjoys a higher status than a second wife (*madewí*), even though she may be of high caste also. Then there are those with a considerably lower status, the wives of low caste (*penawing, slir*), who are regarded as legal concubines. The prince does not usually appear at his wedding ceremony with a bride of low caste, and she is ceremonially married to his kris or to a tree. The wives of a prince live together in the *puri* and each has her own *balé*, placed according to rank, where the prince visits them by turns. A low-caste wife of a nobleman receives the title of *jeró*, and there are special titles to establish the status of their children. The son of a nobleman and a woman of lower class is of the caste of the father unless there is a great difference between them.

A man is not morally bound to be faithful to his wife, but infidelity on the part of the woman is a dreadful crime, punished legally in old times with the death of the guilty couple. I was told of the case of a man of the aristocracy of Badung who found his wife in compromising circumstances with a man of his caste, a relative besides. Out of his mind with rage, he clubbed them to death, then sent for the *pungawa* to give himself up. Calmly he asked for the alarm-drum not to be sounded, as is done in cases of violence when a man temporarily loses his mind and runs amuck. His wish was granted and he was led to jail. When the trial came up, his crime was taken lightly by the noble judges and he was given a short jail sentence. It is possible that in "civilized" society he would have gone free.

Ordinarily in a case of adultery the husband simply "throws his wife away" (*makutang*). Divorce laws are simple and easy. A man may claim divorce if his wife is sterile, quarrelsome, or lazy, but a woman has also the right to divorce an impotent man, or one who has some occult illness, is cruel to her, or fails to support her, although many women support themselves and there is no standard established as to what is non-support. A woman who wants a divorce simply leaves her husband's home, although he may try to bring her back by force. In any case she has to return the money dowry.

The divorce is performed by the village authorities (in whose judgment the case rests) by slight ceremonies, the most important of which is the breaking of a "yellow" *kepeng* (*pipis kuning*) by the husband and wife, to represent, perhaps, the breaking of the magic circle (completeness) of marriage.

Outside of caste and incest[9] taboos, there are no great marriage restrictions in Bali and there seems to be no objection to marriage with cousins, divorcees, a woman thrown out by her husband, and even with widows, against whom there was once revulsion on the part of the nobility, due to the now defunct institution of *mesatia* (suttee), by which the widows of a prince had to follow their dead master into the spirit world. A widow may marry when and whom she pleases as long as she has the permission of her family, her relatives-in-law, and her son, or of her own relatives if she has returned to her ancestral home. Marriage of a Balinese woman with foreigners—people of another race or religion—is permitted, although by the marriage the woman loses the right to be called a Balinese—again an emphasis on the importance of ancestral relations.

[9] There is first-and second-degree incest. It is first-degree incest for a man to have relations with his mother, sister, half-sister, or the mother of his half-brother or sister. Second-degree incest is relations with aunts or with his father's or mother's cousins. Jane Belo: "A Study of a Balinese Family." *The American Anthropologist*, Vol. 38, No. 1.

CHAPTER SEVEN

Art and the Artist

THE PLACE OF THE ARTIST IN BALINESE LIFE

EVERYBODY IN BALI SEEMS to be an artist. Coolies and princes, priests and peasants, men and women alike, can dance, play musical instruments, paint, or carve in wood and stone. It was often surprising to discover that an otherwise poor and dilapidated village harbored an elaborate temple, a great orchestra, or a group of actors of repute.

One of the most famous orchestras in Bali is to be found in the remote mountain village of Selat, and the finest dancers of *legong* were in Saba, an unimportant little village hidden among the rice fields. Villages such as Mas, Batuan, Gelgel, are made up of families of painters, sculptors, and actors, and Sanur produces, besides priests and witch-doctors, fine story-tellers and dancers. In Sebatu, another isolated mountain village, even the children can carve little statues from odd bits of wood, some to be used as bottle-stoppers, perches for birds, handles, but most often simply absurd little human figures in comic attitudes, strange animals, birds of their own invention, frogs, snakes, larvae of insects, figures without reason or purpose, simply as an outlet for their creative urge. In contrast to the devil-may-care primitive works of Sebatu are the super-refined, masterful carvings from Badung, Ubud, Pliatan, and especially those by the family of young Brahmanas from Mas who turn out intricate statues of hard wood or with equal ability paint a picture, design a temple gate, or act and dance.

Painting, sculpture, and playing on musical instruments are arts by tradition reserved to the men, but almost any woman can weave beautiful stuffs and it is curious that the most intriguing textiles, those in which the dyeing and weaving process is so complicated that years of labor are required to complete a scarf, are made by the women of Tenganan, an ancient village of six hundred souls who are so conservative that they will not maintain connections with the rest of Bali and who punish with exile whoever dares to marry outside the village.

The main artistic activity of the women goes into the making of beautiful offerings for the gods. These are intricate structures of cut-out palm-leaf, or great pyramids of fruit, flowers, cakes, and even roast chickens, arranged with splendid taste, masterpieces of composition in which the relative form of the elements employed, their texture and color are taken into consideration. I have seen monuments, seven feet in height, made entirely of roasted pig's meat on skewers, decorated into shapes cut out of the waxy fat of the pig and surmounted with banners and little umbrellas of the lacy stomach tissues, the whole relieved by the vivid vermilion of chili peppers. Although women of all ages have always taken part in the ritual offering dances, in olden times only little girls became dancers and actresses; but today beautiful girls take part in theatrical performances, playing the parts of princesses formerly performed exclusively by female impersonators.

The effervescence of artistic activity and the highly developed aesthetic sense of the population can perhaps be explained by a natural urge to express themselves, combined with the important factor of leisure resulting from well-organized agricultural corporatism. However, the most important element for the development of a popular culture, with primitive as well as refined characteristics, was perhaps the fact that the Balinese did not permit the centralization of the artistic knowledge in a special intellectual class. In old Balinese books on ethics, like the *Niti Sastra,* it is stated that a man who is ignorant of the writings is like a man who has lost his speech, because he shall have to remain silent during the conversation of other men. Furthermore, it was a requirement for the education of every prince that he should know mythology, history, and poetry well enough; should learn painting, woodcarving, music, and the making of musical instruments; should be able to dance and to sing in Kawi, the classic language of literature. There is hardly a prince who does not possess a good number of these attributes, and those deprived of talent themselves support artists, musicians, and actors as part of their retinue. Ordinary people look upon their feudal lords as models of conduct and do not hesitate to imitate them, learning their poetry, dancing, painting, and carving in order to be like them.

Thus, not only the aristocracy can create informal beauty, but a commoner may be as finished an artist as the educated nobleman, although he may be an agriculturist, a tradesman, or even a coolie. Our host in Bali was a prince and a musician, but there were others of the common class who were among the finest musicians of the neighborhood. Of the leaders of the famous orchestras of our district, one was a coolie, another a goldsmith, and a third a chauffeur.

Until a few years ago the Balinese did not paint pictures or make statues without some definite purpose. It has often been stated that there are no words in the Balinese language for "art" and "artist." This is true and logical; making a beautiful offering, and carving a stone temple gate, and making a set of masks are tasks of equal aesthetic importance, and although the artist is regarded as a preferred member of the community, there is no separate class of artists, and a sculptor is simply a "carver" or a figure-maker, and the painter is a picture-maker. A dancer is a *legong*, a *janger*, and so forth—the names of the dances they perform.

The artist is in Bali essentially a craftsman and at the same time an amateur, casual and anonymous, who uses his talent knowing that no one will care to record his name for posterity. His only aim is to serve his community, seeing that the work is well done when he is called to embellish the temple of the village, or when he carves his neighbor's gate in exchange for a new roof or some other similar service. Actors and musicians play for the feasts of the village without pay, and when they perform for private festivals they are lavishly entertained and banqueted instead. Foreigners have to pay a good amount for a performance: from five to thirty guilders according to the quality of the show and the pretensions of the actors; but a Balinese who calls the village's orchestra or a troupe of actors for a home festival provides special food, refreshments, *sirih*, and cigarettes for them. If he pays a small amount besides, from a guilder to five, it is not considered as remuneration, but rather as a present to help the finances of the musical or theatrical club. Whatever money they receive goes to the funds of the association to cover the expenses of the feasts given by the club or to buy new costumes or instruments.

Nothing in Bali is made for posterity; the only available stone is a soft sandstone that crumbles away after a few years, and the temples and reliefs have to be renewed constantly; white ants devour the wooden sculptures, and the humidity rots away all paper and cloth, so their arts have never suffered from fossilization. The Balinese are extremely proud of their traditions, but they are also progressive and unconservative, and when a foreign idea strikes their fancy, they adopt it with great enthusiasm as their own. All sorts of influences from the outside, Indian, Chinese, Javanese, have left their mark on Balinese art, but they are always translated into their own manner and they become strongly Balinese in the process.

Thus the lively Balinese art is in constant flux. What becomes the rage for a while may be suddenly abandoned and forgotten when a new fashion is invented, new styles in music or in the theater, or new ways of making sculptures and paintings. But the traditional art also remains, and when the artists tire of a new idea, they go back to the classic forms until a new style is again invented. They are great copyists and it is not surprising to find in a temple, as part of the decoration, a fat Chinese god or a scene representing a highway hold-up, or a crashing plane, events unknown in Bali, that can only be explained as having been copied from some Western magazine. Once a young Balinese painter saw my friend Walter Spies painting yellow highlights on the tips of the leaves of a jungle scene. He went home and made a painting that was thoroughly Balinese, but with modeling and highlights until then unknown in Balinese painting. Artistic property cannot exist in the communal Balinese culture; if an artist invents or copies something that is an interesting novelty, soon all the others are reproducing the new find. Once a sculptor made a little statue representing the larvae of an insect standing upright on its tail; a few weeks later everybody was making them and soon the statue market was flooded with Brancusi-like little erect worms on square bases.

Unlike the individualistic art of the West in which the main concern of the artist is to develop his personality in order to create an easily recognizable style as the means to attain his ultimate goal—recognition and fame—the anonymous artistic production of the Balinese, like their entire life, is the expression of collective thought. A piece of music or sculpture is often the work of two or more artists, and the pupils of a painter or a sculptor invariably collaborate with their master. The Balinese artist builds up with traditional standard elements. The arrangement and the general spirit may be his own, and there may even be a certain amount of individuality, however subordinated to the local style. There are definite proportions, standard features, peculiar garments, and so forth to represent a devil, a holy man, a prince, or a peasant, and the personality of a given character is determined, not so much by physical characteristics, but rather by sartorial details. The romantic heroes, Arjuna, Rama, and Panji, look exactly alike and can only be recognized by the headdress peculiar to each. A strong differentiation is made between "fine" and "coarse" characters; Arjuna, for instance, is refined, with narrow eyes and delicate features, while his brother, the warrior Bhima, has wild round eyes and wears a moustache. He is further identified by his chequered loincloth.

The Balinese obtain their artistic standards of beauty from ancient Java, and for centuries there has been only one way to treat a beautiful face; which they have, curiously enough, come to identify with themselves. Once, discussing the facial characteristics of various races with the Regent of Karangasem, a man of high Balinese education, he asked me how I drew a Balinese. He disagreed with my conception and proceeded to draw one himself, a face from the classic paintings and a type that could not be found on the whole island. Within these conventions, Balinese art is realistic without being photographic—that is, without attempting to give the optical illusion of the real thing. Thus there is no perspective and no modeling in painting, and sculpture is highly stylized. They admire technique and good craftsmanship above other points, and when I showed a Balinese friend a beautiful sculpture I had just acquired, he found fault with the minute parallel grooves that marked the strands of hair because in places they ran together.

Balinese art is not in the class of the "great" arts like great Chinese painting—the conscious production of works of art for their own sake, with an aesthetic value apart from their function. Again, it is too refined, too developed, to fit into peasant arts; nor is it one of the primitive arts, those subject to ritual and tribal laws, which we call "primitive" because their aesthetics do not conform to ours. Their art is a highly developed, although informal Baroque folk-art that combines the peasant liveliness with the refinement of the classicism of Hinduistic Java, but free of conservative prejudice and with a new vitality fired by the exuberance of the demoniac spirit of the tropical primitive. The Balinese peasants took the flowery art of ancient Java, itself an offshoot of the aristocratic art of India of the seventh and eighth centuries, brought it down to earth, and made it popular property.

Although at the service of religion, Balinese art is not a religious art. An artist carves ludicrous subjects in the temples or embellishes objects of daily use with religious symbols, using them purely as ornamental elements regardless of their significance. The Balinese carve or paint to tell the only stories they know—those created by their intellectuals, the religious teachers of former times.

THE STORY OF THE DEVELOPMENT OF BALINESE ART

The art history of Bali runs parallel to the history of the island itself. When Bali became a colony of Java, the conquering aristocracy brought their art with them, and every political event in Java has had a powerful influence in the development of Balinese culture. Thus, the early classic period of Javanese art corresponds also to a classic period in Bali, and when the mother country suffered disturbances and transformations, these were reflected in Balinese art, until Islamism and political chaos severed all connections between the two islands, and Hinduism had to find refuge in Bali. As the island became the center of a new empire and no longer a province of Java, the Balinese natives took over the art of the exiled aristocracy, transformed it to suit their taste, and a typical Balinese art came into being.

Nothing definite is known of the art of pre-Hindu Bali, but we know that the old Indonesia had a culture of its own, perhaps like the present one of the people of Nias and the Bataks of Sumatra, to whom the Balinese are in many ways akin. They worked metals, especially iron for the making of magic krisses; cultivated rice, had a well-organized administration, kept domestic animals, and made splendid textiles. Outside of a stone sarcophagus, some bronze bracelets and arrow-heads found in Petang, probably belonging to people of Hinduistic affiliation, no material traces of their megalithic monuments remain, or have yet been found, perhaps because archeological excavation has hardly begun in Bali. But a great deal of the old Indonesian spirit has remained in the daily life of the people, not only among the Bali Agas, but also alongside the Hinduism of the ordinary Balinese. As we shall see later, there are definite traces of what could have been the art of pre-Hindu times found today in the offerings, in the patterns of textiles, in certain sculptures, and the like.

Antiques are scarce in Bali, although there are thousands of mossy and battered statues all over the island, often of a more primitive style than the usual contemporary art. But a newly made statue appears of great age after six months of exposure to the damp climate of Bali, and, on the other hand, many ancient statues resemble those made in recent years. Many of the innumerable remains found in the temples, in jungles, or imbedded in the trunk of a *waringin* may easily be contemporary.

We made a sport of going out with Walter Spies into remote districts to find objects of what we called "native" Balinese style, and often located figures in wood, stone, and even clay that showed no trace of Hindu influence. There were demons, girls, primitive animals, and alarm-drums with faces carved on them that were reminiscent of Dayak, Batak, and Polynesian art. Spies is an enthusiast for the "megalithic" art and he has discovered many strange stones with primitive carvings, such as the stone in Bebitera, or the magnificent stone altar in Batukandik in the little island of Nusa Penida: a pyramid twelve feet high surmounted by the torso of a woman with large breasts, supporting on her head a stone throne like those from Nias, with two roosters standing on her shoulders, their heads resting on the palms of her hands. The style of the monument is decidedly Indonesian and so are the two little shrines, also in the same village, with well-defined signs of being one male, the other female. I was invited to accompany Assistant Controleur Grader and Spies on an expedition into the wilds between the mountains Batur and Bratan; descending slippery ravines, into jungles, and up steep hills, we found many old statues overgrown with vegetation, some of which seemed from early Buddhist days, while others looked as if Hinduism had never penetrated into those districts. Particularly interesting were the pyramids and strange carvings in wood in Sanda and Selulung; or the Polynesian-looking statues in Batukaang and Pengajaran.

Perhaps the most remarkable of antiquities in Bali is the great bronze drum kept in the *Pura Panataran Sasih* in Pejeng, the former home of the demon-king Maya Danawa. Some Balinese say that it is one of the *subangs* (ear-plugs) of the moon, while others say it is a *Sasih*, the "moon" itself, that fell down to earth and was caught in a tree. It remained there giving a blinding light, preventing some thieves of the neighborhood from performing their nocturnal work. One of them, bolder than the rest, decided to extinguish the source of light and, climbing on the tree, urinated on it. The "moon" exploded, kill-

One of the faces on the Pejeng drum

ing the thief, and fell to the ground in the shape of the present drum, which explains why it is broken at the base. The people rescued it and placed it on a high latticed shrine in the temple. The drum is of the style of the so-called Chinese drums of the Han dynasty often found in Indo-China and even in Java, but it is the largest and most beautiful I have ever seen. The Pejeng drum differs somewhat from the usual Han drums; it is elongated, with three great handles, rather like the bronze drums found in Alor, the island near Timor, where they are still used as money, some being worth as much as three thousand guilders.[1] The drum is decorated on its sounding surface with a beautiful star in high relief surrounded by a border of sweeping spirals, and on its sides with borders between parallel lines rather like the

[1] Ernst Vatter: *Ata Kiwan*.

popular design called "spears" (*tumbak*) by the Balinese: ▼▼▼▼▼▼▼. Furthermore, there are strangely primitive, or rather conventionalized, human faces in low relief that have no obvious relation to Chinese art and that are strongly Indonesian, with the characteristic leaf-shaped ornament worn behind the ears, the lobes of which are exaggeratedly distended by the weight of unusual ear-rings. The general style, the motifs, and the workmanship of the drum are all definitely related to the unique bronze axes from the island of Roti, also near Timor, which were unfortunately destroyed in the fire of the pavilion of the Netherlands in the Paris Colonial Exposition of 1931 where they were exhibited. The axes and the drums seem to belong, rather than to a definitely Chinese culture like the Han, to an ancient, mysterious Indonesian bronze age.[2] The Pejeng drum is regarded with great reverence, and people often bring it offerings.

Another motif which appears to be of native origin is the figure called *cilí*, a silhouette of a beautiful girl with a body shaped like a slim hour-glass (two triangles meeting at their apex), with rounded breasts, long thin arms, great ear-plugs, and wearing an enormous head-dress of flowers. *Cilí* shapes are made in wood, of Chinese coins sewn together, woven into textiles, modeled in clay to surmount tiles for roofs, and made into clay banks for pennies. They are painted on rice cakes for temple ornaments in Selat, and made out of palm-leaf for certain agricultural ceremonies of the old mountain villages or as containers for the soul of the dead (*adegan*) for cremations. *Cilís* form the central motif of *lamaks*, those beautiful but perishable ornamental strips of palm-leaf, about a foot and a half wide by some ten to twenty feet long, made for feasts by the women, pinned together with bits of bamboo strips of *busung*, the tender yellow blades of the sugar or coconut palm, taken from the tree before the leaf opens. This is decorated with a delicate geometric pattern, a mosaic of bits of the green leaf of the same palm, cut with a knife into elaborate ornaments which are pinned on the yellow background, forming borders like the ones on the Pejeng drum, ornamental strips (*bebatikán*), groups of rosettes called "moons" (*bulán*), the *cilí*, and a stylized tree (*kayon*). These magnificent ornaments, perhaps the purest examples

[2] Heine-Geldern attributes the bronze drums and bronze weapons unearthed near Dông-Son in Northern Annam and Tonkin to a peculiar culture of the bronze age which he believes penetrated from northern into southern Asia not later than 300 B.C. and perhaps even as early as 600 B.C. He called this the Dông-Son culture.

of the Balinese native art, last only for one day, and after hanging for an afternoon on an altar or a rice granary, by evening they are completely wilted. Spies has collected every different type of *lamak* design for a period of years and he has hundreds of them. He claims that every community has a peculiar design not found elsewhere.

The figure of a *cilí* seems to have a strange hold on the imagination of the Balinese, perhaps because it is the shape of the "Rice Mother" (*niní pantun*), a sheaf of rice dressed into the shape of a *cilí*. This would indicate that the mysterious figure was connected with, or derived from, the deities of rice and fertility, either Dewi Sri or Melanting, also goddesses of beauty and seed respectively. Again, the shape of the great offerings (*kebógan*), a pyramid of fruit topped by a fan of flowers and palm-leaf, is also a *cilí*, so stylized however that only the pyramidal skirt and the flower head-dress remain. This became evident when we saw in Kesiman, alongside the usual form of offerings, one six feet tall made into a realistic *cilí*, her skirt of melons, ears of corn, oranges, *jambú*, and *salak*, her torso of frangipani flowers (*jepón*), and her face a smiling wooden mask with great ear-plugs and a fan of flowers as a head-dress. *Cilís* are often so stylized that simply a palm-leaf fan with two loops (the ear-plugs or breasts) is called a *cilí*. I became intensely intrigued by the persistence of this shape in so many of the ritual objects and was determined to find in it some religious significance; I asked all sorts of people about *cilís*, from high priests to old women offering-makers, but they all insisted that they were purely ornamental forms appropriate for offerings because they were beautiful. The word *cilí* means "small and nice," rather in the sense in which we use the term "cute." Whatever its origin, the *cilí* is today nothing more than a beautiful abstract feminine motif.

OLD HINDU BALINESE ART

Already in the records of Chinese travelers of the fifth century it is mentioned that in the country of "Poli," perhaps Bali, there were Hindu princes, and that the travelers were received by priests who danced around them blowing conch-shells. Bali was already a colony of the Central Javanese kingdom of Mataram, the earliest recorded ruler of which was, according to Stutterheim, King Sanjaya (A.D. 732) of the Sailendra dynasty, who ruled also over southern Sumatra. The Sailendras where Mahayanic Buddhists, and their

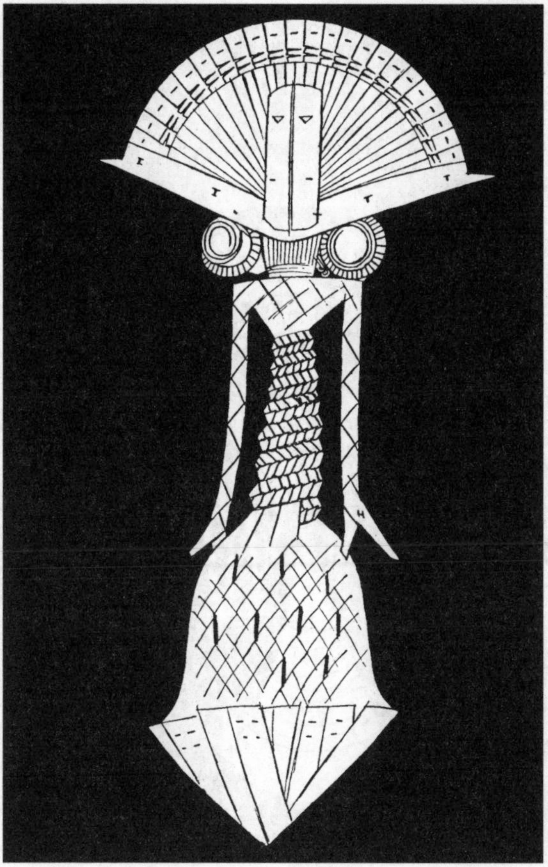

Cilí of woven palm-leaf

highly developed art was like that of the great Gupta period of India. Sivaism was introduced towards the middle of the ninth century and, by degrees, the power of the Sailendras waned, but it was within this period, from the seventh to the ninth centuries, the golden age of Javanese art, that the finest monuments of Java were built, the Buddhist *Borobudur* and the Sivaist *Lora Jongrang* in Prambanan. Soon this great civilization disappeared mysteriously and Bali came under the rule of independent kings in Pejeng and Bedulu. From their time we have remains of the classic style in the neighborhood of the present villages of the same names, some in ruined temples, in caves, or among the rice fields, in the strip

Cilí of palm-leaf from the top of an offering

of land between the rivers Pakrisan and Petanú, where so many of the antiquities of Bali are found. Towards the beginning of the eleventh century there was a renaissance in East Java, in Kediri, brought about by the Balinese-born king Erlangga. Under him Bali became again an integral part of Java and classicism received a new impetus. It was Erlangga who instituted Javanese as the official language of Bali. Tantric black magic seems to have played an important part in Erlangga's time, and while he was having trouble with his greatest political enemy, his own mother, who had sworn to destroy his kingdom by the black arts, Erlangga's brother ruled Bali in his name. This brother was buried (according to

Cilís from *lamaks*

Stutterheim) in the spectacular "Kings' tombs" in *Gunung Kawi* near Tampaksiring.

Among the important relics of the ancient period are the following:

Gunung Kawi: On the banks of the river Pakrisan, descending a steep ravine, is a group of sober, undecorated monuments shaped like the ancient burial towers (*candí*), hewn out of the solid rock, each inside of a niche, four on one side and five on the other. To the right of the main group is a sort of monastery with coves also carved out of the rock, arranged around a central cell with a platform in the center. The monuments are supposed to belong to the eleventh century, when cremation had not yet been introduced into Bali, and Lekkerkerker thinks the cells were probably destined to expose the corpses to be obliterated by decay and wild animals, such as was the custom among Indonesians, and as is still practiced in Sembiran in Bali and by the Torajas in Sulawesi, where it is now forbidden by the Dutch. The monuments were only discovered in 1920, but the Balinese knew them, and saw them with reverence because they attributed them to the giant of mythical times, Kbo Iwá, who is supposed to have carved all the ancient monuments with his own fingernails. The natives formerly called the tombs *Jalú*, but the present placename, *Gunung Kawi*,

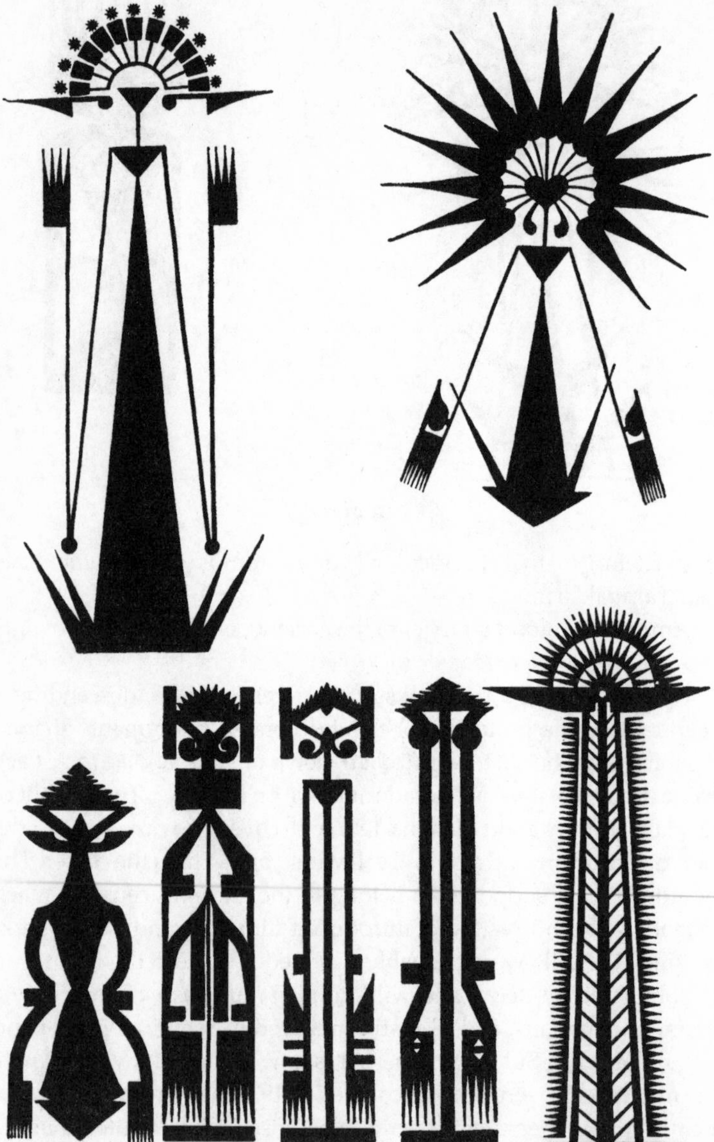

Cilís from *lamaks*

means "mountain of poetry" or "mountain of antiquity."

Bukit Darma: In Kutrí near Bedulu there is another antiquity of the classic period, also related to Erlangga. It is the beautiful statue of Mahendradatta, Erlangga's mother, as the goddess of death, Durga. It is preserved in the sanctuary of *Bukit Darma,* which archeologists believe to be the burial site of Erlangga's mother. The statue is badly worn, but it can still be seen that it was of the purest classic lines.

Goa Gajah: Together with *Gunung Kawi,* the best known relic of the ancient art is the famous "Elephant Cave" near Bedulu. *Goa Gajah* is a great hollowed rock, perhaps the former residence of a hermit,

Sapsap, cilí faces cut out of palm-leaf

elaborately carved on the outside, covered with representations of stylized rocks, forests, waves, animals, and people running in panic because directly over the entrance is the head of a great monster with bulging eyes who splits the rock with his enormous fat hands. Nieuwenkamp says that it may represent Pasupati, who divided the mountain Mahameru into two parts and, taking them in his hands, placed each half in Bali as the Gunung Agung and the Batur. There are a number of ancient stone water-spouts outside the cave, and on the inside is a statue of Ganeça in a central niche, with a *linga* on either side. The *Goa Gajah* dates also from the eleventh century and perhaps receives the popular name of "Elephant Cave" because of the statue, inside, of the god Ganeça, shaped like an elephant. But Goris attributes the name to the fact that the river Petanu, which runs near the cave, was called in old times *Lwa Gajah*, the "elephant river." Elephants have never existed in Bali and the elephant motifs that appear so frequently in Balinese art were importations from India or Java. As of *Gunung Kawi*, Kbo Iwá is also, according to popular belief, the author of the cave. Other hermitages with rock reliefs are the one nearby called *Toya Pulú*; the *Goa Racksasa* near Ubud; *Jakut Pakú*, both on the river Oös (Uwos); and the caves near Kapal in Badung.

Pejeng: In the rice fields approaching Pejeng there is a beautiful stone water-spout in the shape of a youthful hermit holding in his hand a small human figure out of whose body once issued a stream of water. Farther on, in what appears to be the former site of a temple, are scattered fragments of classic statues; an altar of human skulls; the vague silhouette of a slim woman, covered with damp moss, fallen and half buried. The most complete statue is that of a wild *raksasa* crowned with skulls and about to drink from a larger, stylized human skull. In *Pura Panataran Sasíh*, the temple where the bronze drum is kept, there are a number of ancient statues, the majority being commemorative statues of former kings.

Panulisan: In the ruins of *Pura Panulisan* on the mountain of the same name are some fine statues of kings from the eleventh century. The temple was destroyed by an earthquake and, despite the fact that it is regarded as of great holiness, an extravagant stairway of cement has been built to reach it, but the temple has not been repaired. Today one may visit the ruins only with a written permit from the local *pungawa*.

Other statues worthy of mention are the figures of Durga in the temple *Ponjok Batú* on the road to Tejakula in North Bali and the great statue of *Dewa Ratú Pancering Jagat*, over twelve feet high, the largest statue in Bali, kept jealously out of sight in the tower (*meru*) of the temple Trunyan, a Bali Aga village on the eastern shore of Lake Batur. The statue is considered very old and is held to have magic power. No one is allowed even to go into the tower, unless it is the selected "virgin" boys (*truna*) of the village, who on certain dates clean and paint the statue with a mixture of chalk, honey, and water, accompanied by elaborate carefully observed ceremonials. An excellent description of this interesting feast has been written by Walter Spies in "Das Grosse Fest im Dorfe Trunjan" (see Bibliography). The ancient Balinese also left a number of ancient bronzes cast by the *cire perdue* process, some in the form of plates with inscriptions, drums, and little statues of deities and kings, some classic in style like the beautiful ones found in Java, others of a more primitive, perhaps

Cilís painted in black and fuchsia on a rice cake (*jajan*) from Selat

local style. All of these antiquities are not in museums, but are still the property of the people, kept in the temples and honored because of their antiquity, brought out of their wrappings once a year on the occasion of the temple feast of the village.

THE PERIOD OF MAJAPAHIT

After the death of Erlangga, Java went once more into decadence as a power, and various frustrated attempts to regain its former glory followed. During this period the hold on Bali relaxed and the island regained its political independence until the fourteenth century, when the new East Javanese empire of Majapahit finally conquered its enemies and became supreme over the archipelago. Bali was made a vassal of Majapahit, A.D. 1343, after vigorous campaigns against the famed Dalam Bedaulu, last of the Pejeng dynasty and now classed as a mythical demon of great power.

After Bali was conquered, the generals of Majapahit established a new dynasty of Javanese colonial rulers in Gelgel near Klungkung. A century later Majapahit collapsed under the pressure of Islam, and Javanese rule finally gave way to a number of independent Balinese feudal lords, the descendants of the Javanese nobility, who were scattered all over the island. But in the period of years between the classic Sailendras and parvenu Majapahit the art of Java suffered a great transformation, which was similarly felt in Bali. Under King Rayasanagara (Rajasanagara), better known by his native name *Hayam Wuruk,* Majapahit became the most powerful empire of Indonesia, but being strong nationalists, the Javanese of Majapahit had repudiated the esoteric classic spirit and had reverted to native ideas, with the result that their art became strongly Javanized. Having lost its austerity and primitivism in the process, their art became earthly and realistic, taking the character of a sensuous folk-art, intricate and essentially decorative, with a predominance of flaming motifs, volutes and spirals, leaves and flowers, animals and scenes from daily life; losing altogether its religious character.

Balinese art of the epoch of Majapahit and its continuation went even further in the love of unrestrained decoration and developed a freer and more fantastic art than that of Java of the same time. Although resembling the style of the ruins of Panataran in East Java, Balinese art is not the art of Java transplanted into Bali, but a paral-

Cilí from a clay tile

lel art, made even more Baroque by additional decorative elements from China. Tropical vegetation in stone invaded the architecture in the same way that the living creepers and parasites would engulf an abandoned monument in the hothouse atmosphere of Bali.

THE PLASTIC ARTS IN MODERN BALI

Sculpture and Architecture: The primary function of the average sculptor is to enhance the public buildings of his community with florid decoration and judging from the profusion of such carved temple and palace walls, gates, drum-towers, public baths, court houses, and so forth, seen even in the remotest districts, one comes to the conclusion that there must be an enormous number of sculptors in Bali. Domestic architecture is simply of wood and thatch with secondary walls, undecorated for the most part, and is the concern of carpenters and thatch-workers. Formerly the vassals of the feudal princes built great palaces for them, many of which are still among the finest examples of Balinese architecture, but today the artistic activity of the people goes into the care of their places of worship and other communal buildings, still erected and repaired with great intensity.

In Bali there is no special class of architects, and the sculptors are in charge of designing, directing, and even working themselves in the construction of a temple, assisted by a number of stone- and brick-workers. A master carver should be able to plan beautiful gates, which are the most important examples of Balinese architecture. In Mas, a village of Brahmanas, we saw once an architectural drawing, rather resembling our architectural projects, for a temple gate to be erected in the village. The drawing was made by Ida Bagus Ktut, carver, actor, and musician, member of a whole family of artists; the position and shape of the stones and the carvings on what was to be in sandstone were drawn in great detail on European paper with black ink, with the parts to be made of brick painted red. I believe, however, that this drawing was exceptional, and usually the work is started without a drawn plan. For the making of the great towers for cremation, for example, the master builder simply has the design and the proportions already worked out, as the Balinese say, "in his belly."

The only stone to be found in the island is a soft sandstone, a conglomerate of volcanic ash called *paras*, quarried on the banks of rivers. The stone appears to be softer when freshly taken from the ground and becomes harder with time under favorable conditions. Dr. Stutterheim claims that the stone was protected in old times by a coating of cement, but I had no occasion to verify this and I never found evidence of such cement being used by the present-day Balinese. It is perhaps the softness of this, the only stone in Bali, that is responsible for the over-intricate art of the Balinese, making it possible for them to give full vent to their naive delight in covering all available space with decoration.

The stone is cut and shaped with adzes, directly on the spot where it is quarried, and made into blocks of various sizes according to requirements. For the large statues of demons that guard the entrance of temples, the great block of *paras* is roughly shaped to resemble its ultimate form, and when it is considered that enough surplus stone has been removed, it is carried to its destination on stretchers of bamboo—not an easy task, since the quarries are generally at the bottom of deep ravines. I have seen as many as fifteen men struggling up a narrow and slippery path with a great block of stone. The schematic mass of the future devil is placed where it is to remain and is finished on the site.

The blocks of stone for construction are put together without mortar, but it is essential for the stability of the building that the joints should have a perfect fit. This is accomplished by rubbing the two stones together, wearing their surfaces down with great quantities of water. The same process is employed to join baked brick. In this manner the building rises slowly, the workmen protected from the sun by shades made of the woven leaves of the coconut palm and a considerable period of time often elapses before a new temple is finished. The alternate masses of red brick and sandstone are carved last, often leaving the roughly shaped masses of stone for years without decoration.

The stone-carvers follow definite rules when they begin to cover a temple or a palace gate with decoration. For instance, there should be a *karang cewiri* over the gate, the face of a leering monster with a hanging tongue and long canines. On less Important spots the central motif of a pattern is a *karang bintulu,* a curiously popular design consisting of a single bulging eye over a row of upper teeth, the canines of which are developed into fangs, surmounted by the representation of a mountain. To finish a corner there is a special motif, a *karang curing,* the upper part of a bird's beak, also provided with a single eye and pointed teeth. For the same purpose there is a variation of this same motif, a *karang astí,* the jawless head of an elephant. The word *karang* means a reef, a rock, but it also is the word for setting jewels or for a flower arrangement. It has been attempted to give these ornaments an esoteric religious meaning (according to Nieuwenkamp), the representation of the souls of inanimate objects—rocks, mountains, plants—of which they form a part; when a Balinese was pressed to explain why they did not have lower jaws, he replied that it was because they did not have to eat solid food! This is, in my opinion, a typical Balinese wisecrack and not an indication of any such symbolical meaning.

Karang bintulu chiseled on the silver sheath of a kris

These motifs are the starting-point for the intricate volutes, leaves, flowers, flaming motifs, and so forth, strongly reminiscent of those used in ancient Java, but also found in Thailand, Cambodia, and even in the objects of the Dayaks of Borneo, a people uninfluenced by Hinduistic art. All-over patterns are called *karang*, while the carved borders in the moldings are named *patra*, of which there is a *patra olanda* (from the Portuguese word for Holland?) and a *patra cina*, a "Chinese border." Here and there small panels are carved with representations of episodes from their literature: animals from the *tantri* stories, the Balinese Aesop's fables; suggestive scenes from the *Arjuna Wiwaha* in which the nymphs of heaven make passionate love to Arjuna while he is in deep meditation; or a battle from the *Ramayana* or *Mahabharata*, with comic scenes in which the retainers of the heroes, the clowns *Twálen* and *Dé1am*, wrestle and bite each other.

The Southern style of architecture (Badung, Gianyar, Tabanan, Bangli, Klungkung) is characterized by masses of red brick relieved by intricately carved ornaments in gray sandstone in a considerably more restrained style than that of the North of the island (Buleleng),

Karang ceiviri and *karang curing*

where it breaks out into a gaudy riot of gingerbread decoration in a stone so soft that travelers have mistaken it for sun-dried mud. The gates of a North Balinese temple are tall and slender, with a flaming, ascendant tendency as if trying to liberate themselves from the smothering maze of sculptured leaves and flowers, out of which peer, here and there, grotesque faces and blazing demons, their shape almost lost in the flames that emanate from their bodies.

The North Balinese take their temples lightly and often use the wall spaces as a sort of comic strip, covering them with openly hu-

A hold-up, a temple relief in Jagaraga

morous subjects: a motor-car held up by a two-gun bandit, seen undoubtedly in some American Western in the movie house of Buleleng; a mechanic trying to repair the breakdown of a car full of long-bearded Arabs; two fat Hollanders drinking beer; a soldier raping a girl; or a man on a bicycle with two great flowers for wheels. Fantastic pornographic subjects are always a source of hilarious comedy and in many temples in both North and South Bali such subjects are found as temple decorations. As if the mad tangle of stone vegetation were not enough, in North Bali they outline the decorations with white paint to make them even more conspicuous, and in villages like Babetin, Ringdikit, and Jagaraga the overpowering decoration is painted in bright blue, red, and yellow, giving as a result the wildest and most unrestrained effects.

The art of wood-carving has suffered a curious transformation since our first visit to Bali in 1930. Then the majority of the objects carved in wood were made for utilitarian purposes: from carved doors and beams for houses, musical instruments, masks for dramatic shows, handles for implements, to little statues of deities and other ritual accessories. These were of the conventional contemporary Balinese style: flowers and curlicues in high relief for flat surfaces (*ukiran*), and for sculpture in the round (*togog*), statues of divinities, demons, and other characters of mythology dressed in classical attire and profusely ornamented. Furthermore, all wood-carvings were meant to be covered with paint, lacquer, or gold leaf and only in exceptional cases was the wood left in its raw state. There were unusual pieces, but they were freaks among the predominant styles.

Travelers had started to buy Balinese carvings, however, and on our return to Bali three years later, the Balinese sculptors were turning out mass-production "objets d'art" for tourists. Even before arriving in Bali for the second time, we found the curio shops of Makassar and

Relief in the temple of Kubutambahan

Java filled with statuettes of a decidedly commercial style which was totally new to us. Before this we had made acquaintance with Gusti Ngurah Gedé, an old man of Pemecutan rated among the best sculptors of South Bali. Although Gusti Gedé was so old that he talked with difficulty, he could carve the most delicate motifs in hard wood with a precision and sureness envied by the younger sculptors. He had started to make realistic little statues of nude girls, bathing, combing their hair, or in the process of undressing, masterfully carved out of a fine-grained white wood, figures that found ready sale among travelers. This was perhaps the beginning of a new art in which the sculptor began working for a new public: tourists who had little appreciation of the technical perfection demanded by the Balinese, or foreign artists who preferred line and form to intricate ornamentation.

This necessarily introduced the mercenary element into Balinese art, until then non-existent; prices were boosted and the sculptor suddenly became aware that there was a good income in making statues. On the other hand, this same condition gave the art a new impulse, and sculptors sprang up like mushrooms. Soon every important artistic center, such as Denpasar, Mas, Batuan, Pliatan, and Ubud, was turning out quantities of carvings in new styles, mediocre heads of *janger* dancers snatched up by round-the-world tourists, stereotyped slim figures from Mas exported to Java and Holland; while the splendid sculptors from Badung and Batuan carved coconut shells from Bangli and so forth.

Gusti Gedé was also the master of a school of sculptors and every morning boys from the town went to his house to receive lessons and to assist him. Some of his pupils were already fine carvers and could turn out statues almost as finished as those of the master. In his school we had the opportunity to observe the technique of wood-carving, which is considerably more refined and requires greater skill than the carvings in *parás* stone. Hard woods such as teak (*jatí*), jackfruit (*nangka*), and the compact *sawo*, a beautiful dark red wood, are invariably used and the sculptor must have a sure hand, trained by the experience of years, and a good knowledge of the art of cutting into the grain of the wood. He uses every conceivable form of knives, chisels, and gouges: round, straight, slanting, V-shaped, and so forth, some of which are intended for exceptionally deep carving. A complete set of tools consists of some thirty instruments and a wooden mallet. The carving technique consists in chipping bits of wood gradually with the highly sharpened instruments, not by hand pressure, as among us, but with light taps of the mallet, obtaining in this manner delicacy of touch and greater control over the material. If the statue is not to be painted or gilded, it is made smooth with pumice and given a high polish by rubbing it with bamboo.

Painting: Unlike the arts of the theater, music, and sculpture, painting was little in evidence as a living art on our first visit to Bali. Outside of painting artifacts of daily use and scant decorations for temples, the Balinese made only paintings of two sorts: *ider-ider*, strips of hand-made cotton a foot wide by some fifteen or twenty feet long, hung at festivals under the roofs, all around the pavilions in houses and temples; and *langsé*, wide pieces of painted cloth used as hangings or curtains. There were often calendars (*pelelintangan*) used to establish the horoscopes of children, divided into squares with symbolical designs, one for each of the thirty-five days of the month. Often the paintings represented scenes of mythology, episodes and battles from the literary epics; but there were seldom scenes from daily life and never of contemporary subjects. The characters shown were invariably gods, devils, princes, and princesses with their retainers, dressed in the ancient costumes of Hindu-Javanese times. Their attitudes were stilted and the subjects standardized, but at times the restricted artist found an episode where he could give vent to his erotic sense of humor and he took good advantage of a love scene or a mishap to one of the retainers of the heroes. Erotic paintings were met with at times, scenes of fantastic attitudes in love-making, which they assured me would prevent the house where they were kept from burning!

Only the old paintings showed skill and taste; the modern ones sold at the lobby of the Bali Hotel were coarse, hastily made, and with a sad poverty of subject-matter. Painting was at a standstill, no longer in demand from the Balinese themselves and suffering from lack of freedom of expression. Only rarely did we find pictures with style, but the reason for this was the systematic and mechanical manner in which they were made; a master painter drew the main outlines and gave the final touches, leaving his children and apprentices to fill in the colors. Once in Gelgel, center of painters of the conventional style, the two children of a painter had a heated argument because one had painted with blue the flesh parts of a figure and insisted he was right.

The following are among the invariable rules to be followed by

Arjuna

painters of the conservative style: all available space must be covered by the design, even to the blank spaces between the intricate groups of figures, which are filled with an all-over pattern of clouds to indicate the atmosphere. When there are various episodes to a story, each is separated from the next by a conventional row of mountains or flames, with the heroes repeated in various attitudes.

Battle scenes are crowded, bloody, and desperate, a tangle of arms, legs, and blood-spattered bodies, with all the space around filled with flying arrows and strange weapons. Faces are drawn in three-quarters, rarely full face, and never in profile. The characters are "refined" (*alus*)—gods, princes, and heroes—and "rough" (*kasar*) ones—devils, giants, retainers. Coarse characters have wild bulging eyes and fierce mouths full of pointed teeth, their attitudes are vio-

Bhima

lent, their color dark, and their bodies thick and hairy. The refined ones have long, thin arms and legs, delicate hands with curved fingers reminiscent of Indian frescoes, and their attitudes are studied and graceful. Their noses are fine and their mouths full and smiling, even in the midst of a fierce battle. They all wear elaborate clothes and jewelry of a type found only in ancient sculptures.

An important distinction is made between the eyes of men and those of women, which are always downcast—a straight line for the upper lid and a curved one for the lower lid—while the eyes of men are of the same shape but inverted, with the straight line for the lower lid, giving them a proud and inquisitive look:

Eyes, of women, of men, of devils

Everything is restricted for the painter: his subjects, his types, his compositions, and even his colors: light ochre for the flesh of refined characters and darker brown for evil ones; jewelry is yellow, costumes are either in red and blue or more rarely yellow and green. The Balinese painters use five colors: red (*barak*), Chinese vermilion called *kencú;* blue (*pelung*), vegetable indigo; yellow (*kuning*) made from a sort of clay called *atal;* mineral ochre (*kuning waja*); black (*selem*), soot with vegetable juices; and white (*putíh*) from calcined pig's bones. They can make green (*gadang*) by mixing *atal* and indigo, and brown (*tangí*) by mixing black and vermilion. These colors come in the form of stones which have to be laboriously ground together with the medium, a sort of fish gelatin from China called *ancur*. Formerly paintings were made on hand-woven cotton cloth or on bark paper made by the Torajas of Sulawesi, but today imported cloth or paper and even three-ply wood are used. The cloth is prepared with starch and glossed with a smooth shell. The preliminary outline is drawn in ochre with a bamboo style (*penelak*) or with a lead pencil, and the colors then applied with a home-made brush (*penulí*), a piece of sharpened bamboo, the fibers of which have been loosened by pounding with a stone. The picture is finished with steady black lines drawn with the bamboo pen, with a second outline in reddish brown inside the black one for all the parts that represent flesh or wood, and the whole glossed once more.

Highly specialized branches of the graphic art are the illustrations of palm-leaf manuscripts (*lontar*), and the making of leather puppets for shadow-plays (*wayang kulit*). In Singaraja there is a library of these manuscripts, the Kirtya Liefrinck van der Tuuk, where are preserved some splendid old *lontars* with illustrations (or copies of them) such as the famous *Dampati Lelangon*, taken from the palace of the Rajas of Lombok at the time of the war; the *Tetumbalans* of Kamenuh and Sawan, the *Bhima Swarga, Pari Bhasa, Adi Parwa*, and so forth. These are masterpieces of the art of illustration, with miniature pictures incised with an iron style on the blades of the *lontar* palm, the scratch filled in with a mixture of soot and oil. These manuscripts are in the form of books. The *lontar* leaves are cut evenly into strips an inch wide and from a few inches to two feet in length. They are preserved between two boards of some precious wood cut to the size of the leaves and bound together by a cord that passes through a hole in the center of each leaf.

The shadow puppets, the *wayang kulit* (described later in greater detail), are fashioned from buffalo parchment, cut out with special iron dyes into the most delicate lace and painted. The style of the *wayang* is highly conventionalized although it is considerably more realistic than its ancestor, the Javanese *wayang*. It is curious that the art of painting pictures is not altogether dependent on the *wayang* forms, as it happens to be in Java, where the whole of the art consists in reproductions of stylized *wayangs;* their outline is always in profile, while in Balinese paintings a face in profile is never found. However, the influence of these forms in the aesthetic education of children was patent when Jane Belo distributed paper and water-colors among the children of the small village of Sayan, to see what children without artistic training would do; the majority turned out pictures that were arrangements of elementary interpretations of *wayang* shapes.

Together with sculpture, painting underwent a liberating revolution after boys from around Ubud started to paint pictures in a "new" style. These were curious scenes from daily life on backgrounds of Balinese landscapes and village scenes, a mixture of realism and of the formal stylistic, with naïve figures of ordinary Balinese: a woman feeding chickens, men working in the fields, a cremation, and a dance performance, subjects that were never attempted before by Balinese painters.

This developed rapidly into a more mature, naturalistic style, producing a new crop of fine artists, each with a definite individual mark, such as I Sobrat, Madé Griya, and Gusti Nyoman from Ubud, Ida Bagus Anom from Mas, and the group of young painters from Batuan who draw fantastic forests and strange figures in half-tone against solid black backgrounds. These artists were encouraged by Spies and the Dutch painter Bonnet, who bought their pictures and provided them with materials; being careful, however, to keep undesirable influences from them, and helping them to sell their work in the museum of Denpasar, a clearing-house where only pictures of high quality are exhibited.

New materials increased the possibilities of the newly liberated art. The introduction of European paper, Chinese ink, hair brushes, and steel pens resulted in a new style of pictures in black and white, mosaics of delicate black lines with washes of various tones of grays and black, often touched with gold and red. But there are also formal paintings on wood or cloth done in the old Balinese pigments in which they attempted to give atmosphere, and mood through color: night scenes in beautifully harmonized colors that are decidedly a step forward from the limitations of the pure vermilion, blue, and ochre of the old-style paintings. Besides the scenes from daily life, the modern Balinese painters paint episodes of mythology in which the general conception has become freed from the old conventional rules. There are the same elegant gods, beautiful princesses, and other fantastic characters, painted among jungles in which every tree and plant is drawn with each leaf carefully outlined and shaded, jungles that have been wrongly compared with those of the *Douanier* Rousseau, but which resemble more the drawing of Beardsley and Persian or Indian miniatures, none of which the Balinese artists have ever seen. Favorite subjects are from the Balinese Aesop's fables, the *tantri* stories, in which the artists find amusing incidents between animals living in the tapestry-like forests of fantastic leaves and flowers.

The birth of individualism rescued Balinese painting from its latent state and placed it on the same level as the emancipated sculpture—new arts that, considering the searching intensity and liveliness of the Balinese spirit, will perhaps develop unpredictable achievements.

The Crafts: Perhaps one of the most charming qualities of the Balinese mentality is the happy combination of the primitive simplicity in which they live, with a highly refined and rather decadent taste. The Balinese are a people who retain a close contact with the soil, living practically out of doors in simple thatched houses, using artifacts belonging to a primitive culture and going ordinarily almost nude; but they gather for festivals in elaborate buildings of carved stone and dress in silks and gold to enjoy themselves, worshipping the forces of nature by means of flowers, good food, music, dancing, and works of art that only the most highly developed technical skill can produce.

In sharp contrast with their super-elaborated sculpture, painting, and dramatic arts, are the purely functional objects of daily use found in every home: implements of labor, simple but effective tools made of bamboo, wood, and iron, walls of split bamboo, cool mats for sleeping made of finely woven pandanus leaf, light but strong baskets and pocketbooks, and clay vessels to keep water cool. The common objects of daily requirements are beautiful in their simplicity, in the handling of elemental materials such as wood, bamboo, palm-leaf, and clay. In contrast are the lavish taste, labor, and money spent on their objects of luxury: their temples and musical instruments, their jewelry and textiles worn on ceremonial occasions, their weapons, and so forth. Their love of display often goes to extremes, as in the case of the costly towers, biers, and other accessories for the cremation of their dead, which are destroyed in a few minutes after hundreds of guilders and months of labor are spent to produce them.

I have mentioned the *gringsing* cloth, the scarfs from Tenganan, which are one of the rare examples in the world of the art of "double" *ikat*—that in which both the warp and the weft of the cloth are patterned by the elaborate process of dyeing only sections of the threads before weaving by binding them with fibers, the designs of both being made to fit afterwards when the scarf is woven. The *ikat* process is characteristic of Indonesians, although today the laborious double *ikats* are made only in Tenganan in Bali. Single *ikats* in cotton—those in which only the warp is previously patterned—are still made in Nusa Penida and in Mas, but in Klungkung they make "ikated" silks of amazingly elaborate patterns.

Klungkung is also famous for its brocades (*sungket*) in red silk with woven designs in gold and silver thread. The Balinese often decorate pieces of silk by the tie-and-dye process (*plangi*); the fabric is knotted

Motif on a *sungket* cloth of silk and gold brocade

tightly in certain places and dipped in the dyes so that when the knots are loosened, a regular pattern results, leaving uncolored patches where the dye could not penetrate. Interesting also are the striped and chequered cloths in cotton and silk made all over the island, some of which are very popular, and the open-work scarfs (*kamben cerik*) worn by the women around the breasts for feasts. There is a peculiar cloth in black and white checks *(kamben polén)* like the enlarged design of gingham, to which is attributed magic protective qualities. It is worn for certain magic dances like the *baris tekok jago* and is the garment of magic characters such as Bhima, Twalén, and Merdah.

Although not a part of the weaving art, the gilt cloth (*kamben prada*) used for theatrical performances is also important. This is colored silk boldly patterned with applications of pure gold leaf (*prada*) glued onto the fabric with Chinese gelatin (*ancur*) by a special process. It is curious that despite the fact that every Balinese wears Javanese *batik* for everyday dress, there is no evidence of their having adopted this popular process of decorating cloth. I have found strange *batiks* in a rough handwoven cotton of a non-Javanese style, but I could never discover proof that they were made in Bali.

The Balinese also excel in the art of working metals, from the simple agricultural implements of iron, the parts of musical instruments, and the accessories of priests (bells, incense burners, lamps, tripods, and so forth) cast in brass, to the extravagant gold and silver platters (*lelancang*), water-bottles (*kendíh*), and vases (*sangkú* and *batil*), the knives and scissors for cutting betelnut (*caket*) of wrought iron inlaid in silver, and the rich and elaborate rings, bracelets, earplugs, and flowers for the hair in hammered and chiseled gold set with rubies and star sapphires.

But the most important examples of Balinese craftsmanship are their krisses, the famous weapons of important Indonesian men, nowadays worn only as symbols and as ornaments. An inherited kris that has descended in a family for generations becomes not only their most important heirloom, but also the tangible part of the family deity and has come actually to be worshipped as an ancestral god, a *batara kawitan*, in whom the magic strength of the forefathers continues to live. Thus the head of a prominent Balinese family regards his kris as an important appendage and a symbol of himself. Today in the old villages it is compulsory for every man to wear his kris to attend a meeting; the kris must be worn at marriage and for all ceremonial or state occasions. Whoever cannot appear in person sends his kris to represent him, as for instance a judge who is sick and cannot attend a trial. In certain cases the marriage of a prince to a woman of the lower castes is performed by proxy in the form of the kris of her future husband. A new kris must be made "alive" by a priest, who blesses it in a special ceremony, reciting magic formulas over it and inscribing imaginary signs over the blade, while its owner dedicates an offering. Ancient krisses are kept alive with offerings of flowers and incense; a neglected and rusty kris is said to be dead.

The economic status of a man is determined by the richness of his kris, and a good part of his fortune is invested in the gold and jewels that decorate it. Only the blade is sacred, and the gold parts, the precious stones and ivory can be pawned in case of need and turned into cash. There are krisses worth thousands of guilders, covered with beaten gold, with handles shaped like gods or demons and set with enormous rubies and rose diamonds. Such are the famous krisses of the kings of South Bali taken by the Dutch as war booty at the time of the great mass-suicide of Denpasar in 1906, now among the star pieces of the Jakarta Museum. These fancy jeweled krisses were made to be worn on state occasions, while simpler ones were used for actual fighting, with more practical wooden handles shaped to ensure a good grip.

Gold hilts with precious stones are of course the most stylish, but there are also some made of horn, ebony, and other precious woods, with a heavy base (*bebataran*) of gold set with rubies and a small ring, of gold and rubies also, between the hilt and the blade. There is a great variety of kris handles, but a particularly interesting model is that called *kocet-kocetan*, the representation in ebony of the chrysalis of a large beetle with long antennae.

The sheath not only protects the kris from outside influences, both physical and magic, but also insulates the vibrations emanating from the kris itself, which may act dangerously on human beings. The sheaths of the super-ornate krisses are of wood covered with gold and silver, topped by a large crosspiece of ivory or ebony. The Balinese also made krisses of great simplicity, with the sheath and handle of a beautifully mottled precious wood called *pelet* which they obtained from Java. Old men claim that a fine piece of *pelet* for the crosspiece of the sheath or for the handle brought as much as fifty guilders in former times.

The shape of krisses is native Indonesian, free of all Hindu influence. It is found all over the archipelago from the Malay Peninsula to the Philippines and is invariably known by the name of *kris*. The Balinese form differs from that of the other islands only in details, and especially from the Javanese kris mainly in that it is considerably larger and more elaborate, although old Javanese blades are found in Bali, provided, however, with the richer Balinese hilts and sheaths.

The blade is the most important part of the kris; it can be straight and simple at times, but most often is fierce-looking, shaped like a flame, perhaps a form derived from a mythical serpent, a *naga*, since often there are krisses, not only in Bali and Java, but also in other parts of Indonesia, in which the body of the *naga* forms the blade, widening as it nears the top to make room for the curved neck and head of the *naga*. The upper part of the blade is full of barbs, dents, and curlicues wrought into the iron in an endless variety of styles, each with a special name, mysterious shapes that must once have had a now lost significance. There are also krisses with representations in high relief of elephants, bulls, winged lions (*singha*), and geese (*angsa*), which could possibly, at one time, have been related to the family totem. The extraordinary watered patterns (*pamor*) of silvery metal against a background of blue-black iron which have made krisses famous is the result of beating over and over alternating layers of meteoric nickel and iron layers until a fine moiré-like *pamor* is obtained, brought out afterwards by blackening the iron layers with a mixture of antimony and lemon juice. The kris is preserved from rust by a coating of coconut oil.

The blacksmiths, makers of krisses, belong to a special caste, the *pandé,* aristocrats among the lower classes who worship the fiery volcano Batur and are regarded as powerful magicians who understand the handling of iron and fire, two elements held in reverence

Blacksmith at work (*from a Balinese manuscript*)

since earliest times. The distinguished *pandés* are even respected by the proud Brahmanas, who consider themselves the highest form of humanity, and who are required to address a *pandé* in the high language when the smith has his tools in his hands. It is said (according to Korn) that a *pandé* who engaged a Brahmanic priest to officiate for him ("took holy water from a Brahmana") would lose his "*pandé* power" (*kepandean*) and might even become a monkey.

There are many popular beliefs concerning the life and power of krisses. It is said that a witch-doctor, through trance, can communicate with the spirit of a given kris and learn its past history. It is also believed that the strange fascination that a kris has on certain individuals is the cause of the temporary madness of a man who runs amuck (*amok*). He is not responsible for his acts because he is compelled by a bloodthirsty kris to run wild, killing people. Often ancestral krisses are held to have come from the heavens as a gift from the gods, and these krisses are powerful amulets against all sorts of calamities. In Ubud I was told of a man who fell asleep under an old *waringin* tree and dreamed that the spirit of the tree ordered him to cut certain roots for an offering. Imbedded among the roots, he found an old kris blade. Afraid to keep it, he turned it over to the feudal lord of the district, the *Cokorde* of Ubud, who placed it in a special shrine in his family temple. But the temple caught fire, and from then on, every place where the kris was kept soon went up in flames. Through trances and consultations it was learned that it was necessary to placate the spirit of the *waringin* tree by planting a sprig of it in Ubud. Then the fires stopped, but the magic kris would not tolerate anything above it and had to be kept in a roofless shrine. The kris cannot go through doorways, and when it is moved out of the temple it has to be carried over the wall by a bridge.

The historical tale of Ken Arok, the bandit who became a famous Javanese king of the thirteenth century, one of the great classics of Kawi literature, is in reality the story of a magic kris:

The child of simple peasants of Tumapel, Ken Arok ran away from home and joined bandits and gamblers, whom he robbed and deserted after he had learned all he could from them. He continued in his career of crime, holding up people and raping girls, but his personality and charm enabled him always to find someone who would shelter him, until one day he fell in with the great Brahmana Lohgawé, who claimed descent from Wisnú. Lohgawé was so completely won by Ken Arok that he ended by adopting him as a son and introduced him into the court, into the private service of King Tunggul Ametung. The king's wife was the beautiful Ken Dedes, said to be the reincarnation of Dewi Sri because from her womb irradiated a glowing light. She was the daughter of a Brahmana and consequently of a caste superior to the king who had stolen her, causing her affronted father to curse the king to die by a kris.

Ken Arok immediately fell in love with Ken Dedes and she with him. His Brahmanic friends saw the opportunity for vengeance and enticed Ken Arok into making love to her, telling him that he who possessed her would own the world. They did not discourage Ken

BALINESE ART

(*Photos by Walter Spies*)

ABOVE: A *cilí* of fried rice flour that tops an offering from Duda
BELOW: A wood carving apparently representing a water-buffalo's head, from the *balé agung* of Satra

(*Photos by Walter Spies*)

ABOVE: Two alarm drums from Tambakan
BELOW: A wood relief from Selulung, strongly reminiscent of the carvings of Borneo and Nias

Eleventh-century Hindu-Balinese statue in the ruined temple atop the mountain Panulism

Fragment of an ancient statue in the ruins of Purah Gaduh, near Blahbatu

Temple reliefs from North Bali

Contemporary statues used as temple decorations

North Balinese temple reliefs—Hollanders drinking beer and cranking a motor-car

North Balinese temple reliefs

ABOVE: "The princess bathes"—an illustration from the famous palm-leaf manuscript *Dampati Lelangon*
BELOW: Cockfight—an india-ink drawing on paper by a young Balinese artist

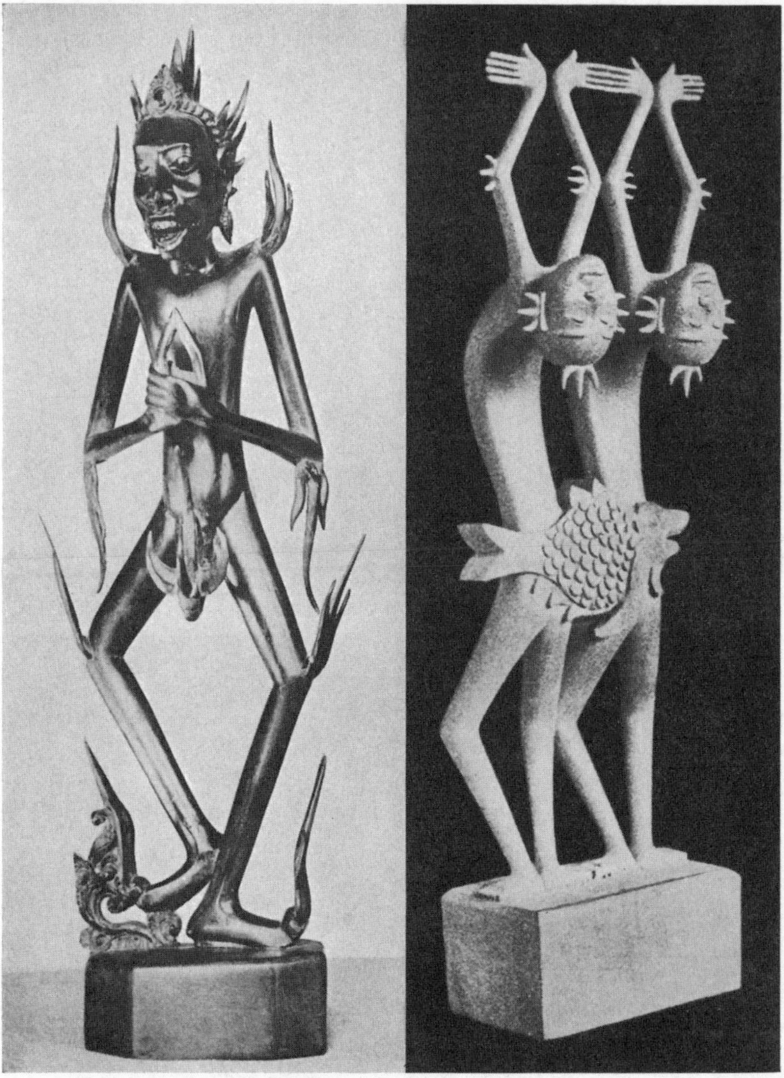

TWO MODERN WOOD-CARVINGS

LEFT: The supreme being, Tintiya, in an angry mood
RIGHT: An amulet to keep thieves away

ABOVE: Fragment of an old painting in the traditional style
BELOW: A modern painting of the *Calon Arang* play,
by I Sobrat, a young artist of Ubud

The Jungle—a black and white drawing by a young Balinese artist

ABOVE: Detail of a fine silk and gold brocade from Klungkung. The *wayang* figures are woven into the fabric by the *ikat* process—the silk threads are dyed with the pattern before the cloth is woven
BELOW: Two *wayang kulit*, puppets of buffalo parchment, cut out with dyes and painted

Arok when he decided to kill the king and marry Ken Dedes. With this purpose in mind, Ken Arok ordered a magic kris from Mpú Gandring, most famous of blacksmiths, whose krisses had the power of killing at the first thrust. The blacksmith asked for six months in which to complete the kris, after which time Ken Arok came impatiently to collect it. In a fit of temper, because the kris was not ready, Ken Arok stabbed the blacksmith with it. Before dying Mpú Gandring cursed Ken Arok to be killed by the same kris, and his children and grandchildren also to die by it.

Ken Arok lent the kris to Kbo Ijo, his best friend, who was so fascinated by it that he wore it everywhere, boasting that it was his. One night Ken Arok took the kris from his friend and killed the king, leaving the kris near the body. Kbo Ijo was accused of the murder and was killed with the kris. Ken Arok could then marry Ken Dedes, who knew who had murdered her husband. The marriage was made possible by a proclamation of the Brahmanas declaring Ken Arok of divine ancestry. The wedding took place despite the fact that Ken Dedes was about to give birth to a child of the dead king.

The child was born and was brought up as a son of Ken Arok, who named him Anusapati, but the young prince always felt an instinctive dislike for Ken Arok. Ken Dedes gave birth to four children by Ken Arok, but he took a second wife, Ken Umang, by whom he had a child, Tohjaya, who became his favorite. Ken Arok grew in power and proclaimed himself Raja of Tumapel, a title nobody dared to challenge. Instigated by Brahmanas who had been humiliated by the ruler of the empire of Singasari, of which Tumapel was a part, Ken Arok made war on him, slaying his troops and causing the king to commit suicide with his whole retinue. Ken Arok became supreme ruler of Singasari, changing his name to Raja Rajasa.

But his reign lasted only seven years. Ken Dedes had grown tired of him, and one day she told her son Anusapati of the secret of his birth and of how Ken Arok had murdered his father. Anusapati obtained the famous kris from Ken Dedes and had Ken Arok stabbed in the back during a meal, by one of his servants.

Anusapati then became King Anusanatha, but his half-brother Tohjaya hated him and one day, in the excitement of a cockfight, Tohjaya grabbed his father's kris from Anusapati and killed him with it. The feud continued between the sons of the two wives of Ken Arok when Tohjaya became king. Anusapati's sons plotted against Tohjaya but they were discovered and killed. A revolt took place, and when Tohjaya was fleeing in a sedan chair, one of the carriers lost his loincloth, remaining naked. The king laughed so, that the carrier became infuriated, seized the king's kris, and killed him with it. The story of the kris proceeds until the full curse of the blacksmith is completed.

CHAPTER EIGHT

The Drama

NO FEAST IS COMPLETE IN BALI without music and elaborate dramatic and dance performances; no one would dream of getting married, or holding a cremation, or even of celebrating a child's birthday, without engaging troupes of dancers and actors to entertain the guests and the neighbors. During the anniversary feasts of the temple there are always dances that last throughout the night and may even continue for days, with a different type of show every afternoon and night. At the great feast of Taman Badung, the death temple of Denpasar, there were shows every night for an entire month.

The Balinese love night-life and it was rare when after ten at night someone did not come to us with news of a show somewhere, or when we did not hear distant music in the village. We became such enthusiastic theater-goers that we had, sometimes, to make a point of staying home to catch up with lost sleep. Even the tired peasant who works all day in the fields does not mind staying up at night to watch a show, and the little children who invariably make up the front rows of the audience remain there until dawn for the end, occasionally huddled together taking naps, but wide awake for the exciting episodes of the play.

MUSIC

THE VILLAGE ORCHESTRAS

Although we had heard enthusiastic reports about the splendid music of Bali, its subtle beauty and vigor came to us as a revelation on our first night on the island. It is customary to hold a concert of Balinese music in the hotel gardens the night that the weekly boat arrives from Surabaya bringing new visitors. We, had experienced disappointments on such occasions elsewhere and we were fully prepared to hear another of the denatured versions of native entertainment usually concocted for tourists. We distrusted the twenty-five or thirty young men who, nude above the waist and wearing sashes of blue silk, sat cross-legged around a square formed by impressive instruments in elaborate carved frames.

There were metallophones, instruments with bronze keys like xylophones, sets of polished bronze bowls arranged from low to high like the notes of the scale, great bronze gongs, and many kinds of small cymbals. There were also two long drums wrapped in black and white chequered cloth.

Quietly, as if to indicate the piece to be played, someone started to beat out a tune on one of the high metallophones; others joined in, gradually increasing the volume of the playful melody, and soon they were all playing music the like of which we had never heard. It was a pure music like tinkling bells, interwoven with the fast humming of the cymbals, onomatopoetically called *céng-céng,* and punctuated here and there by booming gongs, the whole controlled by the masterful leadership of the two drummers, who, with the tips of their fingers, beat impossible rhythms on the double heads of their drums, each differently tuned. Suddenly, with a crash, they all struck a sonorous chord and stopped, all but the four boys playing on the *réyong,* who, in perfect unison and as if moved by a single impulse, beat the inverted bronze bowls with padded sticks, ringing out rippling chords, sinuous melodies that broke at unexpected places into resonant accents or rolled into fast syncopation.

When the *réyong* solo was over, the rest joined in again, building up the themes until they reached a furious climax that faded away into the original theme, but enriched by rhapsodical ornamentation on the high instruments against the measured basses and occasional reverberations of the deep gongs. It was an Oriental ultra-modern Bach fugue, an astounding combination of bells, machinery, and thunder.

All of the pieces they played that evening were masterpieces of musical structure, simple, but rich and alive, violent and at the same time refined, having little in common with the spirit of the over-refined, somewhat precious music we had heard in Java.

The performance, we found out afterwards, was given by one of the finest *gamelans,* orchestras, in the island—the *gong* Belaluan, pride of the quarter of the town that was later to become our home. One of the leaders of the *gong* was Gusti Oka, the young prince who became our host. When he rented us part of his house, we went to bed every night to the music of the orchestra that rehearsed only a few doors away in the *balé banjar*, the communal meeting hall of Belaluan.

The ambition of every *banjar* is to own the best orchestra in the neighborhood. It is only very poor and neglected communities that do not have two or three orchestras of their own to play for their feasts and ceremonies. As soon as they can afford it, after their temples are in good order, the most pressing need is to organize musical clubs, procure instruments, and train musicians. Every member of the village association takes an equal pride and interest in the *gamelan* and they contribute gladly, with labor and even with money, to obtain the expensive bronze gongs and bars, to make and carve the frames of the instruments, and to secure teachers to train the musicians. Often the villagers own the instruments of a former orchestra that has fallen into neglect and have to call upon outside orchestras for their feasts; but let them be spurned by a successful modern group in a rival *banjar*, and they will reorganize their *gamelan* at once—everybody helping with equal enthusiasm. The old instruments are returned, new frames are made, and all the missing pieces are replaced.

To organize a new musical club a community first selects a head man and a treasurer. The new musicians are chosen from among the young men of the *banjar*, who are directed by others with musical experience. It is an honor to belong to such a group, and the members are not paid, but themselves contribute, in whatever way they can, to the acquisition of the instruments. In the group there are even men who do not play, but who are content to carry the instruments from place to place.

The cost of a fine set of instruments often amounts to quite a fortune. The estimated value of the *gong* Belaluan was put at about fifteen hundred guilders. The actual monetary expenses were paid in instalments, and even after four years of profitable playing for the hotel, there still remained four hundred guilders unpaid. Of this apparently exaggerated figure a considerable part goes to buy a good set of large gongs, which are no longer made and are now a rarity and at a premium. The Balinese can make the bars of the metallophones, but the large gongs came from Java, from Semarang, where the last great makers of gongs lived. The richly carved frames of teakwood covered with pure gold leaf are also expensive. In former times it was a favorite hobby of the princes to form large orchestras and play in them themselves, but they are not quite so prosperous now, and today the organizations are more often independent, and it is the community that owns the orchestra. In Bali the orchestra consists of the set of instruments rather than of a group of musicians who own their instruments, as it is understood among us. In their zeal for improvement, the group of Belaluan went even further; fine costumes were made for the players and a special house was built to store the instruments, a shed for rehearsals. They even undertook to finance the repairs of the little temple of the *banjar,* a good example of the love of the Balinese for their music and the pride they show in their orchestras.

When the orchestra is assembled and the musicians are sufficiently trained, rehearsals called by a special tomtom (*kulkul*) are held every night after the work of the day is done. Although it is a requirement in the education of every prince to be able to play many instruments, the musicians are generally ordinary villagers without distinction of caste, and the strict rule that a man of low caste must always sit at a lower level than a nobleman is completely ignored; in an orchestra, at least as long as a performance or a rehearsal is in progress, a prince becomes democratic. Each musician trains a substitute, often a child, to take his place in case of disability; in this way a musical school is formed. A good musician is not satisfied to play one instrument; he must be able to play all equally well and must know the music of other types of orchestras than his own.

The leaders are the two drummers, the best musicians of the group, selected by the group for their musical knowledge. It is generally the orchestra leaders who compose the new pieces. Of the two composers in Belaluan, one was a chauffeur and the other a poor neighbor of ours who worked occasionally carrying loads to the ships. I was told that I Lotring, leader of an orchestra with a great reputation (the famous *pelegongan* of Kuta, revived through the efforts of Colin McPhee), spoke and thought of nothing but *gamelans* and music, and it was said that he dreamed his compositions. I Lotring is the author of a masterpiece of rhythm called *Gambangan.* New compositions are elaborated gradually by the leader through criticism and suggestions from other orchestra members.

Rehearsals often last a period of months before a new piece has been rounded out enough to be played publicly. Modifications and improvements are made during the course of the rehearsal; often a drummer stops the rehearsal, walks to one of the high keyboards, and plays his suggestion for a change. The group either approves or rejects the proposal, and there are no outbursts of artistic temperament.

The Balinese do not write down their music. I asked if it was not difficult to memorize such long and intricate compositions and was

told that "when the piece has been rehearsed long enough, so that it has once entered into a man's liver, he plays it without thinking."

Often the group was visited by the leaders of famous orchestras from other villages who were invited as guests of the community to teach new compositions. The leaders of the *gong* Ringdikit from North Bali came to Belaluan to exchange pieces: while they taught the dynamic and revolutionary style of the North, they learned the classical pieces of the South. The musicians of Belaluan, on the other hand, went to other villages to break in new organizations and were always lavishly entertained. Once in our village we witnessed a contest between two famous *gongs*; the rival orchestras were installed at either end of a large shed specially built for the occasion. A great crowd surrounded them. In the middle sat an impressive jury made up of the local princes and Pungawas. The orchestras in turn played their best compositions while the audience remained silent. At the end the jurors went into deliberation and awarded the decision to the rival *gamelan*, who had come all the way from the district of Tabanan.

Despite the fact that there is no trace of Occidental influence in the music of Bali, even those who hear it for the first time are carried away by it. Musicians who have gone to Bali have become ardent admirers of Balinese music. Walter Spies was the first to take an interest in it and to write transcriptions, Leopold Stokowski wanted to bring a Balinese orchestra to America, and Colin McPhee has spent years in Bali compiling material and writing down the music. However, the laws of Balinese music are different from those of the West. There is in Balinese music a unified range of sonorities tending towards one sound; with the exception of certain bamboo xylophones, an incidental bamboo flute, or a two-string violin, all of the instruments are metals struck with mallets; there is a general tone-color of metallic percussions—tinkling, acid sonorities that can be clashing and violent or soft and delicate, but are never sweet and plaintive. Their musical phraseology is simpler, more confined within a margin of sobriety, than our expansive and unrestrained music.

The Balinese have developed their music to the point of having a special type of orchestra for every purpose, each differing from the others in sonority, in the instruments composing it, in the pieces played, and even in scale. (The Balinese scale, with certain exceptions, consists of five notes, named from low to high: *ding, dong, deng, dung, dang,* corresponding to our E, F, G, B, C.) The "concert" orchestra is entirely different from the one used for feasts, cremations, and processions. The same holds true for the music employed for the various styles of plays and dances; the orchestra for marionette shadow-plays is radically different from the one used for the dances of young girls, which is again different from that used for heroic plays. The general tone of Balinese music does not produce the nervous shock on Westerners such as the more "Oriental" Chinese or Indian music does. Balinese music is readily acceptable to Western ears, perhaps because their compositions are performed by large musical ensembles in polyphonic harmonies and rhythms which are in a way reminiscent of our symphonic music.

SUPPLEMENTARY NOTES ON BALINESE MUSIC AND INSTRUMENTS

In a general way, a Balinese composition is divided into four parts: a light solo to introduce the piece (*geginaman*); an introductory theme (*pengunkab*); a central motif (*pengawak*), the "body" of the piece; and a rhapsodical finale in which the motives are developed (*pengecet*). The melodies are classified by types according to their character: the fluid, delicate motifs (*memanisan*); the playful love themes (*pengipuk*), a sort of "allegretto" or "scherzo"; the strong melodies for masculine dances (*bapang and gilak*) and the violent war music (*batel* or *kalé*). Besides this generic distinction, the pieces have names of their own, such as "the roll of the waves," "*langkwas* flower," and so forth.

The basic instruments of Balinese orchestras can be roughly divided into the following groups: (1) Instruments with metal keys of various sizes and pitch; the higher ones of nine notes (*gangsa jongkok*) that play themes and variations; those of five notes in lower key to play basses (*gangsa gantung, calung, jublag,* and *jegógan*); and the *gendér*, with ten or thirteen notes which are played with both hands. The others are played with one mallet held in the right hand while the sound is stopped with the fingers of the left. (2) The suspended gongs (*gong, kumpur, kemong,* or *bendé*) to play deep accents.

Flute-player

There is also the *reyong* and *trompong*, sets of twelve (or thirteen) and ten bells respectively, which are shaped like the gongs, but which are arranged in a frame in progressive scale. Themes and chord are played on these instruments. (3) Drums (*kendang*) to lead the orchestra, mark the rhythm, and underline the accents. They come always in pairs, a "male" and a smaller "female." The drums are wrapped in black and white chequered cloth to insulate them against evil vibrations. (4) Accessory percussions: a small *gong* (*kempli*) held on the lap and beaten with a stick; sets of cymbals (*cengceng*) to beat fast rhythms; and various sorts of bells and small metal tubes (*kemanak*) to produce incidental tinkling sounds. Besides these, there are other instruments, such as the bamboo flute (*suling*) and the two-string violin (*rebab*), which are used mainly as a lead for the melody. The flute is often a solo instrument. They do not form an essential part of the orchestra.

The *gong kebiyar*, to which the orchestra of Belaluan belongs, is the large modern "concert" orchestra *par excellence*, where the art of ensemble playing, the colorful orchestration, and the vitality of the music show to best advantage. Music played by the *kebiyar* consists for the most part of new compositions based on older pieces, in free variation. The style of the South is more conservative and delicate than that of the North, which is loud, syncopated, and with revolutionary tendencies. Among the most famous *gongs*, during

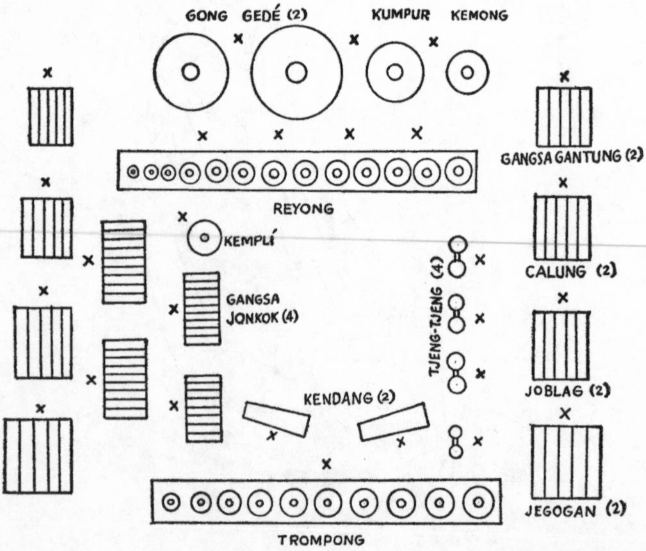

Seating arrangement of the *gong gedé*. x indicates musicians' places

my stay in Bali, were the *gong pangkung* from Tabanan, those of Belaluan, Pliatan, and Selat in the North. The *kebiyar* is obviously a modern form of the *gong gedé*, the old-fashioned grand orchestra indispensable to temple feasts, where they play throughout the night. The melodies of the *gong gedé* have an even, loud stateliness, without the delicate modulations of the *kebiyar*. In the old-fashioned *gong* the drums are beaten energetically with a stick and the hand while large cymbals clash loudly throughout the piece. The *trompong*, which does not appear in the *kebiyar*, plays the leading melody. A forerunner of the *gong gedé* is the *gong luang* or *berong*, an almost forgotten, archaic orchestra using a scale of seven notes. The only one which to my knowledge still exists is in the village of Krobókan in Badung, where it plays occasionally.

The *pelegongan*, the accompaniment for the famous *legong*, the archetype of the delicate, feminine dances, is a large ensemble playing music regarded as fine and classical by the Balinese. The style of the *pelegongan* is basic for a great deal of the music, and some of the finest standard compositions belong to it. It is used also in the *calonarang, jauk, barong*, and other dances of a similar character.

There is another type of orchestra, the *pejogedan*, which has the same tonal style as the *pelegongan*, but much simpler, in which all the sounding keys are made of bamboo slats placed over bamboo resonators. A large, deep-toned bamboo key replaces the *gong* (*kumpur*). (It is used to accompany the light *jogéd* and *gandrung* dances, described elsewhere.) This orchestra and the archaic *gambang* are the only ones in which every sounding key is not made of metal. An ancestor of the *pelegongan* type of orchestra is the ancient *semar pegulingan*, which appears sometimes at temple feasts. The scale of this orchestra resembles that of the *pelegongan*, but it may have seven as well as five notes.

The *gendér wayang* is an orchestra composed of four *gendér* (two in North Bali) to accompany the semi-ritual shadow-plays (*wayang kulit*). The *gendér* is of great importance not only for the fine quality of its music but because it is prescribed for practically all home ceremonials, even in the daytime and without the marionette performance. It appears to be simple, but it is supposed to be the most difficult to master. Its music is perhaps the most refined and delicate, with liquid shades and suspended tempos. The *gendér* is played something like a piano; that is, the themes and harmonies are executed on one instrument with both hands. Its scale is different from the others.

The *angklung*, the most frequently played, is a very ancient portable orchestra used to create excitement and for marching. It has no dancing accompaniment of any sort. The fact that its scale is restricted to four notes is a sign of its antiquity. The *angklung* takes its name from a curious instrument still played in West Java that consists of lengths of bamboo arranged loosely on a frame so that when shaken they produce a certain chord. Colin McPhee located an *angklung* orchestra with a complete set of these strange instruments in the old village of Culik in East Bali, where it is still played. Ancient Javanese records mention that the *angklung* was used in war and to precede the ruler to announce his arrival.

Other archaic orchestras still in existence in Bali are the *selunding*, which has great iron keys, and the *gambang*, already mentioned, played only at cremations in Badung and in Bangli. The keys of the *gambang* are all made of bamboo with the exception of one instrument that has metal keys. A stately melody is played on the metal instrument against an exciting, warlike background played on the bamboos. The Balinese say that it is very difficult to learn the *gambang* because the performer must think of poetical texts (*kidung*) to learn the themes. The poems suggest the melody, and the measure and punctuation serve as guide to the rhythm and pauses, so the player thinks of words as he plays. That the *gambang* is not exclusively Balinese is shown by the fact that there are reliefs in the East Javanese ruin of Candi Panataran depicting *gambangs*.

THE DANCE

A FOCUS OF BALINESE LIFE

Next to having good orchestras, a fine group of dancers is an almost organic need for the spiritual and physical life of the community. Besides the passion they show for their music and dancing and the important part these play in the ritual, to have a skillful and famous group of dancers brings pride and social prestige to the village ward, the *banjar*. The young men of today are fond of football games, but all other attempts to introduce foreign amusements have failed in Bali. The rare movie shows in the two large towns are patronized almost exclusively by the foreign population, and not even the rich princes like phonographs, although there are excellent records of Balinese music. I do not know anyone who has a radio.

Balinese dancing is essentially for exhibition: dancing to entertain an audience and for display of skill, a stage of development that belongs to an advanced civilization, but that in Bali goes hand in hand with the ritual-magic dances characteristic of primitive peoples. Thus the survival of the primitive in a developed society, a characteristic of everything Balinese, shows itself in the dancing as well as in the general mode of life. In the religious dances the community amuses itself at the same time that it tries to propitiate the gods and ward off evil spirits. There are even violent self-sacrificial dances in which the performers in a trance simulate self-torture with knives or walk on fire to appease the bloodthirsty evil spirits and to show their supernatural powers.

The Balinese attribute a divine origin to music and dancing. It is said that Batara Gurú, the Supreme Teacher, invented the first instruments, and that Indra, the Lord of the Heavens, originated dancing when he created the incomparably beautiful *dedari*, the nymphs of heaven, to dance for the pleasure of the gods. In the *Arjuna Wiwaha* it is mentioned that the seven principal *dedari* were made from a precious stone that was split into seven parts. Before dancing for the assembled gods, the nymphs, the legend says, walked three times around them in the usual respectful manner; the gods became lovesick, and since their dignity prevented them from turning around, Indra sprung many eyes, and Brahma developed four faces.

Balinese dancing was, perhaps, originally restricted to the ritual, but the religious dance has become more and more theatrical; characters that were once frightful demons are now tamed to perform for the amusement of the crowd. There are, however, still many purely religious or magical dances; local priests (*pemangku, kabayan,* and so forth) of the old communities still dance solemnly at temple feasts, in front of the altars, holding incense burners, even going into a trance and walking in fire. Only in Bali have I seen wrinkled old women with white hair dancing to amuse the gods, splendidly unashamed of what would be normally the attribute of youth. At temple feasts they perform the *mendét* and the *rejang,* two dances mainly for "aged" women—married women—with offerings of food to the visiting deities.

Although there are dances of a purely demonstrative type that interpret the music, dancing in Bali cannot be considered as an art separate from the theater. In fact, the arts of the theater are so closely allied that there is no word in Balinese meaning "theater." No Balinese would think of separating a show into its component parts or, on the other hand, think a show complete that did not contain music and dancing. They divide their theater rather according to the style of the story, which in turn dictates its music and the style of its technique. So, for example, the stories of the *Ramayana* take the shadow, or *wayang wong,* form, the historical plays are the *topeng,* and love stories the *arja,* and so forth. The following are the most important Balinese dances and plays:

LEGONG Music: full *pelegongan* orchestra. Dance-pantomime by two or three young girls playing Lasem and Semaradhana stories.

CALONARANG *Pelegongan* with large flutes. A great exorcizing drama of the story of Rangda Calonarang, with dialogue, singing, and dancing.

BARONG *Pelegongan* (called *bebarongan* in this case). A dance-pantomime of the adventures of a fantastic, holy animal, ending usually in a wild kris dance (*rebong, ngurek*) by men in trance. Also an exorcism.

JAUK *Pelegongan* orchestra. Dance-pantomime by male masked actors. Danced in the *legong* technique, with any story. Masks do not represent special characters. Characteristic head-dress.

JOGED *Pejogédan,* an orchestra of the *pelegongan* type, but made of bamboo. A purely demonstrative, flirtatious dance without a story. Called *gandrung* when performed by a boy in girl's clothes.

MENDÉT *and* REJANG Orchestra: *semar pegulingan* or *pelegongan.* Two offering dances performed by elderly women and priests during temple feasts.

SANGHYANG Music: songs by a chorus of men and women. An exorcizing trance dance of the *legong* style performed by little girl mediums.

WAYANG KULIT Orchestra: *gendér wayang.* Shadow-plays by puppets. Stories of the *Mahabharata, Ramayana,* and others. A storyteller chants recitative.

WAYANG WONG *Gendér wayang* with drums and other percussions. *Ramayana* episodes by masked actors dancing and singing in classic Kawi.

BARIS *Gong.* Ritual war dances with spears (*baris gedé*). There is a modernized version (*baris pendét*) in which heroic plays are performed in dance-pantomine with incidental dialogue and singing.

TOPÉNG *Gong.* Masked actors playing local historical plays (*babad*); mostly pantomine, but with dialogue by the comic characters.

KEBIYAR *Gong kebiyar.* A modern dance purely demonstrative in character, performed by a boy dancer who interprets musical moods.

GAMBÚH *Gamelan gambúh;* flutes, violin, and percussions. The classic technique for dramatic performances. Stories from the *Malat,* with much singing. Other plays of a similar character are the *tantrí, cupak, basur,* and *parwa.*

ARJA *Gamelan arja;* flutes and percussions. The *arja* is a modernized *gambúh* playing romantic stories like *Candra Lasan, Salya, Sidapaksa, Galolikuh,* and Chinese tales like *Sampik* and *Tuan Wei.*

BARONG LANDONG *Gamelan batél;* flutes and gongs. Giant puppets of a religious character, playing humorous stories, the adventures of an old woman (*jero Iúh*) and a black giant (*jero gedé*).

JANGER *Gamelan janger;* flute, gong, and drums. A modern musical comedy with many foreign elements, performed by boys and girls.

KECAK Large groups of men singing in chorus, moving and dancing to the rhythm of the music. Occasionally performing episodes of plays. Derived from the *sanghyang* and *janger.*

All these forms will be described later, divided for easier recognition according to our custom under the headings of "dance," "plays," "opera," and so forth, by their most characteristic features.

Like music, dancing has developed to a standard of technical perfection that makes of it a difficult science, requiring years of special physical training and practice. Although strict rules are followed and the structure of the dance is made up entirely of traditional gestures that leave no room for improvisation or individualistic styles, there is a certain margin of freedom allowed for the dancer. Sound and gesture become one, definite movements ruled by the most rigid discipline. The excellence of a performer does not depend only on his skill, but also on his personality, his emotional intensity, and the expressiveness of his features. Only clowns (*bebanyolan*) have no special technique and no program. Personality and the spirit of surprise are expected of them.

Obviously there is Javanese influence discernible in the Balinese school of dancing, but they have drifted so far apart in spirit and in social function that they have little in common today. In Bali dancing is still a living popular art, while in Java, where dance of the higher order was dying until rescued in recent years by the sultans, today it is only in the high courts of the Javanese princes that fine dancing can be seen. In Java the fine dancer is a specialist attached to the court,

...n a prince himself; in Bali he is an ordinary villager with talent and skill who performs for the prestige of his community and for the entertainment of his neighbors. In Bali as well as in Java, it is a part of the education of a prince to dance, act, and play musical instruments, but in Bali a prince who organizes a theatrical group mingles with the common people and performs for their amusement. It is amusing to hear the Javanese and the Balinese deride each other's theater: the Balinese think the dances of Java are meaningless, dull, and dead, but the Javanese are shocked at the "noisy" music of Bali and look upon their dancing as the product of rude and primitive peasants.

The Balinese have constantly injected new life into their theater, in contrast to the Javanese, who, perhaps because of Muslim influence, have allowed the art to come to a standstill so that their acting suggests imitation of the movements of their archaic marionette shows (*wayang purwa*). The Javanese actor cannot express emotion except by the most conventional gestures, and his face remains fixed and mask-like. The Balinese act in an exactly opposite manner. They are gay, exuberant, and fond of gestures and slapstick comedy. Javanese masks are stylized, with long, sharp noses and slit eyes that eliminate all sense of the realism frowned upon by Islamism. The Balinese make masks of amazing expressiveness, often realistic in character, studies of standard types. I have seen a masked play with masterfully carved masks that were caricatures of Chinese, Arabs, and Europeans.

A theatrical group is organized by the villagers into a society along the same lines as a musical club. Contributions of money are made, instruments procured, and musicians trained. The future dancers are selected from the boys and girls of the community, taking into consideration their pleasing personal appearance, their physical fitness, and their potential talent for a particular dance. For that most typical of Balinese dances, the *legong*, for example, the little girls chosen should be from five to eight years of age, and if they can be found to look alike, it is taken for granted that they will make a very fine *legong*.

When the dancers are assembled, a teacher is called to train them. He is generally a former great dancer or an orchestra leader who knows the dance to the last detail. The most elementary routines are taught at first, and repeated until the dance has "gone into the pupil." The teacher is often assisted by his more accomplished pupils, slightly older dancers from other villages. The method of training consists in guiding the movements of the pupil, leading them energetically by the wrists until by sheer repetition the pupils acquire the "feeling" of the gesture and can do the movements by themselves. At the beginning the teacher chants the tunes, but formal rehearsals with the full orchestra are held later.

The teacher works tirelessly for weeks and months at a time and it is typical of Bali that he is not necessarily paid for his efforts. If he receives a monetary reward for his work, it is insignificant and is meant rather as expense money while in a strange community. Instead of a fee, he is lavishly feasted and treated as an honored guest. If his home is in another village, he is lodged in the *banjar* where he teaches and at the end of every rehearsal is presented with trays of Chinese cakes, coffee, cigarettes, and betelnut. It is not unusual for a famous teacher like Ida Bagus Boda of Denpasar to be called to give the finishing touches to a well-trained group. The various styles of teaching are so definite that it is not difficult for a Balinese connoisseur to guess the teacher of a given *legong*.

Physical training plays an important part in the dancer's education; while the pupil learns the elemental sequence of the dance, the basic steps, and general movements of the arms, he exercises regularly to acquire suppleness of every muscle and control over each member until his body becomes practically double-jointed. The legs, however, are used with a minimum of importance in the dance, except for locomotion, and in certain sitting dances like the *kebiyar* are not used at all. It is said that such movements are possible only because of the extreme youth of the dancers. It is true that a *legong* dancer retires at twelve or thirteen, or perhaps continues in another type of dance, and that a fully grown girl is often considered too big to dance, but there are old women who are fine dancers and a good *baris* performer is usually a man past middle age. A solo dance often lasts more than an hour, and even children can dance incessantly for long periods of time without showing traces of exhaustion. This resistance often amazes travelers, but the Balinese explain that the dancer is unconscious of the real work and falls into a sort of self-induced trance where only the rhythm of the dance exists, and the dancer then moves in a world where fatigue is unknown. *Legong* dancers are very popular in the community; they are looked upon as people out of the ordinary and are exempt from heavy work. They have many suitors, and a prince frequently marries a *legong* dancer as soon as she becomes of age.

When a society has enough money for costumes and the dancers are ready to make a public appearance, the village association, on an auspicious day, gives an inauguration festival (*malaspasin*). The costumes are blessed before they can be worn for the first time, and the group makes offerings to launch the new organization successfully. An actor, a dancer, or a story-teller undergoes the same ceremony by which a priest or magician adds power to his soul. In the case of a dancer the ceremony is a magic purification and beautification in which a priest with the stem of a flower inscribes magic syllables on the face, head, tongue, and members of the future dancer to make

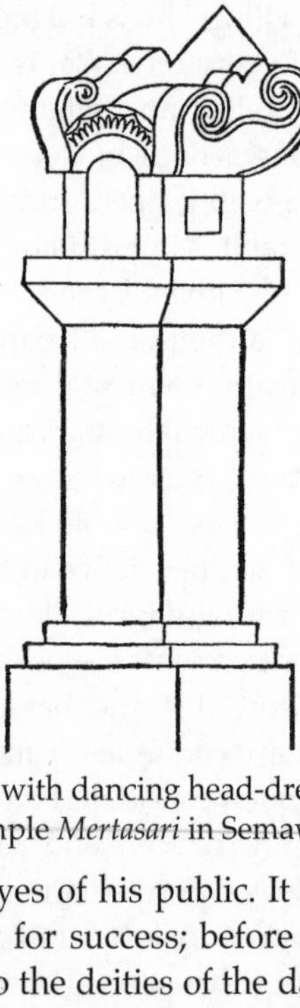

Shrine with dancing head-dress in the temple *Mertasari* in Semawang

him attractive to the eyes of his public. It is not only on this occasion that dancers pray for success; before every performance they make small offerings to the deities of the dance, Dewa Pergina, and to the nymphs of heaven, the *dedari* Supraba and Tilotama. In the temple *Mertasari* in Semawang (near Sanur) there is a small stone shrine shaped like a dancing helmet (*gelunggan*), and often *legong* dancers go there to deposit offerings. Once a year, a day (*tumpak wayang*) is dedicated to the theater, when all theatrical accessories, the costumes, masks, and marionettes as well as musical instruments, receive offerings, perhaps to restore their original effectiveness. On this day theatrical organizations all over the island give feasts, but no performance of any kind is permitted. There is also a day when literary manuscripts receive offerings; the day is dedicated to Saraswati, goddess of learning, science, and literature, when no one may read.

The size of the crowd is the only indication of whether a performance is successful or not. The Balinese do not applaud or show their appreciation of a performer in any other way. This seeming lack of encouragement does not influence the enthusiasm for the art, and it is my impression that the dance and the theater of today are even more developed than in the past. Judging from old reports, it seems that there are more performances, the shows are more elaborate and varied, and there are many new styles besides that of the jealously preserved classic theater. There is hardly a village that does not have some sort of dancing organization, and even the fact that the old custom of exempting actors and musicians from payment of taxes has been abolished by the Government has not diminished interest in dancing and acting. There is not even the incentive of commercial gain for the individual; the small amounts received at private festivals go to the society's fund for new costumes, new instruments, and the communal feasts.

THE LEGONG

As the archetype of the delicate and feminine, the *legong* is the finest of Balinese dances. Connoisseurs discuss the comparative excellence of various *legongs* as intensely as we discuss our dancers, and I have heard solemn arguments among princes as to whether the group of Bedulu was finer than that of Saba, or the school of Sukawati superior to that of Badung.

The *legong* is performed at feasts, generally in the late afternoon when the heat of the day has subsided. At the first rumor that there is going to be a *legong* in the central square or, if it is at a private feast, in the middle of the street, the crowd begins to gather. Women and children come first to secure the best places, crowding around a long, rectangular space left free for the dance. The dancing-space is often decorated with a canopy of palm-leaf streamers or shaded by an awning of black, red, and white cloth, the tail of one of the giant kites. On one end of the "stage" the orchestra entertains the gradually growing crowd with preludes until it is time for the show to begin.

Three little dancers, with an air of infinite boredom, sit on mats in front of the orchestra. They are dressed from head to foot in silk overlaid with glittering gold leaf and on their heads they wear great helmets of gold ornamented with rows of fresh frangipani blossoms. Enormous ear-plugs of gold, an inch in diameter, pierce their

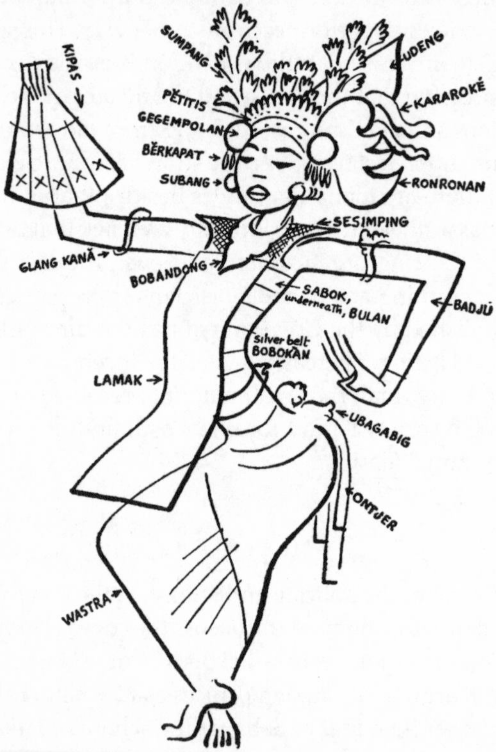

Legong costume

prematurely distended ear-lobes. Their melancholy little faces are heavily powdered, and they wear a white dot (*priasan*), the mark of beauty in dancers, painted between the eyebrows, which are shaved and reshaped with black paint.

The rich costume of the two principal dancers, the *legongs*, consists of a wrapped skirt, a tight-sleeved vest, from which hangs a long, narrow apron, and yards of strong cloth cut in a narrow strip that binds their torsos mercilessly from the breast to the hips. This is in turn covered by another sash of gilt cloth. The tight, corset-like binding gives line to the dancers' bodies and supports their backs. The costume is completed by a stiff short vest of tooled and gilt leather worn over the shoulders, a collar set with colored stones and little mirrors, a silver belt, and scarfs and ornaments of tooled leather hanging from each hip. The little girl who sits between the *legongs*, the *condong*, their attendant, is dressed in simpler clothes.

When a large enough crowd has assembled, the orchestra begins the dance music and the *condong* gets up lazily and stands in the middle of the dancing-space. Suddenly, at an accent from the orchestra, as if pierced by an electric current, she strikes an intense pose: with her bare feet flat on the ground, her knees flexed, she begins a lively dance, moving briskly, winding in and out of a circle, with an arm rigidly outstretched, fingers tense and trembling, and her eyes staring into space. At each accent of the music the whole body of the *condong* jerks; she stamps her foot, which quivers faster and faster, the vibration spreading to her thigh and up her hips until the entire body shakes so violently that the flowers of her head-dress fly in all directions. The gradually growing spell breaks off unexpectedly and the girl glides with swift side-steps, first to the right, then to the left, swaying from her flexible waist while her arms break into sharp patterns at the wrists and elbows. Without stopping, she picks up two fans that lie on the mat and continues dancing with one in each hand, in an elegant winding stride.

At a cue from the music, the two other girls straighten up and begin to dance with their hands, neck, and eyes, still kneeling on the mat. Then they rise and dance with the *condong*, forming intricate patterns with six arms and thirty fingers until the musical theme ends. Then the *condong* hands a fan to each of the *legongs* and retires into the background.

The orchestra plays a more vigorous melody and the *legongs* dance again, with the open fans fluttering at such a speed that their outline is lost like the wings of a humming-bird flying suspended in space. The two dancers seem the double image of one, so much alike are their movements, their necks snap from side to side in such perfect accord, synchronized in double time to the flashes of their eyes. The most absolute discipline controls their sharp, accurate movements. Each motion follows the last in perfect rhythmic sequence, technical perfection transformed into beauty and style. At times the music becomes playful and delicate; the two girls come together, bringing their faces close to each other and delicately "rubbing noses" (*ngarás*), following this by a flutter of the shoulders, a thrill of pleasure. This represents a love scene, a kiss, done to a special musical theme (*pengipuk*).

After a pause the orchestra plays the *Lasem* theme and the actual play begins. The story is based on an episode from the *Malat*, the Balinese *Thousand* and *One Nights*, in which Princess Rangkesari is stolen by the arrogant King Lasem, her despised suitor, while he is waging war against her father. Rangkesari spurns Lasem's advances even after he promises to give up the war if she will yield to him. He threatens to kill her father, but still she will not submit. Enraged, the king goes to carry out his threat, but during the battle that ensues, a blackbird flies in front of him, a bad omen, and Lasem is killed.

The dancers enact the various characters of the story that everyone in the audience knows by heart. The acting of the *legong* is abstract pantomime with such stylized action and economy of gesture that it becomes merely a danced interpretation of the literary text, which is recited by a story-teller, who chants the episodes and dialogues while the dance is in progress.

The dancer who plays Lasem enters, followed by Rangkesari (the two *legongs*). Lasem, tugging at her skirt, tries to force the princess, but she strikes him with her fan. This is repeated until Lasem grows impatient and, after a struggle, retires enraged. The princess is left alone, wiping her tears with the edge of her apron and slapping her thigh with a fan, a gesture of grief. As the girl kneels, Lasem reappears, angry and defiant, on his way to continue the war against Rangkesari's father; the closed fan becomes a kris which he points threateningly at his imaginary enemy. In the following episode the attendant, the *condong*, puts on her arms a pair of golden wings made of leather, to portray the unlucky crow; she dances sitting on the ground, fluttering her wings with lightning speed, advancing on her knees with birdlike leaps, and beating the earth with her wings. Lasem hesitates for a moment at sight of the ominous bird, but goes on with his kris drawn; the bird dashes at him, obstructing his progress and hampering him in the battle. The dramatic end of the episode is left to the imagination, and the three little girls end with a relaxed dance of farewell. The performance has lasted well over an hour and at the end the girls appear perfectly calm, unfatigued after their strenuous dance.

From the treatment of the story, conventional dance formulas to represent actions and emotions explained by a story-teller, one could

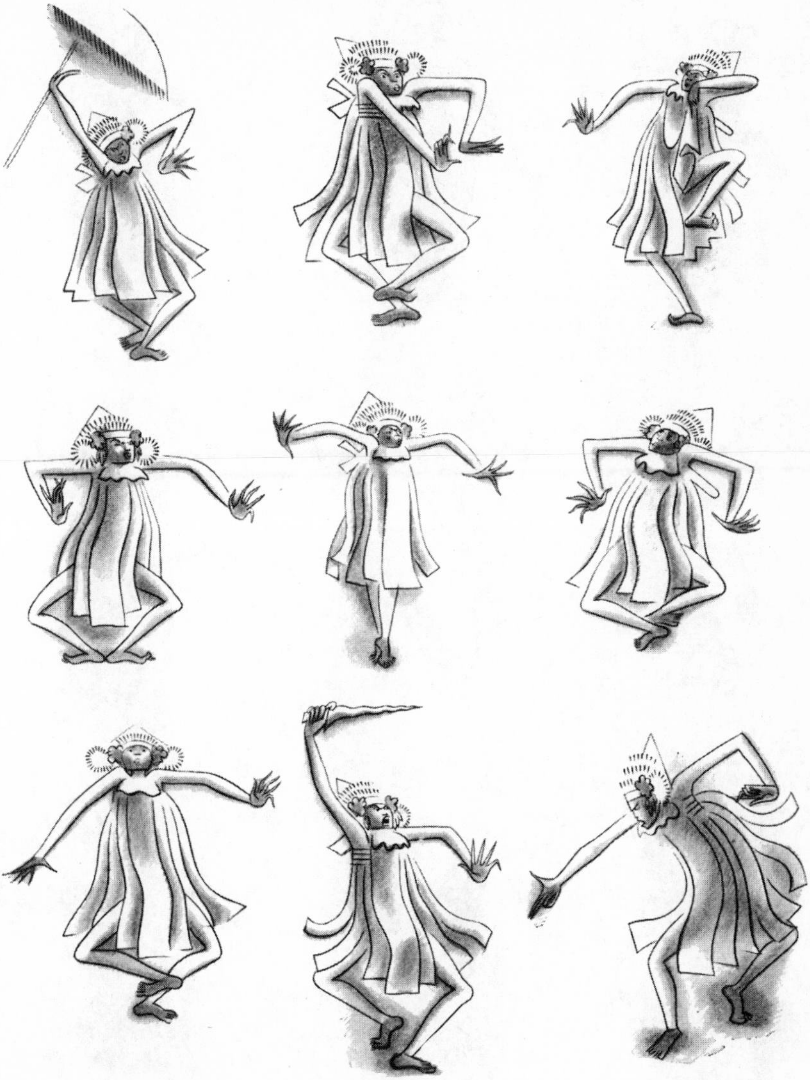

Movements of the *baris*

Movements

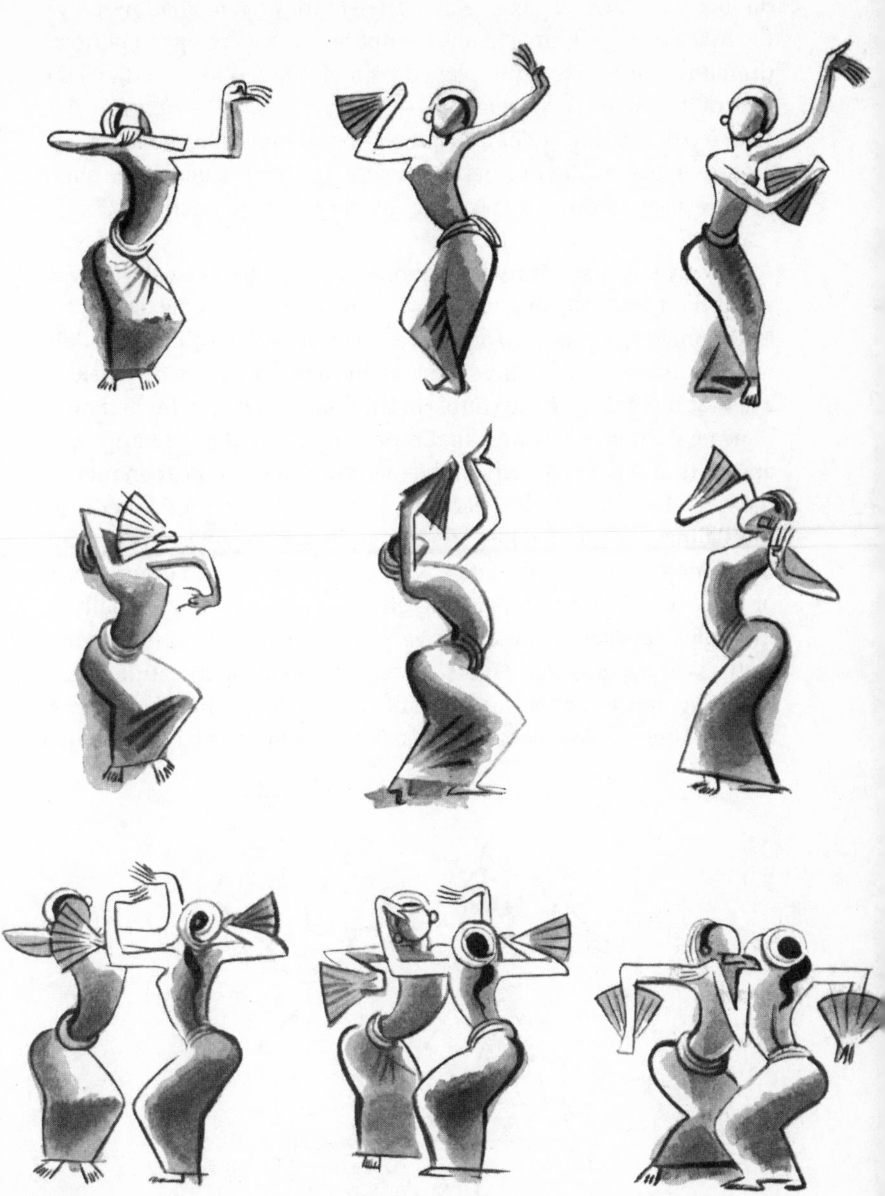

of the *legong*

deduce that the *legong* is an elaboration of the archaic shadow-plays, the *wayang kulit*. It hints at an attempt by human beings to perform dramatic stories like those played by marionettes, as is perhaps the case of the Javanese *wayang wong*—"human *wayang*"—or actors that play in the *wayang* style. It is interesting to note that while the old records speak of other forms of Balinese theater, no mention is made of the *legong*, which may not, after all, be an ancient dance.

A very popular dance that seems related to the *legong* is the *jogéd*, performed by a girl in a variation of the *legong* costume and in the traditional *legong* steps. The dance is considered erotic by the Balinese because the girl entices the men from the audience by "making eyes" at them during the course of the dance. The man invited must dance with her in postures that represent a love game of approach and refusal (*nibing*), in which the man tries to come near enough to the girl's face to catch her perfume and feel the warmth of her skin, the Balinese form of a kiss. As the audience becomes worked up, other men "cut in" and dance with her. I have seen performances of *jogéd* that had an intoxicating effect on the crowd, especially in the more decadent form called *gandrung*, when it is a boy in girl's clothes who performs. Fights among the men of the audience at *gandrung* dances are not unheard of, a procedure which is extremely un-Balinese. The *jogéd* could easily be a modernized, decadent

version of the ancient mating dance still to be found in the village of Tenganan, stronghold of native tradition. There, once a year, a dance called *abuang* is performed in which the unmarried girls of the village appear dressed in their best, wearing gold flower head-dresses (reminiscent of the paper scallops that decorate the back of the *jogéd* head-dress) and meet bachelor boys who posture with the girl of their preference in a short dance in which the gestures make one think of a chaste and restrained *jogéd*. Curiously enough, the *jogéd* is forbidden in Tenganan.

But there is still another dance, undeniably of ancient origin, that is even more closely related to the *legong*: the *sanghyang dedari* (to be described later), a magic dance in which the little girls dressed in *legong* costumes go into trance, supposedly to be possessed by the spirits of the heavenly nymphs, to bring luck and magic protection to the village through their performance. The steps of the *sanghyang* are exactly the same as those of the *legong* and it is disconcerting and eerie that at no time have the little girls received dance training, and that when in trance they are able to perform the difficult steps that take months and even years of practice for an ordinary *legong*.

THE BARIS

An indispensable part of the ritual feasts of the old villages is the *baris gedé*, a stately war dance in which ten or twelve middle-aged warriors with their heads covered with flowers, wearing magic scarves, and carrying long spears tipped with peacock feathers, dance in double line, grimacing and striking heroic poses until the music becomes violent, when they enact a sham battle with their black and silver spears.

No dance in the world can be more manly than the *baris*. Just as the *legong* is the representative feminine dance, so the *baris* typifies the strong elegance of the male and is the source of material for all masculine dances. When the first turkey came to Bali, the Balinese inmediately named it *siap baris*, the "*baris* bird." Remaining essentially a war dance, the style of the ritual *baris* was later adapted to the performance of heroic plays in the *baris pendét*, in which individual dancers play the military heroes, using dramatic dialogues to accompany their movement.

Every well-educated prince must be able to dance the *baris* when he enters middle age, having undergone a rigorous training to obtain the necessary skill and flexibility. To be in trim to dance the *baris*, one must be able to sit on one's heels keeping the knees spread wide apart in line with the body. A good dancer of *baris*, besides a finished physical training and an expressive face, must also have a cultivated, sonorous voice. It is essential that an actor with a "fine" face, who plays youthful heroes, have a high-pitched voice, while an actor who plays "strong," rough characters should have a deep, resonant voice to match the qualities of his face. A good dancer of *baris*, according to Balinese standards, is rare. We never tired of watching the princes Dewa Gedé Rake of Batuan and Gusti Ngurah Regog of Tegaltamú when they acted together.

The music for the *baris*, played by a *gamelan gong*, consists of striking standard melodies with contrasting interludes that indicate the steps and the moods portrayed by the dancer. Every part of his body, from his toes to the tips of his fingers, is in action during the dance. Every muscle of his face is controlled at will to render the storm of passions expressed by the quick-tempered warrior; expressions of admiration and wonder at an invisible magic world all around him, surprise and rage at imaginary enemies, pleasure, tenderness, and love. But as the music grows more violent, the dancer becomes more and more tense, raising himself on his toes until he gives the impression of growing in height; his eyes seem ready to jump from their sockets, his whole body trembles, making the flowers of his headdress shake violently. So raised on his toes and with his whole body at high nervous tension, he slaps his thigh and points an accusing finger at his enemy, as with wild yells of "Wah!" "Adoh, adoh!" he draws his kris and struts aggressively towards his foe, who comes forward at the same moment; before they meet, the dancers stop defiantly, cursing each other, and when the clash comes, with tiger-like grace they perform a stylized duel to music, in which the routing of one of the characters indicates the end of the dance.

The ritual *baris gedé, baris tumbak*, has an exorcizing character and is invariably danced at important cremations and in the feasts of the un-Javanized villages. It appears to be a native of Bali. There is a particularly magic *baris*, called *baris tekok jago*, in which the dancers are dressed in magic black and white chequered cloth (*polén*) and *gringsing* scarfs, which is prescribed for cremations in Badung; but in Sanur there is a group that dances in all-white clothes.

The characteristic part of the *baris* costume is the head-dress with its high triangle of white cloth (*udeng-udengan*), worn at the back of the head, and a diadem of fresh *cempaka* flowers in the front, set in wires and arranged in rows, ending in spirals at each side of the head. The dancer of *baris pendét* wears skin-tight trousers (*jalér*) and a little coat with tight sleeves (*kwací*). Over his breast a scarf (*umpal*) is tied, and from it hang many narrow strips (*lelancar*) of cloth overlaid with gold leaf, giving the dancer the aspect of an enormous gilt cabbage. On his back he wears a kris with gold handle. The word *baris* means "in line," "military formation."

THE KEBIYAR

Individualism is not encouraged in the essentially communal Balinese society, but from time to time the genius of an artist breaks through the conventional mold and emerges as a powerful personal influence. Some years ago a young man of humble birth startled South Bali with a new dance which combined the rugged manliness of the heroic dances (*baris*) with the delicacy of the *legong*. Its novelty consisted in the fact that the dancer never raised himself from the ground, moving only from the waist up, giving greater emphasis to the movements of the torso, arms, and hands and focusing attention on the dancer's facial expression. In using his body like a sensitive musical instrument, the young dancer interpreted even the most delicate moods of the island's finest orchestra, the *gong* Pangkung of Tabanan. Eventually he joined the *gong* Belaluan, and his fame spread to the foreign visitors on the island. The name of Mario became as well known to the world traveler as that of Mei Lan-Fang, Shan Kar, or Escudero.

At the regular weekly concerts of the Belaluan *gong* given at the hotel, Mario sat cross-legged in the center of a square formed by the instruments of the orchestra. He was dressed in a long piece of brocade wrapped around his waist like a skirt, with one end trailing on the ground, and a sash of gilt cloth bound his torso. Jasmine and *cempaka* flowers were stuck in his small turban, and over his left ear he wore a trembling great hibiscus of hammered gold mounted on springs. In his right hand he held a brocade fan. He sat there motionless, in concentrated intensity, until at a signal from the drummers the orchestra struck a sudden crashing chord. Mario straightened like a startled cobra, tense and nervous, holding the fan over his head as if to shade his eyes. The opening theme was fast and furious, and

Mario dancing *kebiyar*

Mario began to dance, waving his fan energetically, darting glances from side to side as if at an imaginary enemy. The tempo increased to a frantic climax, broken suddenly by a melodious solo on the *reyong*. Mario relaxed and danced delicately, his expression softened, and his movements became languid. With half-closed eyes he swayed from left to right, his elbows almost touching the mat, fanning himself or deftly arranging the flowers on his head-dress with quivering fingers. The high keys introduced the main theme; Mario flung his train to one side and hopped on his crossed legs around the square, bobbing up and down. In a coquettish mood he paused in front of the musicians, a smile on his face and his head jerking from side to side, finally centering his attention on the leading drummer, who, captivated by the infectious rhythm, beat his drum, furiously swaying and shaking to Mario's movements. Throughout the dance there were sharp contrasts, changing moods that followed the music, alternating "strong" motives with amorous, playful ones, the dancer wriggling like a trained cobra, swaying in a way that recalled the dance of a praying mantis to fascinate its prey, or stiffening with commanding elegance.

We became great admirers of Mario and never missed his Friday performance. We even bought picture postcards of him which we tacked on the wall. One day a serious young man with a flower over his ear and his pink shirt-tails out came to the house to see Gusti, the orchestra leader and our host. He bowed politely and sat down to wait. After a short while I went into the house and found Gusti's old aunt trying eagerly to say something to me in Balinese, which in those days we had not learned to understand. She repeated the phrase over and over, each time pointing first to the postcard on the wall, then to the veranda, until it dawned on me that our visitor was the dancer Mario. After that we became close friends, and when he came from Tabanan he spent a good deal of his time with us. One day Mario did not come; someone said he was very ill, so we went to Tabanan and brought him to the Dutch doctor in Denpasar. The doctor forbade him to dance and he was ordered to the hospital. Twice he ran away to Tabanan because he missed his wife and also because he would not drink milk. We went again to Tabanan and brought her along and arrangements were made so she could stay at the hospital to take care of Mario and so that he could have *bubur*, rice porridge, instead of milk. After leaving Bali we had word occasionally that he had not improved and had been sent to a specialist in Java. Mario never danced again. On our return to Bali two years later, he was still in a Surabaya hospital, and although some months later he came back, partly cured, he was unable to ever dance again and is now teaching dancing in Tabanan.

Interest in *kebiyar* waned after Mario's illness. To dance the *kebiyar* it is necessary to have what the Balinese call a "good" face, expressive and mobile, and to possess elegance, intensity and personal magnetism, besides highly finished technical training. Mario had great musical knowledge and one of his specialties was to play the *trompong* while he danced, twirling the sticks in his fingers and moving with great agility along the scale of inverted bronze bowls. The *kebiyar* was very popular during Mario's time, especially among the men. It was frequently performed as an interpretation of *kekawin*, epic poems chanted in the archaic language by expert story-tellers, while Mario translated into movement the episodes of the poems with that curious detachment of pure rhythm and abstract gesture so typically Balinese. Good dancers of *kebiyar* are rare today; of Mario's pupils, only one, I Gusti Rake, also of Tabanan, has inherited Mario's intensity and style, and he is becoming as famous as Mario once was.

THE SHADOW-PLAY

MYSTICISM AND SLAPSTICK

Perhaps poetry and the drama were born in Bali with the introduction of the great epics of the Hindus, the famous *Ramayana* and *Ma-*

habharata. They came by way of Java as propaganda for the ancient Hindus and as part of their religious teachings. The semi-divine protagonists of the poems, the princes Rama and Arjuna, gods reincarnated to save the world, soon captured the popular imagination with their romantic adventures and their fantastic wars against evil. They not only became the idols, the heroes, models of conduct for the Balinese, but were accepted as the ancestors and ideal of the race.

The early religious teachers of Java rewrote the great Indian works into the local literary language, the Kawi, archaic Javanese, in which nine out of every ten words are Sanskrit. The rich and flowery Kawi is today the classical language of poetry (*kawi* means "poet") used by Balinese intellectuals, who have continued to practice it, keeping it as alive as it was in Java during the golden age of Hinduism before it fell into neglect at the advent of Islamism. It was not without reason that Raffles wrote in his *History of Java:* "The ancient mythological poems are preserved in Bali in more correct form than in Java."

The poems are written in stanzas based on the Sanskrit meter (*sloka*), which the Balinese have developed into as many as forty-seven different poetical measures that are particularly well suited to singing. These are given out to the masses by story-tellers who chant the Kawi texts while an interpreter explains them in ordinary Balinese. The people soon learned the Kawi poems by heart, although they do not understand the actual words and chant them purely for the sake of their musical meter. Today even boys of the common classes gather at night for hours to sing in Kawi, though the meaning of the songs may be obscure to them. Musical accompaniments were eventually added to the epic songs, and story-telling developed into a fine art in the form called *kekawin*, in which a large orchestra plays interludes between the episodes and dialogues recited and translated by two story-tellers.

The episodes from the *Ramayana* and the *Mahabharata* remain the most important literary works that the Balinese have appropriated for their own literature, and they have influenced the theater to a great extent. But there are countless other stories, Javanese, native, even Chinese, that make the bulk of the literature of Bali, now being compiled by the Kawi scholars of Bali, Java, and Holland.

Out of an ancient shamanistic performance in which the ancestors were brought to this world in the form of shadows to communicate with their descendants, came the *wayang kulit*, the shadow-plays—a performance by marionettes (*wayang*) that cast their shadows on a

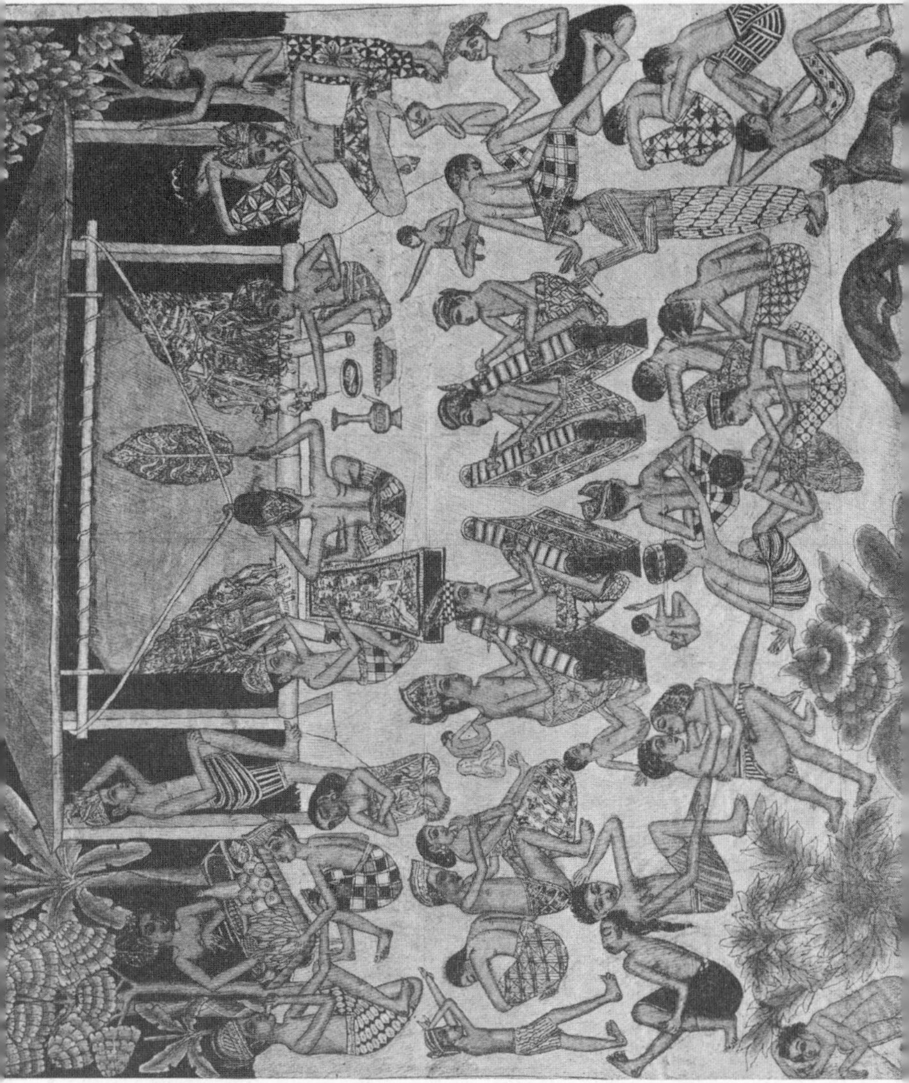

Wayang kulit—a performance of the shadow-play drawn on hand-made paper by Ida Bagus Madé Nadera, a youthful native artist

ABOVE: A make-up artist preparing dancers for a performance
BELOW: The *Arja*, romantic Balinese opera. The prince is instructing his prime minister, the *patih*

screen and are manipulated by a mystic story-teller, the *dalang*. In olden times the *wayang* may have represented the forefathers and the *dalang* the priest, but in all probability the Hindu teachers of early times took advantage of this form of expression to propagandize religion and adapted the stories of Hindu mythology into dramatic performances for the masses, illustrating the episodes of the life of Rama and Arjuna with marionettes. As the popularity of the *wayang* grew, it became stylized theater with a moral lesson, but it has never lost its mystic function. A performance of *wayang* is prescribed in ceremonials at important stages of the life of the Balinese like children's anniversaries, the coming of age of girls, teeth-filings, marriages, cremations, and temple feasts. The *wayang* may be performed in the daytime, without a screen and without an audience, but with a specified story, as magic support to the ceremony. Hardly a night goes by when the fluid music of the *wayang* cannot be heard somewhere. The fantastic adventures of the little leather puppets have a powerful hold on the imagination of young and old alike, who seem to prefer a *wayang* show to the more spectacular performance by human beings.

Travelers watching a shadow-play become bored after a short time and cannot understand why the great crowds sit listening with profound attention to the plays that do not end till dawn. But to the Balinese the *wayang* is more than vague shadows on a screen. It is the medium of their classical poetry, for their ribald humor; and, most important of all, it is the greatest factor in the spiritual education of the masses. In a performance given by an inspired story-teller, there prevails the curious mixture of mysticism and of slapstick humor that the Balinese love so. Every object and every move of the marionettes has a symbolical significance aside from the purely entertaining aspect of the show. The *dalang* is an artist and a great spiritual teacher. Years of training, a thorough knowledge of the stories and their moral value, are required of a good *dalang*. His popularity depends on his inspiration, his humor, and his ability to handle the marionettes while he improvises comic dialogues. But his reputation also depends on his *sakti*, his magic power. He is invariably the star of the show.

Before the *dalang* can perform publicly, he must be ordained by a priest in the *mawinten* ceremony, when mystic syllables are inscribed on his tongue with the stem of a *cempaka* flower dipped in honey. Then he can perform the magic *calonarang* and may wear the knot (*prucut*) worn on the hair by priests.

There are no announcements made when a *wayang* show is to take place. Somehow the rumor spreads from person to person and there is a crowd even before the *dalang* arrives. By the time he begins to stretch his screen, a great mob has gathered, sitting quietly on the ground, giving no signs of impatience at the customary endless wait for the play to begin. It seems as if they deliberately waited until midnight to start, timing the show to end at dawn. Women and children sit in the front ranks facing the screen, the men are divided between the last rows and "backstage," the side of the screen where the *dalang* sits, where they can watch the actual puppets. In Java it is a rule that the men look at the puppets, while the women see only the shadows.

The screen (*kelir*) is a piece of white cloth stretched on a wooden frame and lit by a primitive oil lamp (*damar*) that hangs directly above the *dalang's* head. The shadows are thrown on this screen by means of the lamp. At the foot of the screen is a section of the soft trunk of a banana tree, where the supports of the marionettes are stuck to hold them in position when they are not in motion. The *dalang* sits cross-legged next to a long, coffin-shaped wooden chest (*kropak*), where he keeps his puppets. Behind the *dalang* is the orchestra, the *gendér wayang*, four xylophones, each played by a musician. Between the toes of his right foot, the *dalang* holds a piece of horn, a hammer, with which he knocks out rhythms on the wooden chest—indications to the orchestra.

When everything is ready, at the tock-tock of the *dalang's* toe-hammer, the orchestra begins to play the delicate, watery music of the *wayang*, rich tone-colors and suspended tempos like bells and fountains playing a Debussian melody. A strange shadow appears suddenly on the screen. It is a leaf-shaped silhouette in which the trunk, branches, and leaves of a tree can be distinguished. There are various theories as to its significance; it may represent a mountain, a forest, the Tree of Life, or the gate to the Supernatural; but in Bali it is simply called *kayon*, a tree, or *babad*, the story. The mysterious shadow sways in circles and waves to the compass of the music, its trembling shape distorted and thrown in and out of focus by the flickering flame of the lamp, until it stops and is fixed motionless in the middle of the screen. Whatever mystic significance the *kayon* may once have had, it is now only the link that connects the various parts of the play; standing still in the center of the screen it indicates the beginning and the end; by its motions or by the angle at which it is set it may show the mood of the scene to follow or represent wind, fire, water.

When the *kayon* is removed, the *dalang* brings the marionettes out of the chest, one by one, taking his time to introduce the characters. The shadows of each puppet are fixed on the screen by sticking the ends of their support into the banana stem. On the right the *dalang* places the good and noble characters: the gods, kings, princes, princesses, and their attendants. On the left the evil characters are lined up: giants, demons, witches, and the villains of the play in general. The puppets are lacy silhouettes in profile, delicately cut out of buffalo parchment and beautifully painted. They are handled by three long supports of horn or bamboo, one for the body and one for each arm. Only their arms are jointed, and their acting is reduced to rhythmical arm gestures, while the *dalang* recites their lines. In Bali, but not in Java, some comic characters can move the lower jaw.

The puppets are then removed, leaving the screen empty, and the play begins. It may be the episode from the *Ramayana* in which the

Hanuman

divine prince Rama tries to rescue Sita, his beloved bride, from the clutches of the giant Rawana, the *raksasa* king, a monster of wickedness and lechery. Here Rama is assisted by a great army of monkeys in terrific battles in which "they discharged so many arrows that they could not see each other any more." Millions of monkeys and *raksasas* alike are slain before Rawana is killed and Sita rescued. The most picturesque hero of the war is the monkey-general, Hanuman, who performs miraculous feats of agility and strength, as, for instance, his famous leap across the ocean to Rawana's island to discover where Sita is held. When Hanuman is sent to bring healing herbs from the forest he is unable to recognize the magic plants and, angered, tears out the entire mountain top and brings it back with him.

Or the episode represented may come from the *Mahabharata*. Then the plot deals with the feud between two rival princely houses: the Pandawas, five brothers who are models of virtue (the mystic Yudistra, Bhima, uncouth warrior and powerful magician, the romantic lover Arjuna, and Nakula and Sahadewa), against their hundred cousins, the jealous and treacherous Korawas, headed by the unprincipled Duryodana. The Korawas, through trickery and intrigue, succeeded in ousting the Pandawas from their kingdom and banishing them into the forest for twelve years. During their exile the princes acquire the magic strength to wage the Great War, the Barata Yudda, against the evil Korawas, who are finally exterminated after a battle so fierce that it makes "the rivers stand still, the sun pale, and the mountains tremble."

The symbolical struggle between absolute virtue and absolute evil is the backbone and the characteristic of the Hinduistic literature of Bali. Each character is sharply defined; he is either a fiend or a hero. But the figures of Hindu origin have always remained aloof and esoteric to the Balinese, who have provided the *wayang* with more interesting and amusing characters of their own.

These are the *parekan*, the servants or attendants of the principals. On the side of truth and righteousness are Twalén and his son Merdah, while Délam and Sangut are the retainers of the "left," the villains. Twalén is a ponderous black monster with a pot-belly, a great wit, and a magic air about him. He is the really intelligent character of the *wayang*, who by his resourcefulness and knowledge of the occult saves every situation and makes the hero appear as the conqueror of every combat. His rival, the wild-eyed, stiff-mustachioed red

monster Délam, with his little legs and enormous mouth, assisted by his Sangut, is a well-matched foe for Twalén. They fight constantly by magic means, by words, or by action in bawdy slapstick clowning; the puppets are banged together as the *dalang* improvises riotous dialogues, keeping the audience in hysterics. But in the end Twalén always wins, the triumph of the magic of the "right" over the "left."

The fascinating *parekan* are the favorites of the people and it can be said that the whole show is a pretext for their mad fun making. Twalén and Délam, and their Javanese equivalents, are unknown in the original Hindu epics; they are undoubtedly native characters, perhaps ancient deities degraded to the rank of retainers of the Hindu hero-gods, reshaped by the adapters of the stories into ridiculous, clumsy monsters of ill manners to establish their relation to the Hindu gods. Certain legends mention Twalén as having a divine origin. The Balinese say that he was a son of Tintiya, the Original God, and consequently a brother of Siva; but being given to worldly pleasures and liking forbidden foods too well, he did not care to become one of the high gods and preferred to remain a servant, so that he could eat and drink all he wanted. In exchange for his renunciation, he was given the power always to come out victorious over his enemies. Because of his exorcizing powers, Twalén can purify the country of evil. He probably represents the old Indonesian magician who vanquishes evil monsters, and his role was adapted

to assist the prince against the forces that stood in the way of his spiritual improvement. With its elaborate magic, religious significance, its undiminished popularity, and as the probable ancestor of the Balinese theater, the *wayang* remains the most important form of Balinese entertainment.

THE CLASSIC DRAMA

KINGS AND WARRIORS

Conservative Balinese, fond of the classic literature in the fine old language, like to watch archaic dramas with long dialogues in Kawi and with a great deal of singing. There are various styles of classic plays, each with its own technique, and with special stories and costumes. For instance, episodes from the *Ramayana* are played only in *wayang wong* style (perhaps a development from the shadow-plays) in which masked actors in elaborate costumes enact the struggle between Rama and Rawana, while the rowdy monkeys play tricks on each other and the clowns Twalén and Délam provide hilarious comedy. The music of the *wayang wong* is, like that for the shadow-plays, mellow and delicate, played by the same *gendérs* augmented by drums and gongs to provide dramatic accents. The human *wayang* is not, however, as popular today as the shadow *wayang* and is rarely played.

Semar, as Twalén is called in the ancient *wayang gambúh*

The romantic and heroic adventures of Panji, the native Arjuna, the dashing young prince of the *Malat* stories, are played in the *gambúh*, the ancestor of the Balinese opera. The *gambúh* is played by middle-aged actors who represent kings and prime ministers, singing and chanting long Kawi recitatives to the accompaniment of great bamboo flutes or a two-stringed violin, and drums and cymbals. The style of singing *gambúh* is curiously dissonant and archaic, with great contrasts of deep voices mingled with high falsettos, whines, and loud cries that grow into a jumbled chorus at the exciting moments of the play. There are other classic plays, more or less in the style of the *gambúh*, but with their own stories, such as the *tantrí cupak* and so forth.

A great favorite is the famous *Arjuna Wiwaha*, one of the Kawi classics, a masterpiece of romantic poetry, but when played in the *baris pendet*, it becomes a mixture of love story and roughhouse. The favorite episode of the Balinese is the one in which Arjuna, in deep meditation on a mountain top, seeks to obtain a divine weapon with which to vanquish the demon Deyta Wata Kewaca, who has insulted the gods by demanding that the most beautiful *dedari*, the nymph Supraba, be given to him in marriage. The long penance of Arjuna worries the gods, who decide to send the most beautiful *dedari* to bring him out of his abstraction so that he may help them to make war against the demon. The nymphs find him in a deep trance and all immediately fall in love with him. They display their charms and employ every artifice to attract his attention, but they cannot break his penance.

In the play the main *baris* dancer sits with closed eyes and hands clasped in an attitude of prayer while his *patih* and Kertalah make poor attempts at meditation. Two beautiful girls appear; they are Supraba and Tilotama, the nymphs, who dance in front of him, embracing and kissing Arjuna, who remains unmoved, while the clowns appear indignant at his indifference. The *dedari* go away broken-hearted, when suddenly a blood-curdling roar is heard off-stage. The clowns are paralyzed with fear. A monster with the head of a wild pig leaps into the arena. He is Mang Mang Murka, the *patih* of Deyta Wata Kewaca. Arjuna shows signs of coming to life as the clowns run madly about trying to find a place to hide and getting caught unexpectedly in the path of the monster. Arjuna wakes, takes his magic bow, and kills the hog with a symbolical arrow given him by the gods.

THE TOPÉNG

The most popular afternoon (matinee) entertainment, especially with the more serious type of men, is the *topéng*, a masked play dealing with the exploits of local kings and warriors, episodes of the wars and intrigues of Balinese history (*babad*). Two or three actors, usually aged men, play all the parts and impersonate all sorts of characters with great skill, from the half-witted servants and petulant prime ministers to the heroic kings and cultured young princes. It was like magic to see an old man transform himself into a graceful young prince simply by putting on a mask and dancing with delicacy, only to come out again as a lisping and idiotic clown.

There is a curious variety of *topéng*, the *pajegan*, played by a single actor who impersonates all the characters. For this the usual curtain booth for the actors' changes is erected at one end of the "stage," while the orchestra plays at the other end. The actor sits inside the booth, already in costume but not yet wearing a mask; there he prays, making an offering to the characters about to be played. He lights a stick of incense, dedicates the small offering he has brought with him, and decapitates a small chicken, spilling the blood on the ground. The *gamelan* begins to play. The masks are arranged in the required order on a basket, each wrapped in a piece of cloth. The actor takes the first mask, puts it on, still wrapped, holding it with his teeth by a wooden knob, or a leather strap, fixed to the back of the mask. Before uncovering it, he stiffens and seems to go into a sort of trance, "to enter into the character," making dancing gestures with his head and hands. Suddenly he tears off the cloth, gets up, and after dancing for a short while behind the curtain, makes his appearance. This is done for each character, and each mask is carefully wrapped and put away after it is used. This is not for showmanship since it is always done inside the booth and out of sight of the public.

Comic characters in the *topéng*

As the play develops, the various characters are introduced, starting with the usual clowns, the servants of the prime ministers of the kings involved.

Only the clowns speak in *topéng* performances and they wear half-masks that leave the mouth free, while the finer characters use pantomime. The absurd clowns are clumsy, with stiff wild hair and bulbous noses: one is a shy little man with eyes bulging, who lisps and moves with birdlike gestures; the other is a coarse character with terrifying hollow eyes, large holes in his mask, through which the actor's own eyes can be seen. He has an unkempt moustache and a monstrous hare-lip. After them appear the refined old men with red faces and masses of white hair, high-tempered prime ministers, and young princes with smiling, delicate white features. The personality of each character is sharply defined, with peculiar mannerisms expressed in stylized acting and through extremely realistic masks.

But the curious part of the performance comes at the close. Children in the front ranks begin to show alarm and, when the play is

The *pengejokan*

about to end, some get up and leave. The *gamelan* plays a special melody and the curtains part again. This time the *pengejokan* appears; he wears the white mask of a grinning old man with protruding teeth, a mysterious smile, friendly and terrifying at the same time. He shakes constantly with laughter and shows a large roll of *kepeng*, pennies, with which he tries to lure the children, who all run as if for their lives. He goes after them, chasing them far into the road, and if he captures one, carries him back to the dancing-place and gives the money to his frightened victim. I asked repeatedly for the significance of this curious character, but I never received a satisfactory explanation. The *pengejokan's* other names are Jero Dalam Pegék and Jero Dalam Truna (*truna*: bachelor), perhaps derived from some authentic character, a bachelor king of legend who liked children, but frightened them because of his appearance. To be a bachelor after middle age is considered abnormal in Bali. The mask is very holy, or rather has magic power, and no one would dream of selling it. In general a good set of *topéng* masks is a treasure, since only the best sculptors can make them. Learned Balinese have a high regard for the *topéng* as an art.

THE BALINESE OPERA: THE ARJA

A performance by a good *arja* ensemble is a social event in the village. It is at *arja* shows that young people meet and love affairs are started, helped by the romantic atmosphere of the love stories and the late hours. The performance never begins before midnight, and the villagers wait patiently, gossiping, flirting, listening to music, or munching peanuts until the actors have eaten their interminable dinner and are finally dressed.

The play begins with the appearance of the *condong*, the female attendant of the *putri*, the eternal princess. The part of the *condong* is usually played by a middle-aged, homely, male actor dressed as a girl, who walks in an effeminate way, singing praises to his mistress and begging her to come out. She is finally persuaded; the curtains of the little booth at the end of the dancing-space part and the much heralded beauty appears. In progressive *arjas* she may be a young girl dressed in gold, with a great flower head-dress; but generally beautiful young girls cannot sing very well and in "good" *arjas* the part is played by a male actor famous for his high falsetto. Slowly the two work their way across the stage, dancing and posturing, the servant occasionally kneeling before the princess, all the while singing and talking in high, wailing voices. After this, they go "off-stage" simply by sitting on a mat in front of the orchestra.

Deep hollow laughter is heard from behind the curtain, followed by a song announcing the *patih*, the prime minister of the great prince, the hero of the play. The *patih* draws back the curtain and after what seems like unsuccessful attempts to come out, he finally emerges, very impressive and sure of his importance. He struts and grins, singing his own praises, laughing pompously. His abused and brow-beaten younger brother Kertalah comes out meekly after him. He is a pitiful little figure dressed in an old football sweater and what look like the old clothes of the *patih*. Instead of a gold kris, he carries a stick or some sort of agricultural implement. His face is crossed with dabs of white paint over his nose and upper lip to indicate that he is a clown. They hold long dialogues, giving hints of the story to follow. The *patih* in his hollow, pretentious manner postures and struts like a turkey; Kertalah lisps or stutters. They joke about topical and local matters, much in the style of circus clowns, with the *patih* playing "straight" and acting as foil for the clown. They are the favorites of the crowd and every time an "off-color" joke is made, it is the women and children who laugh the loudest, while the men blush.

Finally it is time for the prince, the *ratú*, to appear; the *patih* recites his praises and with clasped hands begs him to enter. He describes the prince's beauty as contrasted with his own ugliness, and flatters him, in standard phrases such as: "I am so happy to be the *patih* of such a prince, ha, ha, ha! Come out, Excellency, the road is clear, please come out, I wait for my master."

The prince appears, glittering with gold and tinsel, singing in Kawi, dancing in the refined style. The *patih* and Kertalah follow every one of his gestures in awe, trying to imitate them, but succeeding only in a burlesque. By now it is about three in the morning and time for the story to begin. The *arja* stories are romantic episodes of memorable love affairs of princes and princesses, generally full of fantastic situations and with a distinct erotic flavor. The distinguished characters speak and sing in Kawi, which is translated into common Balinese by the comedians for the benefit of the unscholarly crowd. The comedy is incredibly funny and rough slapstick, sprinkled with all sorts of bawdy jokes.

Besides the traditional stories, there are popular new plays such as *Sampik* and *Tuan Wei,* adaptations of Chinese love stories that started in 1924 as bastard performances with actors in European clothes playing on mandolins. Eventually these stories became thoroughly Balinese and were incorporated in the *arja*.

THE JANGER

An inevitable sight for the newly arrived tourist every Saturday morning was the *janger*. Under the hanging roots of a great *waringin,* or banyan tree, in the central square of the village, sat a dozen boys and a dozen girls in groups of six, forming a square, the girls facing the girls, the boys opposite each other; a dance master, the *daag,* sat in the center. The boys wore blue sashes and red hibiscus over their ears; the girls had great fan-shaped head-dresses of flowers and were wrapped in gilt cloth from the armpits to the feet. The boys shouted and shook while the girls sang with baby voices, flinging their hands and flashing their eyes. After a while a girl appeared dressed as a prince, singing and posturing, quarrelling with a wild-looking bird, an actor with a frightful mask, wings, and a bright-colored tail. The show ended with the death of the bird, shot by an arrow of the prince. Half of the tourists looked on, while the other half snapped pictures furiously. The performance was picturesque and justified the fee, but somehow it did not ring true. Despite the fact that the elaborate show was held on the open road, it attracted only a few children, and the dancers seemed bored and indifferent.

On our first night in Bali, strolling on the outskirts of Denpasar, we heard again the same syncopated, persistent beat of drums and gongs we had heard in the morning. Following the sound, we came upon a great crowd watching a show, and after a good deal of pushing, we managed to make our way to the front rows. There were the dancers of the morning, but it was the *janger* for the Balinese. Instead of tourists comfortably seated on folding chairs, the nude torsos of a great mob of eager people pressed us on all sides until we could not move a hand and were nearly suffocated by the constant blast of human breath, overpowered with heat and the heavy perfumes that emanated from the dense crowd. Children climbed on walls and trees or crawled over our feet, trying desperately to see something. Instead of the "traditional" costume worn for tourists, the girls wore tight chiffon blouses, their flower crowns framing their heavily powdered faces. The boys were dressed in European shirts, neckties, shorts, golf socks, and football shoes. Over their shoulders they wore a sort of chasuble of black velvet with appliqués of gold braid, spangles, and epaulets of gold fringe. They had red flowers on their bare heads and incongruous false moustaches on their chalky faces. Only the dance master wore the usual theatrical costume of brocade, but with an added shirt and bow tie. Like the others he wore a huge moustache.

We never discovered the purpose behind the absurd costume; perhaps it was only fun, perhaps to caricature Europeans. But the insanity of the costume was surpassed by that of the performance: to the serpentine melody of a bamboo flute and the syncopated beat of drums and gongs, the girls sang nonsensical songs about flowers, rice cakes, and so forth, many words without meaning, simply to create

Kecaks in a *janger* performance

rhythm: "jange—jange—jangerere . . ." while their hands flew, the flowers on their head shook, and their eyes snapped in unison with their necks. The boys, the *kecak*, swayed and shook, shouting: "Kecak-kecakkecak—cak! cipo—*oh!* cipo—*oh!* a-ha-aha!" much in the manner of a college yell, but growing faster and faster, underlinning the tempo of the gongs and drums. The dance master darted wild glances in all directions with gestures of anger and astonishment, moving like a frantic automaton. The whole moved with the rhythm of a locomotive at full speed—Balinese jazz that intoxicated both performers and audience in a spell of syncopated movement. At calmer moments two girls stepped out of the ranks and danced around the dance master, who registered amazement when the girls made love to him. Then the most incongruous nonsense ensued: like a flash, the *kecaks* jumped to their feet in acrobatic poses, athletic pyramids, a boy in a back-bend while another stood on his chest. They climbed on each other's shoulders, shaking and shouting. Suddenly the dance master whirled on his seat as if he could not stand it any longer, and yelled: "*Daaag!*" The whole show stopped dead. After a pause the play began, an *arja* story with the usual princes, prime ministers, and clowns.

Later I found out that the *janger* was a recent development. It had started suddenly, when, about 1925, the first company of Malay operettas (*stambul*) visited the island. The Balinese immediately created their own version of the pantomime, and the *janger* spread like an epidemic; everywhere *janger* groups were formed and soon every *banjar* could boast a *janger* club. It was the first time that boys and girls joined to dance for the fun of performing together, their first social dance. Every district developed its own style. In Buleleng there was a group in which the girls wore shorts, showing their legs, a rather shocking exhibition for the Balinese, who called it *janger melalong,* the "naked *janger,*" but it was popular among the rich Chinese of Buleleng. The *janger* was then the most popular entertainment. Nobody cared to see anything else and every girl in Bali hoped to become a *janger* and hummed the songs all day. We feared that the *janger* would kill other forms of Balinese dancing, but on our return two years later, we were surprised to find that there was no more *janger;* all the famous groups had stopped. Some of the girls had married, and since there was no more demand, the groups were not reorganized. The most exhilarating show of the Balinese was dead and forgotten. Only a sleepy group remained: the *janger* for the tourists, still avidly photographing what they called "temple dancers."

With the passing of the *janger,* the classical forms of theater regained popularity, and during our second visit it was the *arja* that had again become the favorite. The style of the *janger* was a puzzling departure from the refinement of the Balinese theater. The singing was obviously derived from the magic *sanghyang* songs, and the costumes and acrobatic figures might have been copied from the Westernized Malay shows, but the general mood, the seating arrangements, and the movements can only be explained as a throw-back to the Polynesian spirit.

The case of the *janger* was an interesting example of the attitude of the Balinese towards their arts: their love of novelty and easy following after all new ideas, which are soon assimilated into their traditional forms. This enables the islanders to create new styles constantly, to inject new life steadily into their culture, which at the same time never loses its Balinese characteristics.

Part II

CHAPTER NINE

Rites and Festivals

RELIGIONS WERE BORN OF MAN'S DESIRE to understand and control the mysterious process of nature. Fear of the eerie, unseen forces that cause birth, reproduction, and death, awe before the power of fire, wind, and water, made him worship the elements of the teeming world in which he lived. Only by the existence of psychic forces and powerful spirits could he explain the perpetual motion of the sun and the moon, the roll of the sea, and the movements of the clouds, the wind that shakes the trees, lightning, thunder, and rain. Health, fertility, and success he attributed to his magic harmony with these forces, while for earthquakes, volcanic disturbances, epidemics, and the loss of crops he blamed the anger of spirits whom he had failed to propitiate.

Eager to place his fate in the hands of superior beings who would take care of his needs and on whom he could place the responsibility for his failures, man created a pantheon of supernatural beings—protective gods and adverse evil spirits—whose goodwill he aimed to gain by rites, offerings, and sacrifices. Unconsciously, by elaboration and by the adoption of new elements into the pantheon, he ended by developing an elaborate system of ritual and magic acts. Thus the primitive Balinese made of their island a magic world populated by gods, human beings, and demons, each occupying a level allotted by rank: the deified spirits of their ancestors dwelling in the summits of the volcanoes that form the island; ordinary human beings living in the middle world, the land that lies between the mountain tops and the sea, which is the home of devils and fanged giants, the enemies of mankind.

Placed between these two poles from which emanate opposing forces (the positive from the mountains and the negative from the underworld), the entire life of the calm and sensitive Balinese—their daily routine, social organization, their ethics, manners, art; in short, the total culture of the island—is molded by a system of traditional rules subordinated to religious beliefs. By this system they regulate every act of their lives so that it shall be in harmony with the natural forces, which they divide eternally into pairs: male and female—the creative principle; right and left; high and low—the principles of place, direction, and rank; strong and weak, or healthy and sick, clean and unclean; sacred and powerful or unholy and dangerous; in general: Good and Evil, Life and Death.

SOCIETY AND RELIGION

The conglomerate of religious principles manifests itself in elaborate cults of ancestors and deities of fertility, of fire, water, earth, and sun, of the mountains and the sea, of gods and devils. They are the backbone of the Balinese religion, which is generally referred to as Hinduism, but which is in reality too close to the earth, too animistic, to be taken as the same esoteric religion as that of the Hindus of India. Since the earliest times, when Bali was under the rule of the great empires that flourished in the golden era of Hinduistic Java, the various forms of Javanese religion became in turn the religions of Bali, from the Mahayanic Buddhism of the Sailendras in the seventh century, the orthodox Sivaism of the ninth, to the demoniac practices of the Tantric sects of the eleventh century. In later times Bali adopted the modified, highly Javanized religion of Majapahit, when Hinduism had become strongly tinged with native Indonesian ideas. Each of these epochs left a deep mark in Balinese ritual; to the native Balinese cults of ancestors, of the elements, and of evil spirits, were added the sacrifices of blood and the practices of black magic of the Tantric Buddhists, the Vishnuite cult of the underworld, Brahmanic juggling of mystic words and cabalistic syllables, the cremation of the dead, and so forth, all, however, absorbed and transformed to the point of losing their identity, to suit the temper of the Balinese.

It is true that Hindu gods and practices are constantly in evidence, but their aspect and significance differ in Bali to such an extent from orthodox Hinduism that we find the primitive beliefs of a people who never lost contact with the soil rising supreme over the religious philosophy and practices of their masters. Like the Catholicism of some American Indians, Hinduism was simply an addition to the native religion, more as a decoy to keep the masters content, a strong but superficial veneer of decorative Hinduistic practices over the deep-rooted animism of the Balinese natives.

Religion is to the Balinese both race and nationality; a Balinese loses automatically the right to be called a Balinese if he changes his faith or if a Balinese woman marries a Muslim, a Chinese, or a Christian, because she takes leave forever of her own family gods when she moves into her husband's home and instead worships his gods from that time on. The religious sages, the Brahmanic priests, remain outsiders, aloof from the ordinary Balinese, who have their own priests, simple people whose office is to guard and sweep the community temples, in which there are no idols, no images of gods to be worshipped. These temples are frequented by the ancestral gods, who are supposed to occupy temporarily the little empty shrines dedicated to them, when visiting their descendants. The Balinese live with their forefathers in a great family of the dead and the living, and it would be absurd for them to try to make converts of another nationality, since the ancestors of the converts would still remain of another race apart.

Rather than a sectarian Church system, separate from the daily life and in the hands of a hierarchy of priests to control and exploit the people, the religion of Bali is a set of rules of behavior, a mode of life. The resourceful Balinese fitted their religious system into their social life and made it the law (*adat*) by which the supernatural forces are brought under control by the harmonious co-operation of everyone in the community to strengthen the magic health of the village. Like a human being, the community possesses a life power that wears away and must be fed by the regular performances of magic acts of the "right," the side of righteousness. The life power is seriously impaired by the magic evil, that of the "left," or by the polluting effects of sickness and death. Bestiality, incest, suicide, and temple vandalism are among the acts of individuals that would make the entire village *sebel*, or magically weak. The spiritual health is also undermined by the gradual predominance of evil forces, the demons and witches that haunt the village. Some of these are easily disposed of, but the main concern of the Balinese centers in the propitiation of the protecting ancestors who descend to this earth on special holidays and at the anniversaries of the innumerable temples, when they receive offerings and entertainment from the people. By these ceremonies and temple festivals the populace hopes to entice the spirits to remain among them; the beauty of the offerings, the pleasant music, the elaborate theatrical performances, aim to keep them from growing bored and leaving.

Motivated by this background of religious beliefs, the Balinese found it necessary to establish a system of communal co-operation to provide for the magnificent festivals that are such an important part of their life. The spirit of co-operation soon extended to their personal and economic life and developed into a primitive agrarian commune in which every village was a socially and politically independent little republic, with every citizen enjoying equal rights and obligations. These villages were ruled by councils of village members and officials who governed as representatives of the ancestral spirits. Since the land, source of all wealth, also belonged to the ancestors, individual ownership of land was not recognized, and it is remarkable, but typical, that the village officials still govern as a duty to the community and without remuneration.

Furthermore, the Balinese have been extremely liberal in matters of religion. Every time a new idea was introduced into the island, instead of repudiating it, they took it for what it was worth and, if they found it interesting enough, assimilated it into their religion, since no one knew what power there might be in the new gods. In this manner, from all the sects and cults that at one time or another reached the island, they selected anew the principles that best suited their own ideas and accumulated a vast store of religious power. Buddha became to them the younger brother of Siva, and if the efforts of the Christian missionaries who are attempting to convert the Balinese succeed, it is not unlikely that in the future "Sanghyang Widi," the exalted name that the missionaries have adopted for Jesus, will become a first cousin of Siva and Buddha and will enjoy offerings and a shrine where he can rest when he chooses to visit Bali.

TEMPLES AND TEMPLE FEASTS

The temple is certainly the most important institution on the island and the clearest illustration of the spirit of the Balinese religion. There are temples everywhere, from the modest family shrines in every household, to the extravagant temples of the princes and great town temples; large or small, plain or richly carved temples found in the rice fields, in the cemeteries, in the markets, on the beaches, in caves, among the tangle of gnarled roots of old *waringins*, on deserted hill tops and even on the barren rocks along the coastline.

When we discovered that the Balinese did not seem to mind in the least our going in and out of the temples, we started visiting them systematically, looking for unusual statues or reliefs, and although from the beginning we received the impression that there were not two temples exactly alike, we became aware that there were features common to all; unlike the forbidding, somber temples of other Oriental countries, the Balinese temple is a gay, open-air affair; one, two, or three open courtyards surrounded by a low wall, each court leading into the next through more or less elaborate stone gates, and with a number of empty sheds, pavilions, and shrines in varied styles, the majority covered with thatch, some with only one roof, others with as many as eleven superimposed roofs like pagodas.

There were no soot-blackened rooms filled with incense smoke for mysterious rites performed in front of great idols; as a matter of fact, there were no idols at all worshipped in any of the hundreds of Balinese temples we visited. In many there were ancient statues from former times, together with many shapeless stones kept as amulets by the community, which, because of their antiquity or because they were found in extraordinary circumstances, came to be regarded as gifts of the gods, or as their name (*peturun*) indicates, as heirlooms from their ancestors. The gods are invisible and impalpable and in all Bali there is not an image of a Hindu deity worshipped for the sake of its representation. Most often not even the priests in charge were aware of the names of the divinities represented.

Our interest in temples grew when we tried to understand the rules that dictated their intriguing design, but the first attempts left us only more confused than before. Explanations by the *pemangkus*, the temple-keepers, did not agree and the discrepancies were often greater than the points of agreement. With Spies I started into a more systematic search; we went into a temple, sought the *pemangku*, and drew a plan in which the names and purposes of each unit were indicated. Repetitions started to appear in many plans, and when we had gathered many ground plans of various sorts of temples we traced the common features in them. From those that appeared most frequently I set myself to the task of reconstructing one "ideal" Balinese temple.

Most typical was the temple with two courtyards, the outer court called *jaban*, "outside," and the other the *dalam* the "inside." Entrance into the first court was gained through the *candí bentar*, the "split monument" or split gate (A. See plan), which was like the two halves of a solid tower cut clean through the middle, each half pushed apart to give access into the temple. That the *candí bentar* represented the two halves of a unit was obvious; in most of them each side was elaborately carved, often with the design also cut in two, as in a temple near Mengwi where half of a monstrous face adorned each side of the gate. Furthermore, the two inner sides were invariably left smooth, clean surfaces that shone by contrast with the elaborately carved rest of the temple. This we decided was an inviolable law until we found one *candí bentar* in *Pura Bangkung*, in Sukasada, North Bali, with its inner sides carved. This exception, however, is not im-

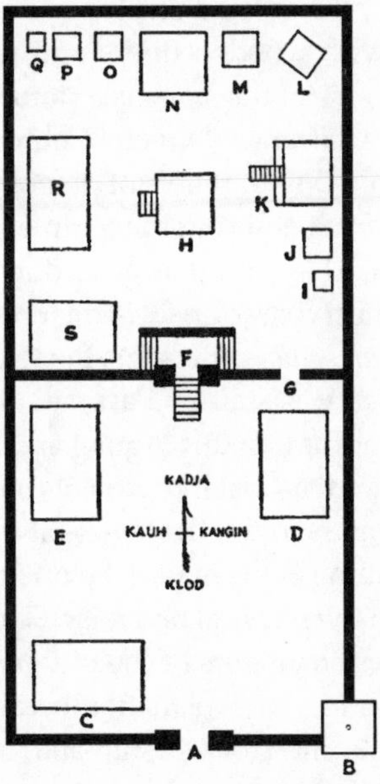

Ground plan of a typical Balinese temple

A – Split gate, *candí bentar*
B – *Kulkul* tower
C – Kitchen, *paon*
D – *Balé gong*
E – *Balé* for pilgrims
F – Ceremonial gate, *padú raksa*
G – Side gate
H – *Paruman* or *pepelik*
I – *Ngrurah alit*
J – *Ngrurah gedé*
K – *Gedong pesimpangan*
L – *Padmasana*
M – *Gunung agung*
N – *Meru*
O – *Gunung batur*
P – *Maospait* (*menjangan seluang*)
Q – *Taksú*
R – *Balé piasan*
S – *Balé*

portant, given the anarchy that prevails in North Balinese temples, and since there is no rule in Bali without its exception.

In the right-hand corner of the first courtyard, or outside the gate, is the high tower (B) where hang the village drums (*kulkul*). Inside the outer court are a number of simple sheds: a kitchen (*paon*) where the food for feasts is cooked (C), the *balé gong*, a shed for the orchestra (D), and another *balé* (E) used as rest-house by the people and for the making of offerings. The outer courtyard is generally devoid of ornamentation except for a number of decorative frangipani trees.

Another monumental gate, the *padú raksa* (F), leads into the second court, the temple proper. This gate is a massive structure identical in shape and design with the reunited halves of the *candí bentar*, but raised high above the ground on stone platforms, with a narrow entrance provided with wooden doors and reached by a flight of stone steps. On each side of the stairs is a statue of a fierce giant, two *raksasas* to guard the entrance. Directly behind the door is a stone wall (*aling aling*) covered with reliefs of demons. These are meant to keep evil influences from entering the temple.

All sorts of theories have been advanced as to the significance of these two gates, the most characteristic structures in the temples. It has been said that the *candí bentar* represents the two halves of the mountain Mahameru, which was split by Pasupati (Siva) in order to place each half in Bali, one as the Gunung Agung and the other as the Batur. A scholarly Balinese told me that it represents the two halves of a complete thing, the male at the right, the female at the left; or it is perhaps symbolical of the splitting of the material world to permit the entrance into the mystery with the physical body. Dr. Goris suggests as the origin of these gates the remainders of the old *candís*, the burial towers of the former kings, a logical explanation because of the cult of deified kings linked to the ancestor worship and, further, because of the identical shape of the Balinese temple gates and the old *candís*, a shape of temple gates which dates back to the most ancient of Javanese temples. The *candí* form appears throughout Balinese ritual as the symbol for the universe: a pyramid of receding platforms—the foundation of the earth and the mountains—the intermediate space between heaven and earth, and the stratified heavens, represented by the pagoda-like roofs (*tumpang*), or by gradually decreasing stone moldings.

The first courtyard is only an antechamber for the preparation of feasts and for other social purposes. It is in the inner court that are

A typical Balinese temple

erected the altars and shrines that serve as rest-houses for the gods during their visits to this earth. The principle of orientation—the relation of the mountains to the sea, high and low, right and left—that constitutes the ever present Balinese Rose of the Winds (*nawa sanggah*), rules the orientation and distribution of the temple units. The principal altars and shrines are arranged in two rows on the honored sides of the court: *kaja*, upward to the mountain, and *kangin*, to the right of this direction.

First in importance is the *gedong pesimpangan* (K), built in the middle of the *kangin* side, a masonry building closed by wooden doors dedicated to the local deity, the ancestor founder of the community, often named after the village, as, for instance, in *desa* Dedap he is called Ratú Dalam Dedapan. Inside there is often a stone phallus (*lingga*) and, since the building can be locked, there the relics and heirlooms of the temple are also kept: ancient statues of stone, wood, or gold, old bronzes, and so forth.

Most impressive are the *merus*, high pagodas of wood resting on stone platforms, always with an odd number of superimposed receding roofs (from three to eleven) made of thick layers of *ijuk*, the everlasting and costly fiber of the sugar palm. These roofs are arranged along an open shaft through which the gods are supposed to descend into the *meru*. The temple of Besakih, the greatest in all Bali, on the slopes of the Gunung Agung, consists practically of *merus*, and other important temples have three, five, seven, or nine *merus*, but our typical temple has one, built in the principal place, the center of the *kaja* side of the courtyard. The *meru* is supposed to represent the great cosmic mountain Mahameru and is the seat of the high Hindu gods. A curious feature of *merus* is the miniature iron implements buried under the building, together with little gold and silver roast chickens, lotus flowers, crabs, shrimps, and so forth. Again, where the rafters of the uppermost roof meet, there is a vertical beam of sandalwood with a hole in which is deposited a small covered Chinese bowl of porcelain containing nine precious stones or nine *pripih*, plates of various metals inscribed with magic words.

Never missing are two shrines for the great mountains: one for the Gunung Agung (M) and other for the Batur (O) (or for the Batukau in the villages in its neighborhood). They resemble little *merus* of one roof, also made of *ijuk* and ending in tall phallic points. Of great importance is the *padmasana* (L), the stone throne for the sun-god Surya, which stands invariably in the uppermost right-hand corner of the temple, with its back directed always towards the Gunung Agung. The form of the *padmasana* is again the representation of the cosmos. On a wide platform shaped like the mythical turtle *bedawang,* with two stone serpents coiled around its body, rest three receding platforms, the mountains, the whole surmounted by a stone chair with a high back.

Other shrines that are never missing are the little houses for *Ngrurah Alit* (I) and *Ngrurah Gedé* (J), the "secretaries" of the gods, who watch that the proper offerings are made, and the stone niche for the *Taksú* (Q), the interpreter of the deities. It is the *Taksú* who enters the bodies of mediums when in a trance and speaks through them to make known the decisions of the gods to the people. There is still one more shrine, the *Maospait* (P), dedicated to the totemic gods of the settlers from Majapahit, the "original deer" (*menjangan seluang*). This can be recognized by a small sculpture of a deer's head or by the stylization of antlers carved in wood.

There are, besides, other pavilions; one in the middle of the temple which serves as a communal seat for the gods, the *pepelik,* or *paruman* (H), and the *balé piasan* (R, S), simple sheds for offerings.

This lengthy description is still far from complete and is limited to the main features of a would-be average temple, but unfortunately such typical temples could hardly be found in Bali. Despite the rules, practically every temple has curious contradictory individual features; besides, such is the variety of types of temples and so great the local differences, that only for the purpose of a general understanding of the spirit of Balinese temples can this "typical" temple be of use. To note down all the variants of Balinese temples would require a great volume.

Besides the family shrines, every Balinese "complete" community, a *desa,* should have at least the three reglementary temples: first a "naval" temple, *pura puséh,* the old temple of the original community from which the village sprang; a second, *pura desa,* the town temple for official celebrations of the entire village, which, in case it has a *balé agung,* the old-fashioned assembly hall of the village Elders, receives the name of *pura balé agung;* and third, a *pura dalam,* the temple of the dead, built out in the cemetery, dedicated to the deities of death and cremation. It often happens that the *pura puséh,* despite its being the most important center of worship, is located in another village or even in another district, because it was from there that came the settlers of the later village. In some places the *pura puséh* and the *pura desa* are combined into one, with only a wall separating the two departments. There are still the private temples of the princes; the royal temples (*pura panataran*), and the *pura dadia*, the private temple of origin of the family, the connecting link between the scattered branches of a common stock. Other important temples are the *pura bedugul*, the rice temple of each agricultural guild; the *pura pamaksan*, little temples of each village ward (*banjar*), from which the *pura puséh* evolves; hill temples (*pura bukit*), sea temples on the beaches (*pura segara*), temples for the deities of seed and markets (*pura melanting*), bathing-temples, temples in lakes, caves, springs, trees, and so forth. (See additional Note 1, page 278.)

Except for the old *pemangku*, the keeper and officiating priest of the temple, who can be seen there occasionally sweeping the yard, the temples are ordinarily deserted because the Balinese go into them only for public gatherings, festivals, and meetings, *Pemangkus* are simple people of the common class with old-fashioned manners, polite, good-natured, and with a charming modesty, who live near the temple and perform all of its duties, from sweeping it to invoking and impersonating the deities. The haughty Brahmanic priests, the *pedandas*, refer to them contemptuously as *jero sapúh*, "sweepers," but the *pemangkus* are the really active priests of the people's ritual and alone officiate at temple feasts, when the *pedandas* do not take an active part. Furthermore there are villages where the *pedandas* are even barred from the temple.

The office of the *pemangku* is often hereditary, but he may also be chosen by some mystic while inspired by the spirits. He dresses in all-white clothes with a characteristic coat with tight sleeves and wears his headcloth in the old-style high crest. *Pemangkus* lead a normal routine life without great religious restrictions, attending to their personal affairs until the date for the feast of the temple approaches, when they will become the center of all activity.

Every temple celebrates its birthday (*odalan*) on the anniversary of its consecration, with a great feast that constitutes the principal social event for the entire community and in which everybody in the village takes part with equal enthusiasm.

For days before the temple feast of Kengetan, as typical as any, the men attended to the decorations of the temple, building the temporary bamboo altars, erecting awnings for entertainers, adorning the shrines with flags, pennants, and *penyors*, cooking the food for the feast, and dressing up the statues of the demons that guard the entrance with a skirt of chequered black and white cloth and a great red hibiscus behind each ear. At the same time the women prepared the offerings and made *lamaks*. The *pemangku* was on duty from early morning to receive and bless the offerings that each woman brought. By afternoon a great crowd of people in festival dress had gathered and the *dagangs* had set up their food-stands. All day long the women arrived with offerings on their heads, walking like sailing ships, requiring the help of two other women to support the fifty pounds of fruit and flowers so that the bearer could come out from under the heavy load to deposit it on the special shed erected for the purpose.

The *pemangku* sat in front of the central god-house praying and ringing a bell, surrounded by the new arrivals, who sat in rows behind him after leaving their offerings, the men cross-legged, with bared heads, behind the kneeling women. They prayed (*mabaktí*) three times, taking a flower between the middle fingers of their joined hands, bringing it to their foreheads, and flinging it in the direction of the shrine. The women sang *wangesari* songs in chorus while the *pemangku* and his assistant went around the praying people pouring holy water with long-handled ladles into their outstretched hands, drinking it with reverence, and wiping their wet hands in their hair. Serious babies in silks and gold necklaces also kneeled, repeating every gesture of their elders. Outside the temple the crowd gathered, listening to the stately music of the *gong* or watching a show. Sometimes the men staged cockfights (also a part of the ritual) or flirted with the vendors.

In a quiet corner an old *pemangku* proceeded to imbue with the spirits of the local deities the temple *arcas*, a pair of beautifully carved little statues, male and female, of painted and gilt sandalwood. They were usually locked into the central shrine, wrapped in many cloths and kept in a special basket, but they were taken out on the day of their feast and made "alive." While an old man chanted the ancient song *Sinom Surakarta*, the old *pemangku* recited a special prayer of invitation to lure the deities to occupy the *arcas* so that in this more tangible form they would preside over the feast in their honor, be taken out in procession, and in general serve as a point of sight towards which the ceremony was directed. (See Note 2, page 280.)

The *gamelan angklung* played outside the temple while the people began to form for the great procession to take the gods for a symbolical bath (*melis* or *makies*) to the nearest big river. The march started, headed by many bearers of flags, pennants, and spears, followed by a long line of girls, their torsos wrapped in silk scarfs of yellow, green, and magenta, marching in single file with the offerings and pots of holy water on their heads. Then came the little statuettes of the gods, decorated for the occasion with fresh flowers, carried on cushions on the heads of a group of picked girls and shaded by three-staged umbrellas of state. Older women followed, also carrying offerings; and the procession was closed by the group of men and the orchestra, which played an obstinate marching rhythm on the gongs. The correct thing would have been to take the gods to the seashore, but Kengetan was far inland and there it was customary to go to the river for *melis*. In Denpasar, on the occasion of the great feast of the temple Taman Badung, from a height I saw a great procession over a mile long, a fact verified by the mileage posts on the road, a fantastic spectacle in the late afternoon sun, preceded by hundreds of fluttering flags and tall pennants, white umbrellas, and spears, moving slowly towards the sea to the accompaniment of gongs. On arrival at the beach in Kuta, after a walk of five miles, the *arcas* received offerings, the priests prayed towards them, and the people sang songs of praise and danced *mendet* to entertain the gods, returning at dusk to continue the feast through the night.

In Kengetan it was already dark when the procession returned to the temple, its arrival greeted with exploding firecrackers and clattering *kulkuls*, while the orchestras played furiously all at the same time. The parade stopped at the temple gate in front of the *pemangku*, who waited, seated in front of a mat spread with offerings. He proceeded to welcome the *arcas*, once more addressing a prayer to them, ringing his bell, and offering rice, money, eggs, and wine, decapitating a little chicken to spill the blood on the ground. In that instant an old woman attendant stiffened and became possessed, followed by the *pemangku*, who also fell into a trance. They both danced like somnambulists, the woman with closed eyes, the *pemangku* staring wildly and holding an incense brazier in his hands, in this manner leading the carriers of the *arcas* into the temple.

Inside, they stood in the middle of the lamplit court, and the *gamelan* played a dance theme; elderly women began to dance a solemn *mendet* (or *gabor*), one holding a bottle with a carved spout, another with a piece of banana leaf folded like a spoon containing *arak* (rice brandy), a third performing intricate steps balancing miraculously on her head a brazier filled with glowing coals. They danced back and forth from one end of the court to the *arcas*, each time pouring holy water and *arak* on the ground in front of the deities. At intervals a group of young girls walked forth with silver platters containing offerings and deposited little trays of palm-leaf with food and flowers (*canan*), samples from the large offerings, on the floor, while the *pemangku* fanned their essence in the direction of the gods.

Only a few people witnessed the ceremony because the majority were outside watching a play. Throughout the night mediums went into a trance and became possessed by the spirits of the *jero Taksú*, the "interpreter" of the deities, in order to inform the people if the offerings had been well received and to obtain advice from the gods. The medium was the *pemangku* himself, going into convulsions, rolling his eyes, and foaming at the mouth as the spirit of the *Taksú* entered his body, making incoherent guttural sounds which were taken as the voice of the spirit. Once I saw a *pemangku* become possessed by the spirit of some sort of tiger, growling and running on all fours in the temple yard under exploding firecrackers, picking up fire with his hands and eating the sparks. The medium came out of the trance painfully, and in an epileptic fit, as the spirit left his body. Gradually he calmed down, got up exhausted, and was helped out of the temple. The crowd remained divided, watching the performances or talking in groups outside the temple, not much interested in the ceremonies or in the spectacular trances. Often, especially at the feasts of the death temples, they performed savage kris dances, which will be described later.

In Kengetan the *gong* played all night the stately, ancient music, and as dawn approached the old *pemangku* moved around quietly supervising things, putting out the lights and preparing for the final ceremony, the adoration of the rising sun, when *mendet* was danced again by middle-aged women and offerings were dedicated in the direction of the first rays of sun that appeared on the horizon. This ended the feast, and by morning, when the essence of the offerings had been consumed by the gods, the women came to collect their respective offerings and take them home.

Such is the general pattern along which a temple feast moves, but, again, each community has its own way of doing things and no two feasts are carried out in exactly the same manner. Differences are particularly striking in the villages of the mountains, as in Paksabali and Bugbug, two communities in East Bali, where they stage wild battles of the gods, the *arcas*, which are placed inside baskets wrapped in *polén* cloth and topped with bunches of leaves. The baskets are firmly attached to bamboo stretchers carried by half-naked men who rush at full speed against others carrying "rival" deities, trying to knock each other down. A crowd armed with spears joins in the free-for-all while firecrackers explode, and everybody yells, pushes, and tramples everyone else. The excitement is followed by an equally mad kris dance.

GODS AND DEMONS: OFFERINGS AND EXORCISMS

Good and evil, right and left, gods and demons, are banded into two opposing factions, constantly at war, in which the weapons are their magic powers and the stakes the lives and interests of the Balinese themselves, compelling them to propitiate both sides so as not to attract the wrath of either party. Only by the proper balance between the negative and positive forces are they able to maintain the spiritual harmony of the community. This is particularly important at certain times, such as childbirth, menstruation, death in the village, or when a crime that disturbs the magic balance of the village has been committed; circumstances that weaken and pollute the protective life power of the individual or of the village and render them vulnerable to the attacks of evil.

The antithesis of the state of normalcy, of health and cleanliness (*sucí, éning*) is for a person or a community to be *sebel*, unclean, physically and spiritually polluted and run down, a condition that must be cured by cleansing factors and ceremonies to give added strength to the soul—the making of offerings, the use of purifying water and fire, and the recitation of secret magic words by a qualified priest, the three elements of Balinese ritual.

To counterbalance the healthy influence of the gods who produce cleanliness, luck, and fertility, there are evil spirits responsible for all illness and misfortune. Among the countless demons that crowd the spirit world of the Balinese, some, like the *raksasas*, are inoffensive giants and ghouls that belong to literature, but the invis-

Buta

ible causes of evil are disagreeable *butas* and *kalas*, symbols of malice and coarseness, that haunt desolated places, the seashore, and the deep forests and infest the "dangerous" parts of the village, the crossroads and the cemetery. The *butas* and *kalas* have no other mission on earth than to annoy and persecute humans, making people ill, disturbing and polluting everything. They can go into people's bodies and make them insane or turn them into idiots.

The tangible gifts to the gods, the offerings (*pebantén*) (see page 280) like the presents given to human beings, consist of fruits, cakes, rice, flowers, money, chickens, and pigs. They are given in the same spirit as presents to the prince or to friends, a sort of modest bribe to strengthen a request; but it is a condition that they should be beautiful and well made to please the gods and should be placed on well-decorated high altars. Their devils, however, the Balinese treat with contempt, and the offerings intended for evil spirits are generally a smelly mess of half-decayed food which is disdainfully thrown to the ground. The deities are served with the essence (*sari*) of the offerings, which is fanned towards the place they supposedly occupy, carried by the rising smoke of the incense. Ordinary people take what is left—the material part is later taken home and eaten. Thus both gods and the donors enjoy the banquet. The magic people, the many Balinese possessed by supernatural powers, are not allowed to touch these left-overs from the feast of the gods, the food without the essence.

Offerings to evil spirits are in themselves polluted and are left to be eaten by the village scavengers, the hungry dogs. The devils receive elaborate sacrifices on certain occasions and on special days, every fifth (*klion*) and every fifteenth (*kajengklion*) day; but, as they are greedy by nature, the little offerings given them every day—a few grains of rice, a few flower petals, and a coin or two—are enough to distract them from their evil intentions. They become particularly obnoxious at sundown, and on these special dates the women of each household place in front of their gates trays of food, flowers, and money, next to a burning coconut husk.

Great calamities will fall upon the village when the *butas* predominate or when they are angry. Then they cause epidemics, the loss of crops, and so forth, and only by the most elaborate ceremonies of purification and great offerings of blood sacrifices can the pollution of the village be wiped out.

Nyepí. Once a year, at the spring equinox, every community holds a general cleaning-out of devils, driving them out of the village with magical curses and rioting by the entire population. This is followed by a day of absolute stillness, the suspension of all activity, from which the ceremony takes its name. *Nyepí* marks the New Year (see Note 5, page 283) and the arrival of spring, the end of the troublesome rainy season, when even the earth is said to be sick and feverish (*panas*). It is believed that then the Lord of Hell, Yama, sweeps Hades of devils, which fall on Bali, making it imperative that the whole of the island be purified.

There is great excitement all over Bali at this time, and on the days before *nyepí* everybody is busy erecting altars for the offerings and scaffolds for the priests at the village crossroads. Since no cooking is allowed on *nyepí* day, the food for the next day is prepared and there are *melis* processions all over Bali to take the gods to the sea for their symbolical bath. The celebration proper extends over a period of two days: the *mecaru*, the great purification offering, and *nyepí*, the day of silence. On the first day the Government allows unrestricted gambling and cockfighting, an essential part of the ceremony, because the land is cured by spilling blood over impure earth.

In Denpasar round after round was fought all morning; crowds of men gathered in the meeting hall of every *banjar*, each bringing his favorite fighting cock in a curious satchel of fresh coconut leaves, handle and all, woven over the cock's body, its tail left sticking out so as not to damage the feathers. Each satchel was cut open and the cocks presented to the audience to announce the matches. The betting began; excited enthusiasts waved strings of *kepengs* and silver *ringgit* and yelled at each other. A vicious steel blade five inches long and sharp as a razor was attached to the right foot of each cock in place of the natural spur, which was cut off. When both contenders were ready and the bets had been placed, the referee and the time-keeper went to their places and gave the signal to start, beating a small gong.

The two cocks, held by their owners, were brought to the middle of the arena, provoked against each other and released. The audience became tense, and the cocks attacked each other with such fury that the eye could not follow them; there were only flashes of the polished steel of the spurs in the cloud of flying feathers. Each round lasted only a few seconds; suddenly the two cocks stopped and stood motionless in front of each other, both streaming blood, until one staggered and fell dead, the winner crowing and still pecking furiously at the corpse.

It frequently happens that both cocks are wounded but the survivor is healed and often lives to fight many battles. A cock is disqualified if it runs away at the beginning; otherwise the fight is to death. When a cock is wounded but it is considered that it can go on fighting, its owner gives it strength to go on with special massages, blowing his own breath into its lungs; then it is not rare for a badly wounded cock to come out triumphantly over an apparent winner. Should both cocks refuse to fight, they are placed inside a basket, where one cannot avoid being killed. Hundreds of roosters are sacrificed in this manner in every village on the day before *nyepí*.

The Balinese cannot understand the attitude of the sentimental Dutch, who have forbidden cockfights. To them a rooster is as dead in the kitchen as after a cockfight; besides, cockfights are staged as a religious duty, as a sport that gives an opportunity for a little gambling and as a way to provide food for the next day. The dead roosters are taken home and cooked for the *nyepí* meal. After the cockfights, in Denpasar it is customary to give a banquet for the children of each *banjar*, a double row of beautifully decorated trays filled with sweets and cakes served to them by the *banjar* officials.

Before sunset the evil spirits had to be lured and concentrated at the great offering, the *mecaru*, then cast out by the powerful spells of the priests of the village. Facing towards *kangin*, the East of Denpasar, were tall altars filled with offerings: one for the Sun and for the Trinity (*sanggah agung*), one for the ancestors, and a third for the great *kalas*, the evil gods. In the center of the ground an elaborate conglomeration of objects was arranged: food of all sorts, every kind of strong drink, money and house utensils, hundreds of containers of banana leaf with a sample of every seed and fruit that grew on the island, and a piece of the flesh of every wild and domestic animal in Bali (a small piece of dried tiger flesh was pointed out); all arranged in the shape of an eight-pointed star representing the Rose of the Winds, the whole surrounded by a low fence of woven palm-leaf.

The colors of the four cardinal points were indicated by a sacrificed black goat for *kaja*, the North, a white goose for *kangin*, the East, a red dog for *klod*, the South, and a yellow calf for *kauh*, the West. Small pieces of black, white, red, and yellow cloth were placed over each of the animals to give further emphasis to their color. A chicken with feathers of five colors was placed in the center, next to a small

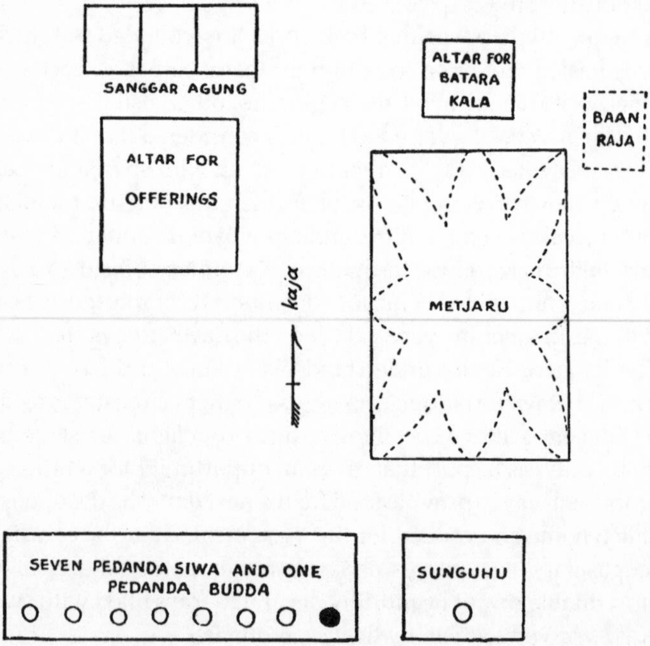

Arrangement of the stage for the *nyepí* festival

circular Rose of the Winds made of rice dyed in the eight different colors of the cardinal directions, with a center of mixed rice of the eight colors. The collection of all these ingredients had taken months and the majority were wilted and decomposing. On the ground at the right of the *mecaru* was spread a bit of rice flour in which an image of Batara Kala was drawn and consecrated by a priest, surrounded by a little bamboo fence to keep the dogs from walking over it.

Facing the offerings were the scaffolds for the priests. First a long shed in which eight *pedandas,* the Brahmanic high priests, sat in a row, wearing their red and gold mitres and with their elaborate paraphernalia of state, ready to pray and dedicate the offerings for the gods. On the end of the shed was a smaller, lower shed where sat the *sunguhu* (see page 282), the low-caste priest in charge of dedicating the offerings to the evil spirits, his specialty. These nine priests chanted powerful *mantras,* accompanied by swift gestures of the hands and fingers, and rang their bells alternately. There were seven *pedanda siwa,* one *pedanda budda,* and one *sunguhu*—a priest for each of the cardinal directions.

The demons were thus lured to the great offering and then expelled from the village by the curses of the priests. The Regent of Badung joined in the prayers with his entire family, kneeling in front of the Sun-altar and making reverences while the nine priests rang bells and chanted formulas. When they finished, "new fire" and holy water were given by the priests to the heads of each *banjar,* and the poor were allowed to loot the offerings for money and other useful objects. Firecrackers exploded in every direction and all the *kulkuls* in Denpasar were beaten furiously, the populace ran all over town in groups, often with their faces and bodies painted, carrying torches on the end of long poles, beating drums, gongs, tin cans or anything that made a noise, yelling at the top of their lungs: "*Megedí, megedí!* Get out! Get out!"—beating the trees and the ground, to scare away the unsuspecting *butas* who had assembled to partake of the offerings. From a dark corner came a deafening din that seemed produced by the frightened devils themselves, but our flashlight revealed a gang of naked children beating empty gasoline cans.

The noisy torch parades swept over town until they were exhausted, long after midnight.

The following day, *nyepí,* was supposed to be one of absolute stillness, a day when no fires, no sexual intercourse, and no work of any sort were permitted. There was no traffic on the roads and only by special permit and the payment of a heavy fine could the cars of foreigners drive through a town. In most Balinese villages the people were not even allowed out of their houses, especially in North Bali, where the *nyepí* regulations are strict. In Denpasar it was forbidden even to light a cigarette, but, people went out visiting as on a holiday. Curious tug-of-war games (*med-medan*) were organized there for the amusement of the young people; in *banjar* Kaliungú, men on one side, girls on the other, pulled a long rattan until one side defeated the other, but in *banjar* Sesétan a shouting crowd of boys stood facing a group of girls; the boys charged as in a football game and captured one girl, who then had to be rescued by her friends in a rough free-for-all. Everybody tugged and pulled and the poor prisoner, wild-eyed and with her hair loose, was so roughly handled in the desperate effort to free her that she fainted. But someone walked over to her and unceremoniously emptied a bucket of cold water on her head so she would revive and the game could proceed; when the girl was rescued the men captured another. Although the unique game is not played outside of the neighborhood of Denpasar and then only on *nyepí* day, the Balinese insisted it had no significance of any sort and that its object was purely play.

THE CALENDAR

The calendar that regulates the social and religious life of Bali is an intricate mechanism by which not only all communal and private festivals are established, but even the most ordinary actions of the Balinese are determined. No Balinese can hope for success in any undertaking unless it is performed on the exact auspicious day set aside on the calendar for the purpose; a wedding, a tooth-filing, a cremation, the occupation of a new house, take place only during special weeks dedicated to the affairs of human beings, while there are other similar weeks and days for activities concerning cattle, fowl, fish, trees, and bamboo (consecutive periods of seven days called *ingkel: wong, sato, mina, manuk, taru*, and *buku*).

The Balinese use two simultaneous systems of time-calculation: one, the *saka*,[1] the Hindu solar-lunar year, similar to ours in duration,

[1] For further information on the Balinese calendar, see Note 5, page 283.

twelve months, "moons," by which they observe the full (*purnama*) and the "dark" or new moons (*tilem*) important for agriculture, for *nyepí*, and for the festivals of the mountain people. The other, the *wuku* year, the so-called native or Javanese-Balinese year of 210 days, is not officially divided into months, but into weeks, ten of them running parallel and simultaneously, from a week of one day in which every day is called *luang*, a week of two days, one of three, of four, five, and so forth, up to a week of ten days. Each day of each of the ten weeks receives a special name, the combination of names determining the character of a date as a lucky or unlucky day. Thus every day theoretically receives ten different names, plus the month of the *saka* year and the "age" of the moon, according to whether it is crescent or waning; for instance, Sunday, the 4th of November of 1934, the beginning of the *wuku* year, was, according to them: *saka* year 1856, *wuku* of *sinta, ingkel wong* (good for humans), *redité, paing, paseh, tungleh, srí, srí, danggu*—only one endowed with the *saktí* and the knowledge of a high priest could keep track of such a tangle of names. Ordinary Balinese reckon simple dates, auspicious days for making offerings and for the principal feasts, by the combination of day-names of the seven-and five-day weeks, by which names everyday dates are recorded. The common people also observe the week of three days by which the village market day is established, held in rotation every day in one of the villages that work in groups of three.

Other date names are used mainly for magic and religious purposes, making of the calendar a science so complicated in itself that it is practiced mainly by specialists, generally the Brahmanic priests and witch-doctors, who, by the ownership of intricate charts (*tika*) with secret symbols painted on paper or carved in wood, and of palm-leaf manuscripts (*wariga*) by which the lucky or unlucky dates are located, make the people dependent on them for this purpose, because the Balinese are obliged to consult them for good dates for every special undertaking and have to pay for the consultation.

Galunggan. Nyepí is the acknowledged New Year feast of the solar-lunar year, but the Balinese celebrate another "new year" in the great holiday of *galunggan,* when the ancestral spirits come down to earth to dwell again in the homes of their descendants. The ancestors supposedly arrive five days before the day of *galunggan,* receive many offerings, and go back to heaven after ten days, five days before *kuninggan,* the feast of all souls.

Every home and all implements were provided with offerings for *galunggan,* the old utensils renewed and the baskets washed. On all the roads, at the gate of every home, tall *penyors* were erected, meant perhaps to be seen from the summits of the mountains where the gods dwell, together with a little bamboo altar from which hung a *lamak,* one of those beautiful mosaics on long strips of palm-leaf. For this occasion the *lamaks* were over thirty feet long and had to hang from the tops of the coconut trees.

Everybody wore new clothes and the whole of Bali went out for a great national picnic. Everywhere there were women with offerings on their heads and many old men dressed for the occasion in old-fashioned style, gold kris and all, although with an incongruous imported undershirt. The younger generation preferred to tear all over the island in open motor-cars, packed like sardines, dressed in fancy costumes, many young men in absurd versions of European clothes, the girls wearing their brightest silks and their best gold flowers in their hair. After visiting the village temple the gay groups went to the many feasts held on this and the following days all over the island. At this time the peculiar monsters called *barong*—a great fleece of long hair with a mask and gilt ornaments, animated by two men—were "loose" and free to go wherever they pleased. Everywhere on the road one met the cavorting holy *barongs,* who had become foolish for the day, dancing down the roads and paths, followed breathlessly by their orchestras and attendants.

In the temple of Gelgel, the former capital, there was a great feast where plays were given and violent "kris dances" were staged—when crazed men in a trance pretended to stab themselves and tore live chickens with their teeth to show their wickedness; but a more serene feast was celebrated in the jungle temple near the summit of the Batukau. There the mountain people brought offerings to the Batukau spirit while the Elders prepared the banquet in the spring underneath giant tree-ferns; performing afterwards a majestic *baris* dance, each dressed in black and white magic cloth, mimicking a stately battle with their long spears.

Ten days after *galunggan* came the day *kuninggan,* when new offerings and new *lamaks* were made and coconut husks were burned in front of every gate. This was the date of the temple feast of *Tirta Empul,* the sacred baths near Tampaksiring, and all morning peo-

The *tika*, key to the wuku calendar

The thirty weeks (*wuku*):

The seven-day week (*saptawara*):

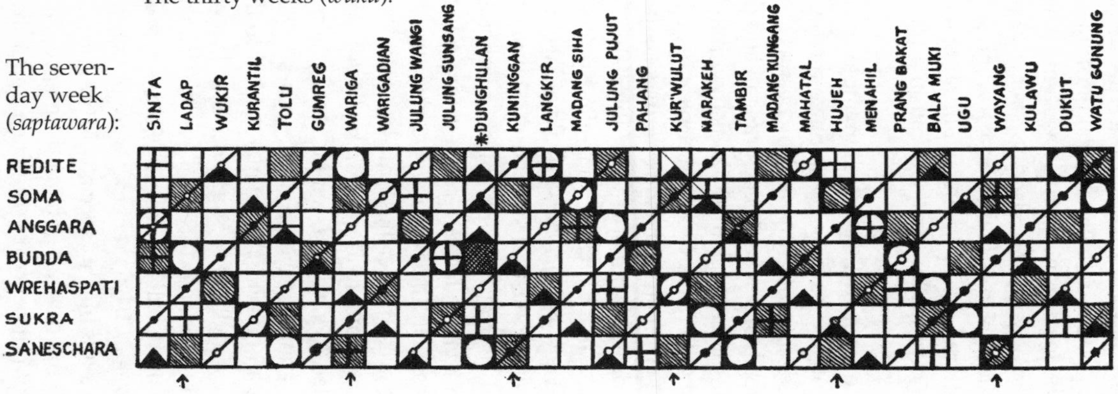

The day *klion*, most important of the five-day week (*pancaware*)

The day *kajeng* of the three-day week (*triwara*)

Also indicates the day *kejeng*, as well as the day *tungleh* of the six-day week (*sadwara*)

The day *guru* of the eight-day week (*astawara*)

The day *kala*, also of the eight-day week. This is repeated three times in the week of *dunggulan*, the three unlucky days before *galunggan* (*).

The day *danggu* of the nine-day week (*sangawara*)

Every time that the day *klion* falls on *kajeng* the day, *kajeng-klion*, is propitious for offerings, especially to evil spirits. This occurs every fifteen days.

When *klion* falls on *saneschara*, it is *tumpak*, an extremely lucky day. It occurs every thirty-five days (↑)

Other lucky days propitious for offerings are *anggara-kaseh*, when *klion* falls on *anggara*; and *budda-chemang*, when *budda* falls on *wagé*.

ple bathed unashamed in the purifying waters, men on one side, women on the other, after leaving an offering for the deity of the spring. They turned their backs on the crowd, unconcerned under the spouts, each of which is supposed to have a special purifying or curative quality. Eventually the local prince arrived with his wives and with an impressive retinue of servants. Also the *barongs* of the district came prancing down the hills to offer their respects and snap their jaws while a *pemangku* offered their prayers, manifesting their temperaments by making the men under the fleece fall in a trance and throw epileptic fits.

The following day was the feast of *Sakenan*, the temple of the little island of Serangan, just off the Badung coast. Since the night before, the island was jammed with pilgrims and orchestras, and the next morning the short stretch of sea between Serangan and the mainland was filled with fantastic boats shaped like fish with their triangular sails up, overloaded with richly dressed people. On arrival they waded to the temple, the women balancing offerings on their heads while lifting their brocade skirts out of reach of the water.

One boat brought the holy *barong landong*, four giant puppets who performed in the temple. They were *Jerolúh*, a ribald old woman with a protuberant forehead, enormously distended ear-lobes, and deep wrinkles outlined in gold all over her white mask; a lecherous black monster with prominent teeth called *Jerogedé*; a young prince, *Manrí*, and his beautiful princess, *Cilí Towong Kuning*, richly dressed in green and gold, who wore great flower head-dresses over their yellow masks. Normal-size attendants held gold umbrellas of state over the giants as they waddled towards the temple in ceremonial procession with music and a retinue of men bearing spears tipped with red fur. After dedicating an offering, the giants danced to the accompaniment of gongs, flutes, and drums; the old rascal *Jerogedé* talked and laughed in a deep thunderous voice, while *Jerolúh* leaped, hooped, and yelled in a shrill falsetto, all behaving in a manner quite undignified for their holy character. Their remarks were of the sort that made my polite Balinese friends blush, especially in the episodes when the prince made love to the princess. The performance over, the men that animated the giant puppets came out from under their skirts, leaving the lifeless forms to rest in a corner of the temple.

The crowds returned home in the late afternoon, this time on foot, because the tide had gone out, leaving solid ground where before only the white boats could pass. There was a long line of happy people in the orange light of the sunset, walking on the mud among thousands of strange vermilion crabs that peered out of their holes, constantly waving a mysterious single purple claw.

When a Balinese speaks of his gods, collectively called *dewas*, he does not mean the great divinities of Hinduism, but refers to an endless variety of protective spirits—*sanghyang, pitara kawitan*, all of whom are in some way connected with the idea of ancestry. The rather vague term *dewa* includes not only the immediate ancestors worshipped in the family temple, or the nameless forefathers, founders of his community, to whom the village temples are dedicated, but also certain Hindu characters of his liking whom he has adopted into the Balinese race and has come to regard also as his ancestors. Rama, for instance, the hero of the *Ramayana*, is Wisnu reincarnated into a brave prince who came to earth to save the world. In a later crisis the god once more took human form and came to Bali to put things in order (as Gajah Mada, according to Friederich), becoming the ancestor of the present Balinese. From the cult of deified dead kings the nobility has accepted the idea of their divine ancestry so naturally as to assure one in all earnest from which god they trace their descent. This notion has extended to the people and I have heard even the Bali Aga Elders of Kintamani invoke Batara Rama as "grandfather" (*kaki*).

The ancestors, being closest to the people, have remained the first gods, and their cult formed the link between this earth and the spirit world. The introduction of great ceremonies for cremation of the dead was easily correlated to this idea because the purpose of it was to consecrate the soul of a deceased family-head in order to release and convey the soul to the heaven where it will dwell as a family god, a *dewa yang* (see Note 6, page 286), when it receives a place in the family shrine.

The deities of the Hindu pantheon are mostly those worshipped in India, the high "Lords"—*batara*—but in Bali they acquire a decidedly Balinese personality. Centuries of religious penetration did not convince the Balinese that the *bataras* were their gods; they were too aloof, too aristocratic, to be concerned with human insignificance, and the people continue to appeal to their infinitely more accessible local *dewas* to give them happiness and prosperity.

The *bataras* remained remote in the popular mind, regarded

rather as deified foreign lords like their princes, and as far as the Balinese are concerned, their functions ended when they created the world with all that it contains. The *bataras* appear in Balinese literature with such human characteristics and are so susceptible to the passions of ordinary mortals that they become merely mythological figures losing their esoteric significance. Typical is the amusing episode in the *Catur Yoga* in which Batara Gurú, the Supreme Teacher, quarrelled with Batara Brahma for the privilege of making men:

"After Siwa had created the insects, Wisnu the trees, Isora the fruits, and Sambu the flowers, Batara Gurú discussed with Brahma the creation of human beings to populate the new world. Brahma admitted he did not know how and asked Batara Gurú to try first. The latter then made four figures, four men out of red earth, and went into meditation so that they could talk, think, walk, and work. Brahma remarked that if those were human beings, then he could make men, and taking some clay, he proceeded to make a figure that resembled a man. Batara Gurú was annoyed and made the rain, which lasted for three days, destroying the figure Brahma had made. When the rain stopped, Brahma tried again, this time baking the figure. On seeing the man of baked clay, Batara Gurú boasted he would eat excrement if Brahma could give it life, but Brahma succeeded in making it alive by meditation and demanded that Batara Gurú make good his boast. Enraged, Batara Gurú took some clay and made images of dogs that became living dogs, and wished that forever after they should walk, whine, bark, and eat excrement."

SIWA

An average Balinese knows, however vaguely, the names of countless *bataras*. He is well aware, for instance, that Batara Brahma is the god of fire, that Surya is the Sun, Indra the Lord of Heaven, and Yama that of Hell, Durga the goddess of death, Semara the god of physical love, and so forth (see Note 7, page 286); but unless he has had a certain amount of theological education, to him the Batara Siwa is simply another of the remote high gods, although the highest in rank; a sort of Raja among the *bataras*.

However, to the learned Brahmanic priests Siwa represents the abstract idea of divinity that permeates everything—the total of the forces we call God. Siwa is the source of all life, the synthesis of the creative and generative powers in nature; consequently in him are the two sexes in one—the Divine Hermaphrodite (*Windú*), symbol of completion, the ultimate perfection. As male Siwa is the mountain, the Gunung Agung, the Lingga, Pasupati, the father of all humanity, all phallic symbols. He is also the Sun, the Space, and as Batara Gurú, the Supreme Teacher, he is the maker of the world. As female he is Uma, mother of all nature, Giri Putri, goddess of the mountains, Dewi Gangga and Dewi Danú, deities of rivers and lakes. These, his feminine manifestations (*saktí*), are taken by the common people as his literal wives, but the learned interpret these wives, and his connubial relations with them, as the two eternal principles: male and female, spirit and matter, united for the constant production and reproduction of the universe, the exaltation of the union of the sexes for procreation.

The well-known Indian trinity, the supreme gods Brahma, Vishnu, and Siva, are in Bali expressions of the one force called Siwa, but there is also a trinity in Bali: Brahma Siwa (Brahma), Sada Siwa (Wisnú), and Prama Siwa (Iswara). In the mind of the common people even this trinity becomes, with typical Balinese miscomprehension, a deity in itself called Sanghyang Trimurti or Sanggah Tiga Saktí, "the Shrine of the Three Forces."

Thus Siwa "is fire (Brahma) who through smoke (vapor) becomes water (Wisnú)," which in turn fertilizes the earth (Pertiwi) to produce rice (Srí). Ideas such as this, juggled cleverly by the high priests, repeat themselves in endless sequence to form the intricate Brahmanic philosophy. All the gods that overcrowd the Balinese pantheon are thus manifestations of Siwa, but they are not always on the side of righteousness, because the good creative and reproductive forces can be polluted and turn into evil and acquire a destroying, angry form. Thus the reversed form of Siwa is Kala, Lord of Darkness, born out of Siwa to destroy the world, just as Siwa's wife Uma became Durga, goddess of death, completing the cycle from life to death. In the Balinese manuscript *Usana Jawa* we find the story of the birth of Batara Kala:

Siwa had created creatures with no ethics and without a code of morals, who went naked, lived in caves, and had no religion. They mated under the trees, left their children uncared for, and ate whatever they found, living like beasts. This made Siwa so angry that he decided to create a son to destroy the unworthy human beings and told his wife Uma of his intentions while mating with her. She withdrew indignant and in the struggle Siwa's sperm fell on the ground. He then called the gods together and told them, pointing to the sperm, that should it develop life the result would bring them into great difficulties. The alarmed gods began to shoot arrows at it; the sperm grew a pair of shoulders when the first arrow struck it, hands and feet sprang out after the second, and as they continued to shoot arrows into it, the drop of sperm grew into a fearful giant who stood as high as a mountain, demanding food with which to calm his insatiable hunger. Siwa called him Kala and sent him down to earth, where every day he could eat his fill of people, and the human race rapidly dwindled away. Wisnu, alarmed, called upon Indra for help to save mankind, and it was decided to civilize them by sending several of the gods to teach them the law of life, agriculture, and the arts and to provide them with the necessary tools.

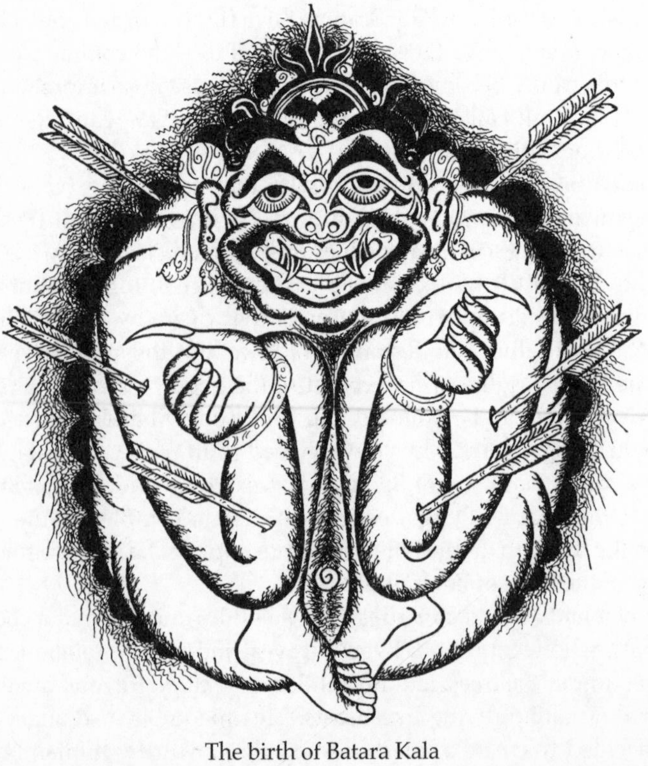

The birth of Batara Kala

THE HIGH PRIESTS AND THE BRAHMANIC RITUAL

The ultimate stage of perfection in the evolution of man on this earth, from the Balinese point of view, is to reach the Brahmana caste and to be ordained as a *pedanda*,[2] a high priest: from simple human being, to warrior, statesman, scholar, priest, and after death a god. Simply having reached this position, the highest during life in the long and arduous scale of evolution, endows *pedandas* with a magic character and justifies —in their own eyes at least—their superiority over all living men.

Thus the high priests are, to the Balinese, extraordinary beings who, by their caste, knowledge, systematic preparation, and old age, are immune in handling the dangerous secret formulas of the higher ritual. An ordinary person, unprepared and not possessing the capacity to store the necessary surcharge of magic energy, would be destroyed, blown out like a weak fuse under a high charge of electricity, should he attempt to use this magic to control the unseen forces. With the proper training, however, people of all castes may become priests; a common man can study to become a witch-doctor, for *pemangku* or for *sunguhu*, and a mystic prince with a vocation may become a *resí*, but only a Brahmana can be an authentic *pedanda*. Although the low-caste priests control the ordinary temple and community ritual, have direct dealings with the ancestors, and are able to intimidate demons with formulas of their own, they are restricted to officiating for people within or below their caste, while the Brahmanic priests serve all those who can afford their fees.

The *pedandas* still exert a powerful influence on Balinese life despite the fact that their relations with the people were never intimate; they represent the law, and the judges of the high native courts (*raadkerta*) are still *pedandas* in the majority. They purify persons or dwellings, bless people after illness or accident, and can avert curses or spells. On account of their knowledge of the calendar they must be consulted every time it is necessary to determine the exact lucky or unlucky date on which to begin or to which to postpone a significant undertaking. Mountain people ignore them entirely, but they are essential to all ceremonies of the nobility, and even the poorest commoner will make great sacrifices to be able to call a *pedanda* to of-

[2] The Word *pedanda* comes, according to Friederich, from *danda*, "a staff"—"staff-bearer," the law. The Balinese call high priests also *pandita* or *penita*, "the Learned."

ficiate at his private affairs, particularly at cremations, to assure his dead ones of the correct send-off into the nether world. To use the services of a *pedanda* is a luxury that brings social prestige.

A *pedanda's* life is strictly regimented and full of prohibitions. We visited occasionally the good-natured, sociable *pedanda* of Sidan, who often remarked with a deep sigh of regret that the life of a priest was a difficult one because he had always to think of the gods. At lunch in his house, when he had a goose "cut" in our honor, he condescended to eat with us, but had to sit at a higher level, "otherwise the gods would not like it." With a grand disdainful gesture he threw a few grains of rice at the hungry dogs that surrounded us, explaining that he had to share his food with these evil spirits in disguise; then he proceeded to enumerate the many taboos he had to observe when eating: he could not sit at a public eating-place or eat in the market; he ate facing east and not until he had made his morning prayers. Beef, pork, and food from offerings were forbidden to him and he could not touch alcohol. Under no circumstances could he walk under dirty water. He was fat and old and he loved to ride in motor-cars, but since so many drain-pipes have been built recently at high points over the roads to connect the rice fields, he encountered great difficulties when traveling by motor-car. Every time he came to a pipe the car stopped. He stepped out and climbed to the top with great effort, to come down panting on the other side.

A *pedanda* marries, generally only once, a woman of his own caste, who becomes automatically a priestess (*pedanda istrí*), who must help her husband in the ritual and who may herself officiate on certain occasions. High priests do not observe sexual abstinence, although it is recommended in the scriptures. Ancestry is one of their great concerns, and the standing of the various Brahmanic families is determined by their purity of lineage. Balinese Brahmanas all claim descent from the mythical Wau Raúh, the highest priest of Majapahit, who in coming to Bali took wives from the various castes. His descendants established themselves at various places in Bali and founded the Brahmanic clans we find today, from the purer *Kamenúh*, to the *Keniten, Gelgel, Nuaba, Mas, Kayusunia, Andapan*, and so forth.

Pedandas should dedicate their entire life to meditation, the study of theology, and the practice of the ritual. During life they are supposed to be models of knowledge, purity of thought and of actions, but unfortunately this is not always the case and, as everywhere else, there are priests who take advantage of their position and by their mysterious hocus-pocus exploit the people. In Bali, however, this occurs on a considerably smaller scale than in countries dominated by an organized clergy. The Brahmanas jealously keep the inner knowledge of the official religion for themselves and the common people believe in them, but continue to regard them, like their princes, as foreigners aloof from the true life of Bali.

The Brahmanic priesthood is today divided into two great groups: the Siwaites (*siwa* or *siwa sidanta*), and the so-called Buddhists (*bodda*); not true followers of Siwa and of the Buddha, but simply sectarian divisions of the same religion (see page 287). The *pedanda siwa* wears his hair long, tied in a knot on the top of his head, while the *pedanda bodda* has his cut shoulder-length; otherwise their office and ritual are the same with only small differences in detail, in phraseology, and in the texts used by each. To the average Balinese this division means so little that he will call a priest of either sect to officiate for him regardless of whether he is *siwa* or *bodda*, simply because of personal preference or family tradition or because the priest's house may be nearer. To him two priests of two sects are undoubtedly more effective than one, but this is an expensive luxury that only the princes can afford. The present Regent of Gianyar always engaged both a *pedanda siwa* and a *pedanda bodda*, who sat side by side. He went even further and had also a Satria priest, a *resí*, and a *sunguhu* to take care of the evil spirits, so that every sort of priest was represented. In Badung I have seen ceremonies with nine priests officiating, one for each of the cardinal points.

From India the Brahmanic priests inherited a good portion of the sacred Sanskrit writings of the Hindus, such as portions of the *Vedas*, called in Bali *Weda*, containing the most powerful secret formulas for the private use of the priests; the *Brahmanda-Purana*, a treatise on cosmogony, mythology, and mythic chronology; and the *Tuturs*, the doctrinal writings of the *pedandas*. In this manner the priests preserved the knowledge of Sanskrit, the really sacred language of Bali, which is, however, only known by the name of *sloka*, the meter in which Sanskrit works are written. The learning of Sanskrit is kept a secret among the priests and should not be confused with the Kawi, which is only the classic language of poetry, well known to the nobility and to scholars in general.

From the scriptures the priests obtained the all-powerful *mantras*, formulas of magic words recited, or rather mumbled inwardly, accompanied by special gestures to give added emphasis to this abracadabra. *Mantras* consist of litanies of praise, each phrase preceded by mysterious sounds, syllables that are repeated in rhythmic se-

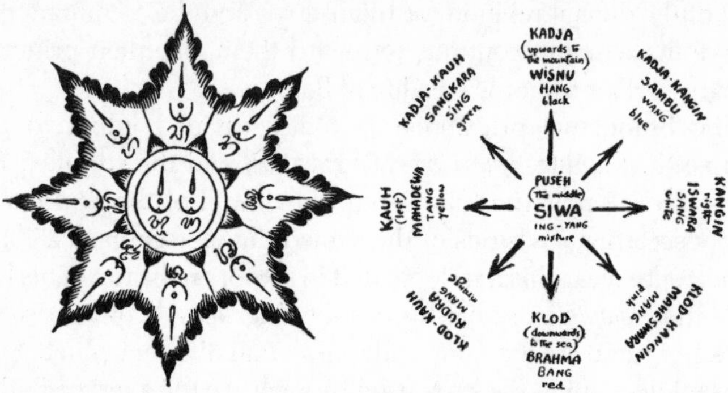

The Rose of the Winds, the *nawa sangga*, with the cardinal directions, their patron Gods, their corresponding syllables, and the color of each

quence and that perhaps produce the ecstasy by which the priests commune with the gods. There are ten of these magic syllables (*adasa aksara*), the proper use of which is kept a strict secret, because "they can become extremely dangerous in the hands of the ignorant." They form an integral part of the *nawa sangga*, the ever present Rose of the Winds, together with the gods, patrons of each direction, and the color of each point of the compass.

The synthesis of this is contained in the Word of Words of the Yogis: *Om*, pronounced in Bali *ong*, consisting of the sounds ah—*u*—*m*, or, as the Balinese say, *ang, ung, mang*, and again *sada siwa, prama siwa*, and *maha siwa*, or, further still, Brahma, Wisnu, Iswara, the eternal Trinity manifested throughout the universe: heaven, earth, and underworld; fire, water, and wind; male, female, and hermaphrodite. The symbol for this sound, called *ongkara:*

is composed of an upright dash (*nada*), a *lingga* or phallus; a crescent moon (*arda candra*), symbolic of the female creative organ; and the circle (*windú or wandú*), symbol of completion—the hermaphrodite—thus the word *ong* is Siwa.

Typical of the Balinese attitude on secret religious science are the endless juggling and speculations of Brahmanas with these symbols. The *ongkara* is used in countless ways in personal magic as an amulet and in practically all accessories of the ritual; for instance, two *ongkaras* facing or turned away from each other:

ongkara madú muka

ongkara pasha

Like a living being, the *ongkara* has a crown (the upright dash), a forehead (the circle), eyes (the half-moon), besides a mouth, trunk, stomach, and legs—the various sections of the lower character.

The magic formulas are the essential part of the religious service of the high priests, the often mentioned *maweda,* through which the *pedandas* make the "pure" holy water (*tirta*) used in such profusion in the ritual that the Balinese have come to call their religion *agama tirta,* the "science of the holy water." The making of this holy water is the principal function and main source of income of the *pedandas,* who sell it to the people, often for exorbitant prices.

There are various kinds of holy waters in varying degrees of power depending on the standing of the priest who makes it, the ritual undergone, the formulas used for its consecration, and, of course, the price paid for it. Simple *yeh ning,* clean water, can be procured from a holy spring such as the one high up on the slopes of the Gunung Agung or near the crater lakes, or can be made by a low-caste priest by placing flowers of three colors in ordinary water and reciting a mild prayer over it. Water from a "yellow" coconut (*nyoh gading*) may be used in an emergency, but all these are poor substitutes for the real thing, the *tirta* made by a Brahmanic priest through the complete performance of the *maweda,* the religious service. Thus *tirta pelukatan,* the water that has the power of curing almost any sort of spiritual impurity, is sanctified by the embodiment of the gods in it, through the person of the high priest, and is the water essential to important ceremonies. Humans may procure a more expensive and considerably more powerful *tirta:* the *toya pangentas,* in which only the holiest formulas are employed and which contains ingredients such as rice dyed yellow, powdered sandalwood, inscriptions (*pripih*) on thin plaques of gold, a ring set with a jewel, and even powdered rubies.

There is still another holy water of limited power that gives immortality, the *toya amreta* or *amerta,* which is, however, reserved exclusively for the gods. In relation to this elixir of immortality there is

An eclipse—Kala Rahu swallowing the moon

a legend that gives the cause of eclipses: "The demon Kala Rahu came once, out of curiosity, to take a peek at heaven; there he saw a vessel of *amreta* and, thinking himself unobserved, stole it and tried to drink from it. But Wisnu saw him and with a single blow cut off the demon's head. Kala Rahu had taken one drink in his mouth, but did not have time to swallow it, so his body died, but his head continued to live, and now, as revenge, he swallows the sun and the moon, producing the eclipses. Thus when an eclipse occurs, the Balinese are frightened and they all go out of their houses to make all the noise possible, beating *kulkuls,* tin cans, drums, and gongs, to frighten away the bodyless head of Kala Rahu and free the threatened sun or moon.

The religious service of the *pedandas,* the *maweda,* consists in the recitation of the *mantras,* the magic formulas, accompanied by ritual actions and significant gestures of the hands and fingers (*mudra*) to give a physical emphasis to the spoken word. Through concentration culminating in a trance, the priest becomes the deity itself, entering the body of the priest and acting through it to consecrate the water and emanate divine vibrations.

A performance of *maweda* by an able priest is one of the most beautiful sights in Bali. Such finished training, such showmanship, enters into its execution, and the hand gestures of the priest are so thoroughly imbued with rhythm and beauty, that the *maweda* is more than a simple prayer; it is a whole spectacle, a pantomimic dance of the hands. I have once seen a revealing film of a Nepalese Buddhist priest dancing with his entire body while he recited Sanskrit *mantras* and performed the symbolical hand gestures, and I have wondered if this was not the origin of the great art of Balinese dancing. Volumes have been written on the hand expression of the Hindus; *The Mirror* of *Gesture* of Comaraswami is already a classic; the beautiful hands of Indian, Tibetan, Chinese, and Indonesian Buddhist statues and frescoes are well known, and in Java we find the statues of the Buddhas of Borobudur in the positions of the *mudras*. De Kat Angelino in his *Mudras* gives us the most thorough study up to date of the Balinese *maweda*, painstakingly illustrated by Tyra de Kleen. Only a moving picture, however, could give an idea of its eerie beauty.

The most important activity in the everyday life of the *pedandas* is the performance of a domestic *maweda*, done every morning and on an empty stomach. Every fifth day (*klion*) and on days of full and new moons, the *maweda* is essential and more complete, with the full regalia of important occasions. The priest has first to purify himself thoroughly by reciting cleansing *mantras* for each action of his morning toilet. He washes his hair, rinses his mouth, polishes his teeth, and rinses his mouth again; washes his face, bathes, rubs his hair with oil, combs it, and then dresses. For each move he has to recite a short *mantra*, one for each garment he wears.

Meantime on a high platform his wife has arranged his paraphernalia (*upakara*): trays with flowers (night-blooming flowers if the ceremony is to take place at night), gold or silver vessels containing grains of rice and sandalwood powder, his holy-water container (*siwamba*) with a silver sprinkler (*sesirat*) and a long-handled ladle (*canting*), his prayer bell (*gantha*), an incense burner (*pasepan*), and a bronze oil lamp (*pedamaran*). Put away in baskets at one side of where the priest will sit are the attributes of Siwa he will wear during the ceremony: the *bawa*, a bell-shaped mitre of red felt with applications of beaten gold and topped by a crystal ball, the "shimmer of the sun" (*suryakanta*), and a number of strings of *genitri* seeds (ear-rings, bracelets, neck and breast beads) ornamented with pieces of gold set with *linggas* of crystal, phallic symbols.[3]

Once seated cross-legged among the *upakara*, the priest proceeds to purify his person; he lays a prayer cloth over his lap and with his hands on his knees he mumbles a formula and asks of Batara Siwa to descend into the water-vessel and into his body. He stretches his hands over the incense smoke, uncovers the tray in front of him, and mumbles the *mantra asta mantra*, the hand-cleansing formula, rubs the palms of his hands with a flower and sandalwood powder, "wiping out impurity," and recites a formula for each finger as it is passed over the palm of each hand, taking flowers which he holds over the incense smoke and then flinging them away saying: "Be happy, be perfect, be glad in your heart."

To induce trance, the priest uses *pranayama*, breath control, closing each nostril alternately with a finger, breathing deeply, and holding his breath as long as possible, then exhaling through the other nostril. With a blade of grass he inscribes the sacred *ong* in the holy water, prays again with a flower which he drops into the water-container, then takes his bell in the left hand and strikes the clapper three times with another flower held in his right hand. Now his breath, his voice, and his spirit (*idep*) are in unison with the deity.

The priest proceeds, mumbling his guttural prayers, ringing the bell alternately with swift, intricate gestures of the hands and fingers, taking flowers at intervals, dropping them into the holy water or holding them over the lamp and the incense, and flinging them away. He rings the bell louder and quicker and stops suddenly.

During these preliminaries he gives signs of the oncoming trance; he gasps, his eyes roll back, and his movements take on a tense, unearthly air. Now the deity is within him and he sprinkles holy water and flings flowers, not away, but towards himself. He touches his forehead, throat, and shoulders with sandalwood powder and puts

[3] These are the attributes of the *pedanda siwa*; the *pedanda bodda's* holy water vessel is called *pamandiyanga*, and in place of flowers for praying he uses a "thunderbolt," a *bajra* of bronze identical with those used by the Tibetan lamas and the priests of the Shingon Buddhist sect of Japan. He has a sort of banner on a stand made of bronze which is turned successively to the four winds during the course of the ceremony. The *pedanda bodda* wears his hair loose and remains throughout the service with his head uncovered.

on the attributes of Siwa: he ties a long blade of *alang alang* grass around his head, wears the beads over his ears, across his breast, and on his wrists, and places his red and gold mitre on his head. He mumbles inwardly his most sacred prayers and, with apparent physical effort, he leads his soul from his "lower body" into his head, holding a rosary of *genitri* seeds and raising his hands slowly upwards. This brings him into the complete trance; he trembles all over and, rolling his eyes in ecstasy, he pronounces the prayers "for the world" in a deep, strangely changed voice. Thus the water in the container becomes *toya pelukatan*, Siwa's water.

Such is the power of concentration of the *pedandas* during these trances that once, at the preliminary ceremonies for the cremation of the Regent of Buleleng's daughter, a small pavilion caught fire near where the high priest performed the *maweda*, almost burning, prematurely, the corpse lying in state; the priest went on with his prayer totally unmindful of the wild screams of the women attendants and the rushing relatives, who extinguished the flames.

To become himself again, the priest sprinkles water towards him and "drives back his soul into the stomach." He takes off his ornaments and pins a little bouquet of multi-colored flowers over his hair knot. This ends the ceremony, and he sprinkles his relatives and neighbors with the remaining holy water.

Despite the secrecy with which the priests surround the knowledge of the Sanskrit *mantras*, a good many of them have been studied and translated by Dutch and Javanese scholars, such as De Kat Angelino, R. Ng. Poerbatjaraka, and Dr. R. Goris, and I refer those interested in *mantras* to their works. Most sacred of all the aphorisms of the *pedandas*, and as typical as any, is the *kuta mantra:* "OM, HRAM HRUMSAH, PARAMA-SHÎVA-DITYÂTANAMAH: Om, hram hrumsah, praise be to the all-high Shiva, the Sun" (Goris).

Religious knowledge is transmitted from father to son or from teacher (*gurú*) to pupil (*sisiya*). The priest then becomes his pupil's absolute master and his father; even in case there be no blood relationship between them, marriage with the teacher's daughter would be considered as incest, a most dreadful crime. All Brahmanas are eligible to become *pedandas* with the exception of lepers, madmen, epileptics, the deformed, and those who have received dishonorable punishments. The pupil learns Kawi first, the classic language, to study the preparatory texts; is taught the moral principles by which to rule his life, which are, according to De Kat Angelino, the capital sins: crime, greed, hypocrisy, envy and ill temper, morbidness; the five commandments for the outer world: Thou shalt not kill, not steal, be chaste, not be violent, adhere to the principle of passive resistance; and those for the inner self: avoid impure foods, or anger, remain conscious of the teachings, and be in unison with the teacher.

Later on, he studies Sanskrit (*sloka*) and learns the Wedas. Eventually he is initiated by his teacher in a most elaborate ceremony, which I know only by hearsay, in which the teacher leads the hands of his pupil with his own hands to perform his first *maweda*. The pupil makes repeated reverences (*sembah*) to his teacher and to the sun, washes and kisses his teacher's feet, and receives his priestly credentials, a secret document containing powerful formulas written on a blade of *lontar* palm. I have been told that the pupil "dies" symbolically during the ceremony and is reborn as a priest, and that his body is then washed and treated exactly like a corpse.

As conclusion, we find that the amazing conglomerate of traditions, beliefs, and philosophies that together constitute the Balinese religion, one that is as complex and tangled as can be found anywhere today, alone is the most powerful motivating force to the entire life of the island. Our knowledge of Bali is as young as the history of its contacts with the West, and a good deal will have to be unraveled before we can have a clear picture of that unique product of tropical Asia, the character of the Balinese, which is reflected in the fantastic interpretation of religious ideas from India, China, and Java. These were at times assimilated with a sense of practical logic, at times obviously misunderstood; but the result was a healthy and thoroughly Balinese manner of belief. Despite Hinduistic deviations, religious symbols and ideas retained much of their original, primitive simplicity, and fanaticism and idolatry did not overshadow the ancient animist worship of nature and of the elements.

Whatever the source of these ideas may be, the Balinese worship the sun, the earth, and water as sources of life-giving fertility; fire is a purifying element. The sea receives offerings once a year in a great feast in Lebih on the Gianyar coast. Also sources of fertility, and the dwellings of the gods, are the mountains, which are venerated in every temple and private shrine. The highest mountain, the Gunung Agung, is the navel, the focal point of their world. A cult in itself has developed around the planting, growing, and harvesting of rice; old banyan trees are seen with respect, and many contain a little altar among the maze of their aerial roots where passing people leave offerings. Once a year all food vegetation, and coconut trees in particular, have a feast in their honor; they are given offerings and each tree is "dressed up" with a gay skirt and a scarf. We have seen that wood for house posts must be erected in "correct" position, the way the tree grew and not "upside down." Not everyone can cut down a tree; specialists are called because they know the formulas and the magic to be performed after a tree is felled (placing a small green bough in the stump) to prevent the tree spirit from taking revenge, making the cutter lose his hair or be reincarnated in a prematurely bald-headed person. It would be dangerous for a person who is *sebel* (spiritually unclean) to climb trees. Everywhere there are temples dedicated to the nameless spirits of the mountains, of the sea, of old caves, ancient trees, lakes, springs, and even shapeless stones and other inanimate objects.

Although invisible and elusive, the gods of the Balinese are not unlike living human beings; they can be invited to dwell on this earth, to visit the temples and homes, when they are received as honored guests with music, banquet food, and entertainment. They are not opposed to coming in contact with ordinary mortals, and to help them they often take part themselves in the ceremonies. But the gods are worshipped only in spirit and nowhere are their images or representations considered as holy in themselves unless it is supposed they are temporarily occupying them. By contrast, they have to tolerate and pacify evil spirits, who are as unavoidable as illness and trouble, but whom they treat with contempt. These evil forces at times pollute and disturb everything: people, temples, houses, the whole organism of the island in general, are subject to critical moments, becoming weakened and unclean, and it is the office of their priests to cure this condition by neutralizing the evil forces, cleansing and strengthening the village or the individual thus defiled by spiritual sickness.

Thus, Balinese religion remains a colorful animist cult in which are interwoven the esoteric principles and philosophy of Hinduism, but this condition is by no means limited to Bali; Javanese Hinduism was of this sort, and even in India we find a parallel in the simultaneous worship of primitive demons, ancestors, and elements, belonging to the Dravidian lower classes, intermingled with the Brahmanic philosophy. To the Indian masses as with the Balinese, Siva and Vishnu may be dignified gods of a higher rank than the more accessible local deities, who remain, however, closer to the common people, perhaps because, like themselves, they are of a lower caste.

For the purpose of a general insight into the mechanics of Balinese religion we have prepared the following chart:

LEFT (*KIWA*) Evil, negative forces	RIGHT (*TENGEN*) Good, positive forces
The forces of the left produce the state of magic uncleanliness, weakening the soul power. A dangerous vibration called SEBEL in human beings makes unholy (TENGET OR ANGKER)—that is, charged with dangerous vibrations—the places they frequent.	As opposed to the state of SEBEL, the forces of the right produce the spiritual and physical health, cleanliness(ENING,SUCI,NIRMALA), that can be developed by acquisition of magic power (SAKTI, WISESA) to resist the evil forces.
DEMONS:	GODS:
KALAS and BUTAS, producers of impurity and ill health, living in the low, unholy grounds like the sea, the beaches, the forests, and the crossroads. Symbols of malice, coarseness, failure, misfortune, sickness, and destruction. Exorcized with offerings of purification and blood sacrifices (MECARU) made when the community or the individual is SEBEL or vulnerable to their attacks, owing to weakening causes such as death of relatives, birth of twins, incest, menstruation, etc. Accumulation of evil forces requires the periodical purifica-	BATARAS and SANGHYANG, but primarily the ancestral spirits (PITARA), sources of life and magic power, dwelling on mountain tops, at the origin of the rivers and lakes. Ancestral gods, mountain gods, gods of fertility, of the earth, of water, the sun, male and female gods, symbols of righteousness, beauty, good harvests—in general, of prosperity and health. Harmony with the gods is achieved by propitiation through the "clean" (SUCI) or "pure" (SUKLA) offerings and the proper rituals, observance of the traditional

tion of the land, the village, or the individual.

village law (ADAT), of the relation of man with the cardinal directions: high and low, right and left; furthermore, by the use of water and fire for purification, together with magic formulas.

The sharp division between the forces of the right and left, clean and unclean, weak and strong, high and low, day and night, sickness and medicine, the sun and the moon, in total, LIFE and DEATH, male and female, become reunited into a supreme force: The Hermaphrodite (WINDU), that which contains the male and female creative elements:

SIWA

ADDITIONAL NOTES

1. *Balinese Temples.* Perhaps the aboriginal form of Balinese temple was a square of consecrated ground in which were erected sacrificial altars, piles of stones, surrounded by a rough stone fence. Temples of this sort are still to be found in Tenganan and Sembiran, two villages that preserve much of the ancient religion. There are temples along the coast in the vicinity of Sanur reminiscent of these primitive temples, like the one on the beach of Sindú that consists of rough pieces of coral in shapeless piles, with a number of primitive statues as the sole decoration. The owners afterwards added shrines of dressed stone; then lately, to be modern, they built altars of cement, resulting in what looks like an object lesson in the progress and evolution of Balinese temple architecture.

There is a strong Polynesian flavor in these primitive temples. Ralph Linton (*Ethnology of Polynesia and Micronesia,* The Field Museum, Chicago) says: "In the Cook groups the temples were usually stone enclosures or platforms often without houses. . . . In the Society group . . . they were low walled enclosures with a platform or pyramid at one end. . . . In the Marquesas there were two sorts of temples, the public ones . . . and the mortuary stone platforms which bore houses . . . that had excessively high roofs so that the early writers often refer to them as obelisks. In Hawaii . . . the most important temples were stone walled enclosures containing a number of houses for the priests and images. . . . None of the images or objects symbolizing the gods seem to have been considered divine in themselves. They were simple bodies which the gods could occupy at will." These striking similarities between the Balinese and Polynesian religious spirits extend into the cult, into the social organization, and even into the physical type of the Balinese.

The Bali Aga, who were never subjected to the political and religious influence of the Javanese lords, build great austere temples with peculiar features such as the little bridge (*tití gonggang*), a stone placed over a hole directly in front of the temple gate, over which can pass only the "pure"—the gods and the virgin boys and girls of the village. Interesting also are the divisions of the Bali Aga communities: first into two great groups, right and left, each with its priests; then into four separate groups that meet in representative halls built in the temple: the married men who sit in council at the *balé agung;* the married women who sit in the *balé loh;* and the adolescent boys and girls with their special clubhouses, the *balé truna* and the *balé daha.* In Bali Aga villages the *balé agung* is still the heart of the political and religious life of the community and great *balé agungs* can always be seen in the first courtyard of their temples. Most striking examples of such temples are in Taro in the Gianyar mountains, where the largest and the most beautiful *balé agung* in Bali is to be found, and in Trunyan on the shores of Lake Batur.

North Balinese temples depart considerably from the normal structure of the Southern temples already described. They are built on the slope of a hill with the temple proper placed on the highest part in a curious ascendant tendency, culminating in high monuments of carved stone reached by successive flights of stairs.

Typical is the *Pura Medrwé Karang*, the "temple of the Owner of the Land" in Kubutambahan. Here steps lead into a wide, totally empty court, and more steps give access into the second court, the temple proper. In this court there are only two small *balés* for offerings, one on each side of a great monumental stone base consisting of three wide platforms strongly reminiscent of a pyramid. In this temple the essential little shrines of South Balinese temples do not exist; instead, the pyramid is surmounted by a great *padú raksa*, the great gate of other temples, with a stone throne, a *padmasana*, in place of the customary doorway. On each side of the *padú raksa* are two god houses with roofs of sugar palm fiber. There is, besides, a great split gate, *candí bentar*, but instead of serving as the outer entrance to the temple, it is built over the second platform of the pyramid, directly in front of the central monument.

There are no *merus* in North Balinese temples, and many of the most important elements of the Southern temples are lacking. It is usual, however, to find the *padmasana*, the throne of the sun-god, the split gate, and the great monumental gate occupying a place and with a function quite different from those in other Balinese temples. It seems as if the North Balinese adopted these features of the temples with a curiously distorted point of view.

Balinese texts often mention the *sad-kahyangan*, the six holy national temples, over the significance of which no one agrees. Most important of these is the great *Besakih*, situated exactly half-way up the slopes of the Gunung Agung. *Besakih* is Bali's most impressive temple in its austere simplicity and its grandiosity, with hundreds of black *merus* rising from everywhere to the misty sky and with a single unadorned great gate. Rather than one temple, *Besakih* is a cluster of temples, one for each of the different Balinese states, and once a year (at the full moon of the "fourth" month), the Rajas of Bali, now the regents, make offerings there for the whole of the Balinese people.

Other temples classed among the *sad-kahyangan*, some of which are debatable, are: *Pura Batukau*, near the summit of the mountain of the same name; *Uluwatu*, magnificently situated at the edge of a projecting cliff with a perpendicular drop into the sea of 250 feet, on the limestone tableland called Tafelhoek (Bukit Pecatu) (a great festival is held there on the day *anggara-klion* of the week *madang siha,* twenty-one days after *galunggan*); the bathing-temple of *Tirta Empul* in Tampaksiring; *Pura Panataran Sasíh* in Pejeng; *Pura Sakenan* in the island of Serangan; *Yeh Jeruk* in Gianyar; *Giralawa* in Klungkung; *Pakedukan* in Tabanan; *Samantiga* in Bedulu, and so forth.

2. *Arcas.* The concept that the spirits can be brought down to earth to be embodied in a receptacle, a stylized human figure or a mask among the primitive animists such as the Africans and Oceanians, appears in Bali in the *arca* cult. *Arcas* are generally statuettes of sandalwood, of gold, or of old coins sewn together, always male and female, and often represent Rama and Sita, the reincarnations of Wisnu and Sri.

Arcas of ancient Chinese cash, *kepeng,* with faces and hands of carved wood or gold are called *dewa rambut sadana* and are supposed to bring luck and riches to their owners. Our having acquired an old *rambut sadana* created considerable disturbance among our neighbors; when our servant first saw it, he asked us excitedly to sell it to him at twice the price paid for it. He told others in the house and they often came asking to see it. Someone even offered to make me a new one since "mine was already falling to pieces." We had to hide it, and it was some time before the matter was forgotten.

The statuettes fit into a base carved like an animal, the "mount" or vehicle of the deities when taken out in procession. Most often these bases are shaped like bulls, deer, or mythical animals, *nagas* or *singhas,* but often the mount is a composite animal, as for instance half-bull, half-fish, in all probability the ancient totems of the families who own the *arcas.* There is still a trace of totemism in Bali; people of the *ngatewel* caste claim descent from a jackfruit tree, and my friend Gusti Oka told me members of his family may not eat singing doves.

That the *arcas,* when imbued with the spirit of the deity, become highly temperamental was shown at the temple feast of *Taman Badung,* the death temple of Denpasar, when about forty of the town's *arcas* were taken out in procession. Absent was the feminine deity from the Civil temple, who "refused to join in the procession because she was not on good terms with her husband, the *arca* of *Taman Badung.*"

3. *Offerings.* The ever present offerings (*pabantén*) made to the gods and evil spirits should not be taken literally as factual food for them, but rather as a tax, a traditional habit of the people to give back something of what right-

fully belongs to the spirits; from the simplest, the little squares of banana leaf with a few grains of rice (*ngejot, canan*) made daily to the house or left in passing a magically charged spot; the more complete portions of food (*kawisan, pangulapan, prasajengan, sorohan*); to the great pyramids of fruit,

Ratna Menggali
(*from a Balinese manuscript*)

flowers, and roast chickens (*kboogan, pajegan*), the intricate constructions of cut-out palm-leaf (*sampian, jerimpan, sesayut*), and the great monuments of cooked pig's meat (*saté gedeh*) decorated with lacy garlands of pig's fat and stomach tissues (omentum) which can be seen at great festivals.

Ordinary offerings to the house and for temple feasts are made by any woman; but for special occasions an offering, to be effective, must conform to certain specifications based on the influences that rule the day: the calendar, the cardinal directions, numerology and so forth. Each day of the week has its color and numerical value that dictate the flowers to be used and the number of units in the offering. These rules are often specified in the *adat*, the traditional village law, but they are better known to professional offering-makers, Brahmana women (*Idayú*), who are engaged for a fee to direct the making of them.

Offerings are sharply divided into "unclean," evil-spirit offerings (*mecaru, banten sor, pasegan*) and "pure" (*sukla*) offerings for the gods.

4. *The Sunguhu. Sunguhus* are low-caste priests whose main office is the dedication of devil offerings in ceremonies of purification. Although Sudras, the *sunguhu* are a proud caste in themselves and claim descent from Sanghyang Tunggal and from Sanghyang Meleng, the Sun. The paraphernalia of the *sunguhu*, although generally poor and in deplorable condition, and their ritual are practically identical with those of the high Brahmanic priests; but accessories peculiar to *sunguhus* are the conch-shell blown by an assistant during his prayers, and the double drum similar to that of the Tibetan lamas, which in Tibet are made of two sections of the top of human skulls.

Like the high priests, they wear their hair long and in a knot, worn low at the back of the neck and not on top like the *pedandas*, because the worthy I Tusan, patron saint of blacksmiths and the greatest ironworker of ancient Gelgel, was unjustly exiled by a *pedanda*, who in time repented and, troubled in his conscience, tried to restore I Tusan, going into the forest in search of him. The blacksmith agreed to return only on condition that the *pedanda* carry him on his back. He had to comply and all the way the blacksmith hung on to the priest's topknot, pulling it down his neck (De Kat Angelino: *Mudras auf Bali*).

Dr. Goris (*Secten op Bali*) is of the opinion that they were the priests of the *wesnawa* sect, now disappeared, the worshippers of Wisnu and Sri. His attributes—the conch-shell, the turtle, the fiery wheel (*cakra*)—are all Visnuite symbols. Furthermore, his spoken formulas, like those of the high priests, are in Sanskrit. He is in charge of the offerings of the Underworld, in contrast to *pedandas*, who dedicate the offerings to the Sun and Sky.

All legends of the origin of *sunguhus* agree that they were high priests degraded in rank because of some fault or because they worshipped demoniac characters. The *Usana Jawa* mentions that they were Brahmanas degraded because they worshipped the devil Dalem Mur Samplangan. *Sunguhus* also claim to be descended from the two sons of the great religious teacher Mpú Bharada; one branch of the family was degraded. They claim further that they were pupils of Mpú Kuturan, Bharada's brother, but never attained great wisdom and did not become full-fledged high priests, but only *bujangga bali*, a term for *sunguhus* for which there is no satisfactory explanation (a child of a Brahmana and a Sudra becomes a *bujangga*). Another manuscript states that the *sunguhus* were descendants of I Guta, a fallen dweller of the sky, who on earth became a man-eating *raksasa*. He became a servant of Mpú Jijaksara, cousin of Mpú Kuturan and Bharada. He imitated his master at office, but was caught in the act and from then on was allowed to officiate as priest of the devil offerings (Korn: *Adatrecht van Bali*).

5. *The Calendar. The Solar-Lunar Year.* The Hindu *saka* (Sanskrit: *çaka*) year by which the mountain people, the Bali Aga, still reckon time and set the dates for their temple festivals is divided into twelve months (*saséh*) the names of which are simply the Balinese numbers from one to ten: 1, *kasa*; 2, *karo*; 3, *katiga*; 4, *kapat*; 5, *kalima*; 6, *kanam*; 7, *kapitú*; 8, *kaulú*; 9, *kasanga*; 10, *kadasa*; with two additional names, *desta* and *sada*, to make up the twelve months. These two last names are corruptions of the Sanskrit names of the eleventh and twelfth months. The ritual Sanskrit names of the months are, as the Balinese pronounce them: *s'rawana, badra wada, asujé, kartika, margasira, posya, maga, palguna, madumasa, wesaka, jiesta,* and *asada*.

These months consist of 29 or 30 days counted from each new moon. The year has either 354, 355, or 356 days, a difference of 9 to 11 days from the true solar year. This is corrected by the addition of an extra month (*saséh nampeh*) every thirty months, corresponding to about two and a half of our years. There are thirty lunar days in each month, but one day is jumped over every 63 days (nine weeks of seven days) to correlate them with the 29 or 30 solar days in each month (Goris: "Bali's Hoogtijden").

Nyepí, the most important yearly feast, the purification of the entire island, marks the spring equinox and is the only national festival of the *saka* calendar. It falls on the first day, the "dark moon" of the ninth month (*tilem-kasanga*), despite which it is regarded as the beginning of the year. The *nyepí* ceremony here described, which took place on the 17th of March 1934, marked the end of the *saka* year 1855 and ushered in the new year 1856.

The Javanese-Balinese Year. The *wuku* year probably came into use at the time of Majapahit's domination of South Bali, and today it is the system used universally in Bali, except for the mountaineer Bali Agas, who still reckon their feasts by new and full moons. The *wuku* is simply divided into weeks (*wukus*) and does not obey any astronomical or other natural rules. Of the ten simultaneous weeks contained in a *wuku* year, the most important is the week of seven days, corresponding to ours, the names of each day being, like our days, dedicated to the planets: Sunday (*redité*), the Sun; Monday (*soma*), the Moon; Tuesday (*anggara*), Mars; Wednesday (*budda*), Mercury; Thursday (*wrespati*), Jupiter; Friday (*sukra*), Venus; Saturday (*saniscara*), Saturn.

There are thirty seven-day weeks in a *wuku* year (*sinta, landap, wukir, kurantil, tolú, gumreg, wariga, warigadian, julung wangí, julung sungsang, dunggulan, kuninggan, langkir, madang siha, julung pujut, pahang, wurkulut, marakeh, tambir, madang kungkang, mahatal, ujeh, menahil, prang bakat, bala mukí, ugú, wayang, kulawu, dukut,* and *watú gunung*).

The origin of the names of these weeks is told in the legend of Sinta, a woman who became pregnant after she dreamed she slept with a holy man, giving birth to a beautiful child. One day Sinta lost her temper when the boy became unruly and struck him, wounding him on the head. The boy ran away and his grieved mother searched for him in vain for years afterwards. The grown boy had in time become the powerful ruler of the country of Giling Wesí, where he was known as Watú Gunung, "Stone Mountain," because he was supposed to have obtained his powerful magic from the mountain where he had undergone penance. One day the wandering mother, always in search of him, came to Giling Wesí accompanied by her sister Landap. The two women were still beautiful and Watú Gunung became so impressed by the strangers that he married both, having in due time twenty-seven children by his mother and aunt. By a scar on the head of Watú Gunung, one day Sinta became aware of the incest committed, and to avert disaster it was decided that Watú Gunung had to marry the goddess Srí, the wife of Wisnu, thus becoming himself like a god, free of the curse on incest. He had the audacity to request her in marriage, but was, naturally, refused, causing Watú Gunung to declare war on the gods. Wisnu took personal command of the armies sent to punish his arrogance and finally defeated Watú Gunung after obtaining the secret of the magic that gave him his powers. To celebrate the victory it was decreed that his twenty-seven sons be killed, one every seven days. Sinta wept for seven days and was received into heaven, so Wisnu added her name as well as that of her sister Landap and of Watú Gunung to the twenty-seven and established the thirty weeks as everlasting signs of his victory.

Parallel and simultaneous to the seven-day week run the other nine weeks—from the week of one day to one of ten days—of which those of five, three, and six days are the most frequently used by the people. The ten weeks are as follows:

1-day week, *ekowara,* in which every day is *luang.*
2-day week, *duwiwara,* the days of which are called: *m'gá* and *p'pat.*
3-day week, *triwara: paseh, beteng, kajeng.*

4-day week, *caturwara: srí, laba, jaya, mandala.*
5-day week, *pancawara: manis, paing, pon, wagé, klion.*
6-day week, *sadwara: tungleh, ariang, urukung, paniron, was, maulú.*
7-day week, *saptawara: redité, soma, anggara, budda, wrespati, sukra, saniscara.*
8-day week, *astawara: srí, indra, gurú, yarna, ludra, brahma, kala, uma.*
9-day week, *sangawara: danggú, jangur, gigis, nohan, ogan, erengan, urungan, tulus, dadí.*
10-day week, *dasawara: penita, parí, suka, duka, srí, manú, menusa, eraja, dewa, raksasa.*

Galunggan comes on the day *budda-klion,* week of *dunggulan,* when the ancestral souls of those cremated receive offerings in the temple, or in the cemetery for those still buried, while the evil spirits are also given offerings, although thrown on the ground. It is believed that the three days before *galunggan* are dangerous and unholy because Batara Kala (or Batara Galunggan) then comes down to earth in the form of Sanghyang tiga Wisesa to eat people. The ancestors go back on the day called *ulihan balí* (*soma-klion, kuninggan*), but the offerings are renewed on the day *tumpak kuninggan* (*saniscara-klion, kuninggan*), ten days after *galunggan* day. This festival is, perhaps erroneously, called the New Year of the *wuku* calendar, and, like *nyepí,* it falls somewhere in the middle of the year and not in the week of *sinta,* the first of the year.

Other holidays, or, rather, important days propitious for offerings and other activities, are: *Kajeng-klion,* every 15 days; *Tumpak* (*saniscara-klion*), every 35 days; *Budda-klion,* every 42 days; *Anggara-kasih* (*anggara-klion*), every 35 days; and *Budda-wagé,* also every 35 days.

If one asks an ordinary Balinese for the number of days in a month, the answer is that it has 35 days, thus conflicting with the knowledge that *saka* months have 29 or 30 days and that there are no months in the *wuku* year. This confusion is perhaps because 10 months of 35 days total almost the correct duration of one solar-lunar year—354 days; then, 6 months of 35 days make exactly 210 days: one *wuku* year. Furthermore, there are many holidays, like the important *Tumpak,* recurring every 35 days, or 6 times during a *wuku* year.

From this is deduced that in the original Balinese calendar there were probably only 10 months of 35 days and that the two extra months of the *saka* were added later when the calendar was modified and the Hindu calendar was adopted, leaving memory of a month of 35 days. We have seen that there are only Balinese names for ten of the twelve months, and Dr. Korn mentions that in Tenganan they say that the last two months were given to them as a present by Begawan Seganin Ening. Thus it is easily possible that the Balinese compromised and divided their year of 210 days into 6 months of 35 days. They do not make astronomical observations to calculate the solar-lunar year, but use special tables and charts called *pengalihan bulan*.

6. *Ancestors*. It is interesting that after cremation a deified ancestor becomes a *dewa-yang*, a word that bears a striking resemblance to the term *wayang*, over which there is a controversy. The *wayang* are the shadow-play puppets which are recognizedly related to the ancestors. Other names for the ancestral souls are *pitara, kawitan*, and *m'pú wayangan*, and the "heaven" where the ancestors live is called *langit gringsing wayang* "the flaming heaven of the *wayang*." The local gods, also ancestors, are called *Sanghyang*, a word made of the old relative pronoun *sang* and *hyang*, or *yang*, a native term for divinity, from which the word *wayang* could easily be derived. *Dewa* is a Sanskrit synonym of *yang*, and *dewa-yang* could have become *'wa-yang*.

7. *The following are among the most important Balinese Gods:*

SURYA—The Sun, chief of the Balinese pantheon. The only Hindu god actually worshipped in the temples.

BATARA GURU—The Supreme Teacher, master of Brahmanas. Most generally identified with Siwa. Represented as a bearded hermit seated on a lotus (*padma*). Batara Gurú has four arms, two clasped in attitude of prayer and the other two holding a rosary on the right, a brush for swatting flies (*pecut*) on the left.

BRAHMA—Who is the fire itself (AGNI), and who as lord of cremation is called PRAJAPATI. Brahma has no particular cult except as "fire." Represented in Bali with only one head; the deity with four faces, CATUR MUKA, is, in the popular mind, a deity in itself, not identified with Brahma.

WISNU—God of waters, giver of fertility, and lord of the underworld. His wife is DEWI SRI, goddess of beauty and agriculture; their daughter, DEWI MELANTING, goddess of seeds, gardens, and markets. Wisnu is represented as a young man riding on the mythical bird Garuda, Srí as a beautiful woman with full breasts, long hair, and slim arms. The agricultural temples are dedicated to her.

INDRA—The active and warlike lord of heaven, of winds and storms, guardian of the heavenly spirits, the WIDEDARAS and WIDEDARIS.

DURGA—The terrible goddess of death who receives the souls of the deceased and turns them over to YAMA for judgment. She is worshipped in the temples of the dead in the cemeteries.

KALA—God of darkness, the destroying form of Siwa, good turned into evil. Kala is represented as a fearful giant, always hungry, living in the center of the earth.

YAMA—Lord of hell, demoniac judge and punisher of souls.

UMA—Mother of all nature, wife of Siwa. Uma is Durga as Siwa is Kala in their beneficial form. Other wives of Siwa are GIRI PUTRI, goddess of the mountains, DEWI GANGGA and DEWI DANU, deities of the rivers and lakes.

SEMARA—God of love (the physical form), whose wife is DEWI RATIH, the moon.

SARASWATI—Goddess of science and literature.

ISWARA, SORA or ISORA, MAHADEWA, SAMBU, RUDRA or LUDRA, and KWERA, are lesser gods, deities of the cardinal points, the NAWA SANGGA.

PASUPATI—Siwa as a phallic symbol.

KUMARA—the god protector of children.

WARUNA—god of the sea.

ANTABOGA—The World Serpent guardian of the nether world, also known as BASUKI or GASUKI.

SANGHYANG IBU PERTIWI—Mother Earth.

SANGHYANG DUWRING AKASA—the space, the firmament.

TINTIYA—(CINTYA, SANGHYANG TUNGGAL), the Almighty. Frequently represented as a nude white male figure, flames emanating from his head, temples, shoulders, elbows, penis, knees, and feet. A figure that appears in endless variety in magic amulets (see *tumbals*, page 312).

GANA—the elephant-headed god, once worshipped in Bali, but now remaining only as a protective magic amulet; also called GANAPATI, the Ganeça of India.

BATARA BUDDA—not the Buddha, but in Bali a sort of protective, although malignant, deity, not clearly defined. Not generally known, but some of those people who knew the name identify it with the BARONG.

8. Dr. Goris (*Secten op Bali*) points to traces of former sects that were in time absorbed or that became obsolete and disappeared. All Brahmanic priests outside of the *bodda* belong to the *siwa* sect and all knowledge of former divisions is now lost to them. The classification of Dr. Goris is:

a) *Ciwa Siddhanta*, the most important group, to which the majority of the priests belong. Characteristic of this group is the use of formulas. The *siwa* priest prays with a bell and flowers, and wears a red and gold mitre topped by a crystal ball. His receptacle for holy water is called *siwamba*. A typical text of this sect is the manuscript *Bhuwana Kosa*, one of the *tuturs*, from which many of the later manuscripts were taken.

b) *Paçupata*, now totally disappeared, with but a trace of it in the cult of the *lingga*, the phallus, as a symbol of Siwa.

c) *Bhairawa*, a sect given to black magic of the left and worship of deities of death. Now extinct as a separate group, but that it was important is revealed in the witch cult, with its *leyaks, rangdas,* and *barongs*. Much of the ritual terminology comes from the Tantric manuscripts to which this black magic of Buddhism belonged. (See Note 1, page 320.)

d) *Wesnawa*, traces of which are the cults of Wisnu and *Srí*, deities of agriculture, fertility, and success, with the pecularity that Wisnu appears as lord of the underworld.

e) *Boddha* (or *Sogata*). The *bodda* priest officiates with his head bare, prays with a bell and a special weapon (*bajara*) instead of flowers, and his holy-water container is called *pamandiyanga*. He uses special *mantras*, his hand positions are different in the prayers, and he has his own literature.

f) *Brahmana*, now thoroughly merged with the Siwaites, but typical *Brahmana* are the speculations about the sacred syllable *ong*, the Om of India.

g) Rsi (*resí*), Satrias who by study and meditation become high priests, *pedandas*, who are not, however, Brahmanas, but princes who through a model life and renunciation of their earthly privileges acquire holiness. They may recite ordinary Brahmanic *mantras* like the *pasucian*, the purifying formula, but are forbidden to use the Wedas. The only *pedanda resí* to my knowledge was the old priest of Sidan, Tabanan, who died recently, although he probably left disciples. Friederich relates that in 1845 the prince Ngurah Gedé Pemecutan had himself ordained as a *resí*, but retained his state.

h) *Sora*, the old sun-worshippers, now merged with the Siwaites. The cult of Surya, the sun god, is, according to Goris, an ancient cult related to the Indian sun cult, which is in turn of Persian origin. The *pedanda siwa* is supposedly the Sun Priest, Sun Servant, and Son of the Sun.

J) *Ganeça*, worshippers of Gana, the "Disturber of Disturbances," an ancient Hindu cult of pre-Majapahit times and now extinct. The only traces of it are occasional ancient statues of Ganeça, the elephant god, and the images of this god that appear in magic amulets.

CHAPTER TEN

Witchcraft

WITCHES, WITCH-DOCTORS, AND THE MAGIC THEATER

A PERFORMANCE OF *WAYANG KULIT*, the shadow-play, is such an ordinary occurrence in Denpasar that it was unusual and intriguing one evening to find the town aroused by news of a shadow-play to take place that night in the outskirts, and we tagged along with the Balinese members of our household to watch the show. The streets were filled with people from the neighboring villages, all going our way, and we found the open square of Pemecutan, where the show was already in progress, jammed with an eager crowd trying to push their way within hearing-distance of the little screen, a focus of flickering light for a restless, dark sea of human heads.

We were accustomed to see sober groups sitting quietly even at performances of the most famous story-tellers, but on this occasion the crowd was so great that we could not approach the screen near enough even to distinguish clearly the shadows of the leather puppets. So unusual was the sudden interest in the performance that the high-collared, helmeted Dutch officials, ordinarily unconcerned with the "nonsense of the natives," asked nervous questions among the crowd. Everything in the performance went on as usual, except for a line of Balinese characters painted across the screen which said: "I, Ida Bagus Ktut, dare to tell." . . . We inquired what he dared to tell and from various sources we pieced together the following story:

For many months a feud had raged between two enemy factions of *leyaks*, witches, the spirits of living people given to black magic. This everybody knew because in Pemecutan the *leyaks* in battle were seen every night in the form of blue flames darting among the coconut trees. The villagers fell sick by the score and many died suddenly of mysterious, unexplained deaths, but the wounds that had killed them became evident if the bodies were washed with specially blessed coconut water. The leader one faction of witches was a well-known dealer in coffee, a woman of low caste named Makacung, famous for her strong character and her natural magic powers. Her child had suddenly died, and in her despair Makacung refused to leave his grave; night came and she fell asleep over it. In a dream the child spoke to her and blamed for his death a princess of Jerokuta, also reputed in the neighborhood to be a powerful witch. Mad with rage, Makacung went to the princess and accused her of the murder of her child. The princess did not deny it, and the *leyak* war was on.

It was supposed that the tide had turned against the faction of the noblewoman, and Makacung, to make her victory known to the public, had engaged the daring story-teller to re-enact the events in a *wayang* performance and give out the names of her enemy's allies. To add to the suspense, it was rumored that the story-teller, the son of Badung's most famous witch-doctor, had stolen the names he was about to make public from his father's records of clients for formulas of witchcraft. Everybody had gathered to learn the names of the village's *leyaks*, whispering advance guesses, and many were in fear of being named. The show dragged on through the night and we did not stay for the outcome. The next day people were reluctant to talk about it and someone remarked indignantly that it was wicked to make public accusations in this manner. We heard no more of the feud until three years later when we assisted at the cremation of the princess of Jerokuta, believed by everybody to have been killed by the superior magic of the low-caste Makacung.

A Balinese prince well known for his eccentric intrigues once announced he was to give a demonstration of how a man became a *leyak* and invited the entire foreign population of Bali to witness the phenomena. He seemed particularly anxious to attract even the casual tourists that came to the Bali Hotel. On the appointed night not only the Government officials, tourists, and illustrious Balinese had congregated in the darkness of the cemetery, but a great rowdy crowd of Balinese who had heard the rumor had gathered, equally curious, although less skeptical of the supernatural performance than the whites. They climbed trees, tearing branches and flashing lights into each other's faces, until the infuriated prince banned all flashlights. The prince's motive came out clearly when before starting the demonstration, he asked the guests for a contribution of one guilder and twenty cents to pay for the offerings that had to be made, should the man succeed in becoming a *leyak.*

After an endless wait the crowd gasped when a greenish light became visible at one end of the graveyard. As it approached it looked more and more suspiciously like a piece of banana leaf with a light behind it. A Dutch official next to me, who had retained his flashlight, aimed it suddenly at the ghost, who disappeared behind the low mound of a convenient new grave. The undaunted prince contended indignantly that the *leyak* was frightened and would not appear again, so he did not collect the fee. Thus ended our only opportunity to make the acquaintance of a *leyak.*

Leyak (from a Balinese manuscript)

The existence of these *leyaks* is to the Balinese an incontestable fact. They are held responsible for most of the evils that afflict Bali, including sickness and death. Like the vampire, they suck the blood of sleeping people and are particularly fond of the entrails of unborn children. Every Balinese has stories to tell of personal encounters with *leyaks* in various forms, and from my friends I often heard stories such as these:

"Walking on a lonely road at night, a man from Sayan was confronted with a monkey that seemed intent on blocking his path. He moved to the right of the road, but the monkey stood In front of him and leaped to the left when he tried to pass on the left side. In sheer desperation he grabbed the monkey's tail, but the animal disappeared, leaving the panic-stricken man with the tail in his hands. He dropped it and ran for his life; the following morning he went back to the place of his adventure to reassure himself that it was all a hallucination, but there he found a scorched loincloth exactly where he had dropped the monkey's tail."

"Another night, in similar circumstances, three men stole a chicken apparently lost on the road. They took it home, killed it, cleaned it, and stuffed it with leaves and spices, ready to cook the following day. Next morning they found an unknown dead man in place of the chicken, his stomach and intestines removed and the cavity filled with leaves and spices."

"A tiger once ran into the school of the mountain village of Baturiti. The alarm-drum was sounded and the tiger was killed. When the villagers proceeded to skin the animal, they found, between the skin and the flesh of the tiger, a *kompet,* the palm-leaf bag with betelnut, tobacco, and pennies that every Balinese carries."

"Rapung's uncle, the temple-keeper and a famous story-teller, had great magic powers but he did not practice evil magic. When he was deprived of his office as keeper of the temple because of a scandalous love affair, he created such a disturbance that he was thrown into jail. Although supposedly locked up in a cell, he was seen at night in the village and it was said that often he slept in his own house. He used his magic knowledge mainly as a defence against his enemies, and, as in the case of the Pemecutan *wayang* show, he gave the names of *leyaks* in *wayang* performances through the Twalén puppet. Once his lamp went out during the performance and, without stopping, he spit on the wick and the light flared up again. He held a memorable battle with a *leyak* chief disguised as a one-winged *garuda* bird and fought him in the form of a bald-headed *raksasa*. He was defied by the chief of Blahbatoeh, a famous witch; the story-teller took up the challenge and turned into a sea that engulfed the *leyak*, turned into a mad motor-car."

Most frequently *leyaks* appear as dancing flames flitting from grave to grave in cemeteries, feeding on newly buried corpses, or as balls of fire and living shadow-like white cloths, but also in the shapes of weird animals: pigs, dogs, monkeys, or tigers. Witches often assume the form of beautiful mute girls who make obscene advances to young men on lonely roads at night. *Leyaks* are, however, progressive and now they are said to prefer more modern shapes for their transformations; motor-cars and bicycles that run in and out of temples without drivers and whose tires pulsate as if breathing. There are even *leyak* airplanes sweeping over the roof-tops after midnight. Children cry during the night because they see *leyaks* that become invisible on approaching to gnaw at their entrails. Then the child becomes sick and soon dies; that explains the high death-rate among children.

The ever unwilling patients of the modern hospital in Denpasar claim to have seen strange shadows under doors and flocks of monkeys that grimace at them through the windows; the congregation of sick, magically weakened people naturally attracts legions of *leyaks* and for this reason they fear having to go to the hospital. Witches congregate under the *kepuh* trees always found in cemeteries, but they are also attracted to the "male" papaya tree (that which bears no fruit) and like to carry on their orgies of blood and their love affairs under its shadow; consequently these trees are never permitted to grow within the village limits.

I was told that to see the *leyaks* that happen to be about, one must stand naked and, bending over suddenly, look between one's legs. They can be recognized by the flames (*endéh*) that issue out of their hanging tongues and from the top of their heads. This does not work with foreigners, because the *leyaks* "are shy and do not show themselves to outsiders;" thus, even the Balinese who fear *leyaks* so that they dare not mention the word *leyak* are not in the least impressed with the bravery of a skeptical stranger who walks alone at night into a cemetery or some such *leyak*-ridden place.

THE RANGDA AND THE BARONG

Queen of the *leyaks* and undoubtedly the most interesting character on the island is the blood-thirsty, child-eating Rangda, the witch-widow mistress of black magic.

A curious ceremony in the temple of a neighboring village introduced Rangda to us. It was well after midnight, and although the date for the temple feast was still far off, there was a crowd, mostly women, in the courtyard sitting in a circle around a man who appeared to be in a trance. Next to him sat the old *pemangku*, the temple priest, quiet and concentrating, attending to the incense that burned in a clay brazier before a monstrous mask with enormous fangs. The community, it seemed, was having a wave of bad luck and they were asking Rangda to advise them, through the medium, of what she required to leave them alone. The stillness of the night, the incense, and the dim light of the petrol lamp, all aided the feeling that the spirit of the dreaded witch was really there. Soon the oracle began to twitch and foam at the mouth, making painful efforts to talk. The mask was placed on his head and the priest listened with intense interest to the incoherent groans, muffled by the mask, which he translated in a monotonous voice as the words of Rangda, now in the body of the medium. After the offerings that she demanded were enumerated, she reproached the villagers for neglecting to give a performance of *Calon Arang*, the play in which her triumphs are enacted. To end the ceremony the musicians played and Rangda danced; then the man was taken out of the trance and Rangda, presumably, went back to her abode in the summit of the highest mountain, the Gunung Agung.

Time and again we saw Rangda appear in various magic plays; she was invariably represented as a monstrous old woman, her naked white body striped with black. Rings of black fur circled her long, hanging breasts, realistically made of bags of white cloth filled with sawdust. She was entirely covered by her white hair, which reached to her feet, allowing only the bulging eyes and twisted fangs of her mask to be seen. Her tongue hung out, a strip of leather two feet long, painted red and ending in flames of gold. A row of flames came from the top of her head. She wore white gloves with immense claws and in her right hand she held the white cloth with which she hid her horrible face to approach her unsuspecting victims. This

Rangda (from a Balinese manuscript)

cloth became a deadly weapon if it struck.

The character of Rangda has its origin in historical facts, now interwoven with fantastic myth. (See page 320.) At the beginning of the eleventh century a Balinese prince became the king of Java, the great Erlangga. His mother, Mahendradatta, was a Javanese princess who ruled Bali with her Balinese husband, Dharmodayana, until the husband, suspecting her of practicing evil magic, exiled her to the forest. When Erlangga's father died, leaving Mahendradatta a *rangda,* a widow, she conspired to use her band of pupils trained in the black arts to destroy Erlangga's kingdom. Professor Stutterheim says that her chief grudge against Erlangga was that he had failed to bring pressure upon his father not to take another wife. Moreover, none of the nobility would marry Rangda's beautiful daughter, Ratna Menggali, out of fear of the old witch, and her caste as a Javanese princess required a noble marriage or none at all. Before Rangda was vanquished by the superior magic of Mpú Bharada, Erlangga's teacher, she had killed nearly half of Erlangga's subjects by plagues brought by her *leyaks.* (According to Stutterheim, the sanctuary of Bukit Dharma near Kutri, Gianyar, is the burial place of the famous witch. There is kept a weather-beaten but still beautiful statue of the witch, remembered as the Queen Mahendradatta in the shape of the goddess of death, Durga.)

The following is an extract of the current Balinese version of the story of Rangda (translated from the Kawi by R. Ng. Poerbatjaraka, in *De Calon Arang*):

"The old witch *rangda* Calon Arang had sworn to destroy the happy and prosperous Daha, Erlangga's kingdom, because of fancied insults to her beautiful daughter Ratna Menggali—the noblemen of Daha had refused her in marriage for fear of her mother's evil reputation. Calon Arang went with her pupils to the cemetery and they prayed and danced in honor of Begawati, the deity of black magic, to help them destroy Daha. The goddess appeared and danced with them, granting her permission, warning the witch, however, to preserve the center of the kingdom untouched. The witches danced at the crossroads and soon people fell ill in great numbers.

"On discovering the cause of the epidemic, Erlangga ordered his soldiers to go and kill the witch. They stole into her house while she slept and stabbed her in the heart, but Calon Arang awoke unhurt and consumed the daring soldiers with her own fire. The witch went once more into the cemetery and danced with her pupils, dug out corpses, cutting them to pieces, eating the members, drinking the blood, and wearing their entrails as necklaces. Begawati appeared again and joined in the bloody banquet, but warned Calon Arang to be careful. The witches danced once more at the crossroads and the dreadful epidemic ravaged the land; the vassals of Erlangga died before they could even bury the corpses they bore to the cemeteries.

"The desperate king sent for Mpú Bharada, the holy man from Lemah Tulis, the only living being who could vanquish the witch. Mpú Bharada planned his campaign carefully. He sent Bahula, his young assistant, to ask for the witch's daughter in marriage. Highly flattered, the mother gave her consent and after a happy and passionate honeymoon Bahula learned from his wife the secret of Calon

Arang's power, the possession of a little magic book, which he stole and turned over to his master. The holy man copied it and had it returned before the disappearance could be noticed. The book was a manual of righteousness and had to be read backwards. The holy man was then able to restore life to those victims whose bodies had not yet decayed. Armed with the new knowledge, he accused the witch of her crimes, but she challenged him by setting an enormous banyan tree on fire by a single look of her fiery eyes. Bharada foiled the enraged witch by restoring the tree, and she turned her fire against the holy man. Unmoved, he killed her with one of her own *mantras;* but she died in her monstrous *rangda* form and Bharada, to absolve her of her crimes and enable her to atone for them, revived her, gave her human appearance, and then killed her again."

It is only in the legend that Rangda could be vanquished; the Balinese perform the story of her struggle with Erlangga in a play, but always stop before the point where the tide turned against the witch.

THE CALON ARANG PLAY

It is in a performance of *Calon Arang*, the legend of Rangda, that the Balinese theater reaches the height of its magnificence. It combines the fine music and delicate dancing of the *legong* with the elaborate staging, the acting, singing, and comedy of the classic plays, besides the element of mystery and suspense.

The *Calon Arang* is not an ordinary play, but a powerful exorcism against *leyaks*, because by dramatizing Rangda's triumphs, the Balinese aim to gain her goodwill. Preparations for staging the great show start days before; it is essential that a "male" papaya tree, which bears no fruit, be first transplanted from the wilds to the middle of the dancing-grounds, because such a tree is the favorite haunt of the *leyaks*. A tall house on stilts is built at one end for Rangda, reached by a high runway of bamboo, flanked by spears, pennants, and umbrellas, all symbols of state. The entire dancing-space is covered by a canopy of streamers made of palm-leaf and tissue-paper flags; as many petrol lamps as are available in the village light the stage.

By midnight the audience is assembled, waiting patiently, listening to the special *Calon Arang* music, perhaps the finest in Bali, played by a full *legong* orchestra augmented with large bamboo flutes. A full moon is propitious for the performance and the company waits until the moon comes out from behind the black clouds, silhouetting the temple roofs, the palm trees, and the long aerial roots of the village banyan tree, a hanging black curtain of long tentacles against the sky, the perfect setting for the magic play. Offerings are made beforehand and consultations are held so as not to offend Rangda and to ascertain whether it is safe to hold the performance.

The show begins after midnight and lasts until dawn, when the witch makes her appearance. The play approaches our dramatic literature more nearly than anything else in Bali. It relates the episodes of the struggle between Rangda and the great Erlangga. Dancing interludes by six little girls, the pupils of the witch, alternate with slapstick, the encounters of the king's subjects with *leyaks*, and with dramatic songs by the prince sent to kill Rangda. She is impersonated by an old actor gifted with such great powers that he is able to withstand, in his own body, the dangerous spirit of the witch herself.

Towards dawn the atmosphere becomes surcharged with mystery as the old actor goes into Rangda's house to enter into the trance. Watchmen are appointed to wake all the children that have fallen asleep lest their tender souls be harmed; a priest stands ready to conjure Rangda, who will make her triumphal appearance at the end of the play. A flickering lamp can be seen through the curtains of the house, and there is an occasional groan from the actor as he undergoes the painful transformation. Meantime below, as the music becomes violent, the prince advances across the dancing-space with his kris drawn. With a yell of defiance he starts up the bridge, just as a blood-curdling howl is heard inside the house, the voice of Rangda. Unexpectedly, fireworks, strung on invisible wires all over the trees, begin to explode over the heads of the crowd. The audience is on edge as the curtains part and the frightful form of Rangda appears, shrieking curses upon the prince, who is put to flight as the old witch descends, bellowing, amidst clouds of smoke, sparks, and explosions.

The climax is a critical moment, as it is never known what will happen next. It is not unusual for Rangda to run wild and go about the village moaning, or to disappear into the blackness of the rice fields. The actor, who is possessed by the spirit of the real Rangda, is hard to bring under control. I have been told of an old actor from Tejakula who, after impersonating Rangda, ran amuck and went insane when captured. He is said never to have regained his mental balance. To the Balinese this was, once more, the evidence of the danger of releasing uncontrolled magic powers.

THE BARONG

The witch has a contender for supremacy in a fantastic animal, a mythical "lion" called Barong. Because of an ancient feud with Rangda, he sides with human beings to thwart her evil plans, and the Balinese say that without his help humanity would be destroyed. While Rangda is female, the magic of the "left," the Barong is the "right," the male. Rangda is the night, the darkness from which emanate illness and death. The Barong is the sun, the light, medicine, the antidote for evil.

Every community owns a set of the costumes and masks of both characters. These masks have great power in themselves and are kept out of sight in a special shed in the death temple of the village. They are put away in a basket, wrapped in a magic cloth that insulates their evil vibrations, and are uncovered only when actually in use, when the performer-medium is in a trance and under the control of a priest, and not before offerings have been made to prevent harm to the participants. At the feasts of the death temples their masks are uncovered and exhibited in one of the shrines. It is a good precaution to sprinkle these masks with holy water when someone is sick in the village.

Like the Rangda, the Barong is treated with great respect and the Balinese address him by titles such as Banaspati Raja, "Lord of the Jungle," or as Jeró Gedé, "The Big One," rather than as Barong, which is only a generic name for his sort of monster. (See Note 1, page 320.)

Despite his demoniac character, the Barong materializes in a trance play in which he is made to act foolishly and to dance for the amusement of the crowd. His costume consists of a great frame covered with long hair, with a sagging back of golden scales set with little mirrors. A beautifully arched gold tail sticks out of his rump and from it hang a square mirror, a bunch of peacock feathers, and a cluster of little bells that jingle at every move. Under a high gilt crown is his red mask, too small for his body, with bulging eyes and snapping jaws. The power of the Barong is concentrated in his beard, a tuft of human hair decorated with flowers. The Barong is animated by two specially trained men who form the front and hind quarters of the animal, the man in front operating the mask with his hands.

In Pemecutan the Barong play began with a performance of *jauk*, a group of boys wearing grinning white masks, who danced to the delicate tunes of a *legong* orchestra called in this case *bebarongan*. After the dance the two Barong performers went under the costume that lay inanimate on two poles, the mask covered by a white cloth. Like a circus prop-horse, the Barong danced, wiggling his hind quarters, lying down, contracting and expanding like an accordion, snapping his jaws, and in general behaving in a comic, rather undignified manner for his awesome character. After his gay outburst of animal spirits, he began a long dance, staring around as if astounded by magic visions that filled the air. He was constantly on the alert for invisible enemies, growing more and more alarmed, clicking his teeth like castanets as the tempo of the music increased. Firecrackers began to explode at the far end of the arena, startling the Barong, and when the smoke cleared, the figure of Rangda appeared, yelling curses at the Barong, who appeared humiliated by her insults. But eventually he reacted and they rushed at each other, fighting and rolling on the ground until the Barong was made to bite the dust.

In the meantime a group of half-naked men sitting on a mat went into a trance. They were the assistants of the Barong against Rangda. A priest consecrated some water by dipping the Barong's beard into it, and sprinkled the men, who shook all over as if in an epileptic fit. With their eyes glued on the Rangda, they got up, drawing their krisses, advancing like fidgety automatons towards the witch, who awaited them ready with her white cloth, her weapon, ready in her raised hand. Suddenly he ran after them, but just then one of the priests on watch noticed something unusual in her behavior and passed the Word that she was out of control. She was caught by a group of strong men and led away, but not before she had put a spell on the entranced men by joining the thumbs of her outstretched hands and yelling a curse.

By the spell, the krisses in the hands of the men turned against them, but the magic of the Barong hardened their flesh so that, although they pushed the sharp points of the daggers with all their might against their naked chests, they were not even hurt. This was the explanation the Balinese gave of the strange exhibition and it seemed inconceivable that they were faking, such was the earnest force with which they seemed to try to stab themselves. Some leaped wildly or rolled in the dust, pressing the krisses against their breasts and crying like children, tears streaming from their eyes. Most showed dark marks where the point of the dagger bruised the skin without cutting it, but blood began to flow from the breast of one, the signal for the watchmen to disarm him by force.

It is said that only by a complete trance can the dance be performed with impunity; otherwise a man will wound himself or hurt others. They were closely watched and if one of them gave signs of returning to consciousness he was quickly and violently disarmed. Possessed as they are, they have supernatural strength and it takes many men to hold them down. Even after the kris has been wrenched away they continue to dance with a blank stare and with the right fist still clenched as if grasping the kris handle. To take the men out of the trance, they were led, one by one, to where the Barong stood; someone sucked the bleeding chest of the wounded man and stuck a red flower in the cut. The *pemangku* wiped the face of each man with the beard of the Barong dipped in holy water, and gradually the hysterical men came out of the trance, dazed, simply walking away as if they did not know what had happened to them.

THE SANGHYANG

Towards the end of the Balinese year, during the last months of the rainy season, epidemics of malaria and tropical fevers make their appearance because evil spirits and *leyaks* are in the ascendancy; then even the earth is said to be sick. It is believed that the fanged demon living on the little island of Nusa Penida, Jeró Gedé Mecaling, comes to Bali then in the form of a fiery ball that, upon coming ashore, explodes into a thousand sparks that spread in all directions. As their glow dies, they release evil forces that go to spread illness and misfortune. This is a propitious time for *leyaks* to prey on human beings; because of the predominance of evil forces, the village is then magically weakened. The dogs gather at the crossroads and howl all night and the owls hoot, predicting deaths in the village. Quantities of offerings are made to placate the devils, and the benign spirits are implored to come down to earth, through the body of a medium, to advise and protect the distressed community.

A performance of *sanghyang dedari* (see page 323) is one of the

Rangda, queen of witches

ABOVE: The *sanghyang* is about to start
BELOW: Three old women performing the *mendét*

most effective exorcisms; two little girls, trained to go into a trance, are chosen from all the girls of the village for their psychic aptitudes by the temple priest, the *pemangku*, to receive in their bodies the spirits of the heavenly nymphs, the beautiful *dedari* Supraba and Blue Lotus (Tunjung Birú). Choruses of men and women are formed and the training begins. Every night, for weeks, they all go to the temple, where the women sing traditional songs while the men chant strange rhythms and harmonies made up of meaningless syllables, producing a syncopated accompaniment for the dance that the little girls, the *sanghyangs*, will perform. By degrees the little girls become more and more subject to the ecstasy produced by the intoxicating songs, by the incense, and by the hypnotic power of the *pemangku*. The training goes on until the girls are able to fall into a deep trance, and a formal performance can be given. It is extraordinary that although the little girls have never received dancing lessons, once in a trance they are able to dance in any style, all of which would require ordinary dancers months and years of training to learn. But the Balinese ask how it could be otherwise, since it is the goddesses who dance in the bodies of the little girls.

When the girls are ready, they are taken to the death temple, where a *sanggar agung*, a high altar, has been erected, filled with offerings for the sun. The *pemangku* sits facing the altar in front of a brazier where incense of three sorts is burned. The little girls wear ear-plugs of gold, heavy silver anklets, bracelets, and rings. Their hair is loose and they are dressed in white skirts. They kneel in front of the altar on each side of the priest. The women singers sit in a circle around them, while the men remain in a group in the back. Their jewelry is removed and is put in a bowl of water; small incense braziers are placed in front of each girl. After a short prayer by the priest the women sing:

> Fragrant is the smoke of the incense, the smoke of the sandalwood, the smoke that coils and coils upwards towards the home of the three gods.
>
> We are cleansed to call the nymphs to descend from heaven.
>
> We ask Supraba and Tunjung Birú to come down to us, beautiful in their bodices of gold.
>
> Flying down from heaven, they fly in spirals, fly down from the North-East, where they build their home.

> Their garden is filled with golden flowers that grow side by side with the pandanus, the scorpion orchids, the *tigakancú,* pineapples, *solí* and *sempol,* their tender leaves gracefully drooping; drooping they spread their perfume through the garden.
>
> Our thoughts shall rise like smoke towards the *dedari,* who will descend from heaven. . . . (See Note 3, page 323, for the Balinese text.)

Soon the girls begin to drowse and fall in a sudden faint. The women support their limp bodies in a sitting-position, and after a while the girls begin to move again, as if suffering intense pain, then trembling all over and swaying faster and faster, their heads rolling until their loose hair describes a wide circle. From this time on the girls remain with closed eyes and do not open them until the end of the ceremony, when they are taken out of the trance. With their bare hands they brush off the glowing coals from the braziers, making inarticulate sounds that are taken to be *mantras,* magic formulas, mumbled by the heavenly nymphs that have entered their bodies. From now on they are addressed as goddesses. Women attendants remove their white skirts and replace them with gilt ones. Their waists are tightly bound in strips of gold cloth, and each girl is given a jacket, a golden bodice, and a silver belt, in all a *legong* costume. The jewelry that lay in the bowl of holy water is put on again. The holy head-dresses of gold are brought in on cushions decorated with fresh frangipani flowers, and the girls are guided so that they can put them on themselves while the women sing about the beauty of the head-dresses and the elegance of their clothes:

> The head-dress, the head-dress circled with jasmines, the *garuda mungkur* ornament on its back, enhanced with *sempol* and *gambir* flowers, crowned with fragrant *sandat* and yellow pistils of *merak.*
>
> Tightly bound in their sashes they dance in the middle of the court, they dance slowly and glide from side to side, sway and swing in ecstasy. . . .

The *pemangku,* until then motionless and concentrating, now takes a coconut with the holy water about to be sanctified, water in which have been placed various sorts of flowers and three small branches of *dadap* bound in red, black, and white thread. Then he asks the *sanghyangs* to turn the water into an amulet.

The *sanghyangs* begin to dance with closed eyes, accompanied by alternating choruses of the men who sing in furious syncopation: "Kechak-kechak-kechak—chakchakchak-chak!—and by the women who sing:

> The flower *menuk* that makes one happy, the white flower, it is—it is—it is white and in rows, like the stars above, like the constellations, like the constellation *kartika,* that scintillates, they scintillate, scintillate and fade away, fade away and disappear, disappear, disappear because of the moonlight.
>
> *Lengkik, lengkik, lengkik,* says the plaintive song of the lonely *dasih* bird that was left behind. Oh, how he cries! He cries, cries like the cry of a child who must be amused, amused by the dancing of the *dedaris*. *Lengkik, lengkik,* swing and sway in ecstasy. . . .

The *sanghyangs* may suddenly decide to go to another temple or tour the village, chasing the *leyaks,* followed by the singing men and women. The *sanghyangs* must not touch the impure ground outside the temple and are carried everywhere on the shoulders of men. They stop at a second temple, where a pile of coconut shells burns in the center of the court. The *sanghyangs* dance unconcerned in and out of the fire, scattering the glowing coals in all directions with their bare feet. They may even decide to take a bath of fire, picking up the coals in both hands and pouring them over themselves.

When the fire is extinguished, the girls climb onto the shoulders of two men who walk around the courtyard, the girls' prehensile feet clutching the men's shoulders, balancing themselves and dancing gracefully from the waist up, bending back at incredible angles. In this manner they give the illusion of gliding through the air. The temperamental girls may suddenly decide that the dance is over. Then they must be taken out of the trance with more songs; and the *sanghyangs* become ordinary girls again, they distribute the flowers from their head-dresses as amulets and sprinkle the crowd with holy water:

> Beautiful goddess stand up, goddess, stand up. The singers have come and are singing the *sanghyang*.

Come, goddess, goddess, we ask of the nymphs to come to us for a while and go around, go around.

Oh, beautiful goddess! take the holy water from the altar, the holy, the clear, the immaculate water with frangipani, white *madurí*, white hibiscus and blue *teleng*. The water in the gold coconut, the liberating water, the water made in heaven.

Sprinkle it over yourself and go and spray the singers. Then go home, go home to the Indraloka.

Go and bathe in the garden and adorn yourself with white orchids, then go home, goddess, go home, back to heaven, and disappear into space, go into space.

The wind blows, fly with the wind goddess; the body remains to take again its human form. . . .

The ceremony lasts for two or three hours, but despite the intensity of the performance the little girls give no evidence of exhaustion and the explanation they give comes back to our minds: the dancers, fascinated by their own rhythm, move in a supernatural world where fatigue is unknown. In ordinary life the little girls are normal children. However, they are forbidden to creep under the bed, to eat the remains of another person's food or the food from offerings, and must be refined in manners and speech. Their parents are exempt from certain village duties and are regarded highly by the rest of the community.

BLACK AND WHITE MAGIC

Every Balinese believes that his body, like an electric battery, accumulates a magic energy called *saktí* that enables him to withstand the attacks of evil powers, human or supernatural, that seek constantly to undermine his magic health. This *saktí* is not evenly divided; some people are born with a capacity to store a higher charge of magic than others; they become the priests, witch-doctors, and so forth, endowed with supernatural powers. The *saktí* can be trained to serve them at will by the systematic study of the arts of magic and meditation, but people whose hearts are contaminated by evil use the magic science to harm their enemies, or simply to satisfy their lowest instincts.

The Balinese use the term *sakrí* like our "holy" or "sacred," but meaning, rather, charged with a magic (positive or negative) power that emanates from people as well as from objects like Rangda and

Barong masks, or from places regarded as magically dangerous (*tenget* or *angkér*), like caves, rivers, and ancient remains. One often hears of the *saktí* of living people who could hardly be regarded as holy, like our coffee-dealer Makacung; I was told of an old prince who was so *saktí* he could floor anyone by simply staring at him.

The normal way to bring out the dormant *saktí* is to undergo *mawintén*—the initiation ceremony of priests, magicians, dancers, and actors, to give them the luck, beauty, cleverness, and personal charm that enable them to be successful. Story-tellers and singers of epic poems (*kekawin*) have magic syllables inscribed on their tongues with honey to make their voices sweet. The ceremony is performed by a priest who, after cleansing and purifying the person through a *maweda,* writes invisible signs over his forehead, eyes, teeth, shoulders, arms, and so forth, with the stem of a flower dipped in holy water.

An explanation of the Balinese attitude in regard to personal magic can be found in the principle that constantly obsesses them—strong and weak, clean and unclean. Thus, the individual is magically strengthened when he is in the state of psychic purity (*éning, sucí, nirmala*) acquired through the performance of the cleansing ritual. The antithesis of this is the often mentioned *sebel* condition, uncleanliness, when a run-down soul renders one vulnerable to the attacks of evil. A person becomes *sebel* automatically at the death of relatives, during illness or menstruation, after having children, and so forth. In cases of bestiality, temple vandalism, incest, the birth of twins of each sex, the entire community becomes polluted and has to be purified by complicated and expensive sacrifices. Not even the deities are free from becoming *sebel,* and, like any other woman, Rangda and the death goddess Durga are *sebel* once every month.

The ancient Indian idea that a positive force, when temporarily distorted and reversed, is turned into an evil, negative power is the backbone of the magic science of Bali. Even the gods have phases of wickedness, their *krodha* or *rodra* manifestations, when a creative spirit becomes a fearful deity of death and destruction. Siwa in his angry form is Kala, and Uma, Siwa's wife, becomes Durga; Wisnumurti or Brahmamurti are the *krodha* manifestations of the gods Wisnu or Brahma, and the average Balinese has come to regard them as many-armed, ten-headed demons of mythology, because their freakish appearance is incompatible with his idea of divinity. The notion remains, however, that a formula of magic intended to give the spiritual health for which they strive, if turned backwards (as in the case of Rangda's book on magic), becomes a powerful source of evil magic. Thus magic is sharply divided into good magic of the "right," *penengen*, and magic of the "left," *pengiwa*, black and evil; both based on the same principles and almost identical in procedure.

THE PENGIWA: HOW TO BECOME A LEYAK

The learned, those possessing a highly trained mystic power, often become "infected in their heart" and misuse their knowledge to transform themselves into werewolves who revel in crime and blood, reverting to the wicked instincts of demons. They instruct pupils in the secret magic and become chiefs of legions of *leyaks*.

When I first became interested in magic, my Balinese friends tried to dissuade me, claiming that unending calamities would befall me if I persisted. None would admit he knew anything about how to become a *leyak* and in general the subject was delicate as a matter of conversation. Eventually someone brought me a manuscript for sale, probably stolen, obviously belonging to the magic lore. The very sight of it frightened them, and it was with certain difficulty that I induced my usually skeptical teacher of Balinese to help me translate the text. Even he deliberately distorted the order of the syllables and I had to orrect them afterwards, checking and rechecking individual words. Later on I obtained another palm-leaf book which was considerably more accessible because it contained magic of the "right," and from the two I tried to procure a general cross section of magic procedures.

The process of becoming a *leyak* is long and arduous and can only be achieved gradually. First the pupils learn by heart magic words from the old manuscripts, which, repeated in rhythmical sequence while in the attitude of meditation, *nglekas*, put the student into a state of feverish trance. This is done while making an offering—cones of steamed rice dyed in certain specified colors, special structures of palm-leaf, amounts of old bronze coins, and a sacrificed chicken of a defined color. These rites should be performed after midnight in a propitious place for the transformation. Most frequently named locales for becoming a werewolf were the cemeteries, the death temple, the crossroads, the place where two rivers meet (*campuan*), where corpses are cremated, in the *balé agung*, in empty lots where people have never lived, in the family shrine, magic spots of any kind.

The pupil achieves communion with the evil deities by degrees, but before he is successful, he undergoes strange tests of fortitude: giants appear to him and pretend to chop off his head with great axes, monstrous snakes will coil around his body, but he must remain unmoved. Should he laugh if mice appear from all corners playing on great flutes, the fruit of his efforts will be lost. The formulas recited during the early stages of training are simple repetitions of the standard holy syllables (*ong, ang mang, ong, ang, mang*) or meaningless words such as: "*ong, ngong breng nengang, ring pang ring pung, sigang sigung, m'ngang m'ngang bem mengung, jingal jingul, leng her.*" Often strange words appear that seem to be onomatopoetic sounds of the animal one wishes to become, as in the case of transforming oneself into the monkey Luntung Bengkur, a favorite of *leyak* women, the formula for which is: "*AH! hrenh* hrang *hrung, UH! hek kwek kwek,*" repeated three times.

So much for the simple *leyaks* that turn into birds, pigs, monkeys, snakes, or even tigers. There are more powerful and dangerous transformations for the later stages of training, for more defined demons and "*rangdas,*" able to cause all sorts of supernatural phenomena. In my manuscript for black magic there ere forty-eight sorts of transformations, each more powerful than the last, but also more difficult to attain, often with minute instructions for the favorable conditions in which to try them safely and with repeated warnings that they were not to be attempted by the unprepared. The offèrings required were elaborate and expensive; the amounts of money specified often mount into the many thousands of *kepengs*. In these the formula becomes a forceful prayer of self-exaltation:

> "ONG! My will is [to become] Sang Kundewijaya-murti. Fire from my immaculate abdomen, ONG! White fire from my heart, red fire from my liver, yellow fire from my kidneys, black fire from my lungs, fire from my navel, fire from the crown of my head—ang ang ang ang ang, fire from my head flare up to heaven, fire of five olours rise as high as a mountain. All you witches (*leyak, destí, telúh, trangyana*), all devils of the universe, collapse! Fearfully they all pay homage to me, the whole world reverences me. ONG! Nothing can outshine my brilliance—go

on [the power of the formula], go on, go on!"
(ONG, *idepakú rumawak Sang Kundewijaya-murti, mijilaken gení ring serira sasti.* ONG, *gení putih ring pepusuh, gení abang ring hatí, gení kuning ring ungsilan, gení ireng ring amperú, gení perebuta ring nabí, metú ring siwedwarankú, ang ang ang ang ang, jemijil gení ring siwedwarankú, murub dumilak ring akasa, mancewarna rupanira miber akú ring akasa, dumilak tejankú ring jagat, murub kadí gení segunung, sarwa leyak, destí, telúh, trangyana, sarwa buta pisaca, dengen, sarwa mambekan ring jagat, rep sirep, pada nembah ring akú,* ONG, *sidi swasti bawankú, ser, ser, ser.*)

The release of this magic fire that comes from the lower interior being is an important factor in the transformation. It is sent off to go and cause the destruction of the victim. In the manuscripts often appear phrases like this to drive this force:

"... fly through the air, soar in the sky, ascend, ascend, ascend, fly in circles, go on, go on, go on, go and burn so-and-so [the victim's name], launch my invincible formula."
(*... teka ber, angawang ring gegana, bijur, bijur, bijur, ser, ser, ser, teka geseng sianú, angenter mantra mawisesa.*)

With every formula comes a prayer so that the witch can return to normalcy—that is, become human again and reacquire cleanliness. This is done by driving the magic fire back into one's abdomen. Here is a typical example:

"ONG! Brahma (fire) return to my abdomen and disappear [the abnormal state], become human again, clearly human, and there shall be no trouble. Lost, lost, lost, clean, clearly a man."
(ONG, *Brahma mulih ring serira teka sedep telas, muksaning jatí, teka purna, teka udep, teka udep, teka udep, èning janma jatí.*)

Every witch-doctor and even high priests should undergo these transformations in order to know what they have to fight against. I was told by an old medicine-man, who claimed to have tried them often, that the process is extremely painful; it starts with violent headaches; gradually the tongue swells, becoming longer and heavier until it hangs out of the mouth uncontrolled. He added that the transformations are dangerous because, with each, one's life wears away and becomes shorter, like burning up one's soul-power. The Balinese claim that certain people have greater aptitude for becoming *leyaks* than others; women, for instance, require less study than men, and persons devoid of the groove between the lips and the nose have *leyak* tendencies. The *leyak* cult is full of rowdy sexual manifestations; *leyaks* appear naked and with tremendously exaggerated sexual organs that emanate fire. Like the witches of the West, they fly naked over housetops and hold orgies and black masses.

PENENGEN: THE MAGIC OF THE RIGHT

Against the dreaded *pengiwa* there is a neutralizing magic used by priests and witch-doctors to protect their clients from *leyaks,* a magic as powerful as that of the witches and consisting of the same elements as the magic of the "left"—formulas (*mantra*) charms (*serana*), and amulets (*penawar, sikepan, pergolan, tetulak*). Typical charms are "yellow" coconuts, *dadap* leaves, onions and salt, flowers, rubbings of gold, rain-water that collects in plants, camphor, a lamp burning perfumed oil, twin bananas and twin coconuts, over which a formula is recited. These amulets are often pictures of monsters and fantastically distorted deities, surrounded with cabalistic symbols, drawn on a piece of new white cloth or on a thin plaque of silver or copper, worn at the waist, hung over the house gate or in front of the rice granary. The images drawn on these little flags, called *tumbal,* may represent the weapons (*senyata*) of the gods, or may be pictures of Batara Kala, Batara Gana, or curious represensations of that intriguing and abstract Balinese divinity Tintiya, known also as Sanghyang Tunggal—the Unthinkable, the Solitary, the Original God. Tintiya appears often in ritual objects in the form of a nude male white figure, bristling with trident-shaped flames emanating from his head, temples, shoulders, elbows, penis, knees, and feet. His hands are clasped in an attitude of prayer and his right foot rests on a fiery wheel, a *cakra.* The Tintiyas used as amulets of magic are fantastically distorted, often in absurd positions, with many heads, or simply Tintiya heads attached to abstract and geometrical shapes. "*Rangdas*" and monsters of all sorts used as *tumbals* are aimed to ward off, by sympathetic magic, the ghosts and werewolves that annoy and persecute the Balinese.

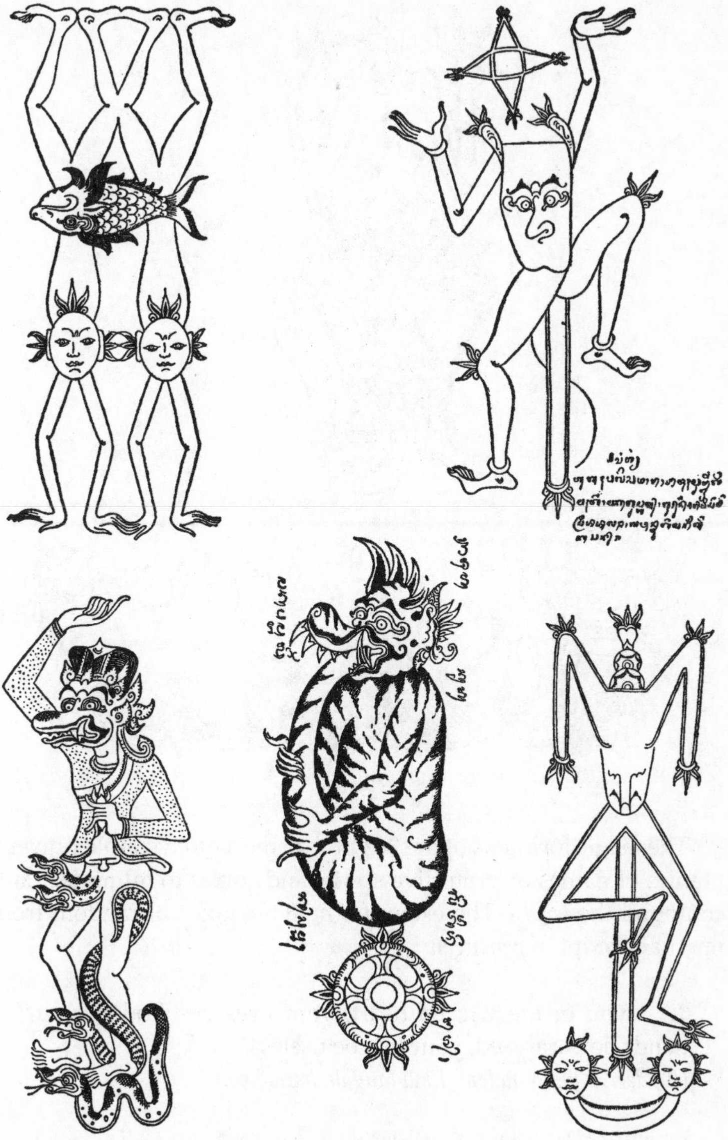

Tumbals, amulets against witches

Tumbal

The magic formulas of the "right" are most often simple prayers, litanies of names of protective spirits and curses to intimidate and confound the *leyaks*. The examples here are taken at random from my manuscript of *penengen:*

> ". . . you of the wicked heart, your eyes be blinded, your hands be paralyzed, your feet be useless."
> (*Ih, deriya mata malem, lima langah, batis jojo*.)

> "... The high and learned who understand the formulas watch over my body day and night, in good and in bad, they watch over me so that I shall not die in my dreams, die in health. Do not be afraid."

(*Ne manusa luwih pengurúh merta sandi mantra, ngijing sai, ring swakú petang lemah, ala-ayú, ané nunggú akú apangeda matí ngipi, mati ngawag-ngawag, tan kuwasa molah.*)

". . . ONG! the Original Word, whose brilliance is like the air that fills the sky, a spell is on my house, a great forest surrounded by tigers. A thousand witches bow down to me meekly and fearfully [because] the amulet given to my enemies by the gods is worn out and spoiled. . . ."
(ONG, *saremula, sutejaniya kadi kangin ngibehing akasa, tulah tumpur umahkú alas agung macan mengidèrim, lèlo tumpuragung siú leyaké membah, sing serana punah pegawen sandelung, paweh dewa punah, teka punah.*)

". . . ONG! ang ung mang ang ah. I am Sanghyang Sukla the Powerful. I descend with the sun and the moon, I am above Kala Rahú. My head-dress has a white diamond and the gods love me. Sanghyang Tintiya and Sarad Manik contemplate me, my parasol is yellow and Brahma admires me. Fire descend! Clean the country and burn all the devils, burn all the witches, burn Banaspati Raja, burn them all! . . ."
(ONG, *ang ung mang ang ah. Arankú Sanghyang Sukla Wisesa, tumurun akú ring Surya amor ring Sanghyang Ulan, anunggang akú Kala Rahú, gelunganakú wintén petak, sarwa dewa kasih, anelengakú Sanghyang Tintiya, wetú Sarad Manik, apayong akú jenar, anelang akú ring Brahma, metú gení melesat sejagat, sekuwihning buta peresel geseng, leyak geseng, Banaspati Raja geseng, teka geseng. . . .*)

In many of these formulas the *leyaks*, demons, and even the higher spirits are mercilessly abused and there are often phrases by which the exalted magician places himself on equal footing with the gods and even above them. Thus it is easy to understand why the Balinese fear uttering the formulas and why they feel that only the highly prepared or the naturally magic people like the priests may do so with impunity. Many priests and witch-doctors sincerely believe they possess in themselves powers equal to the spirits', but the ordinary people, who look in awe at all this hocus-pocus, either buy the amulets already strengthened by the formulas of a priest or witch-doctor or, always resourceful, depend on offerings, trances, and dramatic exorcizing performances of plays and dances like the *Calon Arang* or the *sanghyang*, when the deities themselves provide the necessary amulets.

THE WITCH-DOCTORS, MAGIC, AND MEDICINE

There were two medicine-men, two *balians* among the friends that often visited us. One of these was a learned, serious, middle-aged man who practiced medicine and was progressive enough to adopt some Western medicines like quinine tablets for malaria, to which, however, he added Balinese magic by reciting formulas over them. He liked to discuss the methods of foreigners and often came to us to ask for medicines. The other *balian* was the extreme reverse; he enjoyed the terrifying reputation of teacher and chief of bands of *leyaks*, and our friends had warned us in whispers that many of the old women of our *leyak*-ridden neighborhood were his pupils; nobody had the slightest doubt of his great magical powers. His appearance was as demoniac as his reputation: enormous fingernails on knotty long fingers, half-extinguished little eyes burning still with a wicked gleam, and a great, bloody cave for a mouth, entirely toothless and always crimson with betel juice. He dressed smartly in a blue silk *saput*, and his gestures showed a rather studied elegance. He was gay and solicitous, but he loved to appear mysterious at times.

Our two friends belonged to the two arch-types of Balinese *balians*. One was the inspired mystic who works through fits of temperament and trances to fight the evil forces and who by his inherent *saktí* is able to dominate the supernatural spirits. Shamanism is his medium; he can see "far away" by going into a trance and looking into a mirror or a container with water. Through his self-induced trances he comes in contact with his assisting spirit, perhaps his father's, a former great *balian*, whose reputation establishes the prestige enjoyed by the son; thus possessed by his assisting spirit, he is able to go into the spirit world and fight the wrongdoer. During the trances the *balian* growls and mumbles monologues similar to those in plays, in which he relates his adventures in Hades. Often he dances entranced, elegant versions of duels with malignant spirits. I was told that such a *balian* can see a guilt in the eyes of a boy or a girl who is still "pure"—that is, uncontaminated by sexual intercourse. By going into a trance, *balians* are also able to trace the past history of an old kris or some similar object.

While the intuitive witch-doctor (*balian ngengengan*) works mainly through his inspiration and his inherent *saktí*, the learned *balian* (*balian wisada*), "who can read," depends for his effectiveness on a mixture of practical medicine and religious magic learned from palm-leaf manuscripts (*lontar* or *rontal*). Although not a priest, he knows all the good and evil gods and the manner of their approach; he understands the calendar and knows the proper formulas and magic words, cabalistic symbols, and so forth, which he combines with real medical knowledge, of massage, herbs, and roots. Thus, assisted by the faith of his patients, he can perform real cures.

A *balian* inherits his father's wisdom, his *saktí*, and the accessories of his ritual: magic stones and coins which are placed in water that is given to the patient to drink, calendars and charts for horoscopes, but mainly old treatises on magic and medicine, the possession of which alone already gives *balians* certain powers. Besides the aforementioned manuscripts on "right" and "left" magic, they own special books on love magic (*pengaséh*), collections of models for pictorial amulets (*tetumbalan*), and books on medicine and medical recipes (*wisada* and *tetulak*). These are copied when the old ones have become too worn, and the discarded palm-leaves are burned to prevent them from falling into the wrong hands; the burned remains are then eaten by the owner in order not to waste any of their magic power.

Balians do not divulge their secrets readily; they claim that they would lose their power to recover their human identity after a trance and would go insane if they revealed their formulas or sold their books. They have successfully injected fear of their dangerous practices among the common people, who shudder even at the sight of their magic books. The profession of *balian* is surrounded with an air of mystery, and although there are many kindly and respectable *balians*, it is believed that there are also wicked ones who use magic to do physical harm to a client's enemy. For this purpose they are said to employ the universal system of sympathetic magic by which through the possession of something that belonged to or formed part of the victim—clothes, locks of hair, nail-cuttings, saliva, and even the soil taken from a footprint—they can gain control of the physical and mental condition of the person. Through sympathy between the victim and something of his—his image, a photograph or a doll containing any of the above ingredients—his soul is captured and tortured because he feels the harm done to his image. Consequently the Balinese carefully collect and bury all nail-cuttings, hair, tooth-filings, and so forth.

Just as the Balinese believe that foreigners are immune from the attacks of witches simply because they are of a race apart, so they believe that European medicines and the knowledge of white doctors, pills, liquids in bottles, and bitter or smelly powders, can be effective only to cure the people who invented them. Furthermore, the lack of showmanship of doctors, of dramatic hocus-pocus with which to paralyze the evil forces which they believe cause illness, leave them without faith in their curative ability. Many refuse absolutely to be cured by Europeans, others accept treatment out of politeness, and the few that go to the hospitals do so only after everything else has failed them. It is natural that medical treatment fails then to cure an advanced stage of illness.

In case of serious sickness a folded leaf of pandanus is hung on the gate as a sign of taboo (*sawén*) to inform the village. Then only relatives may enter the house and may only approach the sick person after stamping their feet on the kitchen floor to shake off whatever evil influences may still cling to them. A *balian* is called, and if his magic succeeds in effecting a cure, the patient gives many offerings and has to undergo purifying ceremonies to lose the *sebel*.

The Balinese attach great significance to any sort of physical sickness and, having no great hardships to discuss, to complain of illness, no matter how slight, is a favorite subject of conversation. Colds, cough, stomach-ache, neuralgia, and other minor ailments make them miserable, although they can cure them effectively with domestic concoctions of herbs, roots, barks, flowers, and especially by massage, which they have developed into a real science. However, despite the appearance of being an unusually healthy race, the Balinese are victims of many serious afflictions for which they know no cure.

Worst among these are the widespread venereal diseases; syphilis and gonorrhoea seem to prevail although in an inherited, latent state. Supposedly of ancient introduction, the diseases do not appear in malignant forms and the Balinese seem to have developed a certain immunity that makes them carriers despite a healthy appearance. It is common to see the whitish veil of gonorrhœa in the eyes of elderly people and often a boy or a girl of our *banjar* broke out in sores of an unmistakable origin and had to be sent to the hospital for inoculations. But the reluctance of the Balinese to undertake foreign treatment, the forbidding cost of Salvarsan, and the natural promiscuity do not. help the situation.

The violent rainy seasons bring epidemics of tropical fevers, and malaria takes many lives, especially of children. The Balinese attempt to cure the fevers with concoctions of *dadap* leaves, onions, anise, salt, and coal from the hearth, which, after straining, is given to the patient to drink, and he is put to sleep. It is also effective to rub the sides with a paste of mashed *dadap* leaves, onions, anise, and *tinké,* a sort of nutmeg, and to rub the back with coconut oil with scrapings of *dadap* bark; but quinine is rapidly gaining popularity. The Balinese love a clear skin and they are disturbed by the prevalent skin diseases, from the ugly but harmless *kurab,* a skin discoloration produced by a parasitic fungus, to itches, frambœsia, and tenacious tropical ulcers. The *kurab* (called *bulenan* when in small patches) appears as whitish spots on the brown skin and spreads all over if not checked. It is cured by rubbing the affected areas with *lalang* grass, but it has been discovered that it disappears quickly with salycilic alcohol from the Chinese druggists. Itches are cured with lemon juice, coconut oil, and frequent baths in hot water in which *legundí* and *ketawalí* leaves are macerated.

People after middle age complain of "bone trouble," rheumatism, due to the extreme humidity of the island, and as a preventive they wear bracelets of *kayú ulí,* a sort of black coral from Borneo. It is said that the pain can be driven out by marking the feet with a hot iron, which does not hurt the patient because "the teeth of the fire are taken away by a *mantra.*" Headaches are cured by massage, but it helps to spray the forehead with a mixture of crushed ginger and mashed bedbugs. For stomachache they drink the red infusion of *medaiáh* bark from Java. A cough is relieved by drinking an infusion of *blimbing buluh* flowers mixed with parched, grated coconut, also sprayed externally on the throat. Head colds are cured by massage, but it is good for sneezing to smell a piece of *telor* bark three times. Such are the most common of domestic remedies, but for each illness there are seven medicines used consecutively when the preceding ones fail to give relief. The keystone of Balinese medicine is the principle of "hot" and "cold," irritating and refreshing, also applied to foods. Thus a heated or irritated condition is cured by a cooling medicine.

The Balinese are helpless in the case of infected wounds, but it is always a means of breaking the ice with a foreign neighbor to ask for medicine for an infected cut covered with a greenish mess and wrapped in a dirty rag. Rose treated many such cases soon after our arrival in Belaluan and eventually we had a great circle of faithful friends who brought presents of food to show their appreciation. On our return trip we found that the full responsibility for such cases had fallen on our American friends Jack and Katharane Mershon, former dancers, who had settled on the malarial Sanur coast, where they conducted an improvised but effective free clinic. They spent their spare money on medicines and took turns every day treating scores of people, often coming from afar with the most frightful sores. The disinterested work of the Mershons made them the idols of the neighborhood and they are known only as *tuan doctor* and *nyonya doctor*. There is of course a fine modern hospital in Denpasar, but the Balinese prefer the more informal, sympathetic clinic of the Mershons.

ADDITIONAL NOTES

I. *Rangda and Barong*. The origin of the fascinating Rangda is now confused, fantastic myth, a sample of which is the following tale as it was told to me by an old man of Denpasar:

A concubine of King Erlangga gave birth to a pair of pigs, a dreadful omen of approaching calamity. The Brahmanas were consulted and they advised turning the pigs loose in the forest. The pigs played havoc with the trees, and to prevent further destruction, Sanghyang Berawi (Begawati) turned them into two beautiful women, whom she named Cumpu Mas and Tanting Mas. She gave them a small book of *lontar* palm and ordered them to study the powerful magic formulas contained in it. Cumpu Mas decided to remain in the jungle, keeping the book with her, but Tanting Mas went to the country of Lemah Tulis, where she married the holy man Begawan Mpú Gandu. "Because the holy man could not bear the fire of Tanting Mas," he went to live in the forest as a hermit. There he met an *endéh*, the dancing flame of a witch, that turned out to be Cumpu Mas, his wife's sister, now a proficient witch. So impressed was the holy man with her beauty that he married her on the spot, but on the following day, when he went to perform his daily purification, he found among his cleansing paraphernalia the entrails of a corpse, freshly dug out of the cemetery by Cumpu Mas. Enraged at the profanation, the priest declared a magic war on the witch and turned into a great cremation tower to intimidate her. She became fire that consumed the tower, leaving her a *rangda,* a widow. The Rangda later became pre_ changed her name to Sirowalú (also meaning "widow"), and lived on as queen of the forest of Alas Trung in the country of Dirah, becoming known as the "Widow from Dirah" (Rangda ning Dirah, or Girah). Her child was born in the jungle and grew up to be the famed beauty Ratna Menggali.

There are many varied versions of the tale, in one of which Tanting Mas and Cumpu Mas are the result of the dreaded male and female twins, Tanting Mas the male who struggles with his twin sister for supremacy, becoming Banaspati Raja, "Lord of the Jungle," the Barong's name. This would explain the origin of the Rangda and Barong if it were not for the fact that the Balinese are thoroughly confused in regard to their identity; I have been told that Erlangga himself turns into a Barong to fight Rangda and that Batara Budda and the Barong are the same. It is obvious, nevertheless, that they are not purely Balinese: Rangdas are unknown in the oldest villages and the character and appearance of the witch presents a striking similarity with the wild-eyed, fanged demons of Tibet and northern India, where Tantric Buddhism holds sway. In Nepal there is a long-haired devil called *lakahe* who dances like Rangda, holding a white cloth which it uses as a weapon. Both the Rangda and the Barong seem to belong to the Tantric Buddhist lore, perhaps to the now disappeared Bhairawa sect that flourished in Bali in Erlangga's time.

Bhairawa Buddhism remains the deliverance element in the Hindu-Balinese religion, a short cut to the release of the soul from the cycle of reincarnations, attained not by simple propitiation of gods, but by direct control of the supernatural by man's own magic powers. The Bhairawas paid homage to a sort of Durga—Sanghyang Berawi or Begawati, their deity of evil and death—and they influenced the higher cult with a new demonology, death cult, magic science, and magic terminology. It imparted a strong magic flavor to the national religion, but it disappeared as a separate sect. According to Lekkerkerker and Stutterheim, Buddhism, or, rather, Buddhist magic, was introduced in Bali about A.D. 96, perhaps by the apostles, the brothers Mpú Kuturan and Mpú Bharada from Kediri (Daha). To them is attributed authorship of the civil and religious laws of Bali. Mpú Bharada, hero of the *Calon Arang* and teacher of Erlangga, was the magician who vanquished Rangda and today remains the most important figure in the magic lore.

A good deal of speculation revolves around the significance of the word *Barong,* for which there is no acceptable explanation. The Malay for "bear," *baruang,* has been suggested, but Malay was a recently introduced language and there were no bears in Bali. The classic Barong is called *barong ketet* or *kekek,* but there are also Barongs in the form of tigers (*barong macan*), of pigs (*barong bangkal*), of lions (*barong singha*); and once we saw one in the shape of an elephant (*barong gajah*). There are also Barongs in human shape like the giant puppets (*barong landong*) who, holy as they are, perform ribald slapstick comedy. The main characters of the *barong landong* are Jero Gedé, "The Big One," an evil giant identified with the fanged monster Jero Gedé Mecaling, the demon of Nusa Penida, and Luh, "The Female," a lewd old woman. Most intriguing Barongs are those reported in Trunyan by Walter Spies (*Das grosse Fest im Dorfe Trunjan*): in this ancient Bali Aga village a great festival is held in which the *trunas*, the virgin boys, with their naked bodies covered with dried banana leaves, which give them the appearance of great cabbages, and wearing frightful primitive masks, run around the temple grounds whipping savagely anyone who comes within their reach. These fierce monsters are called *barong berutuk*, a term for which there is no interpretation. Two of these are the *druwené*, the male and female *berutuk* Rajas, and are reminiscent of the Jerogede and Jeroluh of the *barong landong*. They are seen with respectful awe by everybody, and leaves from their dresses are supposedly infallible amulets. Daring people try to steal bits of leaf from their dresses, but are mercilessly whipped by the other *berutuks*, who seem to respect only the village elders and the small children. The ceremony ends at sunset, when the monsters are disarmed of their whips and the now confident crowd can approach to watch the lecherous love dance of the male and female *druwenés*, after which the entranced performers tear off their banana-leaf coverings and, completely naked except for their grimacing masks, jump into Lake Batur and swim for a while with the masks on, returning in the dark to have the sacred masks respectfully put away after the priests make offerings to them.

In behavior and appearance the ordinary Barong resembles the Chinese lion or chimera called *gee-ling* that performs wild antics during the Chinese New Year to the tune of gongs, drums, and firecrackers. In Bali during the first month after *galunggan*, considered as the New Year, the Barongs are permitted to wander over the streets and roads making *upa*—that is, performing for pennies. The most sacred part of the Barong is its beard of human hair coquettishly decorated with fresh flowers. *Penawar* water, a protective amulet, is made by dipping this beard into ordinary water while saying a prayer. Hairs from this beard are worn around the wrists as amulets. There are also extraordinary Barongs that are covered with crow and even peacock feathers instead of the usual fleece of horses' tails or fibers. I was told of a village who wished to have a Barong of crow feathers; the villagers only had to pray for them and one morning they found the temple yard strewn with the most beautiful shiny black feathers.

Balinese with imagination have told me that the Barong is Mpú Bharada, who fights Rangda in this form; that he is Banaspati, the Lord of the Jungle, who is madly in love with Sanghyang Berawi and who assumes the Barong shape to make love to her, but she will have none of it and turns into a Rangda to punish his insolence.

2. *Sanghyang*. A variety of *sanghyang* is the *sanghyang déling* found in Kintamani and other villages around the crater of the Batur. The girls are put into the trance by means of two dolls representing the deities, strung through their middles by a cord, the ends of which are attached to short sticks tensely held by two boys. The string with the dolls is thus held taut in front of the two kneeling girls, songs are chanted, and the boys go into trance; their arms become rigid and commence to shake, causing the dolls to dance back and forth across the cord. As the boys shake more and more violently, the vibration increases and the dolls leap, whirl, and clash against each other. The girls have become drowsy and suddenly faint, going into the trance to be dressed and dance as in the ordinary *sanghyang*.

Another variety is the *sanghyang jarán*, in which the temple priest, the *pemangku*, becomes himself the *sanghyang*, possessed by an ancestral deity, a Gandarwa on horseback. We saw a *pemangku* in Bedulu go into the trance with two boys, his assistants, each riding on small prop horses and dancing in and out of a great blazing pile of burning coconut shells. The *sanghyang jarán* is reminiscent of a trance performance from Central Java called *kuda kepang*—men wearing dark glasses and riding on beautifully stylized horses woven out of bamboo.

3. SANGHYANG SONGS (*gending sanghyang*):

1. *Wau nusdus:*
   Merik sumunung asep, menyan majegau, ia cendana hukus maulekan, ia lelinggan Betara Tiga; ia wus matinining, ia menusa ngasti pukulum, ia nurunan Dedarí kendran, ia Sang Supraba, Tunjung Birú, ia Tunjung Birú, ia mengerangsuk meanggóanggó, ia sesalukin baju mas-masan, ia melicat miber magegana, ia mengelo ngaja-kanginan, ia jalan Dedarí metangun jeró, ia tamané bek misi sekar, ia sekar emas sandingin pudak, angrek gringsing, ia tigakancú, manás, solí, sempol, ia, kedapané malelepe; malelepe makebiyur ketaman sarí, lamun nudus Kadewatan, turun Dedarí kendran.

2 *Nyaluk gelung:*
   Gelung, ia gelung agung, mebulingker ia sekar gadung, metitis Garuda

mungkur, ia, sekar sempol, ia, sekar gambir, sandat gubar anggen susun, merak mekuncir kuning, payas dané ia mepulilit, mengigal tengahing natar, ia igal dané manggu-pipir, metanjek megulu wangsul

3. *Mangunan sanghyang:*
Sekar menuk mengedanin, ia ia putih, ia ia ia ia putih mengarnbiar, buka bintangé diduúr, bintang kartí, bintang kartikané sedih; ia liyer, ia ia ia liyer, liyer, buka twara bakat ruruh, ruruh nujú, ruruh nujú, galang sasih; ia ia lengkik, ia lengkik lengkik, sayang san munyin dasihé; dasih nika, dasih nika, tut kalanin, ia ia aduh! ia ia ia ia aduh mirah! Idewa dadí pangelipur, lipuranda, lipuran Dedari kalé; ia ia lengkik, ia ia ia ia lengkik, metand/ek megulu wangsul.

4. *Wus mengigal; meketis toya:*
Dewa ayú metangí, Dewa metangí, juru kidung sampun rauh mengambelang gending sanghyang; ih! Yang Yang Dedarí munggah kepesilih, ia ia mider, ia mider, mider dané; aduh! Dewa Sang Ayú, ngambil, ia ngambil tirta sanggar agung, tirta empul, yeh ning Sudamala, sekar jepun angkitang ratna madurí, ia pucuk petak, teleng birú, iwa mekaria tirta, tirta ning sibuh mas, toya pemastú, pekarian saking Swarga, siratin Ragan I Dewa, raris ketisin juru kidungé, wus meketis mantuk maring Inderaloka; Mesiram lungga kataman, wus mesiram, mesekar angrek saseh mepatuhan pemarginé muleh; mantuk Dewa mantuk, mantuke ka Suralaya, mantuk maring ileh ileh, angin tarik, kurungania, waluya dadí manusa. Puput.

CHAPTER ELEVEN

Death and Cremation

STRANGE AS IT SEEMS, it is in their cremation ceremonies that the Balinese have their greatest fun. A cremation is an occasion for gaiety and not for mourning, since it represents the accomplishment of their most sacred duty: the ceremonial burning of the corpses of the dead to liberate their souls so that they can thus attain the higher worlds and be free for reincarnation into better beings.

At cremation ceremonies hundreds of people in a wild stampede carry the beautiful towers, sixty feet high, solidly built of wood and bamboo and decorated with tinsel and expensive silks, in which the bodies are transported to the cremation grounds. There the corpses are placed in great cows (hewn out of tree-trunks to serve as coffins and covered with precious materials), and cows, towers, offerings, and ornaments are set on fire, hundreds and even thousands of dollars burned in one afternoon in a mad splurge of extravagance by a people who value the necessities of life in fractions of pennies.

To the Balinese, the material body is only the shell, the container of the soul. This soul lives in every part of the body, even in the hair and nails, but it is concentrated in the head which is near-holy to them. A Balinese observes the rank of his head in relation to the rest of his body, and for this reason no one would stand on his head or take any position that would place his feet on a higher level. It is an offence even to pat a small child on the head and there is no worse insult than "I'll beat your head!" One's soul wanders away during sleep (dreams are its travels and adventures), without becoming, however, entirely detached from the body, and it is considered dangerous to awaken a person too suddenly. Children are never beaten, so as not to shock their tender, still undeveloped souls.

Madness, epilepsy, and idiocy are the results of a bewitched soul, but ordinary sickness is due to a weakened, polluted soul rather than to mere physical causes. Life vanishes when the soul escapes from the body through the mouth, and death occurs when it refuses to return. The relatives of a dying man who has lost consciousness go to the temple of the dead and, through a medium, beg the deities for the release and return of his soul. By force of habit, the soul lingers near the body when death comes, and remains floating in space or lives in a tree near by until liberated by the obliteration of the corpse by the elements: by earth, by fire, and by water, to destroy the last unclean tie that binds the souls of the dead to this earth. By cremation the soul is released to fly to the heavens for judgment and return to be reborn into the dead man's grandchildren. Failure to liberate the soul by neglecting to perform the cremation or by incomplete or improper rites would force the soul to turn into a ghost that would haunt the careless descendants.

Cremation rites were probably not introduced into Bali until the time of Majapahit, about the thirteenth century, but the ancient Balinese animists already believed that their life-fluid was immortal and that after death it returned to animate other beings. They practiced the obliteration of the corpse by burial or, as is still done in the primitive village of Sembiran, simply by abandoning the bodies in the forest at the edge of a ravine to be eaten by wild animals. A man in Bali is born into a superior state—a higher caste—if his behavior on this earth has been good; otherwise he will reincarnate into a lower stage of life to begin over again the progressive march towards ultimate perfection. A man who is guilty of serious crimes is punished by being reborn, often for periods of thousands of years, into a tiger, a dog, a snake, a worm, or a poisonous mushroom.

Between incarnations, until the time comes for its return to this earth, the soul goes to Indra's heaven, the *swarga,* a reservoir where "life is just as in Bali, but devoid of all trouble and illness." But this process does not go on forever; when the individual has attained the highest wisdom and has reached the highest position among men, that of a Brahmana who has been ordained as a priest, he hopes to obtain liberation from this cycle of births and become a god. The man of low caste attributes his state to former misconduct, redeemable in future lives only through a virtuous existence, which entitles him to be reborn into a higher and higher caste.

A man's life on this earth is but an incident in the long process of the soul's evolution.

The grand send-off of the soul into heaven, in the form of a rich and complete cremation, is the life-ambition of every Balinese. He looks forward to it, often making provision during life with savings or property that can be pawned or sold to finance his cremation. The greatest happiness that comes to a Balinese family is to have, in this way, accomplished the liberation of the souls of their dead, but complete cremation ceremonies are so costly that a family of limited means have to wait often for years, haunted by the fact that their dead are not yet cremated, and are sometimes obliged to sacrifice their crops and their lands in order to pay for the ceremonies. The expenses of a cremation are enormous; besides the priest's fees, the great amounts of holy water used, and the costly towers, coffins, offerings, and so forth, there is the food and entertainment provided for days for the hundreds of guests and assistants that help in the ceremonies.

A rich cremation adds greatly to the prestige of a well-to-do family, giving occasion for gay, extravagant festivities that are eagerly anticipated despite the financial burden they represent. A good average for a great cremation is seldom less than a thousand *ringgits* or about two million *kepengs* (a *ringgit* is worth about one gold dollar in normal exchange), but there have been cremations of princes that cost as much as fifty thousand guilders (at the time of writing, about twenty-five thousand dollars).

The cremation of the mother of Naséh, a former servant of ours, was the poorest we ever witnessed. She was burned three days after her death with only the most essential rites, but even then the costs amounted to more than the fifty guilders that Naséh had succeeded in borrowing. A unique and rather improvised cremation of a nobleman of Pemecutan cost only three hundred and fifty guilders because the body had to be burned on the same day the death occurred and I was told by the relatives that had the corpse been kept for the reglementary forty-two days, the cremation would have cost over two thousand guilders. The extraordinary decision to cremate a man of high caste immediately became possible only because the festival that the community was preparing for, their greatest in a decade, could not have taken place had there been an important uncremated corpse in the village. The family was in difficult financial circumstances and they welcomed the decision.

A Brahmanic priest is essential to a proper cremation, and only the destitute would call upon a lesser priest. The quality of the ceremonies the priest performs is determined by the fee paid to him. There is a choice of three kinds of cremation: *utama*, the highest, costing an average of fifty dollars in fees for the priest alone; *madia*, the medium-class cremation, for about twenty-five dollars; and *nista*, the low, for about five dollars. The rites for each are about the same, the difference consisting in the quality and power of the magic formulas and symbols and the sort of holy water used, the credentials given by the priest to the soul entering heaven, and the more or less thorough purification of the soul.

It is always a good resource, in a great cremation of a prince, to provide a retinue of souls for his trip into the beyond and to profit at the same time by the magical and social advantages of a more elegant cremation. In Krobokan we witnessed the release of two hundred and fifty souls of commoners who accompanied a member of the royal family. It is of extreme importance, however, to keep within the rules prescribed for each caste, the breach of which would bring dreadful punishment upon guilty relatives who in their craving for ostentation should use rites or materials for the accessories allotted to a higher caste. These rules are at times infringed and it becomes the source of malicious gossip if a family use a cow instead of a lion to burn their deceased, or if they have more roofs in their tower than is their right. In a few cases the right of cremation is denied, as in the death of exiles from the island. Lepers are buried in hidden places and their redemption is carried out by pious persons, secretly and through an effigy.

THE BODY

To the Balinese only the soul is really important, the body being simply an unclean object to be got rid of, about which there is no hysteria. Details which would be considered weird and shocking elsewhere are regarded naturally and with great indifference. I have seen a corpse poked, to help it burn, by relatives who were making loud jokes and scolding the body because it would not burn quickly enough, so they could go home.

When a man dies, his relatives, near and far, are expected to assemble and bring presents of food to the immediate family of the deceased. It is believed that the ghost of the dead man will bring them bad luck if they are not informed within three days. Automatically all relatives of the dead man become impure, *sebel,* and cannot enter the temples until the complete purification rites have been performed. This impurity extends to the house and even to the entire village, and the higher the position of the dead one, the greater the degree of uncleanliness of the village.

A sign of death in a house is the lamp called *damar kurung,* made of white tissue paper stretched over a bamboo frame and hung outside the gate. This lamp hangs from a bird, also of bamboo and white paper, which is suspended from the end of a tall bamboo pole, high over the roofs. Every night while the corpse is in the house the lamp is lit to show the way to the wandering soul. The corpse is placed in one of the pavilions of the house to await an auspicious day to be treated and purified for burial, or to be mummified if it is to be kept in the house. High priests may not be buried and it is customary to keep their bodies within the house until time for their cremation comes; this was also done to the corpses of princes, and in the great palaces there is even a special court devoted to this purpose, but this is becoming rare nowadays because of the extraordinary expenses it involves. (See Note A, page 350.)

On the first auspicious day after the death occurs, two altars are erected in the courtyard of the house for the purification of the body; one for the sun and another for Prajapati, the deity of cremation. These are decorated with *lamaks* and filled with offerings that are renewed daily. The naked corpse is then placed on a stretcher with its sexual parts covered with a small square of cloth or by the hand of the wife or husband. The priest sprinkles the body with holy water and recites prayers; the hair is combed and anointed with perfumed oil and the teeth are filed off if this had not been done during life. The body is then rubbed with a mixture of rice flour and turmeric, with salt, vinegar, and sandalwood powder. The toes and thumbs are bound together with white yarn, and rolls of *kepengs* are tied to the hands, which are folded over the breast in an attitude of prayer. Then come the *bantén sucí:* shreds of mirror glass which are laid on the eyelids, bits of steel on the teeth, a gold ring with a ruby in the mouth, jasmine flowers in the nostrils, and iron nails on the four limbs—all symbols of the more perfect senses with which the person will be reborn; stronger and more beautiful, "with eyes as bright as mirrors, teeth like steel, breath as fragrant as flowers, and bones of iron" (according to Wirtz). The head is covered with a white cloth, and an egg is rolled all over the body to signify its newly acquired purity. The corpse is next wrapped in many yards of white cloth, in a straw mat, and again in more yards of cloth, and finally bound tightly on the *ranté*, an external covering of split bamboo tied with rattan.

If the corpse is to be buried and not mummified, it is taken to the cemetery with music, accompanied by singing relatives, who carry offerings and bamboo tubes with holy water. Before lowering the body into the shallow grave, the offerings are dedicated to Mother Earth, a prayer is recited, and money is thrown in to pay for the ground used. The corpse is laid in the grave with an open bamboo tube in the place of the mouth to let the soul out, the grave is filled, and a bamboo structure with a roof of white tissue paper is erected over it. A small altar of bamboo is placed next to the grave for offerings, brought daily for a period of twelve days. Offerings are brought again forty-two days after the date of death, when it is considered that the soul has been completely detached from the body and the cremation can take place, provided there is money available; otherwise it has to be postponed until means are obtained, often years later.

The high priest is next consulted to determine the propitious day on which to hold the cremation—a date far enough in advance to allow for the elaborate preparations. A few days before the date named, the relatives start for the cemetery to dig up the remains. The grave is opened and the body removed or as much of the body as remains after an interment which lasts from a month and seven days to even two years and longer. Sometimes there is not more than a few bones to be found, but even these are collected and arranged as nearly as possible in the form of the human body. These are wrapped in a bundle of new white cloth and carried back to the house. It was an eerie sight when on a rainy day the men of Pemecutan were opening the graves for a mass cremation, searching the mud-filled trenches, cavorting and shouting with delight at the discovery of a blackened jaw-bone or a femur.

At home, the bundle containing the remains is placed again on the pavilion reserved for the corpse, now strewn with silks and brocades and ornamented with the family's heirlooms: gold and silver vessels, peacock feathers, jeweled krisses, and so forth. The remains are covered with many cloths bearing magic inscriptions, over which are placed the offerings and the many ritual accessories that symbolize or contain the dead man's soul.

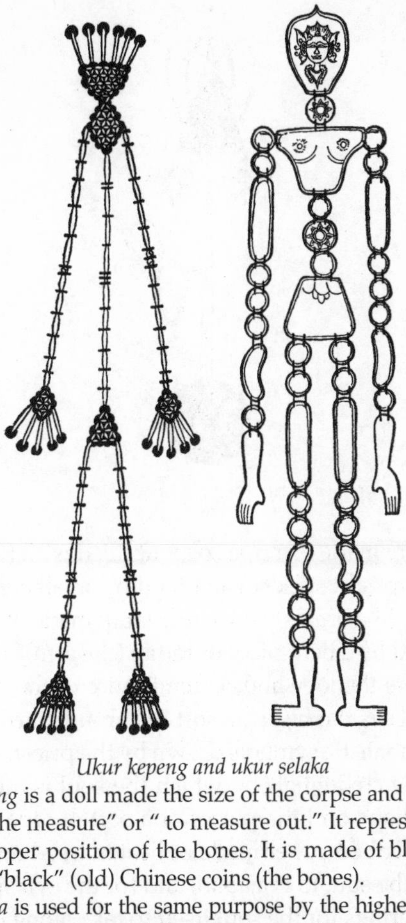

Ukur kepeng and ukur selaka

The *ukur kepeng* is a doll made the size of the corpse and cremated with it. "*Ukur*" means " the measure" or " to measure out." It represents the skeleton, indicating the proper position of the bones. It is made of blessed white yarn (the nerves) and "black" (old) Chinese coins (the bones).

The *ukur selaka* is used for the same purpose by the higher castes and prosperous people in conjunction with the *ukur kepeng*. It is made of silver plaques strung on silver wires, and is not cremated with the corpse, but is used over and over as a family heirloom. A similar figure is sometimes made of gold (*ukur mas*).

Among these are the *kekreb sinom*, a sort of lattice of coconut leaves with flowers in the crossings; and the *ukur*, a human representation showing the proper position of the bones and nerves, usually simply *kepengs* (the bones) strung on ropes of white yarn (the nerves), but the prosperous use *ukurs* made of silver or gold plaques representing the head, hands, feet, and bones, held together by wires of the same metal. These are used for display and are replaced by an ordinary *ukur* of coins for the actual burning. An interesting accessory is the *angenan*, a

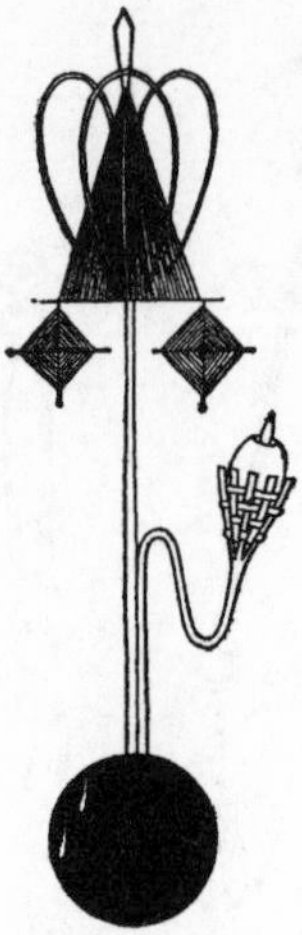

Angenan

curious structure made of a ripe coconut filled with rice (the heart) as the base of an upright stick surmounted by an elaborate structure of colored threads (the brains) and a little lamp made of an eggshell (the soul), supported by a bent piece of rattan (the arm). This is supposed to commemorate the love and remembrance of the dead person. Of great importance is the *kajang,* a sort of shroud, yards of white cloth covered with cabalistic symbols drawn by the priest, who also writes the *ulantaga,* the credentials by which the soul is admitted into the *swarga,* inscriptions on little pieces of a sort of tapa from Sulawesi, a specially prescribed paper made of beaten tree-bark. Offerings are made again to the sun, to Prajapati, and for the evil spirits. There are also special offerings for the soul itself to take along on its trip to the beyond: food for the soul, for its retinue, and for presents to give out along its way. These are the *ponguriagan, pisang jatí, nasí angkab, panjang ilan,* and *bubuh pirata,* the essential cremation offerings.

THE SOUL

By this time the corpse has lost all importance, and from this time on, the family is concerned entirely with the soul of the dead person. A most important accessory for the ensuing ceremonies, and the object around which the rites revolve, is the *adegan,* the effigy in which the soul is embodied to be purified. The *adegan* consists of two images, one silhouetted out of palm leaf in the traditional *cilí* shape, and a more realistic one drawn on a thin tablet of sandalwood, bound together and placed on a silver vase that rests on a silver platter. Betelnut, *sirih* leaves and flowers for praying are placed inside the vase to make the soul comfortable and, nothing being too good for it, the well-to-do add a third image made of beaten gold, bracelets, anklets, and a comb of silver or gold. The person's name is written on a small label of palm-leaf attached to each *adegan*. There is an effigy for each corpse, but only the *adegan* is used should no remains be available; for instance, if no bones should be found on opening the grave, if its location has been forgotten, or if the person died at sea or in a foreign land.

The souls are provided daily with "drinks," holy water from sacred springs. Processions go regularly to distant mountain springs to fill the new clay pots inscribed with a lotus and the sacred syllable

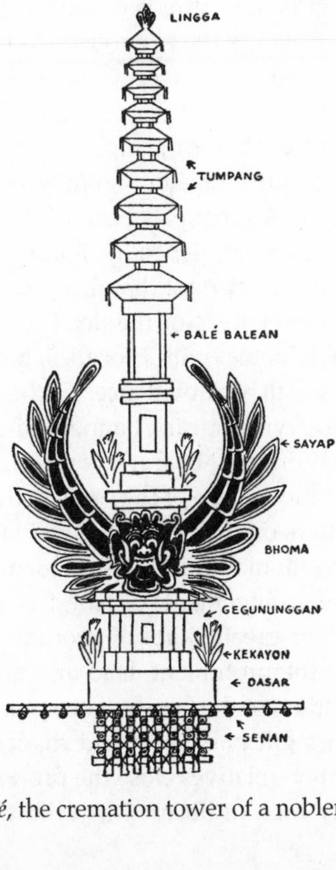

Badé, the cremation tower of a nobleman

ong, while someone casts coins into the waters and recites prayers for the spirit of the spring. Rolls of ancient "black" coppers are tied to the neck of each pot with the special white yarn used in ritual, and each pot is provided with a label bearing the name of the dead. The pots of holy water are then deposited on the pavilions where the bodies lie.

The elusive souls are next "awakened" and captured in the effigies. They are taken to the burial ground, and the company kneels in front of the open graves, strewing offerings on the ground and singing songs. The men dig the earth a little, knocking upon it, and call the souls to awaken, while someone scatters pennies to distract the devils that wait ready to pounce upon the effigies and pollute them. The procession returns home, each effigy, now incorporating a soul, carried on the head of a girl, to be blessed in the shrine of each household. Each effigy is then "cured" as if it were a corpse: it is sprinkled with holy water, the various ingredients (*bantén sucí*) to attain physical perfection (shreds of mirror, flowers, a gold ring, nails, etc.) are placed over it, the egg rolled along its length, and it is decorated with gold and silver objects. The cured effigies are placed near the corpses, *wayang* music is played, and the little egg-shell lamps of the *angenans* are lit for the night.

The ceremonies acquire greater significance as the date for the cremation approaches. A great procession is held on the eve of the cremation day to take the effigies to the house of the high priest for their final blessing. It is important that this procession be grand and luxurious, and all the relatives of the dead parade in it dressed in the finest clothes obtainable, with brocades, gold flowers, jewelry, and jeweled krisses much in evidence. Orchestras, *baris* dancers, and scores of boys carrying spears, banners, and flags, followed by long lines of women offering-bearers, come at the head of the parade; they represent the retinue of the souls in the effigies which are borne on silver platters on the heads of a specially picked group of beautiful girls in ceremonial full dress—diadems of trembling gold flowers on elaborate arrangements of hair, lacy scarfs binding their breasts, and yellow or green skirts of brocade trailing in the dirt. Often the effigies of the prominent dead are carried on the arms of the youngest descendant of the family, a boy or a girl dressed in silks and gold, riding on a gilt palanquin and shaded by gilt umbrellas of state. Groups of men relatives close the procession. In Pliatan we once saw some fifty men uniformed in yellow trailing loincloths, magenta breast-cloths, and white head-dresses, all wearing gold krisses, awkwardly conscious of being admired, marching in triple file to the beat of gongs and drums amidst bursting firecrackers.

The procession goes to the priest's house, where he waits to consecrate the effigies through a performance of *maweda,* the spoken formula emphasized by gestures of the hands. The priest recites his formulas, flings flowers, and sprinkles holy water towards the effigies, which are reverently held in front of him by the kneeling girls. After the ceremony the procession returns home, stopping along the way in the temple of the family's origin to offer a final prayer. At the house, towards dusk, the *baris* dancers perform war dances to cast a protecting net of magic vibrations, and shows are given to entertain the guests. Relatives, guests, and populace spend the night divided between watching an all-night shadow-play and listening to public readings of the Balinese classic *Bhima Swarga,* the tale of the fantastic adventures of Bhima on his visit to Hades. Tradition prescribes that this should be read aloud from beginning to end on the eve of cremation. In dark corners people huddle to steal naps. Outside, the orchestras, among them the *gambang,* only heard at cremations, boom and hum throughout the night.

THE CREMATION

The great towers in which the corpses are carried to the cremation ground and the animal-shaped coffins in which they will be burned, the two most spectacular factors in a cremation, have waited ready for days in some corner of the village, covered with screens of woven palm-leaf.

The cremation tower is a high structure solidly built of wood and bamboo, bound together with rattan and covered with colored paper ornaments and cotton-wool dyed in bright colors, and glittering with tinsel and small mirrors. Shaped like the temple gates and the sun altars, the tower represents again the Balinese conception of the cosmos: a wide base, often in the shape of a turtle with two serpents entwined around its body, the symbol of the foundation upon which the world rests, supporting three gradually receding platforms—the mountains, with bunches of paper flowers and leaves on the corner of each platform to represent the forests. Then comes an open space, the *balé balean,* "rather like a house," the space between heaven and earth. This consists of four posts backed with a board on one side,

and with a protruding platform to which the bodies are fastened. The *balé balean* is topped by a series of receding roofs like a pagoda to represent the heavens. These are always in odd numbers which vary according to the caste of the family: one for Sudras, from three to eleven for the aristocracy, and none for the Brahmanic priests. The back of the tower is nearly covered with a gigantic head of Bhoma, the Son of the Earth, a wild-eyed, fanged monster with enormous outstretched wings that spread some ten feet on each side of the tower. This mask and the wings are covered with bright-colored cotton-wool. As many as seventy-five men are often required to carry the great tower and its complementary bridge, a tall bamboo runway by which the upper stages of the tower are reached. (See Note B, page 351.)

Strict caste rules also dictate the shape of the *patulangan*, the sarcophagi: Sudras are entitled only to burn their dead in open cases shaped like a *gajah-mina*, a fantastic animal, half elephant, half fish. Today the majority of the nobility use the bull for men and the cow for women, animals supposedly once reserved for Brahmanas; Satrias were entitled only to a *singha*, a winged lion; and Wesias used the deer. Towers and coffins are not made by ordinary villagers but by artist specialists who are directed by a master craftsman. The cows are splendidly carved out of wood, the hollow body hewn out of a tree-trunk, the back of which opens like a lid. The whole animal is covered with colored felt or velvet, lavishly ornamented with gold leaf, cotton-wool, and silk scarfs. Caste again decides whether the animal should be black, white, spotted, yellow, orange, or purple. With true Balinese playfulness, their sexual organs are clearly defined and those of bulls often are made so that they can be put into action by means of a hidden string.

From dawn of the day of the cremation the house teems with excited people attending to the last details; the hosts wait on the notable guests, the women see to the offerings, hordes of half-naked men proceed to uncover the towers and the sarcophagi and bring them to the front of the house gate. Delegations are sent to the cremation grounds to put the final touches on the bamboo altars and on the platforms of tightly packed earth, roofed with colored paper and tinsel, where the corpses will be cremated.

When everything is ready and the guests have been served with their final banquet, the village *kulkul* is beaten to start the march to the cremation grounds; the way to the tower is cleared of evil influences by sprinklings of holy water, and a great fire is often made to prevent rain during the day. Eventually the corpses are taken out, not through the gate, but over a bridge or through a hole knocked out somewhere in the house walls. The groups of men in loincloths that carry the bodies are greeted with fireworks, and handfuls of *kepengs* are scattered, as a traditional custom and not because the people actually believe the evil spirits to be interested in pennies.

A second party waits outside ready to snatch the corpse from the first group, and a realistic free-for-all ensues; one group rushes against the other, yelling and hooting like madmen until the attacking party runs off, knocking one another down, turning and whirling the body in all directions "to confuse it so that it can not find its way back to the house." The corpse is disrespectfully rough-handled all the way to the tower, carried up the bamboo runway, and securely tied to the plank on the uppermost stage, the *balé balean*. Meantime the women, unconcerned with the pranks of the men, rush to the cremation place in a disorderly stampede, quite in contrast with the solemn procession of the day before. Instead of silks and gold, they wear ordinary clothes and most of them go with uncovered breasts. They carry the accessories, offerings, and the pots of holy water. The decaying evil-spirit offerings that lay for days near the corpses are piled up on bamboo stretchers and rushed to the cemetery, followed by hordes of hungry dogs that fight for the rotten food that falls on the ground.

Although there is no organization committee, the procession is soon under way. The orchestras that have played incessantly since the day before march at the head of the parade followed by the spear-bearers, the *baris* dancers, and the men who carry the cows; then come the women with the effigies, then the towers and the bridges, carried by a wild mob of half-naked, shouting men who deliberately choose the most difficult paths, falling into ditches and splashing each other with mud, almost toppling the towers over, and whirling them to further mislead the dead. The high priest rides in a dignified and mystic attitude amidst all this hullabaloo. Each tower is led to the cemetery by a long rope tied at one end to the platform where the corpses are fastened, the other end held by the hands of relatives. This rope has a special significance, and in cremations of members of the royal family, the descendants of the Dewa Agung of Klungkung, it takes the shape of a great serpent that serves as a vehicle for the souls. (See Note C, page 351.)

The noisy procession dashes along in disorderly fashion, raising clouds of dust, accompanied by fireworks and war music, until it reaches the cemetery, just outside the village. There the cows are placed on the *balé pabasmian,* the cremation pavilions, their final destination; a canopy of new white cloth, a "sky," is stretched under the paper and tinsel roof directly over the funeral pyre, and detachments from the procession walk three times around the pavilions to do them honor. The bridge is placed against the tower and men run up the runway while the attendant who rode on the tower releases two small chickens that were tied by the feet to the posts of the stage where the bodies are fastened. They are used as a substitute for the doves that in olden times were released by the widows that were sacrificed and cremated with the corpse of a prince. Their significance was probably symbolic, although the Balinese now say that they are only "to teach the soul how to fly." This may be a typical tongue-in-cheek Balinese answer to dodge a complicated explanation for outsiders.

The remains are then handed down by the men lined along the runway until they reach the ground. Each group carrying a corpse is attacked again by another party of yelling men who aim to take the body by force in fierce hand-to-hand battles. Clothes are torn to shreds and men are trampled upon until the victorious party makes away with the corpse. Meantime women attendants spread the *kajang,* the long white shroud which they hold stretched over their

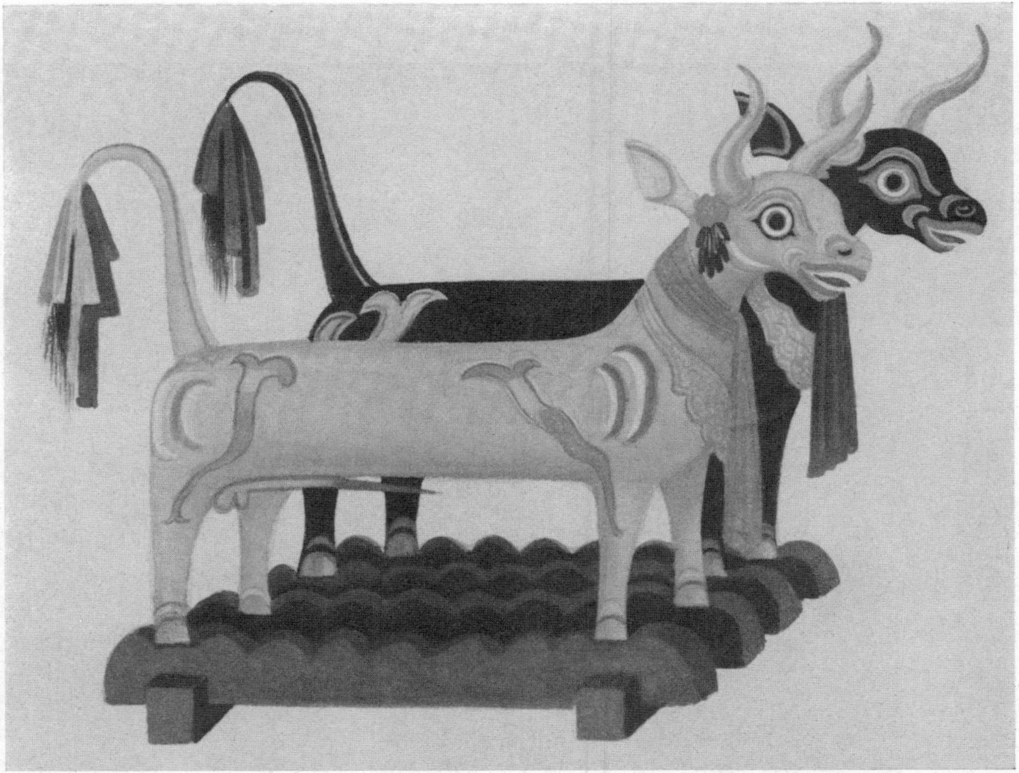

Patulangan, sarcophagi used for cremating corpses of the nobility, and made of hollowed out tree trunks, covered with felt, velvet, silks, and tinsel

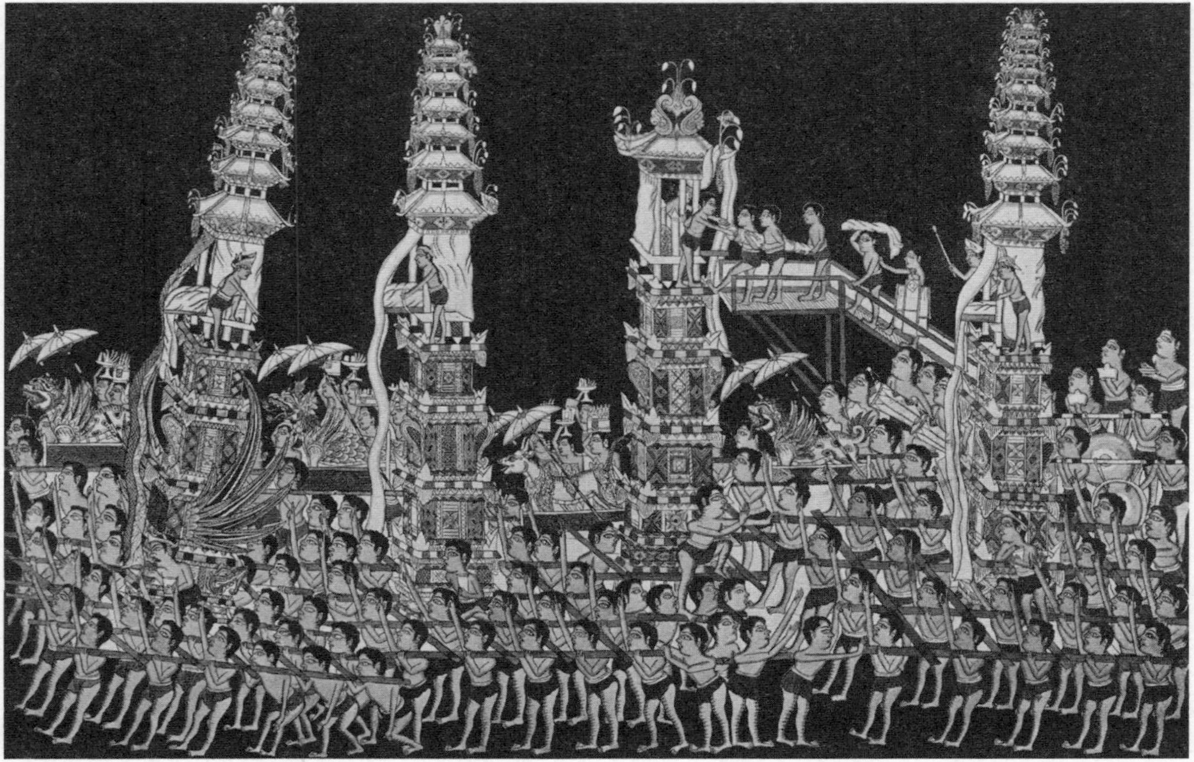

A cremation procession, as seen by a young Balinese artist

heads, attaching one end of the cloth to the corpse, held up high by as many hands as its length permits. Thus led by the *kajang*, the body is taken to the coffin, now opened by lifting the lid that forms the back of the animal, and the corpse is placed inside. Relatives crowd around it to supervise the last details and have a last look at the body, which they expose by cutting the many bindings with a special knife inscribed with magic syllables.

The high priest steps onto the platform and recites prayers over the corpse, at intervals pouring pot after pot of holy water on it, dashing the empty pots to the ground to break them, which is one of the rules. The body is so thoroughly soaked in holy water that one begins to wonder how it is possible that it will burn. Next the important accessories,[1] together with thousands of *kepengs* as ransom to Yama, the lord of hell, are spread over the body; costly silks and brocades are piled on it, and the lid is replaced, while the more voluminous offerings are put under the coffin to serve as fuel. The priest stands facing the closed coffin for a final blessing and often he himself sets off the pyre. Fire from matches is considered unclean and it should be procured by friction or by a sun-glass.

The orchestras play all at once, the *angklung* louder and more aggressive than ever, while the *gambang* hums solemnly near where the old men and the women relatives have assembled to watch the body burn. The air is heavy with the odor peculiar to cremations, which haunts one for hours after, a mixture of decaying organic matter, sweating bodies, trampled grass, charred flesh, and smoke. The mob plunders the towers to rescue the mirrors, silks, and tinsel before it is set on fire. Everybody is tense and they dash about excitedly feeding the fires, all except the high priest, who is in a trance, performing the last *maweda* on a high platform, the elderly men, who drink palm wine from tall bamboo vessels, sitting in a boisterous group, and the daughters and wives of the dead men, who remain unemotionally quiet in the background.

The men in charge poke the corpses unceremoniously with long poles, adding debris from the towers, all the while joking and talking to the corpse. The crowd is neither affected nor touched by the weird sight of corpses bursting out of the half-burned coffins, becoming anxious only when the body is slow to burn. Soon the cow's

[1] The *adegan, kajang, angenan, ukur*, and *ulantaga*.

legs give way and the coffin collapses, spilling burning flesh and calcined bones over the fire until they are totally consumed, often not without a good deal of poking. Small boys are then permitted to fish out the *kepengs* with long sticks after the unburned pieces of wood are taken away. Water is poured over the embers, and the remaining bits of bone with some ashes are piled into a little mound which is covered with palm-leaves. Green branches of *dadap* are tied to each of the four posts of the cremation pavilion, and surrounded by a rope of white yarn, thus closing it "to forget the dead." The remaining ashes are then blessed and placed in an urn, a coconut inscribed with the magic *ong* and wrapped in white cloth. It is customary that this be done just as the sun has begun to set. A new procession is formed for the march to the sea, where the ashes will be disposed of. On arrival at the seashore, or at the river if the sea is too far away, the priest wades into the water to ask of the sea or the river spirit to carry the ashes safely out. The ashes are then carefully strewn over the waters and the whole congregation bathes, to cleanse themselves before returning home in the darkness.

THE SACRIFICE OF WIDOWS

Cremation rites have remained practically unchanged for the last three hundred years, except perhaps for the suppression of the notorious Indian custom of suttee, the sacrifice of widows of deceased notables, burned alive on their husband's pyre. This custom seems to have enjoyed great popularity at one time among the Balinese aristocracy, although today it has become merely a legend. A hundred years ago the pioneer historian of the Malay Archipelago, John Crawfurd, gave us the first English account of a widow-burning that took place in 1633, when the Dutch sent a mission to Bali to gain the prince of Gelgel, then sole sovereign, as their ally against the Sultan of Mataram, who was driving attacks on Jakarta. The Dutch found the Balinese king making preparations for the cremation of his wife and his two eldest sons. The manuscript account of the mission was translated by a Monsieur Prevost and published in an early *Histoire des Voyages*. Among the passages of the Dutch narrative quoted by Crawfurd are the following:

> ". . . About noon, the queen's body was burnt without the

city with twenty-two of her female slaves. . . . The body was drawn out of a large aperture made in the wall to the right side of the door, in the absurd opinion of cheating the devil. ... The female slaves destined to accompany the dead went before, according to their ranks . . . each supported behind by an old woman, and carried on a Badi (tower), skillfully constructed of bamboos, and decked all over with flowers. Before them were placed a roast pig, some rice, betel and other fruits as an offering to their gods, and these unhappy victims of the most direful idolatry are thus carried in triumph, to the sound of different instruments, to the place where they are to be poignarded and consumed by fire. There, each found a particular scaffold prepared for her, in the form of a trough, raised on four short posts and edged on two sides with planks. . . . Some of the attendants let loose a pigeon or a fowl, to mark that their soul was on the point of taking its flight to the mansions of the blessed. . . . They were divested of all their garments, except their sashes, and four of the men, seizing the victim, two by the arms, which they held extended, and two by the feet, the victim standing, the fifth prepared himself for the execution, the whole being done without covering the eyes. . . .

"Some of the most courageous demanded the poignard themselves, which they received in the right hand, passing it to the left, after respectfully kissing the weapon. They wounded their right arms, sucked the blood which flowed from the wound, and stained their lips with it, making a bloody mark on the forehead with the point of the finger. Then returning the dagger to their executioners, they received a first stab between the false ribs, and a second under the shoulder blade, the weapon being thrust up to the hilt towards the heart. As soon as the horrors of death were visible in the countenance, without a complaint escaping them, they were permitted to fall on the ground . . . and were stripped of their last remnant of dress, so that they were left in a state of perfect nakedness. The executioners receive as their reward two hundred and fifty pieces of copper money of about the value of five sols each. The nearest relations, if they be present, or persons hired for the occasion . . . wash the bloody bodies . . . covering them with wood in such manner that only the head is visible, and, having applied fire, they are consumed to ashes. . . .

"The women were already poignarded and the greater number of them in flames, before the dead body of the queen arrived, borne on a superb Badi of pyramidal form, consisting of eleven steps, supported by a number of persons proportioned to the rank of the deceased. . . . Two priests preceded the Badi in vehicles of particular form, each holding in one hand a cord attached to the Badi, as if giving to understand that they led the deceased to heaven, and with the other ringing a little bell, while such a noise of gongs, tambours, flutes and other instruments is made, that the whole ceremony has less the air of a funeral procession than of a joyous village festival. ... The dead body was placed on its own funeral pile which was forthwith lighted. The assistants then regaled themselves with a feast while the musicians, without cessation, struck the ear with a tumultuous melody, not unpleasing. . . .

"At the funeral of the King's two sons a short time before, 42 women of the one, and 34 of the other, were poignarded and burnt in the manner above described; but on such occasions the princesses of royal blood themselves leap at once into the flames . . . because they would look upon themselves as dishonored by anyone's laying hands on their persons. For this purpose a kind of bridge is erected over a burning pile, which they mount, holding a paper close to their foreheads, and having their robe tucked under their arm. As soon as they feel the heat, they precipitate themselves into the burning pile. ... In case firmness should abandon them ... a brother, or another near relative, is at hand to push them in, and render them, out of affection, that cruel office. . . .

"When a prince or princess of the royal family dies, their women or slaves run around the body, uttering cries . . . and all crazily solicit to die for their master or mistress. The King, on the following day, designates those of whom he makes choice. From that moment to the last of their lives, they are daily conducted at an early hour, each in her vehicle, to the sound of musical instruments . . . to perform their devotions, having their feet wrapped in white linen, for it is no more permitted them to touch the bare earth, because they are considered as consecrated. The young women, little skilled in these religious exercises, are instructed by the aged women who accompany them. . . . Those who have devoted themselves, are made to pass the night in continual dancing and rejoicing. . . . All pains are taken to give them whatever tends to the gratification of their senses, and from the quantity of wine which they take, few objects are capable of terrifying their imaginations. . . . No woman or slave, however, is obliged to follow this barbarous custom. . . ."

The remainder of the narrative proceeds like any other of the great cremations that are held today. Another interesting account of widow-burning is given us by an eyewitness, the scholar Friederich, of the cremation of the Dewa Manggis, Raja of Gianyar, which took place in that town on December 22,1847:

"The corpse was followed by the three wives who became Belas. A procession went before them, as before the body. . . . They were seated in the highest stories of the Bades. . . . After the body of the prince had arrived at the place of cremation, the three Belas in their Bades, each preceded by the bearer of the offerings destined for her, with armed men and bands of music, were conducted to the three fires. . . .

"Their Bades were turned around three times and were carried around the whole place of cremation, The women were then carried down steps from the Bades and up the steps of the places erected for their cremation. These consisted of squares of masonry three feet high filled with combustibles which had been burning since morning and threw out a glowing heat; the persons appointed to watch them fed the fire, and at the moment when the women leaped down, poured upon it a quantity of oil and arrak, so that it flared up to a height of eight feet and must have suffocated the victims at once. Behind this furnace stood an erection of bamboo in the form of a bridge, of the same width as the square of masonry, about forty feet long and from sixteen to eighteen feet high; steps of bamboo led up to it in the rear. In the center there is a small house, affording a last resting-place to the victim, in which she waits till the ceremonies for her husband are finished and his body has begun to burn. The side of the bamboo scaffold nearest the fire is protected by a wall of wet Pisang (banana) stems. Upon the bridge lies a plank smeared with oil, which is pushed out a little over the fire as soon as the time for the leap draws near. There is a door at the end of the bridge that is not removed until the last minute. The victim sits in the house on the bridge, accompanied by a female priest and by her relatives. . . . Then she makes her toilet; her hair especially is combed, the mirror used, and her garments newly arranged; in short, she arrays herself exactly as she would for a feast. Her dress is white, her breasts are covered with a white Slendang (scarf); she wears no ornaments, and after the preparations to which she has been subjected, her hair at the last moment hangs loose. When the corpse of the prince was almost consumed, the three Belas got ready; they glanced one towards another to convince themselves that all was prepared; but this was not a glance of fear, but of impatience, and it seemed to express a wish that they might leap at the same moment. When the door opened and the plank smeared with oil was pushed out, each took her place on the plank, made three Sembahs (reverences) by joining her hands above her head, and one of the bystanders placed a small dove upon her head. When the dove flies away the soul is considered to escape. They immediately leaped down. There was no cry in leaping, no cry from the fire; they must have suffocated at once. One of the Europeans present succeeded in pushing through the crowd to the fire and in seeing the body some seconds after the leap—it was dead and its movements were caused merely by the combustion of the materials cast upon the flames. On other occasions, however, Europeans have heard cries uttered in leaping and in the first moments afterwards. . .

"During the whole time from the burning of the prince till the leap of the victims, the air resounded with the clangour of numerous bands of music; small cannon were discharged and the soldiers had drawn up outside the fire and contributed to the noise by firing off their muskets. There was not one of the 50,000 Balinese present who did not show a merry face; no one was filled with repugnance and disgust except a few Europeans whose only desire was to see the end of such barbarities."

It was only the wives of princes that were thus sacrificed; the Brahmanas did not consider it necessary for the redemption of their wives, and the common people were not interested in a practice that was foreign to them. There were two sorts of widow-sacrifice: one reserved for noblewomen, the *mesatia* ("truth," "fidelity"), in which the noble widows stabbed themselves as they jumped into the same fire with their dead husbands; the other, for the prince's low-caste wives and concubines, the *mebela* ("to die together with the master"), the one described by Friederich, which consisted in jumping into another fire apart to be burned alive. A woman who died in *mesatia* became a *Satiawati*, "The True One," a deity.

From the time their decision was made, the widows were regarded as already dead and deified. They lived a life of constant pleasures, exempt from all duties and constantly attended by the other wives. Their feet were not supposed to touch the impure ground and, like goddesses, they were carried everywhere, lavishly dressed and half-entranced. A Brahmanic priestess was constantly at their side, encouraging them to their sacrifice with flowery descriptions of the beauties of life among the gods. Friederich tells that when the time came, they were so thoroughly hypnotized that "they jumped into the fire as if it were a bath."

However shocking this practice may seem to us, it is not difficult to understand why it was acceptable to the Balinese; the scriptures not only sanctioned it, but even encouraged the sacrifices, and to the victims it was a short cut to attain the higher spiritual state ever so much more important than their insignificant physical life on this earth. Both the early Dutch narrative and Friederich make it clear that no compulsion was used and that the women to be sacrificed had to make their decision by the eighth day after their husband's death. They could neither withdraw nor volunteer later.

The Dutch did all that was in their power to stamp out this practice and set a strict prohibition on widow-sacrifices. The last official cremation in which a woman was burned took place just after the conquest of South Bali; we were present, however, at a cremation in Sukawati at which we were told by a reliable informer that the noble wife of the deceased prince had died conveniently in a mysterious manner three days before the cremation in order to be burned together with her husband. Despite the Dutch claim of having suppressed widow-sacrifices, it seems that the custom was already dying out, like many other extravagant practices that became too costly. Nearly one hundred years ago, during two years' residence in the island, Friederich witnessed only one case of widow-burning, that which he describes.

THE AFTERMATH

To have got rid of the corpse that, with its uncleanliness, bound the soul to the material world, despite the strenuous sacrifices of the family and the countless rites performed does not yet mean that the duties of the descendants are over. It is now essential that the liberated soul be consecrated by further ceremonies, often even more elaborate than the cremation itself, as one of the *pitara*, the full-fledged ancestral deities. After this the soul receives the name of *Dewa Yang*, literally a "God," and is allotted a resting-place in the family temple to protect the household.

There are further minor ceremonies within the next twelve days after the remains have been disposed of, such as the *metuhun*, when the relatives congregate and through a medium, usually a medicine-man, a *balian* in a trance, communicate with the soul to ask if all is well. I was told that once the *balian* encountered difficulties in establishing contact with the soul, but an old woman relative suddenly went into ecstasy and spoke to the spirit of the dead man in order to inform the anxious family of the success of the cremation. Then there are the *ngerebuhin,* when the soul receives offerings, and the *mapegat,* the final breaking of the last ties with this earth, symbolized by burning a thread and smashing egg-shells. The relatives, the house, and the precious objects used in the ceremonies that were not meant to be destroyed have still to be cleansed from the impurity they acquired by their contact with the dead. But the greatest of all the funeral ceremonies, the consecration of the soul, is the *mukur,* when the deceased is symbolized by an object called a "blossom," by means of which the ceremonies are performed.

The *mukur* takes place forty-two days after the cremation and consists in offerings and magic incantations by the high priest, meritorious acts to help the traveling soul to attain its highest goal, the heaven allotted to it by caste, and to predispose the supreme judges to overlook minor sins and be lenient. There are various heavens, each on a higher and higher level, the stages of the cosmic *meru,* symbolized by the temple pagodas and by the cremation towers. Each heaven is dedicated to one of the castes: the highest is of course for the Brahmana Siwa, the next for the Brahmana Budda, and the lower ones for the Satrias and Wesias. The common people have to be content to go to the *swarga*, the purgatory where they enjoy a perfect life in pure Balinese earthly fashion.

The *mukur* ceremony is extremely complicated, but is, in a way, so similar to the cremation itself that a detailed description of it would only result in a repetition of the ceremonies already described. The same guests are entertained, similar offerings and accessories are made, the same priests are engaged, and a second tower (*bukur*) is constructed, this time tall and slender and entirely decorated in white and gold. Again many orchestras and troupes of actors are engaged and pretentious banquets of turtle and roast pig are served.

Great stages raised high above the ground are built at the house for offerings and for the priest. The altars are higher and more beautifully decorated than ever, the devil offerings more elaborate than before, and the participants wear their best clothes and jewelry, the women adding a band of white cloth and a little fan of white paper worn on the head as a symbol of the purity of the occasion. The ceremonies begin by the making of new effigies identical to the *adegans* used for the cremation, which are given life, blessed, purified by the priest, and then "killed" by being burned. The ashes are collected and placed in individual coconut shells with a short stick through their middle. These coconuts are then wrapped in white cloth, decorated with flowers, and provided with a gold knob at the top, a gold ring with a ruby, a string of about two hundred *kepengs*, an image representing the dead drawn on a sandalwood slab, and a label of palm-leaf bearing the name of the person. This is the *sekar*, a "blossom."[2] When ready, the *sekars* are placed on silver platters, the relatives make a ceremonial reverence to them, and they are deposited on the high stage, which is now filled with expensive silks and offerings. At the *mukur* of the Raja of Jerokuta we saw glasses of foreign commodities such as whisky, brandy, and gin.

After the night of vigil spent in watching dramatic performances, listening to music, and so forth, the priest performs his most power-

[2] The *sekar* or *puspa*, meaning literally a "blossom," is symbolical of the spirit of the deceased and is the same as the *shraddha*, the urn-like object seen in the hands of the ancient statues of deified Javanese and Balinese kings.

ful *mantras*, the relatives pray, and the *sekars* are brought down, each member of the family placing one over his or her head to absorb their beneficial influence. They are then broken up, burned, and the ashes placed again in a new *sekar* identical with the former. These are placed on the white and gold biers and again a great procession starts off for the sea, often miles away, with the same mad recklessness as when the corpses were carried to be cremated. The procession stops at the seashore and the *sekars* are brought down, placed on a boat, and taken out to the open sea, where they are thrown into the waters, far enough so that they will not be washed ashore. The biers are again dismantled and burned. All the accessories are destroyed; nothing must remain, and what is not broken up is burned. Special patrols are appointed to destroy whatever is returned by the waves.

The ceremony over, the happy participants, now relieved of their strenuous duties, take a general bath just at the water's edge, the women unconcerned in a group just a few yards away from the boisterous men, who play and splash in the breaking waves. There is still the long walk home from the shore, and the crowd returns in the blazing midday sun—hot, exhausted, and considerably poorer than before, but in high spirits and happy to have accomplished their greatest duty to those to whom they owe their existence: the consecration of their dead so that they shall continue to guide them as deities in the same way in which, as ordinary human beings, they helped and protected them. All of this has been achieved by the triple purifying action of earth, fire, and water.

NOTES ON DEATH AND CREMATION

A. A corpse that is to be kept mummified within the house and not buried before cremation remains in the pavilion destined for it (*balé Iayon*), where it is taken care of by female relatives (in old times by a family of slaves), who attend to the collection of the body liquids that flow from the coffin through a bamboo tube into a Chinese porcelain bowl, often a priceless piece of Sung celadon, a family heirloom, to be buried after a sprinkling of holy water.

In old times the slaves appointed to the gruesome task of caring for a noble corpse were regarded as already dead and were treated as such; nobody could talk to them and they could not be denied anything. After the cremation they were set free, but, being "dead," they could not remain in the village. This strange practice, found also among other Indonesians, could be explained as being in the same spirit that caused widow suicides, a symbolical sacrifice of a servant or a slave to accompany his master in the hereafter.

The uncleanliness that emanates from a dead body demands that such preserved corpses be taken outside the village during festivals. Likewise, a carcass of an animal must not remain in the open and must be buried.

B. The great cremation towers used to convey the corpses to the place of burning are called ordinarily *wadah*, but that of a nobleman, which has many roofs, receives the more impressive name of *badé*. In detail the tower consists of a strong bamboo platform (*senan*) by which it is carried by hordes of men; then comes the "base" (*dasar*), which represents the underworld (*bhur*). Next come the mountains (*gegununggan*); three receding platforms that represent our visible world (*bhuwa*), ornamented with bunches of paper flowers and leaves (*kekayon*), the forests. Then comes the *balé balean*, the pavilion for the bodies "not yet in heaven, no longer on this earth"; the whole topped by the number of roofs or "heavens" (*tumpang*) allotted to the family by caste. These are symbolical of the celestial world (*swah*).

High priests become merged at death with the sun, and their cremation bier takes the form of a *padmasana*, a throne for the sun-god. The *wadah* or *badé* and the *padmasana* are, like the stone *candis*, the ancient burial monuments of kings, the modern temple gates and stone sun-thrones, symbols of the three worlds (*tribhuwana*) that constitute the Balinese universe: the upper, intermediate, and lower worlds.

C. The great serpent, the *naga banda*, used at cremations of the descendants of the Dewa Agung, the highest aristocracy in the land, is shot and "killed" by the priest to serve as a vehicle for the royal soul in its flight into heaven. The *naga banda* ceremony commemorates the legend of the strife between the ruling class and the Brahmanic priests (see page 47), when the Dewa Agung's life was saved by a priest who killed a serpent about to crush him.

In Denpasar we had occasion to witness the great cremation of the old king of Jerokuta, killed in the mass suicide of 1906. His body was burned then, hurriedly and almost without ceremony, together with other victims of the war, and it was not until the 12th of February 1934, twenty-eight years later, that his descendants could afford to hold a great ceremonial cremation befitting his rank. He was entitled to use the serpent by a special decree of the Dewa Agung, and the town was aroused because for over thirty years the event of a *naga banda* had not taken place in Denpasar. The cremation rites were performed through an effigy, but there were well over a hundred corpses burned on that afternoon because other relatives of the Raja and many of his former subjects joined in the cremation to accompany their prince.

The *naga banda* itself consisted of a long rope bound in green cloth with an elaborate head of carved and painted wood and with a great mane of *lalang* grass. It measured one hundred yards, although I was told that according to regulations it should have been 1,600 *depa* (a *depa* is about one yard). The *naga banda* is made alive by a *pedanda bodda*, and a *pedanda siwa* kills it, in a sort of battle of wits between the magic of the two sects, but in Denpasar the ceremony had not taken place for a decade and the older priests were afraid to attempt it. The formulas employed for this are the most difficult tongue-twisters and they claimed that the slightest mistake would result in the death of the priest himself. Nobody would undertake it except the young but mystic *pedanda* Gedé of Pemecutan, of whom it was said he was so studious that he once lost his mind temporarily, trying to learn a difficult *mantra*. He agreed to perform both, give life to and then kill the *naga banda*, a great test of his powers.

On the day of the cremation the great serpent was the most spectacular part of the procession; hundreds of people clung to it, and the priest himself, dressed in full regalia, rode on its neck, the bow and arrow with which to kill it in his right hand, in the left his bell, which he rang all the way to the cemetery. The tail of the serpent was held by the present Regent of Badung, a descendant of the old Raja, while in the other hand he held the effigy; he rode on the tower where the corpse should have been. At the cremation ground the priest shot imaginary arrows to the four winds and then towards the serpent. That was a moment of suspense because the great throng watched breathlessly to see if the red hibiscus on each side of the snake's head wilted. It is believed that should the flowers remain fresh until the end of the ceremony, the priest has failed to kill it and he himself will die instead. It was a hot afternoon, the hibiscus soon wilted, and all was well.

Part III

CHAPTER TWELVE

Modern Bali and the Future

"ISN'T BALI SPOILED?" is invariably the question that greets the returned traveler from Bali—meaning, is the island overrun by tourists, and are the Balinese all wearing shirts? The questioners are visibly disappointed to hear of big hotels, fine roads, and motor-cars; there is still enough of the Robinson Crusoe in travelers to make each one of them want to be the "only" white man among picturesque semi-naked, dark-skinned savages, although they would preferably see them from a motor-car or a hotel veranda.

Bali was only conquered by the Dutch in 1908, but long before that the libraries of Holland had been filling slowly with scholarly volumes on the literature, the archeology, and the religion of Bali. However, the remote little island only became news to the rest of the Western world with the advent, a few years ago, of a series of documentary films of Bali with a strong emphasis on sex appeal. These films were a revelation and now everybody knows that Balinese girls have beautiful bodies and that the islanders lead a musical-comedy sort of life full of weird, picturesque rites. The title of one of these films, *Goona-goona,* the Balinese term for "magic," became at the time Newyorkese for sex allure.

The newly discovered "last paradise" became the contemporary substitute for the nineteenth-century romantic conception of primitive Utopia, until then the exclusive monopoly of Tahiti and other South Sea Islands. And lately travel agencies have used the alluring name of Bali to attract hordes of tourists for their round-the-world cruises that make a one-day stop on the island. On this day the tourists are herded to the hotel in Denpasar to eat their lunch, buy curios, and watch hurried performances by bored "temple dancers"—ordinary village actors who hate to play in the midday heat.

The show over, the tourists are rushed back to their ships in numbered cars, satisfied to have seen Bali. An average of five or six such cruises unload every winter some fifteen hundred round-the-world tourists that leave the Balinese puzzled as to why all these madmen come from so far for only a day. They would never willingly leave their island, and once an old woman remarked that surely the foreigners must have done something at home that forced them to leave their own lands.

The great cruise ships come with twice as many visitors as can be taken care of by the island's limited supply of motor-cars, and half the tourists have to remain on board ship until the others return. On one occasion it was planned to send a troupe of dancers and musicians to entertain those who had to remain on board, but the ship's officers objected; "they could not allow natives to overrun the ship; something might be stolen." They were persuaded that the Balinese were an honest people and they let them come to play and dance for the tourists, but when the show was over and the Balinese started packing to leave, one of their large bronze gongs in a carved wood frame was missing! The gong was never found.

Besides the cruises, every week two K.P.M. boats bring a handful of more enterprising visitors that stay for three days or even for a week or two. They land in the northern port of Buleleng, which has been under direct Dutch control for nearly a hundred years. There all the houses and all the temples have tin roofs and all the women wear soiled blouses, "signs of civilization," both supposedly made compulsory by official decree—to the joy of the importers of foreign cloth and of galvanized tin. After the Dutch occupation of Buleleng in 1848, someone decided that the morals of the Dutch soldiers needed protection, and a law was passed requiring the women to wear blouses. Tin roofs also, it is rumored, were ordered to replace the thatched ones because an official became deeply concerned about the possibility of fires caused by "exploding automobiles." Only three years ago the women of Denpasar went to market proudly uncovered to the waist, but the princes' wives wore the ugly blouses and soon they became the dictate of fashion. In Denpasar they now regard those who go habitually with uncovered breasts as "crude mountain people." Young men are growing contemptuous of the simple batik *kain* and headcloth of their forefathers. After dark, in Buleleng and Denpasar, the equipment of the smart young man-about-town consists of a set of striped pyjamas, a Muslim skull-cap, sandals, a bicycle, and a flashlight, although he may still wear flowers behind his ear to stroll on the main street among the food-vendors, the flourishing prostitutes and procurers that haunt the streets around the hotels.

Undoubtedly Bali will soon enough be "spoiled" for those fastidious travelers who abhor all that which they bring with them. No longer will the curious Balinese of the remote mountain villages, still unaccustomed to the sight of whites, crowd around their cars to stare silently at the "exotic" long-nosed, yellow-haired foreigners in their midst. But even when all the Balinese will have learned to wear shirts, to beg, lie, steal, and prostitute themselves to satisfy new needs, the tourists will continue to come to Bali to see the sights, snapping pictures frantically, dashing from temple to temple, back to the hotel for meals, and on to watch rites and dances staged for them. The Balinese will be, to the tourists, guides, chauffeurs, and bellboys to be tipped, dancers on salary, curio-dealers, and tropical beauties to be photographed blouseless for a fee.

The younger generation is rapidly being cut off from a cultural environment which they have learned to regard as below them, considering their parents, formerly their models of behavior, as rude peasants who have not gone to school. This, however, is not the fault of Hollywood. To Bali goes the distinction of being totally uninterested in the movies. Over a decade ago an enterprising Armenian brought the first movies to the island. At first he cleaned up, all the Balinese had to see the miracle; but, not used to paying for entertainment, they soon grew bored with something they could not understand and the movies were a failure. Today there are two small primitive movie houses, one in Buleleng and one in Denpasar, that give Sunday shows of films often twenty-five years old, patronized chiefly by the foreign population. Chaplin may be a favorite of even the Eskimos, but to the Balinese who saw him in the flesh he was simply the funny man who came to Bali with his brother and who, after watching a Balinese play, took the stage and performed for them a hilarious parody of their dances.

In Bali the exalted title of Teacher, *Gurú*, is the name of one of their highest gods and is the most respectful way of addressing one's father. The old-fashioned teachers were the reservoirs of the science and poetry of Balinese culture, but those young Balinese who have gone to Java to become teachers for the Western-style Government schools have returned convinced that what they learned in Java is the essence of knowledge and progress. They have become conscious of the contempt of Europeans for the native cultures and have been influenced to believe that the philosophy, arts and habits of their country are signs of peasant backwardness.

The young *gurus* look upon the graceful and healthful costume of the island, so well suited to the climate, as indecent and primitive and demand that their little pupils wear shirts in school. A little girl once told me her teacher said it was improper to show one's breasts. In at least one case the result has been tragic; in the little mountain village of Kayubihi a child was shamed by his teacher because he did not wear a shirt, but his father, who had never owned one (nor had any of his ancestors), refused to buy it for him. He felt so thoroughly disgraced that one night he hanged himself from the tree in front of the schoolhouse.

The teacher forces his half-digested jumble of European ideas on the little pupils, who from the beginning of their education learn to look down on everything Balinese. They are taught about what a European child learns in primary school; they learn to speak and write in Malay, a language foreign to Bali, which most often their parents ignore, and some even have a smattering of Dutch, so when they come out of school they make good, cheap clerks, totally uninterested in their own culture. Most speak better Malay than Balinese and feel above the everyday requirements of Balinese life. Since there are so few jobs available on the island in which such education would be required, making clerks of the Balinese seems to make European education have a negative and even detrimental effect. Typical was the case of Rapung, the young school-teacher out of work who gave me lessons in Balinese; he was intelligent and rather well informed, yet he wanted to learn to cook or to serve at table or become a houseboy. Of course agriculture was much below him.

It seems too bad that modern education, at least in Bali, where the entire life of the island is so dependent on its traditions, tends to disinherit the future generation from their culture, simply because it is snubbed in the educational program of the schools. It is true that many young Balinese are still taught at home the rudiments of the native education, often by old-fashioned *gurus*, but what is not officially recognized by their teachers will soon become discredited.

There are, however, encouraging rumors that the Government plans a revision of the system.

THE MISSIONARIES

During the past century all efforts to Christianize the Balinese have failed, and the story of Nicodemus, the first Balinese convert, is already well known. Nicodemus was the servant and pupil of the first missionary who came to Bali. He allowed himself to be baptized after some years in the service of the missionary, but time went by and no other converts could be made, so the missionary began to bring pressure upon Nicodemus to baptize others. The poor boy, already mentally tortured because his community had expelled him, declaring him morally "dead," unable to stand the situation any longer, killed his master, renounced his new faith, and delivered himself to be executed according to Balinese law. The scandal aroused in Holland brought about a regulation discouraging missionary activities in Bali.

This, however, did not stop the missionaries; permits were granted to them in 1891, again in 1920, and in 1924, when Roman Catholics requested special concessions, but waves of opposition from the Balinese thwarted these attempts. Meetings were held among Balinese leaders to "stop the catastrophe," and the permits were revoked.

But towards the end of 1930 the American missionaries again succeeded in securing an entrée, supposedly only to care for souls already saved and not to seek new converts. But quietly and unostentatiously they began to work among the lowest classes of the Balinese. The more sincere of the early missionaries had aimed at obtaining converts of conviction and consequently had failed, but these later missionaries wanted quicker results and followed more effective methods. Taking advantage of the economic crisis that was already making itself felt in Bali, they managed to give their practically destitute candidates for Christianity the idea that a change of faith would release them from all financial obligations to the community—all they had to do was to pronounce the formula: "*Saja percaja Jesoes Kristos*—I believe in Jesus Christ." If the man who was induced to pronounce the magic words was the head of a household, the missionaries claimed every member of the family as Christians and soon they could boast about three hundred converts.

Soon enough the new Christians discovered they had been misled; they had to pay taxes just the same, had become undesirable to their communities, and were being boycotted. In Mengwi, where the missionaries had their greatest success, the authorities refused to release converts from their duties, bringing endless conflict with the village and water-distribution boards; lawsuits developed and trouble began. In many villages regulations were written into the local laws to the effect that those who were unfaithful to the Balinese religion were to be declared "dead"; meetings were held to discuss the possibility of banishing the converts to remote places like Jembrana, together with "other criminals." The Christians had also become deeply concerned when they found out that they could not dispose of their dead, because they were not permitted to bury them in the village cemeteries and all the other available lands were either rice fields or wild places. At times the situation became tense and near-riots took place. The alarmed village heads reasoned with some converts and succeeded in bringing back a number of them to the old faith.

Typical is the story of Pan Luting, a convert village headman who had helped the missionaries to increase their fold. He repented, claiming he had been deceived, and being a *topeng* actor of repute, in his performances of masked dramas he now never misses an opportunity to poke fun at the missionaries and to express his joy at not being a Christian any longer. Another soul was lost to the missionaries when a young convert discovered that the venereal disease he suffered from did not disappear when he pronounced the magic formula: "I believe in Jesus Christ," as he had thought it would. Again, a convert who felt himself at the point of death quickly renounced his new faith when the village medicine-man refused to treat him, claiming that his magic would be of no avail to a Christian. He recovered and it is needless to say that he held a great offering feast of thanksgiving. Stories such as these are repeated endlessly in Bali, but perhaps the best illustration of the superficiality of the convictions of the new Christians is the following conversation between a young convert and an enlightened official:

"Why did you renounce your religion?"

"Because I believe!"

"Believe what?"

"I believe in Jesus Christ."

"Who is he?"

"That *Tuan* (European) with the black coat that comes often from Lombok."[1]

Eventually the disturbances became too noticeable and the American missionaries had to leave. Until then the Dutch missions had restrained themselves from further activity in Bali, but when the news came that rival missionaries had succeeded in making a few converts, they went up in the air and are now pulling every rope to have the law modified. Bitter controversy flared up in the papers in Holland and Java; the missionaries claimed that the Balinese were finally ripe for conversion because their religious feeling was, at last, breaking down. A Dr. Kraemer, head of a Protestant missionary sect, went to Bali to investigate and, after a stay in the island of a little over a month, wrote a thick volume in which he aimed to prove the failings of the Balinese religion, and the idea that the Balinese really wished to become Christians, but were opposed by European intellectuals living on the island. This argument was quickly answered by Cokorde Gedé Rake Soekawati, the Balinese representative in the Volksraad, the "People's Court," in Jakarta. Dr. Kraemer's prejudiced "findings" were entirely wiped out by answers and an analysis of his arguments by the real students of Bali, men like Bosch, Goris, Korn, Haga, Lekkerkerker, De Bruyn Kops, and Damsté. Dr. Goris has pointed out that the view of the missionaries is based on the principle that all peoples are by nature "no good" and in a hopeless "soul-conflict" that can only be remedied by the peculiar brand of religion the missionaries preach. Finding little evidence of this "soul-conflict" in the Balinese, the missionaries encourage it or try to create it by stirring up the natural animosity of the lower classes against the high castes and by playing on their poverty, thus encouraging the caste struggle rather than abolishing it, as was their claim. Curiously enough, the same missionaries who accuse the Balinese of religious superficiality approve of the converts made under false pretences who know nothing of Christianity except rubber-stamp Malay phraseology.

In the meantime, while the controversy rages on, the shrewd missionaries are steadily gaining ground. At present a Catholic priest and a Protestant missionary are stationed in Denpasar, and another

[1] *"Knapa Ktoet boeang agama Bali?" — "Sebeb saja percaja!" — "Percaja apa?" — "Saj'a percaja Toean Jesoes Kristos" — "Siapa dia?" — "Itoe Toean jang pake bajoe itam jang sering datang deri Lombok."*

missionary, a Catholic, is stationed in Buleleng, all three undoubtedly discreet but tireless in their efforts to "save" the Balinese.

But Bali is certainly not the place where missionaries could improve in any way the moral and physical standards of the people and it is hard to believe, knowing the Balinese character, that they will succeed. Religion is to the Balinese more than spectacular ceremonies with music, dancing, and a touch of drama for virility; it is their law, the force that holds the community together. It is the greatest stimulus of their lives because it has given them their ethics, culture, wisdom, and joy of living by providing the exuberant festivity they love. More than a religion, it is a moral philosophy of high spiritual value, gay and free of fanaticism, which explains to them the mysterious forces of nature. It is difficult to imagine that it will ever be supplanted by a bleak escapist faith devoid of beautiful and dramatic ritual.

The little island of Bali, now famous for the beauty of its people, its intense religious life, and its colorful arts, music, and theater, is still one of those amazing nations that we shall never know again, one of the so-called primitive countries. It is obvious that the Balinese are by no means a primitive people, although we use the term to differentiate our own material civilization from the native cultures in which the daily life, society, arts, and religion form a united whole that cannot be separated into its component parts without disrupting it; the cultures where spiritual values dictate the mode of living.

Perhaps of even greater importance than the fascinating artistic development, and, in all probability, the factor that motivated the artistic impulse of the population, is the unique manner in which they have solved their social and economic problems. Bali presents the amazing spectacle of a compact nation of over one million hard-working, cultured people living in a deep-rooted, well-coordinated form of agrarian socialism, that has, perhaps because of its elemental directness, until recently, minimized the social and economic evils that today afflict the less fortunate rest of the world. The primitive Balinese socialism flourished parallel to medieval feudalism despite five centuries of domination by an aristocracy that with all its ruthlessness could not break down the inherent unity and co-operativism of the Balinese communities.

The nobility met with insurmountable passive resistance to any encroachments upon the autonomy of the villages and had finally to content themselves with the collection of tribute from their "vassals." The common people tolerated the princes, but even today they consider them as total outsiders and in most social and administrative matters the villages remain entrenched against all interference from the noble landlords, now appointed as go-betweens between the people and the Dutch Government, mainly to the same office to which the threat of boycott reduced them in the past—the collection of taxes.

We have seen that the Balinese are fanatics about organization. From childhood to old age a Balinese joins all sorts of societies, from the clubs of "virgin" boys and girls, of actors, musicians, and even squirrel-chasers, to the great agricultural, fishing, village, and ward associations that control the internal government of the communities. Every one of their activities is managed, not individually, but communally, with every active member having a vote and a voice in every enterprise. Naturally, individualism did not develop in the strict communalistic society; individual names are hardly ever used and they call one another "brother," "father," "teacher," or "grandfather." All art is anonymous and only recently have painters begun to sign their works, owing entirely to the influence of Europeans. This, however, did not kill individuality of expression; it is easy to detect the authorship of a certain painting or a sculpture if one is familiar with the author's work, every notable actor or dancer has his own unmistakable way of performing standard dances or improvising lines for a play, and no two orchestras play alike.

In the larger towns and in the districts where the princes held sway, landownership became more individualistic, but elsewhere the right of landed property is not recognized as absolute and an undesirable member of the community cannot hold property given to him or to his ancestors against the will of the village council. A landowner cannot sell his property within the jurisdiction of the village without authorization from the council and it can be confiscated if he misuses it or if he abuses his privileges.

Instead of the familiar exploitation, enslavement, and economic inequality imposed on the population by a ruling class of aristocrats or bureaucrats so often found in countries where the government is centralized in individuals, in Bali we find an economically independent majority that is truly democratic because every representative villager, regardless of his caste or his wealth, is an active member of the village council with an equal voice in village affairs and with equal duties to perform. The government of the villages remained impersonal and with a minimum evidence of even its existence, because power was equally divided among the members of the various councils, and the executive officials, such as *kliangs*, council heads, treasurers, and so forth, officiated as a duty to the community and without reward. If to the inherent spirit of co-operation and high ethical standards of the Balinese we add their model institutions, we may find the explanation in the fact that the Balinese never actually became wage earners, and even now coolie labor for hire remains unimportant. Despite their poverty the Balinese are freer and live better than do most natives under colonial rule.

However, the contact of Balinese culture, first with the feudal princes and lately with our civilization in the form of trade, unsuitable education, tourists, and now missionaries, has made a deep dent in the simple and logical life of the Balinese. The changes are taking place so rapidly that they were strikingly evident even after a two years' absence, the time elapsed between our first and second visits to the island. Fine roads and new necessities are encouraging the consumption of foreign commodities such as imported cloth, motor-cars, and gasoline, and the islanders will learn to desire more and more the "advantages of civilization," thus creating a gigantic exodus of the island's wealth. The Balinese have lived well under a self-sufficient co-operative system, the foundation of which is reciprocal assistance with money used only as a secondary commodity. Being extremely limited in means to obtain the cash—scarcer every day—necessary to pay taxes and satisfy new needs, it is to be feared that the gradual breaking down of their institutions, together with the drain on their national wealth, will make coolies, thieves, beggars, and prostitutes of the proud and honorable Balinese of this generation, and will, in the long run, bring a social and economic catastrophe.

Unfortunate as this is, the power of our civilization to penetrate can no longer be ignored. It would be futile to recommend measures to prevent the relentless march of Westernization; tourists cannot be kept out, the needs of trade will not be restricted for sentimental reasons, and missionary societies are often powerful. To advocate the unconditional preservation of their picturesque culture in the midst of modern civilization would be the equivalent of turning Bali into a living museum, putting the entire island into a glass case for the enjoyment of hordes of tourists. It is a matter of deep regret to see a million intelligent people, living a simple and logical life ruled by an almost unprecedentedly harmonious co-operativism and with a truly great national culture, be turned into an experimental field for missionaries and a stamping-ground for traders.

In adapting foreign ideas to their own culture the Balinese have shown unusual logic and an intelligent power of assimilation. It is to be hoped that those in control of the island's future will see that progress comes to the Balinese naturally and gradually and that they shall be permitted to decide for themselves what they want to absorb without losing their essential qualities and becoming another vanishing race of coolies. The Balinese deserve a better fate; they are too proud and intelligent to be treated with the prevalent arrogance and patronizing attitude of colonizers who regard the native as a shiftless and treacherous inferior whose contact pollutes the "superior" whites and who regard those who show deference to the native as a menace to the prestige—greatly menaced nowadays—of the often bigoted and insolent whites in the colonies.

The Dutch have been often called the best colonizers in the world, and whatever the verdict may be on the principle of colonization, it is lucky for Bali that of the imperialists it is Holland that rules there. The Netherlands Government boasts of a motto of "Rule with love and wisdom" and a policy of non-interference with the native life. There is no doubt that these principles have been followed in Bali whenever their application did not interfere with colonial interests, and the native has derived definite benefits from Dutch rule: land may not be sold for exploitation by strangers, the autocratic powers of the princes have been considerably curtailed, the Balinese have retained their laws and their courts, and the troublesome missionaries were supposedly barred from the island.

Up to now the Dutch have shown a more humanitarian treatment of the people than most imperialistic colonizers and in many cases have sided with the people against the princes despite the fact that the old system of government of the Rajas was preserved. No more can the despotic princes enslave or exploit their helpless subjects, or as in old times kill or punish savagely someone for such offences as disrespect or disobedience. Only two of the former Rajas, those of Gianyar and Karangasem, because of "loyalty" to the Government, retain their feudal rights—in a considerably limited way, however—while the others are rulers only in name. The Dutch have also stopped the bloody wars between petty chieftains, and widows no longer kill themselves at the pyre of their noble masters. Taxation still burdens the habitually penniless peasants, although now at least they receive certain returns for their money in the form of protection, health services, roads, and so forth.

Dr. Korn (*Adatrecht van Bali*) has already pointed out that the problem confronting the Dutch in regard to Bali is the gradual incorporation of the Balinese into modern life from medieval isolation through a better understanding of their institutions. Fifty years ago, when Liefrink took charge of the administration of North Bali, he understood that it was best to leave things more or less as they were. But in South Bali the change came more suddenly; the ruling houses collapsed overnight and the Dutch had to reorganize the government of their new conquest hastily and without a thorough knowledge of the island's laws and customs.

In late years the Government of the Netherlands has commissioned scholars like Doctors Korn, Goris, and Stutterheim to make studies for a better understanding of the law, the religion, and the history of Bali. Perhaps through these studies those in charge of the colonial policy of the Netherlands will realize, in the first place, that the Balinese have a great culture that cannot be saved by the admiration of the outside world, but only by commanding the respect and appreciation of the Balinese themselves; that the native arts need no encouragement, simply because they are still vividly alive, but that they do need official recognition in the educational program of the schools that are now turning out hybrid Balinese with contempt for whatever does not come from the outside world. Second, that the Balinese are agriculturists living in small communities in which clerks and middlemen have no place. Third, that their social organization not only is the best suited, but is essential to their manner of living. And last but not least, that their whole life, society, arts, ethics—in short, their entire culture—cannot, without disrupting the entire system, be separated from the set of rules which are called the Balinese religion. If this principle is disturbed, the foundation will be knocked from under the structure upon which the culture, the law and order of the Balinese are based, and social and economic chaos will eventually descend upon the happy and peaceful island of Bali.

ALBUM OF PHOTOGRAPHS

The sun sets on the Tabanan coast and rises over the Gunung Agung

Outriggers drying in the sun. Shaped like the mythical *gajah-mina*, half-elephant, half-fish, they have eyes to see at night

Approaching rain and the beach of Sanur at dusk

Giant pandanus in the forest of Batukau

A statue trapped in the roots of a *waringin* tree

The trunk of an ancient frangipani tree

Rice fields ready for planting, seen from terraces above them

ABOVE: Balinese ducks are trained to wait near the little flag on the left until their guardian returns from the fields to take them home

BELOW: Pigs at feeding time

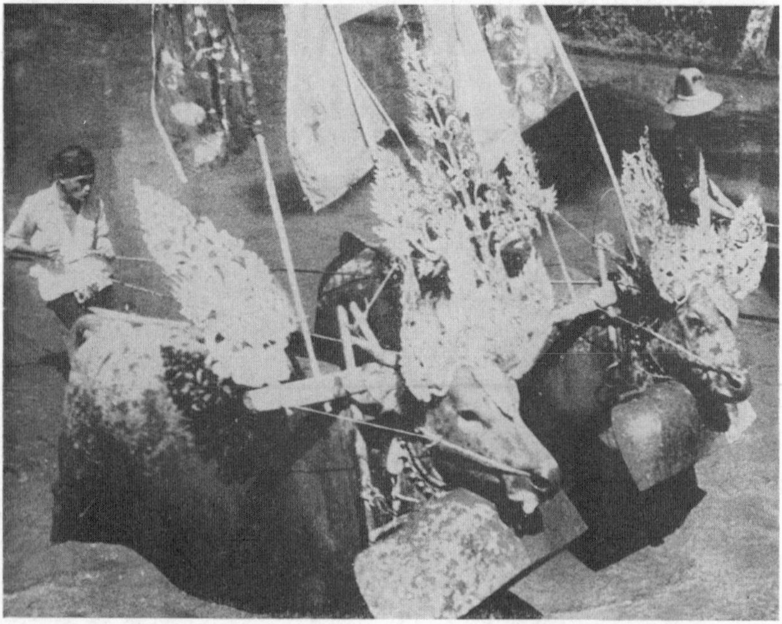

ABOVE: Oxen and a primitive plow are used in the rice fields

BELOW: Plowing can be turned to festive and to profitables uses, made to please the gods and so serve as a basis for bull-racing bets

In the mountain villages rice is dried on tall bamboo poles with conical tops

Planting the rice shoots

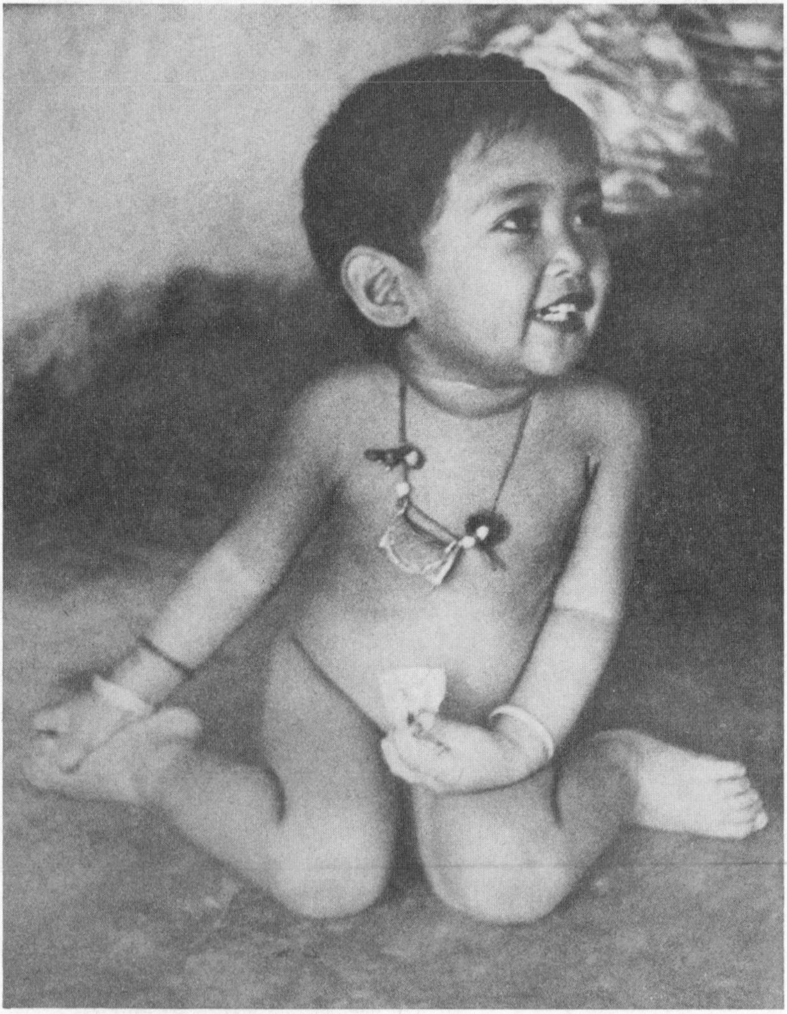

A baby of Denpasar

ABOVE: Old men from Sanur

BELOW: Two boys from Sebatu

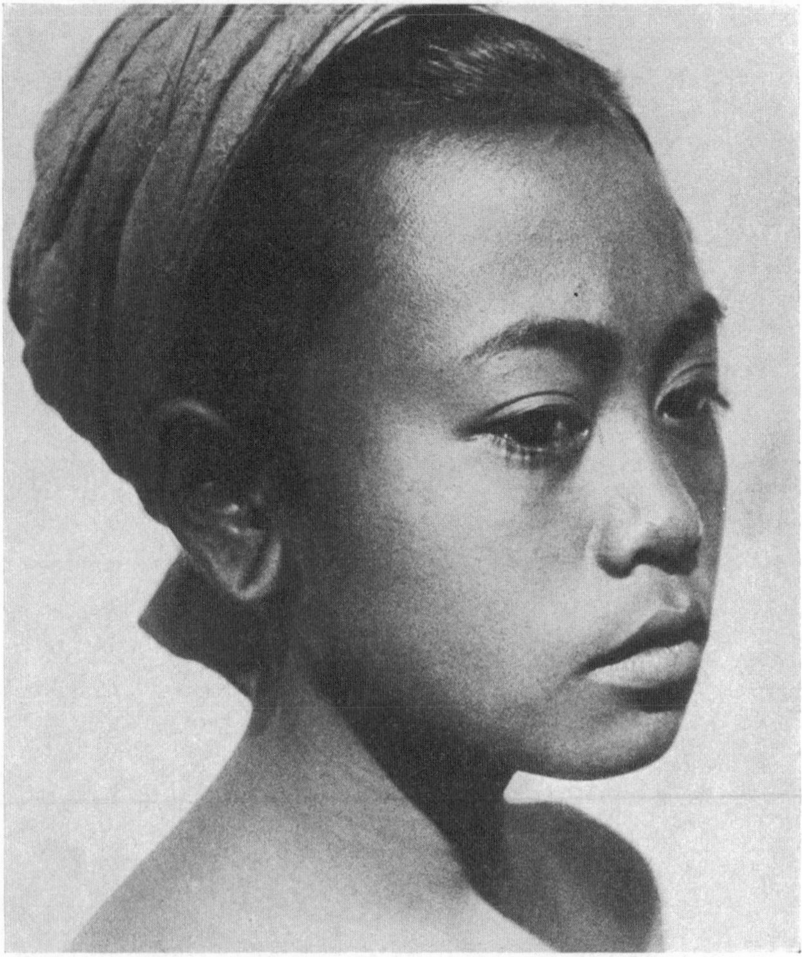

Gebrag, a famous *legong* dancer

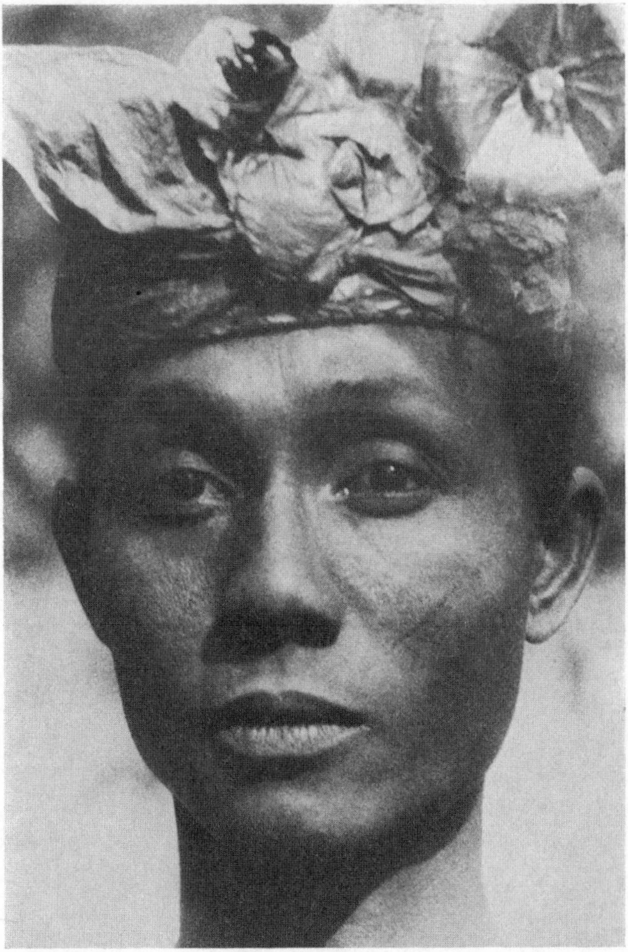

Mario

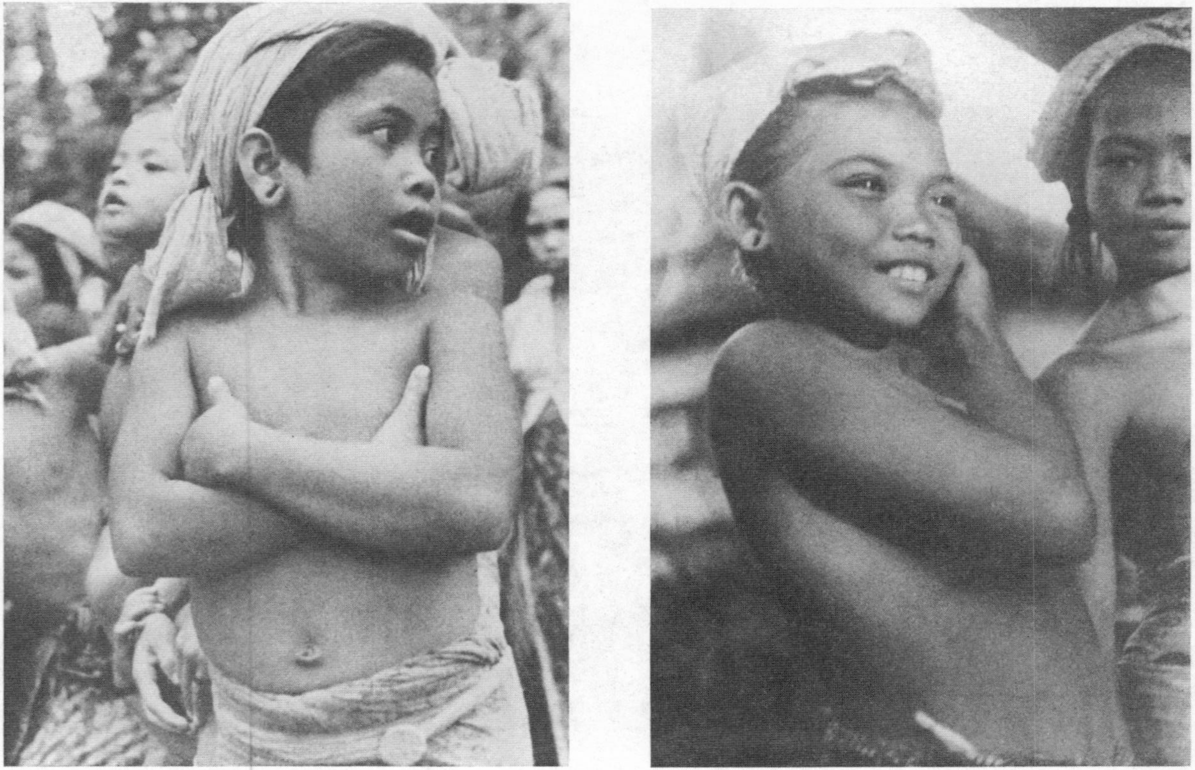

Watching a play

An attentive group

A proud grandfather

The loving sister

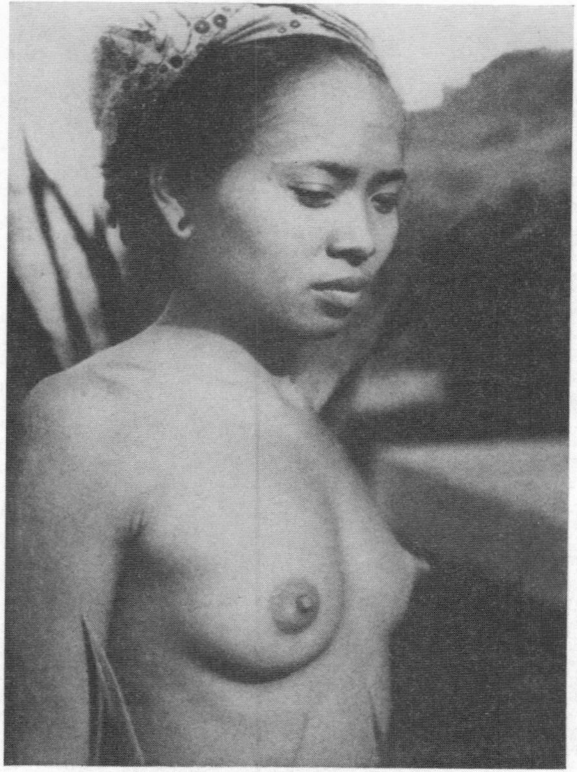

Mukluk

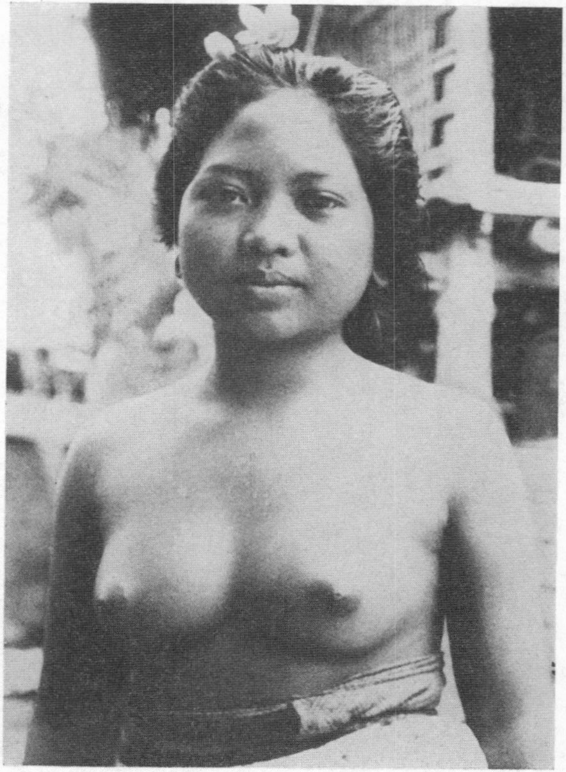

Ciblun

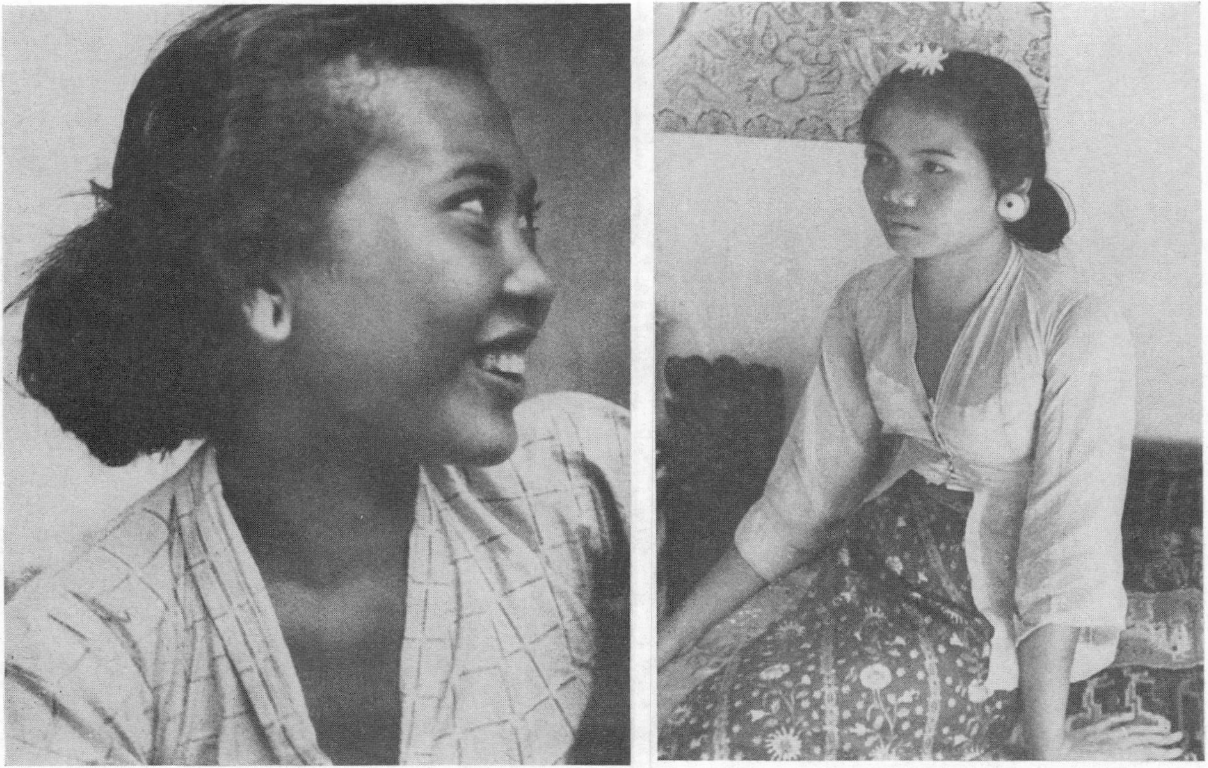

Ayu and Camplong in modern dress

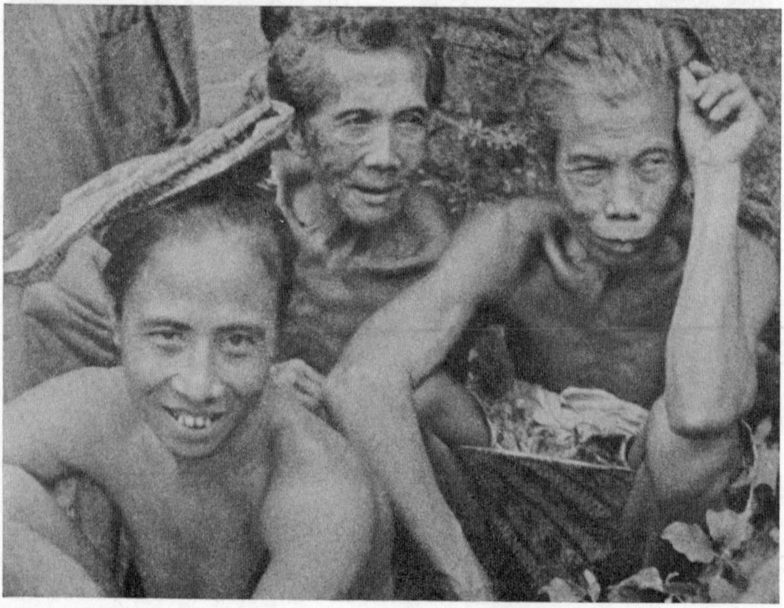

ABOVE: Three generations

BELOW: Three men from the mountains

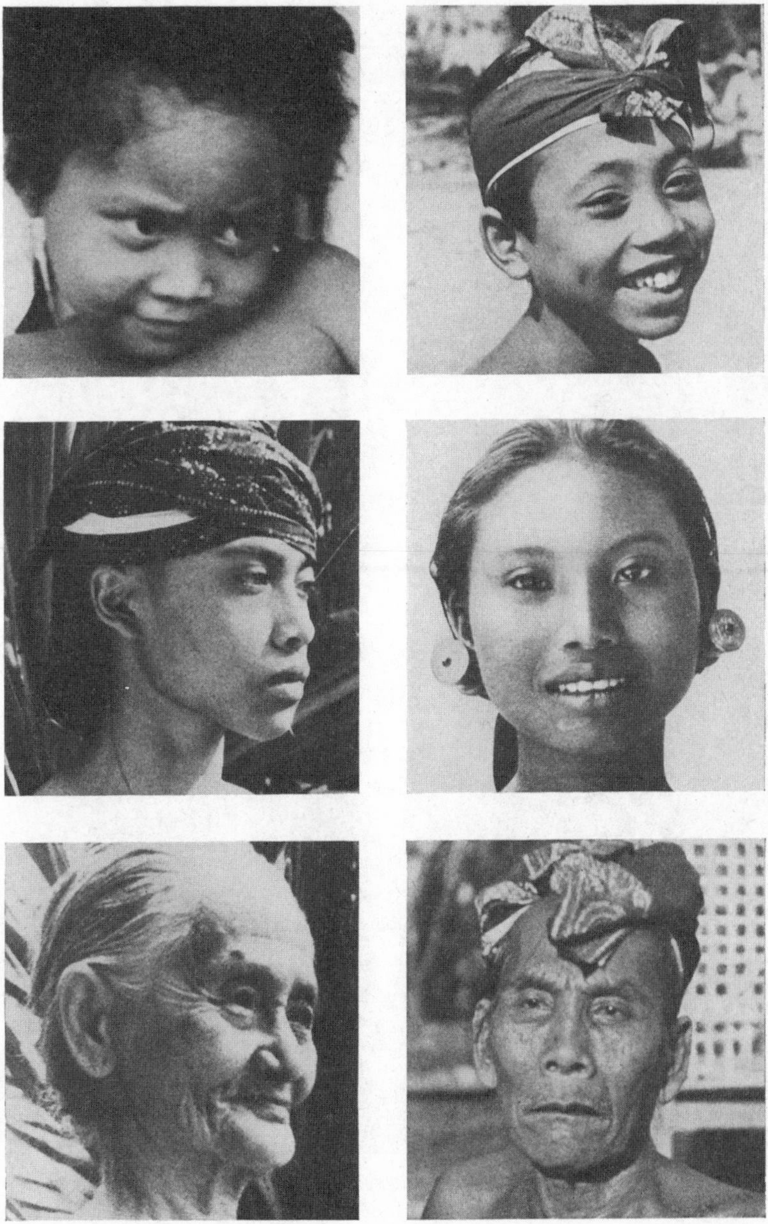

Six Balinese types, the old man a witch-doctor

Irsak with a rice pestle

Girls of Sanur pounding rice

ABOVE: A noblewoman at her loom

BELOW: For banquets men prepare quantities of *saté,* turtle meat *en brochette,* broiled over a bed of hot coals

Women carry loads on their heads, men over the shoulder

ABOVE: Going to market

BELOW: Sweet drinks of crushed leaves are popular in the markets

ABOVE: The old and the young sell their wares side by side

BELOW: At noon the market is at its height

Exchanging news in the market at Denpasar

A *kulkul* or tom-tom calls the villagers together; it has different signals for meals, feasts, meetings. A fast, continuous beating is the signal of a village emergency

ABOVE: Every Balinese home, which houses one family or a number of related families in its many pavilions, is surrounded by a wall of whitewashed mud

BELOW: Not all Balinese kitchens are as elaborate as this, with its carved stone ornaments of crabs, turtles, shrimps

Preparing for the cockfight: tying on the steel spurs; the owners of the cocks

Ready for the fight; the loser

Padu raksa, the inner gate of a temple

The *meru* or tower of the temple Kehen in Bangli rises beside the shrines which the gods use as resting-places

ABOVE: A panorama of *merus* which make up the Mother Temple (Besakih) of Bali

BELOW: Giant puppets for the holy *barong landong*: a wild giant and a prince

ABOVE: The puppets of the *barong landong* land at the island of Sakenan to perform in the coral temple

BELOW: Palm-leaf offering shaped like boat-sails

Temple offering: bananas, custard-apples, oranges, palm-leaves, and flowers mingle to compose a *kbogan* to the gods. The deities are served with the essence of this food, and ordinary people take what is left

ABOVE: A *lamak*, a strip of palm-leaves designed for temple decoration;
a detail of the same.
BELOW: a shrine decorated for a temple feast

Mukluk carrying her offering to the village temple

An exceptionally fine *lamak* and a tall *penyor,* a tall bamboo pole hung with lacy ornaments of palm-leaf decorating the entrance to a temple

The *pemangku* (below) dedicates the offerings brought to the temple by the women of the village

ABOVE: *Mendet* in Sayan, an offering dance of the married women

BELOW: Noble girls of Gelgel making their prayers with flowers

Taking the gods of Denpasar to the sea-shore in Kuta for *mlis,* a symbolical cleansing bath. For this particular temple feast all the women wore white skirts to signify the purity of the occasion

In a coming-of-age costume of gold brocade, with beaten gold head-dress, a Brahmana girl stands by an appropriate offering of fried rice paste, in bright-colored shapes of animals and gods

ABOVE: A bridegroom and his bride stirring the symbolic wedding meal, which they must cook and eat together.
BELOW: Two beds provided with special marriage offerings, ready for a double wedding ceremony

ABOVE: Gusti Alit Oka: prince, carpenter, and musician, who as drummer led the famous ensemble of Belaluan. The boy at the left plays the cymbals onomatopoeically called *ceng-ceng*.
BELOW: Musicians from Klandis

ABOVE: The *pelegongan* from the village of Saba accompanies the famous *legong*

BELOW: The *gendér wayang* orchestra is used as accompaniment to the shadow-play

An experienced *legong* dancer from Kapal comes to train a young *legong* of Belaluan

Legong dancer wearing a head-dress of beaten gold and frangipani flowers

The finest exponents of the *legong*, archetype of the delicate and feminine dance, perform under the *waringin* tree in the village of Saba

Four gestures in the *legong* of Saba

ABOVE: The servant (*condong*), a definite figure in the pattern of the *legong* and a soloist during the introduction, is about to hand fans to the dancers

BELOW: Flashing eyes and quivering fingers are important in the language of the *legong*

ABOVE: Two actors in the *jauk*, a pantomimic dance that precedes the *barong* play. In their masks and dance routine there is a sharp distinction between the uncouth and the refined characters

BELOW: Dancers of *baris gedé*, a ritual war dance, dressed in magic black and white cloth

Mario: originator and finest exponent of the *kebiyar*, a sitting dance that combines the manliness of the *baris* and the delicacy of the *legong*

Before he was ten years old, Sampéh was already adept in the difficult and sophisticated *kebiyar*

A *pedanda siwa*, a high priest of the *siwa* sect, with his bell in one hand and prayer flowers in the other, looking at the tip of his nose as a first step to induce trance

A *pedanda bodda*, high priest of a Buddhist sect, who prays with a *bajra*, a symbolic thunderbolt of bronze, instead of flowers. Below him in the picture, as he is in caste, the lowly *pemangku* is nevertheless of greater importance in the temple and is essential to the ritual, which the high priests are not

The mythical jungle beast, the *barong*, prays for victory against the dread witch Rangda, while the *pemangku*, holding a flower between his fingertips, assists him in his exhortations. Below, the *barong* addresses his assistants before they go into a trance to fight Rangda

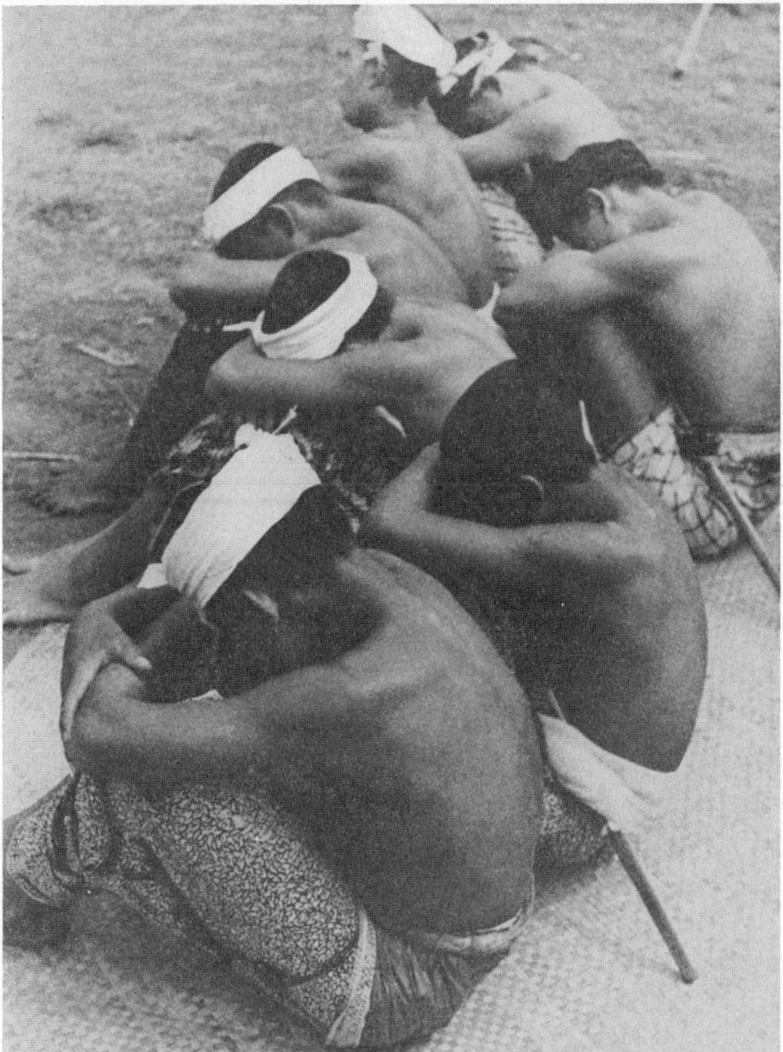

The *barong's* followers are about to enter into the trance

The kris in the hands of the dancer in trance is turned against him by the magic of Rangda

The colorful tower that serves to transport corpses to the cremation ground. It represents the cosmos: the underworld, the earth, and the heavens

Sarcophagi used for cremating corpses of the nobility, made of hollowed-out tree-trunks in the shape of cows. They are covered with felt or velvet, richly polychromed and decorated in gold

Down the bamboo bridge that leads from the tower, the corpses are carried to the sarcophagi, which in the picture below have already been reduced to ashes, leaving only the towers to follow them when the darkness comes

A *mukur* tower of white and gold built a month and seven days after the cremation for the ceremony that consecrates the souls of the dead as family gods. On a tall bamboo pole are the bird and the lamp that guide the soul on its way

GLOSSARY

BIBLIOGRAPHY

& INDEX

Glossary

adat: the traditional religious and social village laws and regulations.

angklung: a portable orchestra present at all celebrations, processions, etc.

balé: a pavilion; a house; a couch or bed.

balé agung: meeting-hall of the Elders' council in the old villages.

balé banjar: the meeting-hall of the *banjar*, the village ward.

balé gedé: the reception hall and guest house in the homes of the well-to-do.

Bali Aga: "the original Balinese"; the mountain people and those of the villages that remain isolated and have resisted the religious and cultural influence of the Javanese Empire of Majapahit.

balian: a witch-doctor and medicine-man who knows some of the magic used by the priests but takes no part in the community ritual.

banjar: a village ward; a social and political community within the *desa*, or village.

barong: a mythical beast of great magic power; most frequently identified with Banaspati (or Bonaspati) Raja, Lord of the Jungle (*barong ketet* or *kekek).* There are many other forms of barongs; described in greater detail in Note 1, pages 320-3.

barong landong: "the tall barong"; giant puppets of well-defined characters endowed with a certain holiness, kept in the temples and brought out occasionally to perform slapstick comedy (see page 260).

bodda (*boddha*): the so-called Buddhists; the members of a sect of Brahmanas that have a ritual of their own, derived from an ancient form of Javanese Buddhism.

Brahmana: a member of the priest (Brahmin in India) caste, highest of the aristocracy, the *triwangsa*.

cilí: a stylized representation of a beautiful girl, an important element of the native decorative art.

dalang: a story-teller; the mystic scholar who specializes in manipulating the puppets of the *wayang kulit,* the shadow-play, while he recites their lines and describes their exploits. In the *legong* dance, a *dalang* chants the story enacted by the young dancers.

desa: a complete, independent community; a village.

dewa: a deity; any beneficent supernatural spirit.

Dewa Agung: the title of the members of the royal family of Klungkung, highest of the Satrias and once regarded as the kings for the whole of Bali. The proud Dewa Agungs dispute caste supremacy with the Brahmanas.

Erlangga (or Erlanggia): a great and famous king of eleventh-century Java; born in Bali of a Balinese father and a Javanese princess, perhaps the most important historical figure and cultural influence in both Java and Bali.

gamelan: generic name for orchestras and music.

Gusti: the title of members of the third (Wesia) caste, lowest of the nobility.

Kawi: ancient Javanese, the classic language of poetry.

kepeng: Chinese perforated coins worth a fraction of a Dutch cent, the smallest coin in use.

kliang (or *klian*): headman; the elected chief of an association.

kulkul: a hollowed tree-trunk beaten to give signals, call meetings, and sound alarms.

leyak (or *leak*): a witch; a person who through knowledge of black magic can assume absurd, weird shapes to harm others.

lontar: a manuscript; a book written on dried leaves of the lontar palm.

Majapahit: The East-Javanese Empire that colonized the Malay Archipelago during the twelfth and thirteenth centuries.

mantra: cabalistic words; a secret spoken formula of great magic power.

maweda: a magic ceremony in which a high priest recites *mantras,* giving them emphasis with symbolic gestures of the hands.

naga: a mythical serpent.

nyepí: a day of prohibition, of stillness, of silence. The *nyepí* festival represents the suspension of all activity in the village preliminary to chasing out the evil vibrations that have accumulated during the year. There are also *nyepí* days for rice fields when no one may work in or even enter the fields.

pandé: the blacksmiths; a caste in itself, proud and supposedly magically powerful enough to handle with impunity such holy elements as fire and iron.

pedanda: a high priest, generally of the Brahmana or Brahmin caste.

pemangku: the low-caste temple guardian and officiating priest of the temple ritual.

perbekel: a lesser official in the village wards, formerly the agent and tax-collector of the feudal lords, now of the Dutch Government.

pungawa: a noble provincial governor who served the Raja, usually his relative, and who now serves the Dutch Government in the same capacity.

puri: the palace of a prince.

puséh (or *pusér*): the navel, the place of origin, the centre. The *pura puséh*, "temple of origin" of each village community is the most sacred social and religious link between the villagers themselves and between those of nearby communities that at one time broke away from the mother village.

Rangda: a "widow," a condition repulsive to the former Balinese. Now the name for the old witch heroine of the *Calon Arang* legend, the narrative of the struggle of King Erlangga to save his kingdom from destruction by the black magic performed by his own mother; to the Balinese, even today, a very real and dangerous spirit (see pages 294-7, 320-3).

ringgit: a silver dollar; two and a half guilders.

sanghyang: a deity, usually a local village god. Also the name of a trance dance in which mediums impersonate the sanghyang.

Satria: a member of the second or princely caste (Ksatriya in India).

sawah: a rice field.

sebel: polluted; a magical uncleanliness that weakens the village, temple, or individual spiritually.

seka (or *sekehe*): a club, an association.

sirih: peppery leaves chewed with betelnut and lime; a word used to express the combination of materials chewed with betelnut.

Siwa: Siva; the abstract, supreme deity.

subak: the village rice-growers' association; a society of all the village landowners for co-operation and the administration of agriculture and irrigation.

Sudra: a member of the fourth caste, the common people, or, rather, one without a caste, outside of the nobility. The term Sudra is seldom used in Bali and the common people are called *jaba* or "outsiders." They constitute the bulk of the Balinese people.

sunguhu: a priest of low caste who performs ritual similar to that of the Brahmanic priests, but whose office is limited to the propitiation of evil spirits (see page 282).

waringin (*bingin* in low-Balinese): a banyan tree.

Wau Rauh: the legendary Brahmanic priest who came from Java and originated the present families of Balinese Brahmanas.

wayang: The meaning of the word is highly controversial, but it is generally applied to any pictorial representation of the figures of mythology, although it appears to have a deeper, more significant religious meaning, perhaps related to the cult of ancestors. For further information see page 286, Note 6.

wayang kulit: the puppet shadow-play.

wayang wong: an archaic style of masked drama performing episodes from the Hindu epic, the *Ramayana*.

Wesia: the name of the third or military caste (Vesiyain in India), the great majority among the Balinese aristocracy. The term Wesia is seldom used in Bali and the members of this caste are known by the title of Gusti.

Bibliography

BAWANAGARA. Monthly devoted to Balinese ethnology and literature. Published in Malay and Balinese in Singaraja, North Bali, organ of the Kirtya Liefrink-van der Tuuk.

BELO, JANE: "A Study of Customs Pertaining to Twins in Bali." *Tijd. Ind. T. L. V.*, Deel LXXV (1935), alf 4.

—: "The Balinese Temper." *Character and Personality*, Vol. IV, No. 2 (1935). Durham, N. C.

—: "A Study of a Balinese Family." *The American Anthropologist*, Vol. 38, No. 1 (1936).

BERNATZIK, H. A.: *South Seas.* New York, 1935.

BEZEMER, T. J.: *Indonesian Arts and Crafts.* The Hague.

BLOEMEN-WANDERS, P. L. VAN: "Aanteekeningen omtrent de Zeden en Gewoonten der Balinezen." *Tijd. B.* G., Deel VII (1859).

BOSCH, F. D. K.: *Bali en de Zending;* Kraemer, H.: *Repliek op Bali en de Zending.* Batavia, 1933.

CARPENTER, BRUCE W.: *W.O.J. Nieuwenkamp: First European Artist in Bali.* Periplus, Singapore; 1997.

COAST, JOHN: *Dancing Out of Bali.* Faber and Faber, London; 1954.

COOL, CAPTAIN W.: *With the Dutch in the East. Outline of the Military Operations against Bali and Lombok.* London, 1897.

CRAWFURD, JOHN: *The Malay Archipelago.* Edinburgh, 1820.

DE KAT ANGELINO, P.: "Het Huwelijksrecht." *Koloniale Studien,* 4(1918).

—: "Over de smeden en eenige andere ambachtslieden op Bali." *Tijd. B. G.*, Deel LXI, alf 3 en 4.

—: "De leak op Bali." *Tijd. B.* G., Deel LX, alf 1 en 2.

— and TYRA DE KLEEN: *Mudras auf Bali, Handhaltungen der Priester.* Hagen in Westfalen, 1923.

DJELANTIK, A. A. M., *Memoirs of a Balinese Prince.* Singapore: Periplus, 1997.

DJILANTIK, GOESTI POETOE and OKA, IDA BAGOES: *Adi Agama, oud Balineesch wetboek. Op last van den Resident van Bali en Lombok in het hoog Balisch vertaald.* Bat Landsdrukkerij, 1909.

ECK, R. VAN: "Schetsen van het eiland Bali." *Tijd. Ned. Ind.*, Deel VIII (1879).

—: "Balische spreekworden." *Tijd. B. G.*, Deel XXI (1875).

—: *Eerste proeve van een Balineesch-Hollandsch worden boek.* Utrecht, 1876.

Embree, E. R., Simon, M. S., and Mumford, W. B.: *Island India Goes to School.* University of Chicago, 1934.

Forbes, Cameron: *Under the Volcano: The Story of Bali.* Black Inc, Melbourne; 2007.

Friederich, R.: "Over den godsdienst van Bali." *Tijd. Ned. Ind.,* Jg. 1849.

—: "Voorloopig verslag over het eiland Bali." *Verh. Bat. Gen.,* Deel XXIII (1850).

—: "An Account of the Island of Bali." *Journal of the Royal Asiatic Society,* Vol. IX. London, 1877.

—: *Arjoena Wiwaha, en oorspronkelijk Kawi werk.* Batavia, 1850.

—: *Boma Kawja; gedickt van Bhauma, in het oorspronkelijk Kawi.* Batavia, 1852.

Geertz, Hildred and Togog Ida Bagus Madé: *Tales from a Charmed Life: A Balinese Painter Reminisces.* University of Hawai'i Press, Honolulu; 2005.

Gobiah, I Wayan: *Nemoe Karma* (a novel of Balinese life, in Balinese). Balai Poestaka, Batavia, 1931.

Goris, R.: *Zie Bijdrage tot de kennis der Oujavaansche-en Bali-neesche theologie.* Leiden, 1929.

—: "Secten op Bali." *Overdruk uit Mededeelingen,* alf 3. Kirtya Liefrinck-van der Tuuk, Singaraja, Bali.

—: "Bali's hoogtijden." *Tijd. I. T. L. V.,* Deel LXXIII (1933).

—: "Sketches of Bali." *The Netherland Indies,* February, November 1935, February 1936.

—: *De Waarde van Dr. Kraemer's boek: "De Strijd over Bali en de Zending."* Batavia, 1933.

(Dr. Goris was editor of and regular contributor to the monthly publication *Bawanagara* (Soerat boelanan oentoek memperhatikan peradaban Bali), published by the Kirtya Liefrinck-van der Tuuk in Singaraja, Bali, dedicated to Balinese studies. Dr. Goris contributed also to *Jawa, Tijd. I. T. L. V.,* and other periodicals.)

Hanna, Willard A.: *Bali Chronicles.* Periplus, Singapore; 2004.

Heine-Geldern, Robert: *The Archeology and Art of Sumatra.* Universität Wien, 1935.

Hitchcock, Michael and Putra I Nyoman Darma: *Tourism, Development and Terrorism in Bali,* Ashgate, Aldershot; 2007.

Hooykas, C: *Tantri Kamandaka.* Bandung, Java, 1931.

—: *Proza en Poëzie van Oud Java.* Batavia, 1933.

Ikle, Ch., F.: *Ikat Technique and Dutch East Indian Ikats.* The Needle and

Bobbin Club, New York, 1931.

JASPER, J. E.: and MAS PINGARDIE: *De Inlandsche Kunstnijverheid in Nederlandsche Indie.* s-Gravenhage, 1912.

JUYNBOLL, H. H.: *Het oud Javaansche Brahmandapurana.* 1900.

—: *Mahabharata, Adiparwa. Oud Javaansche prozageschrift.* Den Haag, 1906.

—: *Kawi-Balineesch-Nederlandsch Glossarium op het oujavaansche Ramayana.* s-Gravenhage, 1902.

—: "Gids voor Ethn. voorwerpen." *Publ. Ethn. Mus.,* Serie II, No. 16c. *Cat. Ethn. Mus. Leiden,* Deel VII Bali en Lombok, 1912.

KATS, J.: *Het Ramayana, op Javaansche tempel reliefs.* Batavia.

— "Dancers and Actors of the Island of Bali." *Interocean.* Batavia, 1924.

KLEEN, TYRA: *Tempeldanser och Musikinstrument på Bali.* Stockholm, 1931.

KORN, V. E.: *Het Adatrecht van Bali.* Tweede herziene druk, s-Gravenhage, 1932.

—: *De dorpsrepubliek Tnganan Pagrinsingan.* Kirtya Liefrinck-van der Tuuk, Singaraja, Bali, 1933.

KRAUSE, GREGOR: *Bali: Volk, Land, Tanze, Feste, Tempel.* München, 1926.

KROM, N. J.: "De Boeddha-belden van Boeroebodoer." *Ned. Ind. Oud en Nieuw.* Ve. Jg., alf X. 1921.

—: "L'Art javanais dans les musées de Hollande et de Java." *Ars Asiatica,* 1926.

KRUIJT, J. and J. A.: *Het Animisme in den Indische Archipel.* s-Gravenhage, 1906.

KUNST, J. and C. J. A.: *De Toonkunst van Bali.* Batavia, 1925.

LAUTS, ULRICH GERHARD: *Het Eiland Bali en de Balinezen.* Amsterdam, 1848.

LEKKERKERKER, C.: *Bali en Lombok, overzicht der literatur tot* 1919. Bali Institute, Rijswijk, 1920.

—: "Les Récentes Découvertes archéologiques dans l'île de Bali." *Revue Anthropologique,* Année 34, p. 237. Paris, 1924.

—: "De Geschiedenis der zending onder de Baliers," *Ind. Gids.,* Deel XLI (1919).

—: "Pedandas op Bali." *Indie Geill. Weekblad van Ned. Kol,* No. XLVI.

LELYVEED, TH. B. VAN: *La Danse dans le théâtre javanais.* Paris, 1931.

LIEFRINCK, F. A.: "Bijdrage tot de kennis van het eiland Bali.'" *Tijd. I. T. L. V.,* Deel XXXIII.

—: *Bali en Lombok.* Gescheiteften, 1927.

LOEB, E. M.: *Sumatra, its History and People.* (With HEINE-GELDERN, R.: "The Archeology and Art of Sumatra"). Inst. Volk. Univ. Wien, 1935.

McPhee, Colin: "The Balinese Wajang Koelit and its Music." *Jawa,* No. 1, 16 jaar (1936).

—: "The 'Absolute' Music of Bali." *Modern Music,* Vol. XII, No. 4 (1935).

—: *Pemoengka; Gambangan, Arrangements of Balinese Wayang Music for Two Pianos.* Schirmer, New York, 1937.

Moojen, P. A. J.: *Kunst op Bali, inleide studie tot de bouwkunst.* Den Haag, 1926.

Nielsen, A. K: *Mads Lange til Bali.* Kovenhavn, 1926.

Nieuwenhuis, A. W.: *Het Animisme in Nederland Indie.* Amsterdam, 1913.

Nieuwenkamp, W. O. J.: *Bali en Lombok.* Edam, 1910.

—: *Bouwkunst van Bali.* s-Gravenhage, 1926.

—: *Beeldouwkunst van Bali.* s-Gravenhage, 1928.

Nyessen, D. J. H.: *The Races of Java.* Batavia, 1929.

Oja, Carol J.: *Colin McPhee: Composer in Two Worlds.* Smithsonian Institution, Washington; 1990.

Picard, Michel, *Bali: Cultural Tourism and Touristic Culture.* Archipelago Press, Singapore; 1996.

Poerbatjaraka, R. Ng.: "Negarakertagama." *Bijdr. T. L. V.,* Deel LXXX (1924).

—: "De Calon Arang." *Taalland en Vol. van Ned. Ind.,* Deel LXXXII alf 1 (1926).

—and Hooykaas, C.: "Bharata-Yuddha." *Jawa,* 14 jaar (1934).

Powell, Hickman: *The Last Paradise.* New York, 1930.

Raffles, Sir Thomas Stamford: *The History of Java.* London, 1830.

Ramseyer, Urs and Tisna I Gusti Raka Panji (eds.): *Bali: Living in Two Worlds.* Schwabe, Basel; 2002.

Robinson, Geoffrey: *The Dark Side of Paradise: Political Violence in Bali.* Cornell University Press, Ithaca, NY; 1995.

Rubinstein, Raechelle and Connor Linda H.: *Staying Local in the Global Village: Bali in the Twentieth Century.* University of Hawai'i Press, Honolulu; 1999.

Schulte Nordholt, Henk: *Bali: An Open Fortress 1995-2005.* Singapore University Press, Singapore; 2005.

Soekawati, Cokoede Gde Rake: *Hoe de Balier zich kleedt.* Ubud, Bali.

—: "De Sanghyang op Bali." *Jawa,* 5e jg., No. 6 (November 1925).

—: "The Romance of the Rice Grain." *Interocean.* Batavia, December 1924.

Spies, Walter: "Das grosse Fest im Dorfe Trunjan." *Ind. T. L. V.,* Deel LXXIII (1933).

STEIN-CALLENFELS, P. V. VAN: "Epigraphica Balica." *Kon. B. G. van Kunst en Wet*, Deel LXVI, st. 3. s-Gravenhage, 1926.

STUTTERHEIM, W. I.: *Oudheden van Bali.* Kirtya Liefrinck-van der Tuuk, Singaraja, Bali, 1931.

—: *Indian Influences in Old Balinese Art.* London, 1935.

—: *Het Hinduisme in den Archipel.* Batavia, 1932.

TUUK, H. N. VAN DER: *Kawi-Balineesch-Nederlandsch Woorden-boek.* Batavia, 1876-1912.

VATTER, ERNST: *Ata Kiwan.* Bibliographisches Institut, Leipzig, 1932.

VICKERS, ADRIAN, *Bali: A Paradise Created.* Penguin, Ringwood, Vic.; 1989.

—(ed.): *Travelling to Bali: 400 Years of Journeys.* Oxford University Press, Oxford; 1994.

—(ed.): *Being Modern in Bali: Image and Change.* Yale Southeast Asian Studies, New Haven; 1996.

WALLACE, ALFRED RUSSEL: *The Malay Archipelago.* London, 1898.

WEEDE, H. M. VAN: *Indische Reisherinneringen* (account of the South Bali Expedition). 1908.

WILLIAMS, ADRIANA: *Covarrubias.* The University of Texas Press, Austin; 1994.

WILLIAMS, ADRIANA and CHONG YU-CHEE, *Covarrubias in Bali.* Editions Didier Millet, Singapore; 2005.

WIRTZ, P.: *Der Totenkult auf Bali.* Stuttgart, 1928.

Index